THE CLAY SANSKRIT LIBRARY

FOUNDED BY JOHN & JENNIFER CLAY

EDITED BY

RICHARD GOMBRICH

WWW.CLAYSANSKRITLIBRARY.COM
WWW.NYUPRESS.ORG

Artwork by Robert Beer.
Dust jacket design by Isabelle Onians.
Typeset by Somadeva Vasudeva.
Printed in Great Britain by St Edmundsbury Press Ltd,
Bury St Edmunds, Suffolk, on acid-free paper.
Bound by Hunter & Foulis Ltd, Edinburgh, Scotland.

THE EMPEROR OF THE SORCERERS VOLUME ONE

BY BUDHASVĀMIN

EDITED & TRANSLATED BY
SIR JAMES MALLINSON

NEW YORK UNIVERSITY PRESS
JJC FOUNDATION
2005

First Edition 2005

Clay Sanskrit Library is co-published by
New York University Press
and the JJC Foundation.

Further information about this volume
and the rest of the Clay Sanskrit Library
is available on the following Websites:
www.claysanskritlibrary.com
www.nyupress.org

Library of Congress Cataloging-in-Publication Data
Budhasvāmin.
[Bṛhatkathāślokasaṅgraha. English & Sanskrit]
The emperor of the sorcerers / by Budhasvamin ;
edited and translated by Sir James Mallinson.– 1st ed.
p. cm. – (The Clay Sanskrit library)
In English and Sanskrit; translated from Sanskrit.
Includes bibliographical references and index.
ISBN 0-8147-5701-4 (cloth : alk. paper)
1. Sanskrit literature–Early works to 1800.
2. Tales–India–Early works to 1800.
I. Mallinson, James, 1970-
II. Title. III. Series.
PK3794.B84B713 2005
891'.21–dc22 2004014626

CONTENTS

A *sandhi* grid is printed on the inside of the back cover

SANSKRIT ALPHABETICAL ORDER

Vowels:	*a ā i ī u ū ṛ ṝ ḷ ḹ e ai o au ṃ ḥ*
Gutturals:	*k kh g gh ṅ*
Palatals:	*c ch j jh ñ*
Retroflex:	*ṭ ṭh ḍ ḍh ṇ*
Labials:	*p ph b bh m*
Semivowels:	*y r l v*
Spirants:	*ś ṣ s h*

GUIDE TO PRONUNCIATION AND PUNCTUATION

a	b*u*t
ā, â	r*a*ther
i	s*i*t
ī, î	f*ee*
u	p*u*t
ū, û	b*oo*
ṛ	vocalic *r*, American p*ur*dy or English p*re*tty
ṝ	lengthened *ṛ*
ḷ	vocalic *l*, ab*le*
e, ê, ē	m*a*de, esp. Welsh pronunciation
ai	b*i*te
o, ô, ō	r*o*pe, esp. Welsh pronunciation; Italian s*o*lo
au	s*ou*nd
ṃ	*anusvāra* nasalizes the preceding vowel
ḥ	*visarga* voiceless aspiration (English *h*), or like Scottish lo*ch*, or aspiration with faint echo of the preceding vowel: e.g. *taiḥ* is pronounced *taih*^{i}
k	lu*ck*
kh	blo*ckh*ead
g	*g*o
gh	bi*gh*ead
ṅ	a*n*ger
c	*ch*ill
ch	mat*chh*ead
j	*j*og
jh	aspirated *j*, he*dgeh*og
ñ	ca*ny*on
ṭ	retroflex *t*, *t*ry (tip of the tongue touching the hard palate)
ṭh	aspirated retroflex *t* (tip of tongue touching the hard palate)
ḍ	retroflex *d* (with the tip of the tongue touching the hard palate)
ḍh	same as the preceding but aspirated
ṇ	retroflex *n* (with the tip of tongue touching the hard

	palate)
t	French *t*out
th	ten*t h*ook
d	*d*inner
dh	guil*dh*all
n	*n*ow
p	*p*ill
ph	u*ph*eaval
b	*b*efore
bh	a*bh*orrent
m	*m*ind
y	*y*es
r	trilled, resembling the Italian pronunciation of *r*
l	*l*inger
v	*w*ord
ś	*sh*ore
ṣ	retroflex *sh* (with the tip of the tongue touching the hard palate)
s	hi*ss*
h	*h*ood

CSL PUNCTUATION OF SANSKRIT

Sanskrit presents the learner with a challenge: *sandhi*. *Sandhi* means that when two words are joined in connected speech or writing (which reflects speech), the last letter (or even letters) of the first word often changes; compare the way we pronounce "the" in "the apple" and "the pear." In Sanskrit the first letter of the second word may also change; and if both the last letter of the first word and the first letter of the second are vowels, they may fuse. This may produce ambiguity. The chart at the back of each book gives the full *sandhi* system.

But it is not necessary to know this in order to start reading Sanskrit. For that, what is important is to know the form of the second word without *sandhi*, so that it can be recognized or looked up in a dictionary. So we are printing Sanskrit with a system of punctuation that will indicate, unambiguously, the original form of the second word, i.e., the form without *sandhi*. This mostly concerns vowel *sandhi*.

In Sanskrit, vowels may be short or long and are written differently accordingly. We follow the general convention that a vowel with no mark above it is short. Other books mark a long vowel either with a bar called a macron (*ā*) or with a circumflex (*â*). Our system uses the macron, except that for initial vowels in *sandhi* we use a circumflex to indicate that originally the vowel was short, or the shorter of two possibilities (*e* rather than *ai*, *o* rather than *au*).

When we print initial *â*, before *sandhi* that vowel was *a*

When we print initial	before *sandhi* that vowel was
â,	*a*
î or *ê*,	*i*
û or *ô*,	*u*
âi,	*e*
âu,	*o*
ā,	*ā* (i.e., the same)
ī,	*ī* (i.e., the same)
ū,	*ū* (i.e., the same)
ē,	*ī*
ō,	*ū*
āi,	*āi* (i.e., the same)
āu,	*āu* (i.e., the same)

’, before *sandhi* there was a vowel *a*

FURTHER HELP WITH VOWEL SANDHI:

When a final short vowel (*a*, *i* or *u*) has merged into a following vowel, we print ’ at the end of the word, and when a final long vowel (*ā*, *ī* or *ū*) has merged into a following vowel we print ” at the end of the word. The vast majority of these cases will concern a final *a* or *ā*.

Examples:

What before *sandhi* was *atra asti* becomes *atr’ âsti*

What before *sandhi* was	becomes
atra asti	*atr’ âsti*
atra āste	*atr’ āste*
kanyā asti	*kany” âsti*
kanyā āste	*kany” āste*
atra iti	*atr’ êti*
kanyā iti	*kany” êti*
kanyā īpsitā	*kany” ēpsitā*

Finally, three other points concerning the initial letter of the second word:

(1) Where a word begins with *r* followed by a consonant, before *sandhi* it began with *ṛ* (vowel): *yathā ṛtu* becomes *yatha” rtu*.

(2) Where a word begins with *ch* and the last letter of the previous word is *c*, before *sandhi* it was *ś* and the previous word ended in *t*: *syāt śāstravit* becomes *syāc chāstravit*.

(3) Where a word begins with *h* and the previous word ends with a double consonant, this is our simplified spelling to show the pre-*sandhi* form: *tad hasati* is commonly written as *tad dhasati*, but we write *tadd hasati* so that the original initial letter is obvious.

COMPOUNDS

We also punctuate the division of compounds (*samāsa*), simply by inserting a thin vertical line between words. There are words where the decision whether to regard them as compounds is arbitrary. Our principle has been to try to guide readers to the correct dictionary entries.

Where others would print:

kumbhasthalī rakṣatu vo vikīrṇasindūrareṇur dviradānanasya /
praśāntaye vighnatamaśchaṭānāṃ niṣṭhyūtabālātapapallaveva //

We print:

Kumbha|sthalī rakṣatu vo vikīrṇa|sindūra|reṇur dvirad'|ānanasya
praśāntaye vighna|tamaś|chaṭānāṃ niṣṭhyūta|bāl'|ātapa|pallav" êva.

PUNCTUATION

Both the Sanskrit and English texts are punctuated. In mid-verse, the punctuation will not alter the *sandhi* or the scansion. Proper names are capitalized, as are the initial words of verses (or paragraphs in prose texts). In the Sanskrit text, we use French *Guillemets* (e.g. «Here I am!») instead of English quotation marks to avoid confusion with the apostrophes used for vowel elision. The deep layering of Sanskrit narrative has also dictated that we use quotation marks only to announce the beginning and end of every direct speech, and not at the beginning of every paragraph.

The acute accent on the cover and in the index marks stress. It is not part of traditional Sanskrit orthography, but we supply it here to guide readers in the pronunciation of these unfamiliar words.

INTRODUCTION

The Emperor of the Sorcerers (*Bṛhat/kathā/śloka/saṃgraha*) is a delightful retelling of the story of the adventures and romantic conquests of prince Naravāhanadatta, the future emperor of the sorcerers. Unfortunately the 4539 verses of the text that we have are but a fragment of the original work. We are told that our hero is to amass twenty-six wives during his travels (5.50), but when the story breaks off in the twenty-eighth canto he is in pursuit of only his sixth bride.

The *Bṛhat/kathā* or "Long Story" mentioned in the title is the work in which the narrative of the *Bṛhatkathāślokasaṃgraha* first appeared. Now lost, it was ascribed to Guṇāḍhya and said to have been composed in Paiśācī, the language of the goblins. The import of the title of the *Bṛhatkathāślokasaṃgraha* is thus that it is an abridgement *(saṃgraha)* into Sanskrit verse *(śloka)* of the *Bṛhatkathā*. There are numerous references to the original *Bṛhatkathā* in Sanskrit literature, and as well as the *Bṛhatkathāślokasaṃgraha* there are two other reworkings of its narrative: the *Kathā/sarit/sāgara* and the *Bṛhat/kathā/mañjarī*.

Nothing is known of Budhasvāmin, the author of the *Bṛhatkathāślokasaṃgraha*. The two oldest manuscripts of the text were copied in Nepal in the twelfth century. The extensive variation between the four manuscripts that were collated to edit the text suggest that a long time passed between its composition and the copying of its oldest manuscript, so we can be confident that Budhasvāmin lived some time before 1000 CE.

Budhasvāmin was a masterful poet. His Sanskrit is polished and easy to understand; although he occasionally shows off his virtuosity by using obscure words and archaic verb forms, he never lets his mastery get in the way of the story. He deliberately eschews elaborate descriptions in favor of a fast-paced narrative and deft characterization. He displays a keen interest in all aspects of ancient Indian society: despite the poem being the story of a divine prince, the stories within the narrative have a wide range of protagonists, from artisans and seafaring traders to courtesans and forest-dwellers.

The many layers of narrative in the text can sometimes lead to confusion, so a brief synopsis of the plot follows. Verse numbers indicate where a story is being told within a story.

Canto 1 (91 verses) Gopāla

Mahāsena, king of Ujjain, dies. Gopāla takes the throne, renounces it and gives it to his brother Pālaka.

Canto 2 (93 verses) Pālaka

Pālaka has a dream about an elephant. He renounces the throne, gives it to Avantivardhana, Gopāla's son, and retires to Asitagiri to be an ascetic.

Canto 3 (126 verses) Avantivardhana

Avantivardhana marries Surasamañjarī.

vv. 46–63 Surasamañjarī tells the story of Ipphaka and her father.

Avantivardhana and Surasamañjarī are abducted by Ipphaka and rescued by Divākaradeva, servant of Naravāhanadatta. He brings them, with Ipphaka, to Kāśyapa's hermitage on Asitagiri, where Pālaka is living. Naravāhanadatta, son of Udayana, arrives. Ipphaka is punished.

Canto 4 (132 verses) The Story of Piṅgalikā

Naravāhanadatta is asked by Kāśyapa to explain how he came to be the emperor of the sorcerers and won his twenty-six wives.

From 4.13 to the end of what we have of the text is Naravāhanadatta's story. Udayana, king of Kauśāmbī in Vatsa, hears the story of a shipwrecked merchant's wife. When she has a son, Udayana realizes the importance of having a son and wants one himself.

vv. 82–131 Piṅgalikā's story of how she gave birth to sons after worshipping Viṣṇu.

Canto 5 (326 verses) Satisfying Pregnancy Cravings

Udayana thus worships Kubera and has a dream portending the birth of a son, as do his wife, Vāsavadattā, and his ministers. Vāsavadattā becomes pregnant.

vv. 89–175 Her mother-in-law, Mṛgayāvatī, tells the story of her pregnancy craving and Udayana's birth at Vasiṣṭha's hermitage.

vv. 115–137 Udayana tells the story of his meeting with the Nāga boys. Udayana comes of age and he and his mother go to Kauśāmbī.

vv. 178–189 Mṛgayāvatī tells the story of Manoramā's pregnancy craving.

Vāsavadattā's pregnancy craving is to ride in a flying machine. The artisans say it is impossible.

vv. 200–272 "A certain landowning brahmin" tells Udayana's court the story of Viśvila, Pukvasaka and flying machines.

A stranger arrives and makes a flying machine. Udayana and Padmāvatī, his other favorite wife, fly to Ujjain and pay respects to Mahāsena, her father.

vv. 298–324 Bhadrā's story.

Canto 6 (33 verses) The Birth of the Prince

Naravāhanadatta and his ministers' sons are born and reach maturity.

Canto 7 (82 verses) Consecration as Crown Prince

Kaliṅgasenā comes to court with her daughter Madanamañjukā. Naravāhanadatta is anointed crown prince. A year passes. Gomukha behaves strangely. Naravāhanadatta and his friends debate whether to go to the festival. Gomukha convinces him to go.

[8–11 The Journey to the Festival]

Canto 8 (55 verses) The Sport of Hunting

Udayana gives his approval and they set off on the journey to Snake Forest Park. Naravāhanadatta sees a girl in a carriage and Gomukha tricks him into waving at her. Naravāhanadatta and his friends go hunting. Naravāhanadatta's arrow goes around the special deer, a predicted sign of his sovereignty.

Canto 9 (108 verses) The Meeting on the Riverbank
They spot footprints by a river. Following them and other clues, they find a sorcerer, Amitagati, impaled on a tree, and bring him back to life with magic herbs.

vv. 81–104 Amitagati tells his story: the sage Kauśika brought him up, and told him that his future lord would revive him after he had been impaled. He won a girl called Kusumālikā, then his friend made advances toward her and he took her off to the river. His friend found them, abducted Kusumālikā and impaled Amitagati.

Canto 10 (274 verses) The Conversation on the Road
The journey continues. Gomukha describes lovers, and says that someone loves Naravāhanadatta.

vv. 30–265 On being asked who, he tells the story of what happened to him during the events described in canto 7. Padmāvatī describes him as mindful. He wanders about in the hope of finding out what mindfulness is. He meets Madanamañjukā, a courtesan. Another of the courtesans, Padmadevikā, seduces him.

vv. 182–241 An attendant courtesan, Mudrikālatikā, describes how everything that has happened since he was first called mindful has been engineered so that he might relate Madanamañjukā's desires to Naravāhanadatta. When Madanamañjukā sat on the king's knee she fell in love with Naravāhanadatta. On not being allowed to visit him she has tried to hang herself.

Gomukha says he will act as go-between. Naravāhanadatta falls in love.

Canto 11 (107 verses) The Winning of Madanamañjukā

The dancing contest between Suyamunadanta and Madanamañjukā is held at the palace. Marubhūtika and Gomukha are sent to Madanamañjukā's house.

vv. 30–63 Marubhūtika gives an account of their visit.

Madanamañjukā arrives and spends that night and subsequent ones with Naravāhanadatta. Madanamañjukā bemoans her status as courtesan. They all return to the city.

Canto 12 (84 verses) The Substitution in the Garden

vv. 2–21 Gomukha reports Madanamañjukā's disappearance to Naravāhanadatta.

vv. 39–57 Marubhūtika tells the story of Aṅgiras, Amṛtā and Sāvitrī.

Naravāhanadatta finds Vegavatī (disguised as Madanamañjukā) in the garden. The king declares Madanamañjukā to be a noblewoman, allowing her to marry Naravāhanadatta.

Canto 13 (52 verses) Vegavatī

Naravāhanadatta and Madanamañjukā/Vegavatī are married. Vegavatī gets Naravāhanadatta drunk. He and his friends pass their time drinking. Naravāhanadatta discovers that Madanamañjukā is Vegavatī.

Canto 14 (125 verses) Vegavatī Revealed

vv. 2–122 Vegavatī tells her story. Her father, Vegavān, king of Aṣāḍha, renounces his throne and goes to the penance grove. His son, Mānasavega, becomes king. Vegavatī goes to learn the magical power of flight from her father. She returns to the city. Mānasavega has abducted Madanamañjukā, but cannot have her because of a curse. Vegavatī meets Madanamañjukā and then goes to find Naravāhanadatta.

Canto 15 (158 verses) The Winning of Vegavatī

Naravāhanadatta stages a repeat of his wedding to please the two queens. His four friends are also married, to four friends of Vegavatī. Naravāhanadatta is abducted by Mānasavega. Vegavatī arrives and fights with Mānasavega. He drops Naravāhanadatta, who falls in a well.

vv. 106–148 Naravāhanadatta remembers the story of Ekata, Dvita and Trita.

He thinks of Amitagati, who appears and shows him the way out of the well.

Canto 16 (93 verses) The Entry into Campā

Amitagati flies off to fight Mānasavega. Naravāhanadatta finds his way to Campā and meets the merchant Dattaka. He pretends to be a brahmin.

Canto 17 (181 verses) Marriage to Gandharvadattā

Hiding his mastery, Naravāhanadatta pretends to learn the lute. He wins Gandharvadattā, Sānudāsa's daughter, by accompanying her in a lute contest.

SANSKRIT TEXT

The Sanskrit text printed here is based on Félix LACÔTE's 1908 edition. He collated four Nepalese manuscripts: two from the twelfth century (denoted by A and B in his edition), and copies (N and M) made in 1906 of two undated mss (N and M). A appears to be a direct copy of B. LACÔTE has not been able to use stemmatic analysis to base his edition on a single manuscript, although a later hand has made several corrections and emendations to B and LACÔTE always adopts his readings. When the evidence of this later hand is unavailable, he makes his own judgement as to which reading of all the witnesses is to be adopted, and he has a preference for the readings of N and M. In general his text is very good: there are few places where it has been necessary to make corrections or emendations.

BIBLIOGRAPHY

Bṛhatkathāślokasaṃgraha of Budhasvāmin. Ed. and tr. FÉLIX LACÔTE & LOUIS RENOU. Paris. Imprimerie Nationale. 1908–1928.

Bṛhatkathāślokasaṃgraha of Budhasvāmin with English Translation by PODDAR, R.P. & SINHA, N. Varanasi. Tara Book Agency. 1986.

KEITH, A.B. *A History of Sanskrit Literature.* Oxford University Press. 1920.

LACÔTE, F. *Essai sur Guṇāḍhya et la Bṛhatkathā.* Paris. 1908.

MATEN, E.P. *Budhasvāmin's Bṛhatkathāślokasaṃgraha. A literary study of an ancient Indian narrative.* Leiden. E.J.Brill. 1973.

SHASTRI, HARA PRASAD. *Old Nepalese Manuscripts.* JASB LXII (1893) No.3 pp.254–5.

VAN BUITENEN, J.A.B. *Tales of ancient India.* Chicago. 1959.

CANTO 1
GOPĀLA

Oṃ namo Vighn'|ântakāya!

MAHĀ|KHĀTĀ MAHĀ|ŚĀLĀ
pury asty Ujjayan" îti yā.
mah"|âmbhodhi|mahā|śaila|mekhal" êva mahā|mahī.
Prāsādān yatra paśyantaḥ saṃtatān haima|rājatān
Meru|Kailāsa|kūṭebhyaḥ spṛhayanti na nāgarāḥ.
Veda|maurvī|vipañcīnāṃ dhvanayaḥ prati|mandiram
yatra saṃnipatanto 'pi na bādhanti parasparam.
Kṛtaṃ varṇanayā tasyā yasyāṃ satatam āsate
Mahākāla|prabhṛtayas tyaktvā Śiva|puraṃ gaṇāḥ!

Tasyām āsīn mahā|seno Mahāsenaḥ kṣit'|īśvaraḥ
yasya devī|sahasrāṇi ṣoḍaśa Śrī|pater iva.
Ciraṃ pālayatas tasya prajāḥ śāstr'|ôkta|kāriṇaḥ
Gopālaḥ Pālakaś c' êti sutau jātau guṇ'|âmbu|dhī.
Bṛhaspati|samaś c' âsya mantrī Bharatarohakaḥ
Rohantakaḥ Surohaś ca tasy' āstāṃ tat|samau sutau.

Nar'|êndra|mantri|putrāṇāṃ catur|vidy"|ârtha|vedinām
prayogeṣu ca dakṣāṇāṃ yānti sma divasāḥ sukham.

Atha gāṃ pālayām āsa Gopālaḥ pitṛ|pālitām
Pālako 'pi yavīyastvād yauva|rājyam apālayat.
1.10 Mantri|putrau tu mantritvam atha bhūmir nav'|ēśvarā
nava|mantri|kṛt'|ārakṣā jāyate sma punar navā.

Gaja|rājam ath' ô rājā dāna|rāji|virājitam
adhiṣṭhāya jagat|sāraṃ nirjagāma bahiḥ puraḥ.

Om! Homage to the Remover of Obstacles!

THERE IS A CITY called Ujjayani, which, with its wide moat and huge mansions, is like the earth with its girdle of wide oceans and huge mountains. When the citizens there see the rows of golden and silver palaces, they have no desire for the peaks of Meru and Kailasa. The sounds of the Vedas, bowstrings and lutes arise together in every house there, yet do not clash with one another. But that's enough description of the city where Mahakala* and the rest of his troop always reside, having abandoned Shiva's heaven!

King Mahasena lived there. He had a great army and, like Krishna, sixteen thousand queens. When he had been ruling the people for a long time in the manner prescribed in the sacred books, two sons were born to him, Gopala and Palaka, oceans of virtue. His minister, Bharatarohaka, was equal to Brihaspati*, and had two sons, Rohantaka and Suroha, who were like him.

The sons of the king and his minister knew the four sciences* and were skilled in their application. The days passed happily for them.

Then Gopala became the protector of the land that had been looked after by his father, and Palaka, because he was
younger, assumed the role of crown prince. The minister's 1.10
sons took over the ministry, and the land, under a new king and protected by new ministers, became young again.

One day the king mounted the best of beasts, a great elephant shining with streaks of the ichor of rut, and went out of the city. Crowds of people came to see him. In fear of

Tad|darśana|āśayā yātam anekaṃ nṛ|kadambakam
bibhyad vyāḍād gajāt tasmād itaś c' êtaś ca vidrutam.
Kanyak" ânyatamā tatra gṛhyamāṇ" âtha hastinā
prāṃśu|prākārataḥ prāṃśor agamyāṃ parikhām agāt.
Khāta|pāta|vyathā|jāta|saṃjñā|nāśā kṣaṇaṃ tataḥ
taṭa|sthā hasti|pṛṣṭha|sthaṃ s" âbhāṣata ruṣā nṛpam.
«Avadhyam avadhīr yas tvam pitaraṃ tasya kiṃ mayā?
adhīta|vedaṃ yo hanti brāhmaṇaṃ tasya ke mṛgāḥ?»
Iti kanyā|vacaḥ śrutvā duḥ|śravaṃ śva|pacair api
cint"|êṣu|bhinna|hṛdayaḥ praviveśa niveśanam.
Ativāhya ca duḥkhena dina|śeṣaṃ samā|samam
jana|vād'|ôpalambhāya pradoṣe niryayau gṛhāt.
Kāla|kambala|saṃvītaḥ s'|âsi|carm'|âsi|putrikaḥ
sa|mantr'|âgada|saṃnāhaḥ saṃcacāra śanaiḥ śanaiḥ.
Atha suśrāva kasmiṃś cid devat"|āyatane dhvanim
abhisārikayā sārdhaṃ bhāṣamāṇasya kāminaḥ:
1.20 «Hataṃ muṣṭibhir ākāśaṃ tuṣāṇāṃ kaṇḍanaṃ kṛtam
mayā yena tvayā sārdhaṃ baddhā prītir abuddhinā!
Iyam etāvatī velā khidyamānena yāpitā
mayā tvaṃ tu gṛhād eva na niryāsi pati|vratā!
Kaumāraḥ subhago bhartā yadi nāma priyas tava
khalī|kṛtaiḥ kim asmābhir vṛth" êva kula|putrakaiḥ?»
Evam|ādi tataḥ śrutvā sā pragalbh" âbhisārikā
vihasya viṭam āha sma: «tvādṛśā hi hata|trapāḥ!
Nanu cittaṃ may" ārādhyaṃ tasy' âpi bhavataḥ kṛte?

the unruly elephant they scattered in all directions. When the elephant tried to grab one of the girls there, she jumped from a high rampart to the safety of a ditch. The shock of falling into the ditch made her faint for a moment. Then she stood on the bank and angrily addressed the king as he sat on the elephant.

"What am I to you who broke the tabu against killing one's father? What are deer to a man who kills a learned brahmin?"

When he heard the girl's words, which would have been hard for even dog-cooking outcastes to hear, he went home with his heart pierced by the arrow of anxiety. After struggling to get through the rest of the day, which seemed as long as a year, in the evening he went out of the house to get to the bottom of what people were saying. Disguised in a black blanket, carrying a sword, a shield and a dagger, and protected by spells and potions, he quietly crept about. In a temple he heard the voice of a lover speaking to his sweetheart:

"In foolishly falling in love with you, I have been punch- 1.20
ing the sky and threshing chaff! I spend all this time waiting anxiously and you, the obedient wife, don't even leave your house! If your husband is young and charming, and you do in fact love him, then why do you needlessly torment a respectable boy like me?"

After hearing these words, and more like them, the audacious adulteress laughed and said to her lover: "Your sort really are shameless! Don't you realize that I have to indulge him for your sake? Unfaithful women cannot have fun with

na hi bhartṝn aviśvāsya ramante kulaṭā viṭaiḥ.
Atha nirmakṣikaṃ bhadra madhu pātuṃ mano|rathaḥ
jahi ghātaya bālaṃ me patiṃ nitya|pramādinam!
Atha pāpād asi trastaḥ! sphuṭaṃ n' âhaṃ tava priyā!
nanu durvāra|rāg'|ândhaḥ sutāṃ yāti Prajāpatiḥ?
Athav" âlaṃ vivādena! vaidharmyaṃ kiṃ na paśyasi
yena rājya|sukh'|ândhena prajā|pālaḥ pitā hataḥ?»

Su|duḥ|śravam idaṃ śrutvā Gopālo dur|vacaṃ vacaḥ
gacchann anyatra śuśrāva dhvaniṃ viprasya jalpataḥ:
«Ayi brāhmaṇi jāgarṣi nandini? krandate śiśuḥ
tvaritaṃ yācate dehi stanyaṃ kaṇṭho 'sya mā śuṣat!»

1.30 Iti śrutvā giraṃ bhartur vi|nidrā brāhmaṇī sutam:
«pitṛ|ghātin mriyasv' êti!» nirdayaṃ nirabhartsayat

«Āḥ pāpe! kim asaṃbaddhaṃ ‹pitṛ|ghātinn iti› tvayā
bālo 'yam ukta ity?» enāṃ brāhmaṇaḥ kupito 'bravīt.

«Kim āryaputra putreṇa yadā rājñā pitā hataḥ
śruti|smṛti|vid" êty?» etad uvāca brāhmaṇī patim.

Śrutv" âivam|ādi kaulīnaṃ praviśy' ântaḥ|puraṃ nṛpaḥ
anayat kṣaṇadā|śeṣam asaṃmīlita|locanaḥ.
Atha gāḍh'|ândha|kārāyāṃ velāyāṃ mantriṇau rahaḥ
apṛcchat «ko 'yam asmāsu pravādaḥ kathyatām iti.»

Tatas tāv ūcatus trastau sa|trāsaṃ nṛpa|coditau,

their lovers without first winning their husbands' trust. So, my dear, if you want to drink wine that doesn't have flies in it, murder my naïve and ever-careless husband yourself or have him murdered! But you're scared of sinning! You clearly don't love me! Did not Prajapati, blinded by insatiable lust, ravish his own daughter? Anyway, that's enough arguing! Don't you realize that life is unfair—that's why the royal father was slain by a son blinded by the pleasures of kingship."

After hearing these awful words, which were so hard for him to hear, Gopala was on his way somewhere else when he heard the sound of a brahmin speaking: "O dear wife, are you awake? The baby's crying. Quickly, he wants you—give him your breast before his throat dries up!"

On hearing her husband's words, the sleep-deprived brah- 1.30
min woman cruelly scolded her son: "Die, you father-killer!"

The enraged brahmin said to her, "Oh you wicked woman! Why did you absurdly address the child as 'father-killer'?"

The brahmin lady replied: "Dear husband, what is the point of having a son when the king, who knows the sacred texts, has killed his father?"

After hearing this and other similar slurs, the king went to his inner apartments and did not get a wink of sleep for the remainder of the night. Then, at the time when it was darkest, he secretly asked his two ministers to explain the slander about him.

Anxiously urged on by the king, the two terrified minis-

«kaulīna|hetu|śrutaye cittaṃ dev' âvadhīyatām.
Su|gṛhīt'|âbhidhānasya Pradyotasya pitus tava
āsanna|vyabhicāriṇy a|riṣṭāny aṣṭau mumūrṣataḥ.
Uddhārye dhavale keśe pramādāt kṛṣṇa uddhṛte
uddhartāraṃ mahī|pālaḥ kartayām āsa nāpitam.
Bhuñjānena ca pāṣāṇe daśan'|âgreṇa khaṇḍite
kula|kram'|āgato vṛddhaḥ sūpa|kāraḥ pramāpitaḥ.
Prakṛter viparītatvaṃ jānann apy evam|ādibhiḥ
prabho vidher vidheyatvād brāhmaṇān apy abādhata.
1.40 Bhartur īdṛśi vṛttānte mantrī tasy' âvayoḥ pitā
adṛṣṭa|bhartṛ|vyasanaḥ pūrvam ev' âgamad divam.
Śruta|mantri|vināśas tu sa rājā rāja|yakṣmaṇā
guru|śoka|sahāyena sahas" âiv' âbhyabhūyata.
Tatas tāte divaṃ yāte yātu|kāme ca bhūpatau
prajāsu ca viraktāsu jātau svaḥ kiṃ|kriy"|ākulau.
‹Prāpta|kālam idaṃ śreya iti› buddhvā prasāritam
kaulīnam idam āvābhyāṃ sarpayanteṣv Avantiṣu:
‹Krodha|bādhita|bodhatvād bādhamānaṃ nijāḥ prajāḥ
bandhayām āsa rājānaṃ rāja|putraḥ priya|prajaḥ.
Śṛṅkhalā|tantra|caraṇaḥ sva|tantrād bhraṃśitaḥ padāt
sukhasya mahato dadhyau sa rāj'|êndro gaj'|êndra|vat.
Cintā|muṣita|nidratvād āhāra|viraheṇa ca
sa kṣapāḥ kṣapayan kṣīṇaḥ saṃvatsara|śat'|āyatāḥ.
Putreṇ' âivam|avastho 'pi prajā|priya|cikīrṣuṇā
na mukta eva muktaś ca yāvat prāṇaiḥ priyair iti.›

ters said, "Your Majesty, please listen carefully to the reason for the rumor. When your father Pradyota*—blessed is his name—was on the verge of dying, the eight undesirable portents of death arose. Then a barber mistakenly plucked a black hair when he was supposed to be plucking a white one, and the king had him chopped into pieces. When he crushed a stone with the point of his tooth while eating, he had the aged hereditary cook killed. Sire, even though he knew that the people had turned against him because of such actions, he was in the grip of fate so he harassed
even brahmins. While the king was behaving like this, his 1.40
minister—our father—preceded him to heaven without seeing his master's plight.

On hearing of his minister's demise, the king was immediately struck down by consumption brought on by violent grief. Our father was dead, the king was about to die, and the people were disaffected. We were at a loss what to do.

Thinking it timely and for the best, we spread the following rumor among the gossip-mongering people of Avanti: 'Because his mind was troubled by anger, the king was troubling his subjects, so his son, to whom the subjects are dear, had him arrested. With his feet in chains, deprived of his freedom and good fortune, the great king brooded like a great elephant. Because his sleep was stolen by worry and he wasn't eating, he became emaciated and struggled through nights that lasted a hundred years. Even when he was in this state, his son wanted to do what was best for the people and did not release him until he had been released by his last dear breath.'

Nidānam idam etasya kaulīnasya vigarhitam
itarad v" âdhunā devaḥ prabhur ity» atha bhū|patiḥ.
Adhomukhaḥ kṣaṇaṃ sthitvā tal'|āhata|mahī|talaḥ
dṛṣṭvā ca s'|âsram ākāśam a|nātha idam abravīt:
1.50 «Tulyau Śukra|Bṛhaspatyor yuvāṃ muktvā suhṛttamau
anapāyam upāyaṃ kaḥ prayuñjīt' âitam īdṛśam?
Kiṃ tu sattvavatām eṣa śaṅkā|śūnya|dhiyāṃ kramaḥ
dṛṣṭ'|âdṛṣṭa|bhaya|grasta|cetasāṃ na tu mādṛśām.
Tasmāt pālayataṃ bhadrau Pālakaṃ pālakaṃ bhuvaḥ
idaṃ tv alīka|kaulīnam aśakto 'ham upekṣitum.»
Tasy' âivaṃ bhāṣamāṇasya vrīḍ"|âdhomukha|mantriṇaḥ
kūjan prakāśayām āsa kṣīṇāṃ tāmra|śikhaḥ kṣapām.
Atha śuśruvire vācaḥ sūta|māgadha|bandinām:
«yaśo|dhavalit'|ânanta|digant' ôdbudhyatām iti!»
Dīna|dīnaṃ tad ākarṇya karṇa|dāraṇam apriyam
pidhāya pārthivaḥ karṇāv uttam'|âṅgam akampayat.
Sa c' âvocat pratīhārīṃ: «nivāryantām amī! mama
kṣate kṣār'|âvasekena kiṃ phalaṃ bhavatām iti?»
Āsīc c' âsy' «âtha vā dhiṅ mām evam ātm'|âpavādinam
nanu praśasyam ātmānaṃ n' âham arhāmi ninditum.
Niryantraṇa|vihāreṇa cira|jīvini rājani
rāja|putreṇa laḍitaṃ ken' ânyena yathā mayā?
Samucchinna|dur|uccheda|bāhy'|âbhyantara|vairiṇā
varṇ'|āśramāḥ sva|dharmebhyaḥ kiṃ vā vicalitā mayā?
1.60 Avantivardhana|samo nij'|āhārya|guṇ'|ākaraḥ

This is the cause of the defamation, be it blameworthy or otherwise. Now the matter is in Your Majesty's hands."

The king stood downcast for a moment before stamping his foot. Then the helpless man looked tearfully up at the
sky and said: "You two dear friends are the equals of Shu- 1.50
kra and Brihaspati and who other than you would have employed a plan as perfect as this? But this course of action is for courageous men whose minds are free from doubt, not for men like me with minds fraught with fears about the present and the future. So, my friends, you must have Palaka rule as king. I cannot ignore this slur on my name."

As he was addressing the ministers, whose heads were hanging in shame, a cock crowed to proclaim the end of the night. Then they heard the voices of the heralds, bards and minstrels: "Arise, you whose glory illuminates the infinite universe!"

The king listened in utter dejection; the hateful sound pierced his ears. He blocked his ears and shook his head. He said to a lady-in-waiting: "Have them stopped! What do you people gain from rubbing salt into my wounds?"

But then he thought, "Shame on me for putting myself down so. Surely I am to be praised and should not reproach myself. What other prince with a long-lived father ever enjoyed himself in unrestrained amusement as much as me? And did I, after completely destroying my formidable enemies both without and within, make men of the various castes and life stages deviate from their traditional duties?
Does anyone else have a son like Avantivardhana, a mine 1.60
of both innate and acquired virtues and my savior from

putraḥ puṃ|narakāt trātā kasy' ânyasya yāthā mama?
Atha v" āstām idaṃ sarvam! eken' âiv' âsmi vardhitaḥ
Naravāhanadevena jāmātrā cakra|vartinā.
Eka eva tu me n' āsīd guṇaḥ so 'py ayam āgataḥ
prasādān mantri|vṛṣayor yat tapo|ana|sevanam!»

Iti niṣkampa|saṃkalpaś codayām āsa mantriṇau,
«sa|siṃh'|āsanam āsthānaṃ maṇḍape dīyatām iti.»
Tayos tu gatayoḥ keśān vāpayitvā sa|valkalaḥ
kamaṇḍalu|sa|nāthaś ca bhū|pālo niryayau gṛhāt.
Viṣāda|viplut'|âkṣeṇa vakṣo|nikṣipta|pāṇinā
dṛśyamāno 'varodhena viveś' āsthāna|maṇḍapam.
Trāsa|mlāna|kapolena dṛṣṭaḥ pṛthula|cakṣuṣā
Pālaken' âbravīt taṃ ca sthita eva sthitaṃ sthitam:
«Prasādāt tāta tātasya Vatsa|rājasya ca tvayā
buddheḥ svasyāś ca śuddhāyāḥ kiṃ nāma na parīkṣitam?
Ato 'nuśāsitāraṃ tvām anuśāsati bāliśaḥ
yena loke ta ucyante viyātāḥ pitṛ|śikṣakāḥ.
Etāvat tu mayā vācyaṃ ‹pitryaṃ siṃh'|āsanaṃ tvayā
varṇ'|āśrama|paritr"|ârtham idam adhyāsyatām iti.›
1.70 Tac c' âvaśyam anuṣṭheyam asmākīnaṃ vacas tvayā
mādṛśāṃ hi na vākyāni vimṛṣanti bhavādṛśāḥ.»

It' îdam Pālakaḥ śrutvā sthitvā c' âdhomukhaḥ kṣaṇam
uttaraṃ cintayām āsa nās'|âgr'|āhita|locanaḥ.

Kṛta|kṛtrima|roṣas tu rājā Pālakam abravīt,
«bhoḥ! siṃh'|āsanam āroha! kiṃ tav' ôttara|cintayā?
Kiṃ c' ôttara|śaten' âpi tvay" âhaṃ s'|ôpapattinā
vegaḥ prāvṛṣi Śoṇasya caraṇen' êva dur|dharaḥ!»

hell*? But forget all that! One thing alone is enough to commend me: my son-in-law, the emperor Naravahanadeva. There was one virtue in which I used to be lacking, but, thanks to my two fine ministers, now I have that too: the life of a hermit!"

His resolve was unflinching and he ordered the two ministers to convene the royal assembly in the hall. When they had gone, the king had his hair shaved off and went out of the house wearing bark and carrying the water pot of an ascetic. Watched by his wives with eyes overflowing with tears of grief as they clutched their breasts, he entered the assembly hall. Palaka's face was wan with worry and wide-eyed as he watched him. When Palaka stood up, Gopala stayed standing and said to him: "Dear brother, by the grace of our dear father and the king of Vatsa, as well as your own keen intellect, there is no subject that you have not studied in detail, so only a fool would teach you, a teacher: as the proverb says, it is the impudent who teach their fathers. But I do have this much to say: in order to protect the castes and life stages, you must sit on this, your father's throne. You really must do as I say. It is not for men 1.70
like you to deliberate the words of men like me."

When he heard this, Palaka hung his head and stared at the tip of his nose for a moment while pondering his reply.

Feigning anger, the king said to Palaka, "Hey! Ascend the throne! There's no point in your thinking about an answer! Why, even with a hundred reasoned answers, it would be as hard for you to stop me as it would be to stop the flood of the Sone in the rainy season with your foot!"

Iti dvi|jātayaḥ śrutvā purohita|puraḥ|sarās
viṣāda|gadgada|giraḥ pramṛjy' âśru babhāṣire:
«Pālakas te niyojyatvād ājñāṃ mā sma vicārayat
tvan|niyogān niyoktāraḥ kasmād vayam udāsmahe?
Dhriyamāṇe prajā|pāle jyeṣṭhe bhrātari Pālakaḥ
mṛg'|êndr'|āsanam ārohan khaṭv"|ārūḍho bhaven nanu.
Rājy'|âgnim ādadhad v" âpi tvayi varṣa|śat'|āyuṣi
parivettāram ātmānam ayaṃ manyeta ninditam.
Tasmād asmān nivartasva saṃkalpād atibhīṣaṇāt
śoka|jāny aśru|vārīṇi bhavantv ānanda|jāni naḥ!»

Baddh'|âñjalir ath' ôvāca kiṃ cin namita|kandharaḥ,
«alaṃ vaḥ pīḍayitvā māṃ vacobhir iti» pārthivaḥ.
1.80 «May" âyam abhyanujñāto rakṣaṇe ca kṣamaḥ kṣiteḥ
khaṭv"|ārūḍho na bhavitā ninditaḥ śabda|vedibhiḥ.
Asamarthe ca rājy'|âgneḥ pālane patite mayi
parivett" âpi n' âiv' âyam bhaviṣyati nar'|âdhipaḥ!
Yac c' âpi pihitāḥ karṇā ākarṇya patita|dhvanim
prajābhis tac ca na mṛṣā mayā hi nihataḥ pitā.
Tad idaṃ pātakaṃ kṛtvā yuṣmat|pīḍā|praśāntaye
prāyaścittaṃ vrajan kartuṃ na nivāryo 'smi kena cit!
Mayā c' â|tyakta|dharmeṇa yat prajānāṃ kṛte kṛtam
tasya pratyupakārāya Pālakaḥ pālyatām ayam.»

It' îdaṃ prakṛtīr uktvā Pālakaṃ punar abravīt:
«Avantivardhanaṃ putram mat|prītyā pālayer iti.»

Hearing this, the family priest and the other brahmins, their voices stuttering with grief, wiped away their tears and said: "As your subordinate, Palaka must not hesitate to obey your order; but you have ruled that we are to give commands, so how can we remain uninvolved? With his elder brother the previous king alive, Palaka will surely be an impostor when he takes the throne. Should you live for a hundred years, Palaka, although he may be feeding the flame of kingship, will all the while consider himself at fault, like a man who marries before his elder brother. So please revoke this most terrible decision, and let our tears of sorrow become tears of joy!"

With his hands together in salutation and his shoulders slightly hunched, the king said, "Stop causing me pain with
your words. He has been approved by me and is capable of 1.80
protecting the land. He will not be reviled as an impostor by those who understand the meaning of the word. When I have abdicated and am unable to tend the flame of kingship, he will not be like a man who has married before his elder brother; he will be king! Those wicked words that made the people block their ears when they heard them were not untrue, for I did kill my father. So, having committed this sin, I am going to do penance to appease your suffering. No one is to stop me! May Palaka here be looked after to repay what I, by adhering to my duty, have done for the people."

After saying this to the people he spoke again to Palaka: "Out of fondness for me, please look after my son Avantivardhana."

Vilakṣa|hasitaṃ kṛtvā Gopālam Pālako 'bravīt,
«Avantivardhano rājā rājan kasmān na jāyatām?
Satsu bhrātṛṣu bhūpāla|guṇa|vatsv api bhū|bhujaḥ
nikṣiptavantaḥ śrūyante putreṣv eva guruṃ dhuram.»
Gopālas tam ath' ôvāca «bhaviṣyati yuvā yadā
tvaṃ ca vṛddhas tadā yuktaṃ svayam eva kariṣyasi.»
Evaṃ niruttarāḥ kṛtvā prakṛtīs tāḥ sa|Pālakāḥ
sarva|tīrth'|âmbu|kalaśair abhyaṣiñcat sa Pālakam.
1.90 Āropya c' âinaṃ tvaritaṃ siṃh'|āsanam udaṅ|mukhaḥ
nirjagāma purāt svasmād eka|rātr'|ôṣito yathā.
Atha rājani kānan'|āvṛtte
puram āspandita|loka|locanām.
nibhṛta|śvāsit'|āmaya|dhvaniṃ
mṛta|kalpāṃ praviveśa Pālakaḥ.

iti Budhasvāminā viracitāyām
Bṛhatkathāyāṃ Ślokasaṃgrahe
prathamaḥ sargaḥ.

Palaka gave an embarrassed laugh and said to Gopala, "Sire, why doesn't Avantivardhana become king? Even kings with brothers capable of ruling have been known to cast the heavy burden of sovereignty upon their sons."

Gopala replied, "When he has become a man and you have grown old, then you will do what is right yourself." Having thus had the last word with his subjects and his brother, he anointed Palaka with pots of water from all the
sacred bathing places. He quickly had him sit on the throne 1.90
and, heading north, left his city as if he had spent just one night there.

When the king had retired to the forest, Palaka entered the city. The quivering eyes of the people and the sounds of sickness and faltering breath made it seem all but dead.

Thus ends the first canto of the
Long Story Abridged into Sanskrit Verse
composed by Budhasvamin.

CANTO 2
PĀLAKA

ATHA BIBHRAD DUR|UCCHEDAṂ
śokaṃ bhrātṛ|viyoga|jam
utsṛṣṭa|pṛthivī|cintaḥ Pālakaḥ kālam akṣipat.
Taṃ purodhaḥ|prabhṛtayaḥ kadā cid avadan prajāḥ:
«utsīdantīḥ prajā rājan n' ârhasi tvam upekṣitum.
Bhrātuḥ puraḥ pratijñāya dū|rakṣyāṃ rakṣituṃ kṣitim
kiṃ śocasi? na śoko 'yam upāyaḥ kṣiti|rakṣaṇe.
Ṣaṣṭhaṃ pāp'|âṃśam ādatte rakṣann api nṛpaḥ prajāḥ
nikṣipta|kṣiti|rakṣas tu sarvam eva na muñcati.
Tasmāj jighāṃsatā pāpaṃ puṇyaṃ c' ôpacicīṣatā
rājan dhanyāḥ prajāḥ kāryāḥ sukhaṃ c' ânububhūṣatā.
Na ced arthayamānānāṃ vacanaṃ naḥ kariṣyasi
dhruvaṃ drakṣyasi saṃkrāntā deśād rājanvataḥ prajāḥ.
Avṛtta|pūrvam asmābhir udāsīne tvayi śrutam
balād agni|gṛhān nītaḥ puroḍāśaḥ śunā kila,
Baṭoś ca bhrāmyato bhikṣāṃ bhikṣā|pātrād anāvṛtāt
baṭutvāt kṣipta|cittasya hṛtaḥ kākena modakaḥ».
Iti śrutvā sa|saṃtrāso rājā tāḍita|dundubhiḥ
mṛg'|êndr'|āsanam adhyāste Sumeruṃ Maghavān iva.
2.10 Tasminn ārūḍha|mātre ca samaṃ vikasitāḥ prajāḥ
uday'|âcala|kūṭa|sthe nalinya iva bhāskare.
Ath' âtīte kva cit kāle viprān papraccha pārthivaḥ,
«dharmam ācakṣatāṃ pūjyāḥ śuddham» ity atha te 'bruvan,
«Sarva|vidyā|vidā dharmaḥ kas tvayā n' âvalokitaḥ?

SUFFERING THE UNSHAKABLE GRIEF of separation from his brother, Palaka passed his time without a thought for the kingdom.

One day the royal chaplain and some of the subjects said to him: "Sire, the people are in distress. You should not ignore them. Having promised your brother to protect this vulnerable land, why do you grieve? This grief is no way to protect the land. Even a king who protects his subjects takes on a sixth of their sins. As for one who neglects the protection of his realm—he takes on all of them. So, sire, you should make the people happy by striving to eliminate wrongdoing, accumulate merit and experience pleasure. If you do not do what we ask, you are sure to see the people leave the area under royal rule. We have heard of unprecedented goings-on while you have been disengaged: a dog snatched an oblation from a sacrificial fire, and a crow took a sweet from the uncovered begging-bowl of a young brahmin on his begging-round (as is the wont of young brahmins, he was distracted)."

After hearing this, the dismayed king installed himself on the throne like Indra installing himself on Mount Sumeru
to the beat of kettledrums. As soon as he had ascended the 2.10
throne, the people blossomed with happiness, like lotus flowers when the sun touches the peak of the eastern mountain.

After some time the king made a request of the brahmins, "Worthy gentlemen, please acquaint me with the true religion." They replied, "You are well versed in all branches of learning. What religion have you not studied? In asking

ācāro 'yam iti vyaktam anuyuktās tvayā vayam.
Rāg'|ādimantaḥ puruṣās tair uktā hy apramāṇatā
sāṃkhy'|ādīnām akāryatvād vedasy' âiva pramāṇatā.
Tasmād vedeṣu vihitaṃ yat tad āsevyatām iti!»
śrutv" êdaṃ nṛ|patir yajñair īje niḥ|saṃkhya|dakṣiṇaiḥ.

Ath' ôtsṛṣṭa|prajā|kāryaṃ dīkṣā|saṃtāna|sevayā
mantriṇau jāta|saṃtrāsau taṃ kadā cid avocatām:
«Uddhṛtaḥ śoka|paṅkāt tvaṃ balibhir dvija|kuñjaraiḥ
uddhāryaḥ sāmprataṃ kena dīkṣā|paṅkād dur|uttarāt?
Kām'|ârthau yady api tyaktau sevyāv eva tath" âpi tau
durlabho hi vinā tābhyāṃ dharmaḥ śuddho nṛpair iti.»

Upapannam idaṃ śrutvā pratiśrutya «tath" êti» ca
devatā|yācana|vyagra|strīkam antaḥ|puraṃ yayau.
Pān'|ābharaṇa|vāsaḥ|srak|priya|vāg|dāna|mānitāḥ
antaḥ|pura|carīḥ praiṣyāś cakāra paritoṣitāḥ.

2.20 Anantaram anujyeṣṭhaṃ devīḥ saṃmānya bhū|patiḥ
Vāsukinyā mahā|devyā nināya saha yāminīm.
Sa tāmra|cūḍa|rutibhir bandi|vṛndair vibodhitaḥ
upāsiṣṭa puraḥ|saṃdhyām ā divākara|darśanāt.

Tato dhavala|vāsaḥ|srag|alaṃkār'|ânulepanaḥ
stūyamāno jay'|āśīrbhir āsthāna|sthānam āgataḥ.
Purodhaḥ|prabhṛtīs tatra prakṛtīḥ prakṛti|priyaḥ

us you are clearly just being polite. Men feel passion and other emotions, so doctrines like Samkhya, which they have formulated, lack authority. Because it alone has no author, only the Veda is authoritative. Therefore, follow that which is laid down in the Vedas!" When he heard this, the king had sacrifices performed and gave innumerable rewards to the officiants.

Because he underwent a constant stream of sacrificial initiations he neglected his duties to the people and one day he was spoken to by the two ministers, who had become troubled: "Like mighty elephants, eminent brahmins rescued you from the quagmire of grief with sacrificial offerings. Now who is to rescue you from the quicksand of sacrificial initiations? Even if they have renounced desire and wealth, kings must still pursue them, for without them the true religion is unobtainable."

Their words were right; when he heard them, he agreed and went to the harem where his wives were busy worshipping the gods. He made the serving women of the harem happy by honoring them with gifts of drinks, ornaments, clothes, garlands and sweet words. Then the king 2.20
paid his respects to his wives in order of their seniority before spending the night with Queen Vasukini. He was woken by cock-crows and bands of bards, and performed his morning worship until sunrise.

Then, wearing white clothes, garlands and ornaments, and anointed with white paste, he was hymned with victory-prayers as he arrived at the assembly hall. He was pleasant

mānayitvā yathā|yogyaṃ s'|ôpacāraṃ vyasarjayat.
Smayamānas tato rājā mantriṇāv idam abravīt:
«āpāna|bhūmir udyāne ramaṇīyā prakalpyatām.
Ko hi yuṣmad|vidha|suhṛd|vihit'|āpat|pratikriyaḥ
viṣayān na niṣeveta dṛṣṭ'|âdṛṣṭ'|âvirodhitaḥ?
So 'haṃ paura|janaṃ bhṛtyān antaḥ|pura|vicāriṇaḥ
ātmānaṃ ca bhavan|nāthaṃ yojayāmi sukhair iti.»
Atha tau prahva|mūrdhānau svāmy|abhiprāya|vedinau,
«pān'|ôpakaraṇaṃ sarvaṃ sajjam ev' êty» avocatām.
Vyāhārya sa tatas tatra sa|bāla|sthavirāṃ purīm
vastr'|ābharaṇa|māly'|ânna|dānaiḥ prītām akārayat.
Padma|rāg'|ādi|śuktiṣṭham utpal'|ādy|adhivāsitam
kṛta|jot|kāram anyonyaṃ pīyate sma tato madhu.
2.30 Madhu|pān'|ântarāleṣu sa|vipañcī|svanaṃ muhuḥ
gīyate sma mano|hāri naṭ'|ādyair nṛtyate sma ca.
Vihṛtya dinam evaṃ ca śīta|raśmau divākare
visṛjya prakṛtī rājā viveś' ântaḥ|puraṃ tataḥ.
Tatr' âpi śruta|saṃgīto dṛṣṭa|strī|pātra|nāṭakaḥ
pāyit'|â|śeṣa|bhāryaś ca paścān nidrām asevata.
Evam āsevamānasya s'|ārtavaṃ viṣayān gatāḥ
vivṛddha|sukha|rāgasya bahavas tasya vāsarāḥ.
Sa kadā cid dvij'|ādibhyaḥ sa|viṣādo nyavedayat,
«svapno may" âdya yo dṛṣṭaḥ praśasyaiḥ śrūyatām asau.

to his people and he paid his respects to the priests and subjects there, before duly and courteously dismissing them.

Then the smiling king addressed his two ministers: "Have a beautiful place for a drinking party prepared in the garden, for who would not indulge his senses when he has friends like you on hand to prevent a calamity, and is thus unhindered by worries about the present or future? So I shall show the townspeople, the servants who live in my inner apartments and myself, your master, a good time!"

The two ministers, who had anticipated their master's plan, bowed and said, "All the preparations for drinking are already in place."

He invited the whole city there, including the young and the old, and delighted them with gifts of clothes, ornaments, garlands and food. Then, with everyone toasting one another, wine scented with lotus and other fragrances was drunk out of goblets made from rubies and
other gems. In between the bouts of drinking, performers 2.30
sang and danced beautifully to the sound of the lute. The king whiled away the day like this, and when the sun's rays became cool he dismissed his subjects and went to the harem. There too he listened to music and watched plays with women as actors. He gave all his wives drinks before finally going to sleep. He spent many days like this, indulging his senses in the manner befitting the season, and his passion for pleasure grew stronger.

One day he dejectedly said to some brahmins and others, "Your eminences, listen to the dream I had today. I had gone out to inspect the animals in the stables when I saw

Vāhy'|âvalokanāy' âhaṃ nirgatas tatra dṛṣṭavān
mattaṃ mahāntam āyāntaṃ mātaṅgaṃ vana|cāriṇam.
Tan|mad'|āmodam āghrāya rājya|hasty api māmakaḥ
krodhād unmūlit'|ālāno yātaḥ prati vana|dvipam.
Vanyas tu hastam utkṣipya kiṃ cid ākuñcit'|âṅguliḥ
āhūtavān iva yudhe sa|garvaiḥ kaṇṭha|garjitaiḥ.
Madīyen' âtha nāgena vegen' āpatya dūrataḥ
saṃnipāto mahān datto dantayor vana|dantinaḥ.
Sphaṭika|stambha|śubhrābhyāṃ
  dantābhyāṃ tena māmakaḥ
dūram utkṣipya nikṣiptas
  tato yātaḥ parāṅ|mukhaḥ.

2.40 Parājitaṃ pareṇ' âtha dṛṣṭvā svaṃ rājya|hastinam
nivartayitu|kāmo 'ham āsannān idam uktavān:
‹Nivartayāmi rājy'|êbhaṃ śīghram ānayat' âṅkuśam!
śikṣito Vatsa|rājena hasti|śikṣām ahaṃ nanu?›
Iti mantrayamāṇo 'ham alabdha|prārthit'|âṅkuśaḥ
pratibuddhaḥ sa|saṃtrāso ‹kim etad iti?› cintayan.
Iti svapno mayā dṛṣṭaḥ kṣaṇadāyāḥ parikṣaye
phalam iṣṭam aniṣṭaṃ vā pūjyair atr' ôcyatām iti!»

Ath' âniṣṭa|phalaṃ svapnaṃ jānanto 'pi dvi|jātayaḥ
rāj'|ôpacāra|caturāḥ sthāpayām āsur anyathā:
«Yo 'sau rājan gajo vanyas taṃ budhyasva Vināyakam
yaś c' âbhiṣeka|hastī taṃ rājya|vighnaṃ śarīriṇam.
Tat te Gaṇapatiḥ prītaḥ prasahy' ôddharati prabhuḥ
tvam apy unmūlit'|ânarthaś ciraṃ pāhi mahīm iti!»

Iti duḥ|śliṣṭam ākarṇya phalaṃ svapnasya kalpitam
sukhaṃ n' âlabhat' âth' âinam abrūtāṃ mantriṇāv idam:
«Śrūyatāṃ deva yad vṛttaṃ vṛddhasya jagatī|pateḥ

there a huge, wild bull-elephant in rut coming my way. When my royal elephant smelt the odor of his passion, he furiously pulled up his restraining post and charged at the wild tusker. The savage beast lifted his trunk, curled his toes a little and with his proud trumpeting seemed to issue a call to battle. Then my tusker charged violently from afar, and came crashing down on the tusks of the wild elephant. With tusks as white as marble pillars, the latter picked up my elephant and hurled him far away. Then mine turned
away and fled. When I saw my royal elephant vanquished 2.40
by his foe, I wanted to bring him back, and said to those present: 'I shall make the royal tusker come back—quickly, bring the goad!—for was I not trained in elephant lore by the king of Vatsa*?' Just as I was saying this, and before I got the goad I had asked for, I woke up terrified, wondering what was going on. This was the dream I had at the end of the night. Tell me, Your Reverences, what it portends, be it good or bad!"

The brahmins were ingenious in their flattery of the king and despite knowing the dream to be a bad omen they interpreted it otherwise: "Sire, the wild elephant is Ganesha; the royal tusker is the embodiment of the troubles of the realm. So Lord Ganapati is pleased with you and has used force to save you. With your problems eradicated, may you rule this land for a long time!"

When he heard this contrived and inconsistent interpretation of the dream, the king was not satisfied. Then the two ministers said to him: "Sire, listen to this story about the old king that we heard our father telling at home. Ap-

āvābhyāṃ śrutam etac ca gṛhe kathayataḥ pituḥ.
Mṛg'|êndr'|āsanam āroḍhuṃ Pradyotena kil' êcchatā
yathā|pradhāna|militāḥ pṛṣṭāḥ svapnaṃ dvi|jātayaḥ:
2.50 ‹Mama siṃh'|āsana|sthasya sthito mūrdhni vihaṃgamaḥ
vicitraiḥ saptabhiḥ pakṣaiḥ ko 'sau vyākriyatām iti!›
Teṣu nir|vacaneṣv eko dvi|jaḥ Śāṇḍilya|nāmakaḥ
sa|kampa|vacano 'vocan nīcaiś cañcala|bhīrukaḥ:
‹Rājñā svapna|phalaṃ pṛṣṭāḥ kiṃ tūṣṇīm āstha? kathyatām!
trasyadbhiḥ paruṣād v" âpi mādṛk kasmān na yujyatām?
An|iṣṭam api vaktavyaṃ sv|anuṣṭhāna|pratikriyam
duṣ|kara|pratikāre tu yuktam ittham udāsitum.›
Iti śrutvā Mahāsenaḥ saṃśay'|āmṛṣṭa|mānasaḥ
Śāṇḍilyam idam aprākṣīd vivakṣuṃ sphurit'|âdharam:
‹Brahman kathaya viśrabdham anujñāto dvi|jātair api
yasmād vyāhartum ārabdhaḥ pratiṣiddho na kena cit.›
Ity uktaḥ kṣiti|pālena vyāhartum upacakrame:
‹ahit'|ādi hit'|ântaṃ ca śrūyatāṃ deva mā kupaḥ.
Yo 'sau sapta|chadaḥ pakṣī so 'śanir duḥ|śrava|dhvaniḥ
sapta pakṣās tu ye tasya sapta pakṣān nibodha tān.
Sarvathā vistareṇ' âlam alaṃ siṃh'|āsanena te!
kaś cid āropyatām etad yasya n' êcchasi jīvitam.
Kaṃ cid ady' êdam ārūḍham ardha|māseṣu saptasu
atīteṣv aśanir hanti patitvā mūrdhani dhruvam.›
2.60 Iti śrutvā sphurat|krodhaḥ prabhur Bharatarohakam,

parently, when Pradyota was wanting to ascend the throne, he asked the brahmins assembled in order of seniority about
a dream: 'I am sitting on the throne and a bird with seven 2.50
brightly colored wings sits on my head. Explain what this means!'

When none of them answered, a brahmin called Shandilya, so scared that he was trembling, spoke softly in a faltering voice: 'The king has asked you about the meaning of a dream; why do you remain silent? Speak! Or, if you are frightened of saying something harsh, why not employ a man like me? Even if an omen is bad, it should be reported if it can be easily remedied, but it is right to remain silent like this if the predicted outcome is difficult to prevent.'

When he heard this, Mahasena's mind was consumed by anxiety, and he asked Shandilya, whose bottom lip was quivering with the desire to speak: 'Brahmin, hold forth without fear; you have the permission of the brahmins too, because nobody stopped you when you started to talk.'

Addressed thus by the king, he began to speak: 'Your Majesty, what I am going to say sounds bad at first, but is ultimately good. Please listen to it without getting angry. The bird with seven wings is a crashing thunderbolt; its seven wings are seven fortnights. I shall not go into the details—you must abandon the throne! Have someone sit on it whom you would not mind dying. Whoever sits on this throne today will be killed after seven fortnights by a thunderbolt falling on his head—I'm sure of it.'

When he heard this, the king shook with rage and ordered 2.60
Bharatarohaka, 'Have this chatterbox's eyes put out!'

‹akṣiṇī mukharasy' âsya khanyetām!› ity acodayat.
‹Yath" ājñāpayas' îty!› uktvā badhnan parikaraṃ dvijān
mantrī s'|âkṣi|nikocena grāhya|vākyān asūcayat.
Mṛdu|pūrvaṃ tato viprā mahī|pālam abodhayan,
‹deva n' ônmatta|vākyāni gṛhyante paṭu|buddhibhiḥ.
Na ca kevalam unmatto brāhmaṇaś c' âiṣa mūḍhakaḥ
ten' âpi nayan'|ôddhāraṃ n' âiva nigraham arhati.
Kiṃ tu tāvad ayaṃ baddhaḥ sthāpyatāṃ vidhavā|sutaḥ
pakṣāḥ sapta gatā yāvat tataḥ prāpsyati nigraham.
Siṃh'|āsanam api kṣipram ārohatu nar'|âdhipaḥ
lagne 'sminn eva sauvarnaḥ parīkṣ"|ârthaṃ dvi|janmanaḥ.
Yadi saty" âiva vāg asya tataḥ satkāram āpsyati
viparyaye khalī|kāraṃ Manv|ādi|paribhāṣitam.
Devo 'pi divasān etān vidvadbhir brāhmaṇaiḥ saha
kurvadbhiḥ śānti|karmāṇi Mahākālaṃ niṣevatām.›
Iti śrutvā dvi|jātibhyo ‹yuktam› ity avadhārya ca
bandhayitvā ca Śāṇḍilyaṃ Mahākālaṃ yayau nṛpaḥ.
Tatra sapta sthitaḥ pakṣān apaśyad divase 'ntime
madhyaṃ|dine payod'|ālīm unnamantīṃ raviṃ prati.
2.70 Atha sā kṣaṇa|mātreṇa vyāpt'|ânanta|dig|antarā
Nīlakaṇṭha|gala|chāyā pravṛṣṭā vṛṣṭim aśmanām.
Caṇḍaṃ caṭacaṭā|ghoṣam udghoṣy' âśanir utkaṭaḥ
rāja|pratikṛtiṃ piṣṭvā tatr' âiv' ântar|dadhe tataḥ.
Atha Śāṇḍilyam āhvāyya kṛtvā vigata|bandhanam
kṣamayitvā ca vipulaiḥ saṃpradānair atoṣayat.
Rājñā c' âsya kṛtaṃ nāma tac ca loke pratiṣṭhitam

The minister replied, 'As you wish!,' but, hitching up his robe, he winked at the brahmins, whose pronouncements had to be taken into consideration.

Then the brahmins gently counselled the king, 'Sire, the wise do not listen to the words of the insane. This idiot is not only mad, he is also a brahmin, so he should not be punished by having his eyes put out. Rather, have this widow's bastard imprisoned until the seven fortnights are up, and then he can be punished. Moreover, you should immediately arrange for a golden image of a king to be placed upon the throne at the crucial moment, in order to test the brahmin. If what he says is true, then he is to be rewarded; if not, he shall get the punishment specified by Manu and others. And during this period, Your Majesty should serve Mahakala in the company of learned brahmins performing rites to ward off evil.'

When the king heard this from the brahmins he decided they were right. He had Shandilya imprisoned and went to the temple of Mahakala. He stayed there for seven fortnights and at noon on the last day he saw a line of clouds
rising up toward the sun. In an instant it filled the whole 2.70
sky with the beautiful dark hue of Nilakantha's* throat and poured forth hailstones. With a terrifying, juddering crash a huge thunderbolt pulverized the image of the king and vanished right there and then. Then the king had Shandilya summoned, released him from his chains, asked his forgiveness, and appeased him with numerous gifts. The

so 'yaṃ mukhara|Śāṇḍilyaḥ siddh'|ādeśo 'nuyujyatām.»
Tena c' āhūya pṛṣṭena niḥ|śaṅkena niveditam,
«śṛṇu rājan na kopaṃ ca pitṛ|vat kartum arhasi!
Yo 'sau vanyo gajaḥ so 'nyo rājā rājan upāgataḥ
bhavadīyo bhavān eva sarvathā śrūyatām idam.
Tvam anyena mahī|pāla mahī|pālena rājyataḥ
svataḥ pracyāvitas tasmād yuktam āsthīyatām iti!»
Iti śrutvā mahī|pāle viṣād'|ānata|mūrdhani
śanair mukhara|Śāṇḍilya|pramukhā niryayur dvijāḥ.
Mantri|mātra|sahāyas tu rājā kṛtv" âvaguṇṭhanam,
«kaḥ syād rāj" êti» cintāvān niṣasāda nṛp'|āsane.
Siddh'|ādeśasya tu vacaḥ śraddadhānaḥ Surohakaḥ
viṣādād dīnayā vācā mahī|pālam abhāṣata,
2.80 «Mahāsenena duḥ|svapnaḥ sa yathā vañcitas tathā
vañcaya tvam api kṣipram aty|āsanna|phalo hy asau.
Tiryag|yoni|gataḥ kaś cid adhyāstāṃ pārthiv'|āsanam
devo 'pi divasān kāṃś cid vana|vāsī bhavatv iti.»
Tūṣṇīṃ|bhūtaṃ tu rājānam evaṃ bruvati mantriṇi
Gopāla|tanayas tatra viveś' Âvantivardhanaḥ.
Tasya saṃkrīḍamānasya dūram utpatya kandukaḥ
nipaty' ôtpatya ca punaḥ siṃh'|āsana|talaṃ gataḥ.
Avantivardhanayaśā bhaginī tena coditā
«siṃh'|āsana|talād eva kandukaḥ kṛṣyatām iti.»
Tay" ôktaṃ «svayam eva tvaṃ kiṃ na karṣasi kandukam?

king gave him the name by which he is famous. Let us consult that same 'Chatterbox' Shandilya, whose predictions have come true."

On being summoned and questioned, he spoke without hesitation, "Listen, Your Highness, and do not become angry like your father! Sire, the wild elephant is another king who has come near; your elephant is none other than you. You must listen to me! Your Highness, the other king removed you from your kingdom, so you must act accordingly!"

When he heard this, the king hung his head in despair, and the brahmins departed quietly, led by "Chatterbox" Shandilya. Accompanied by just his two ministers, the king held his head and slumped on the throne, worrying about who the king might be. Shandilya's predictions had come true in the past and Surohaka believed what he had said.
In a voice wretched with despair he said to the king, "In 2.80
the same way that Mahasena prevented the outcome of his bad dream, so must you quickly prevent that of yours, for its fulfillment is very close at hand. Your Majesty should have some animal sit on the throne, and take to living in the forest for a few days."

But as the minister was saying this to the silent king, Gopala's son Avantivardhana came in. He was playing with a ball and threw it a long way. It kept bouncing up and down until it was under the throne.

He ordered his sister Avantivardhanayasha, "Get the ball out from under the throne!"

She replied, "Why don't you get the ball yourself? Am I

kiṃ c' âhaṃ bhavataḥ praiṣyā yen' ādiśasi mām iti?»
Tato «paśy' êti!» tām uktvā tad utkṣipya nṛp'|āsanam
Avantivardhano 'nyatra sthāpayām āsa nirvyathaḥ.
Sa tu kandukam ādātum ārabdhaś ca nṛpeṇa tu
siṃh'|āsanād avaplutya pariṣvaktas trap"|ānataḥ.
Ath' ânantaram āhūya rājā prakṛti|maṇḍalam
uvāca «rāja|putro 'yam adya rājye 'bhiṣicyatām!
Yuṣmat|samakṣam ukto 'haṃ bhrātrā jyeṣṭhena gacchatā
‹Avantivardhanaṃ putraṃ mat|prītyā pālayer iti.›
2.90 Tad|ādeśāt sutatvāc ca so 'yaṃ saṃvardhito 'dhunā
pitryam āsanam adhyāstāṃ nyāsaṃ pratyarpitaṃ mayā!»
Ath' âsmin saṃkaṭe kārye Pālakena pradarśite
sabhāyām ānat'|âṅgāyāṃ na kaś cit kiṃ cid uktavān.
Tato dharm'|ârtha|kāmānāṃ mātrām ākhyāya Pālakaḥ
putram āropayām āsa siṃh'|āsanam avantiyam.
Kṛṣṇ'|âjin'|âmbara|dharaḥ kṛta|keśa|nāśaḥ
skandh'|âvasakta|karako nṛ|patiḥ purāṇaḥ
adhyāsitaṃ muni|varaiḥ saha Kāśyapena
manda|spṛho 'sita|giriṃ tapase jagāma.

iti Bṛhatkathāyāṃ
dvitīyaḥ sargaḥ.

your servant, that you can order me around?"

Avantivardhana said to her, "Watch this!," picked up the throne and casually put it down to one side.

When he was about to take the ball, the king jumped down from the throne and hugged the boy, who shyly hung his head. The king immediately summoned all his subjects and declared, "Today the prince is to be anointed king! When my eldest brother was leaving, he said to me in front of you, 'Out of fondness for me, please look after
my son Avantivardhana.' Because of his father's order and 2.90
because he is his father's son, may he now, having reached maturity, sit upon his father's throne. I have returned that which was entrusted to me!"

When Palaka announced this difficult course of action, the assembly bowed and no one said a word. Then Palaka explained the relative merits of religious duty, material wealth and worldly pleasure, and put Gopala's son* upon the throne of Avanti. Wearing the skin of a black antelope, his head shaved and a water pot hanging from his shoulder, the old king, his desires dulled, went to live as an ascetic on the Dark Mountain where Kashyapa and other great sages were living.

Thus ends the second canto
of the Long Story.

CANTO 3
AVANTIVARDHANA

ATH' ÂVANTIṢU JANTŪNĀṂ
kṣudrāṇām api kena cit
janyate sma na saṃtāpaḥ pārthive 'vantivardhane.
Evaṃ bahuṣu yāteṣu vāsareṣu mahī|patiḥ
kadā cid vāhayitv" âśvān nivṛtto dṛṣṭavān kva cit,
Tamāl'|ālambi|dol"|ântar vilasantīṃ kumārikām
Kālindī|hrada|saṃkrāntāṃ lolām indu|kalām iva,
Uttarīy'|ânta|saṃsaktam ākarṣantīṃ śikhaṇḍakam
nirmucyamāna|nirmokaṃ bhogaṃ bhogi|vadhūm iva.
Dṛśyamānas tayā rājā tāṃ ca paśyan punaḥ punaḥ
āvṛtto haya|śālābhiḥ svaṃ viveśa niveśanam.
Tatra saṃkṣiptam āsevya majjan'|ādi raho|gataḥ
dolāyamāna|hṛdayo dolām eva vyacintayat.
Mand'|âśan'|âbhilāṣasya manda|nidrasya bhū|pateḥ
manda|dharm'|ârtha|cintasya divasāḥ kati cid gatāḥ.
Kadā cid atha velāyāṃ manda|raśmau divā|kṛti
kṣubhitānām iv' âśrauṣīt sa nirghoṣam udanvatām.
Didṛkṣuḥ kāraṇaṃ tasya samudbhūta|kutūhalaḥ
prāsāda|talam ārohad antaḥ|pura|car"|āvṛtaḥ.
3.10 Nṛ|mātaṅga|turaṃg'|ôṣṭra|gav'|âj'|âiḍaka|rāsabhān
saṃpramardantam adrākṣīn mātaṅgaṃ Saṅghamardanam.
Unmūlita|mahā|vṛkṣaś cūrṇita|prāṃśu|mandiraḥ
bhṛṅga|mālā|parīvāraḥ sa yayau prati pakkaṇam.
Pāna|prasakta|mātaṅga|maṇḍala|prahit'|ēkṣaṇam
mātaṅga|rājam adrākṣīn mātaṅga|grāma|ṇīs tataḥ.
Ādideśa samīpa|sthāṃ kanyakām «avilambitam!
hasti|kīṭo 'yam uddāmo! durdānto damyatām iti!»
Kar'|âmbho|ruha|saṃsparśa|subhagen' âtha s" âmbhasā

WITH AVANTIVARDHANA as king, no one inflicted any suffering on even the tiniest creatures in Avanti. Once, after many days had passed like this, the king was returning from riding his horses when he saw somewhere a young maiden playing on a swing that hung from a *Tamāla* tree, looking like a rippling reflection of the crescent moon in the waters of the Yamuna. Her hair was caught in the top of her robe and she drew it up like a she-snake drawing up her hood as she casts off its slough. She watched him and he kept turning back to look at her as he returned to his quarters from the stables. There he cut short his ablutions and sat alone, his heart seesawing as he thought of nothing but that swing.

For several days the king had no appetite, hardly slept and cared little for religious duty or affairs of state. Then one evening, when the sun's rays had dimmed, he heard a roar like that of a stormy sea. His curiosity was aroused and he wanted to see what was causing it, so he went up to the roof terrace, surrounded by his harem. He saw 3.10
the bull-elephant Sanghamardana* trampling people, elephants, horses, camels, cows, sheep, goats and donkeys. Uprooting huge trees and pulverizing tall buildings, he headed for a settlement of outcastes, followed by a line of bees. A group of outcastes was carousing; their chief noticed the majestic forest beast staring at them.

He ordered a girl standing nearby, "Quick! This lousy tusker is out of control! He's wild—tame him!"

From a brass pot the girl then quickly sprinkled water blessed by the touch of her lotus-like hand onto the ele-

ārāt siṣeca kariṇaṃ kare kuñcita|puṣkare.
Atha saṃrambha|saṃhārāt saṃvellita|karaḥ karī
vavande caraṇau tasyāḥ saṃspṛśya śirasā mahīm.

Tām Avanti|patir dṛṣṭvā dṛṣṭa|pūrvāṃ tathā|gatām
citrīyamāṇa|hṛdayaḥ cintayām āsa cetasā,
«Kiṃ citraṃ yad ayaṃ nāgaḥ saha|rāgaḥ sa|cetanaḥ
vaśī|kṛtaḥ śarīriṇyā vaśī|karaṇa|vidyayā?
Iyaṃ hi vīta|rāg'|ādīn munīn api nirīkṣitā
vaśī|kuryād icchantī ca calayed acalān api!»

Ath' êndr'|āyudha|rāgeṇa s'|ôttarīyeṇa dantayoḥ
baddhāṃ dolām adhiṣṭhāya nāgaṃ «yāh' îty» acodayat.
3.20 Tato mandatar'|âbhyāsaiś caraṇaiḥ Saṅghamardanaḥ
abhistambham agād vīta|bhaya|paura|jan'|āvṛtaḥ.
Tay" ôktam «ātapaś caṇḍaḥ saṃtāpayati mām iti»
aśoka|pallavaiś chāyām atha tasyāś cakāra saḥ.
Bandhayitvā gajaṃ stambhe prāsāda|tala|vartinam
vanditvā ca mahī|pālaṃ mātaṅgī pakkaṇaṃ yayau.

Mātaṅgī|vandanā|pūtam ātmānaṃ prekṣya pārthivaḥ
«k" êyaṃ? kasya? kuto v" êti?» pṛcchati sma Surohakam.

Sa tasmai kathayām āsa «deva na jñāyate kutaḥ
sahas" âiv' êdam āyātaṃ parun mātaṅga|pakkaṇam.
Ṛddhimanto 'tra mātaṅgās, teṣām Utpalahastakaḥ
grāma|ṇīs tasya kany" êyaṃ sutā Surasamañjarī.»

Iti śrutvā praviśy' ântardhyāyan Surasamañjarīm
sva|dehaṃ yāpayām āsa pitta|jvara|cikitsanaiḥ.

phant's trunk, the tip of which had contracted. The elephant's rage subsided immediately: he curled up his trunk and saluted the girl's feet by touching the ground with his head.

When he realized that the girl who had done this was the one that he had seen before, with surprise in his heart, the king of Avanti thought to himself, "What is surprising about this elephant, who has both passion and intelligence, being subjugated by the embodiment of the power of subjugation? For this girl, on being seen, could subjugate even passionless sages, and, if she wanted, move mountains too!"

Then she tied her rainbow-colored robe to his tusks to make a swing, sat in it and ordered the elephant to move.
Sanghamardana strolled gently to a restraining post, sur- 3.20
rounded by the now fearless citizens. The girl said that the ferocious heat of the sun was scorching her and the elephant shaded her with *aśoka* fronds. After tying the elephant to the post and saluting the king on his roof terrace, the outcaste girl returned to her settlement.

The king considered himself purified by the outcaste girl's salutation and asked Surohaka, "Who is this girl? Whose daughter is she? Where is she from?"

He replied, "Sire, her provenance is not known: this settlement of outcastes arrived out of the blue last year. They have supernatural powers. Their headman is Utpalahastaka; this girl is his daughter, Surasamanjari."

When he heard this he went inside thinking only of Surasamanjari, and tried to cure himself with remedies for bilious fever.

Surohakas tu taṃ dṛṣṭvā mātaṅgī|dūṣit'|āśayam
ākhyad Aṅgāravatyai sa tan|naptur vṛttam īdṛśam.
Sā tu sthitvā kṣaṇaṃ tūṣṇīṃ vicāra|stimit'|ēkṣaṇā
smit'|âpagamita|trāsaṃ Surohakam abhāṣata.
«Mātaṅga|rūpa|dhāriṇyo yath" ânyā divya|yoṣitaḥ
tath" êyam api ken' âpi nimitten' āgatā mahīm.
3.30 Kva Saṅghamardano vyālaḥ kva ca tad|danta|lambanam?
vyāpāro 'yam adivyasya prekṣitaḥ kena kasya cit?
Atha v" âlaṃ vimarśena! svayaṃ saṃbandhino gṛham
kanyāṃ varayitum yāmi n' ātma|tuly" âsti dūtikā.»
S" âtha pravahaṇ'|ārūḍhā vṛddha|vipra|puraḥ|sarā
gatvā pakkaṇa|madhya|sthaṃ dadarś' Ôtpalahastakam.
Dūrād eva sa dṛṣṭvā tām ātta|jharjhara|veṇukaḥ
saha mātaṅga|saṅghena vavande dūram utsṛtaḥ.
Ath' Âṅgāravatī yānād avatīrṇā tam abravīt:
«ahaṃ tvāṃ draṣṭum āyātā tvam apy eṣa palāyase!
Kāryaṃ me mahad āsannam ādhīnaṃ c' âpi tat tvayi
dūr'|ôtsaraṇam utsṛjya tena ḍhaukasva mām iti!»
Tam utsārita|mātaṅgaṃ s" āsann'|āsīnam abravīt:
«man|naptre dīyatāṃ rājñe rājñī Surasamañjarī.
‹Cāṇḍālī|sparśanaṃ rājā n' ârhat' îty› evam|ādibhiḥ
na ca grāmeyak'|ālāpais tvam māṃ bādhitum arhasi.
Yaś ca divy'|âbhimānas te tatr' âp' îdaṃ mam' ôttaram
mam' âpi bhadra dauhitraś cakra|vartī bhavādṛśām!»

Meanwhile, after seeing that the king's heart was troubled by the outcaste girl, Surohaka told Angaravati what had happened to her grandson. She remained quiet for a while, her gaze fixed in thought, and then spoke to Surohaka, whose discomfort was dispelled by her smile. "Like other divine women who don the guise of outcastes, this girl has arrived on the earth for some purpose. Sanghamardana is 3.30
such a brute and she swung from his tusks! Who has ever seen such behavior from an earthly being? But I must stop deliberating! I shall go myself to her kinsman's house to ask for the girl's hand: there is no go-between as good as oneself!"

She mounted her carriage and went on her way in the company of some elderly brahmins. She saw Utpalahastaka in the middle of the outcastes' settlement.

He spotted her in the distance. Taking his drum and flute, he and his band of outcastes moved off and greeted her from afar.*

Angaravati got down from her carriage and said to him: "I have come to see you and here you are, running away! I have an important job to do and you are crucial to it. Stop running off into the distance and come here!"

He dismissed the other outcastes and sat close by. She said to him, "Surasamanjari is to be given as queen to my grandson, the king. You must not oppose me with parochial arguments about kings not being allowed to touch outcaste girls. And as for your conceited opinion that you are divine, this is what I have to say to that: me too! Good sir, my daughter's son is the emperor of people like you!"

Ity Aṅgāravatī|vākyam ākarṇy' Ôtpalahastakaḥ
anukt'|ôttara ev' âsyai tath" êti pratipannavān.
3.40 Atha pracchannam āropya yugyaṃ Surasamañjarīm
mṛta|saṃjīvanīṃ naptur asāv oṣadhim ānayat.
Pariṇīya tu mātaṅgīm antar|antaḥ|purād bahiḥ
sa buddhy" âpi na yāti sma pratyakṣam api tāṃ smaran.
«Iyam ev' âsti tattvena mithy" ânyad iti» cintayan
gandharva|nagar'|ākāraṃ sa saṃsāram amanyata.
Gamayan divasān evam.
ekadā saha kāntayā
sa prāsāda|gato 'paśyat pakkaṇaṃ nir|janaṃ|gamam.
Taṃ ca dṛṣṭvā tri|yām"|ânte mandaṃ Surasamañjarī
krandantī parimṛjy' âśrum anuyukt" êti bhū|bhṛtā:
«Kiṃ śūnyaṃ pakkaṇaṃ dṛṣṭvā rudyate sundari tvayā
ut' ânyad asti duḥkhasya kāraṇaṃ kathyatām iti?»
S" âbravīt «kiṃ mam' âdy' âpi pakkaṇena bhavad|gateḥ?
kiṃ tu kāraṇam asty anyad bhīṣaṇaṃ tan niśāmyatām.
Siddha|mātaṅga|vidyo 'yaṃ pitā mama mah"|arddhikaḥ
Saptaparṇapure pūrvaṃ Vāyumukta|pure 'vasat..
Tatra kālaḥ śva|pāko 'sti vidyādhara|gaṇ'|âdhamaḥ
Ipphako nāma tasy' âiva pitr" âhaṃ ca pratiśrutā.
Tātasya viyatā yātaḥ kadā cid atha mārutaḥ
rajaḥ|piśaṅga|bhṛṅg'|âlīm aharat kusuma|srajam.
3.50 Sā tu saṃdhyām upāsīnaṃ Gaṅgā|rodhasi Nāradam
sthāṇu|sthiraṃ bhujaṃg" îva vilolā paryaveṣṭayat.

When he heard what Angaravati had to say, Utpalahas-
taka signalled his consent without saying a word. She put 3.40
Surasamanjari in the covered carriage and brought her, the
elixir of life, to revive her grandson.

After he married the outcaste girl, he did not leave his innermost apartments, even in his mind, and dreamed of her constantly even though she was there before his eyes. He thought that in reality she alone existed and everything else was false, and considered his mundane world to be as illusory as the heavenly city of the Gandharvas*. He spent the days like this.

One day when he was on the roof terrace with his beloved he saw that the outcaste settlement was empty. At the end of the night Surasamanjari also noticed it and sobbed gently. The king wiped her tears and asked: "Tell me, beautiful lady, are you crying because you have seen that the settlement is empty, or is there another reason for your grief?"

She replied, "Why should I care for the outcastes' settlement now that I am with you? But there is another reason and it is terrible. Listen. My father has perfected the magical lore of the outcastes and possesses great powers. He used to live in Saptaparnapura*, the city of Vayumukta. A black, dog-cooking outcaste called Ipphaka lives there, the lowliest of the sorcerer class, and I was promised to him by my father. One day, when my father was flying through
the sky, the wind blew off his flower garland, the black
bees in which had turned golden from its pollen. Narada 3.50
was sitting upright as a post on the bank of the Ganga
performing his evening worship and as it fluttered down

Vyutthitaś ca samādhes taṃ dṛṣṭvā lohita|locanaḥ
Nāradaś caṇḍa|kopatvād uccair idam abhāṣata:
‹Śarīr'|ôpahatā mālā yen' êyaṃ māla|bhāriṇā
kṣiptā mayi manuṣyeṣu caṇḍālaḥ sa bhavatv iti!›
So 'tha śāp'|ôpataptena pitrā vijñāpito mama
‹tīvrasya brahma|śāpasya pratīkāro bhavatv iti.›
atha kṛp"|âmbu|śamita|krodha|jvālā|kadambakaḥ
Nārad'|âgnir uvāc' êdaṃ mlānam Utpalahastakam:
‹Na śakyaḥ pratisaṃhartuṃ śāpa|vahnir may" âpy ayam
utsṛṣṭaḥ kṛta|puṅkhena dhānuṣkeṇ' êva sāyakaḥ.
Kiṃ tu n' êṣu|samāḥ śāpāḥ prājñair abhimukh'|āgatāḥ
svalpen' âpi hi vañcyante tena tvam api vañcaya.
Pariṇeṣyati Gaupālir bhavatas tanayāṃ yadā
tadā tvaṃ dāruṇād asmād asmac|chāpād vimokṣyase.›
Iti śāpe varaṃ labdhvā vayaṃ tvat|pāda|pālitāḥ
uṣitā varjitā duḥkhair aho|rātra|samāṃ samām.
S" âhaṃ muneḥ prasādena jātā tvat|pāda|pālikā
ten' âpi śānta|śāpena svargād asmān nirākṛtā.
3.60 Sa kadā cid ito dṛṣṭvā gatam Utpalahastakam
mat|kṛte tvām api krūra Ipphakaḥ pīḍayed iti.
Nir|mātaṅgam idaṃ dṛṣṭvā mayā pitṛ|niveśanam
caṇḍāla|bhaya|śaṅkinyā ruditaṃ niḥsahāyayā.
Asti c' âtr' âpi sukara upāyaḥ sa tu duṣkaraḥ
mahā|rājasya sādhyatvāt pratikūlo hi pārthivaḥ.

it wrapped itself around him like a snake. Disturbed from his meditation, Narada looked at him with red eyes and, because of his violent temper, shouted:

'This garland has been sullied by contact with a body. Whoever was wearing it and threw it on me shall become an outcaste among men!'

My father was most upset at this imprecation and humbly begged him, 'Would that this harsh curse of a brahmin be overturned!'

With the flames of his rage put out by the water of compassion, the fiery Narada said the following to the despondent Utpalahastaka: 'Even I cannot recall this blazing curse, just as a skilled archer cannot recall an arrow once fired. However, clever people do not consider curses aimed at them to be like arrows, for they are easily avoided—you can avoid this one. When Gopala's son weds your daughter, you shall be freed from this terrible curse of mine.'

We thus received a blessing in the form of a curse. Under Your Majesty's protection we were carefree and passed a year as if it were a day and a night. By the grace of the sage, I came under the protection of Your Majesty. But that same
spent curse has removed me from this paradise. When the 3.60
heartless Ipphaka notices that Utpalahastaka has gone from here, he may harrass you on my account.

After seeing my father's settlement empty of outcastes, I was terrified of that outcaste and, helpless, I began to cry. There is an easy way out of this, but it is made difficult by the fact that it has to be done by a king, and for kings it goes against the grain. If you don't want to dissuade me

Yadi vijñāpayantīṃ māṃ n' ânyathā vaktum iṣyasi
tato vijñāpayiṣyāmi kartavye tu bhavān prabhuḥ.»
Ath' ôktaṃ jana|rājena «yad icchasi tad ucyatām
muktv" ânya|strī|kathāṃ bhīru sarvaṃ saṃpādayāmi te».
Ath' ānanda|ja|netr'|âmbu|sikt'|ānana|payodharā
«atiprasādaḥ ity!» uktv" âbravīt Surasamañjarī,
«Vidyādhar'|âdhirājena vyavasthā sthāpitā yathā
hiṃsitavyaḥ sa|doṣo 'pi n' ântaḥ|pura|gato nṛpaḥ.»
It' îdaṃ nṛpatiḥ śrutvā tām uvāca kṛta|smitaḥ
«anugrahe 'pi ‹yācñ" êti!› yad idaṃ tad idaṃ nanu.»
Tataś c' ārabhya divasād aho|niśam Avanti|paḥ
amāvāsyāṃ śaś" îv' āsīj jana|durlabha|darśanaḥ.
Kadā cid atha niryāntīṃ purīm udaka|dānakam
śrutvā harmy'|āvalī|śeṣāṃ rāj" âpy āsīt samutsukaḥ.
3.70 Śaiśava|prāpta|rājyatvād indriy'|âdhīna|mānasaḥ
tad" âlpa|darśī samayaṃ visasmāra sa taṃ tataḥ.
Prasuptām eva dayitām āropya śibikāṃ niśi
taṭaṃ Śiva|taḍāgasya citra|vṛtt'|ântam ānayat.
Tatas tan makar'|ākīrṇaṃ poten' êva mah"|ârṇavam
plavena vyacarat sārdhaṃ bhāryayā vīta|nidrayā.
Anujñāt'|âvagāhāṃś ca paśyan paura|kumārakān
so 'paśyad dayitāṃ bhītāṃ «mā bhaiṣīr iti!» c' âbravīt.
S" âvadat «pālitā yena prajāḥ sarvā na bibhyati

from telling you, I shall go ahead. Whether it is carried out is up to you."

The king said, "Say what you want, bashful lady, as long as it doesn't involve any other women. I will arrange whatever you want."

Her face and breasts wet with tears of joy, Surasamanjari said, "You're too kind!," and continued, "The king of the sorcerers has decreed that a king, even if he is at fault, is not to be harmed when he is in his harem."

When he heard this, the king smiled and replied, "Even when granting me a favor, you call it a request! I shall certainly do as you say!"

From that day forth the king of Avanti, like the new moon, was constantly out of sight of the people.

Then one day when the king heard that the entire city was on its way to the water-offering festival* and only the rows
of houses remained, he became keen to go too. Because 3.70
he had inherited the kingdom as a child, his mind was subservient to his senses, and the blinkered fellow forgot his promise. That night he placed his still sleeping sweetheart in a palanquin, and took her to the banks of Shiva's lake, where there were wonderful goings-on.

Then, as though in a ship on the great sea-monster-infested ocean, he floated about in a small boat with his wife, who had woken up. While watching the young people of the city, who had been allowed to bathe, he noticed that his sweetheart was scared. "Don't be frightened!" he said.

She replied, "It is not right for me to be frightened when

tasy' âiv' ôrasi tiṣṭhantī bibhem' îti na yujyate.
Kiṃ tu yātr" ânubhūt" êyam idānīṃ niṣ|prayojanam
ih' āsitam ahaṃ manye tasmād āvartyatām iti».

Yātr"|âpahṛta|cetastvāt tad|vākyam avakarṇayan
sabhāryaṃ baddham ātmānam aikṣat' Âvantivardhanaḥ.

Krandatām atha paurāṇāṃ paśyatāṃ c' ōrdhva|cakṣuṣām
Ipphakaḥ sphurita|krodhaḥ samutkṣipya jahāra tam.

Ath' âṅgāravatīṃ mūḍhāṃ pautr'|âpaharaṇa|śravāt
hlādayām āsatur vākyaiḥ sacivau sa|jal'|ânilaiḥ.
Sā tāv uvāca saṃbhrāntā «gatv" Âsitagiriṃ laghu
Pālakaḥ śrāvyatāṃ sūnor vṛtt'|ântam iti» tau gatau.

3.80 Kāśyapa|pramukhāṃs tatra namaskṛtya ca tāpasān
vanditāy' ācacakṣāte Pālakāya hṛtaṃ sutam.
Atha kaṇṭha|gata|prāṇaṃ Kāśyapaḥ samajīvayat:
«sv|antaḥ khalv eṣa vṛtt'|ânta iti» vāky'|âmṛtena tam,
«Sandehaś cen nirīkṣasva nabhaḥ|prasthāpit'|ēkṣaṇaḥ
āyāntīm eva jānīhi putra|vārttāṃ śivām iti.»

Ath' āgacchantam aikṣanta nabhaḥ|prahita|dṛṣṭayaḥ
cakāsad|asi|carmāṇaṃ divi divyaṃ tapasvinaḥ.
So 'vatīrya marun|mārgād a|svatantrī|kṛt'|Êpphakaḥ
saha c' Âvanti|nāthena Kāśyap'|ādīn avandata.
Vadhū|vandita|pāde ca cetanāvati Pālake
vidyādharaḥ kathitavān vṛtt'|ântaṃ muni|saṃnidhau.

I'm resting on the chest of the very man under whose protection none of the citizens are fearful. But we have enjoyed the festival, and I see no point in staying here now, so let's go back."

Because his mind was captivated by the festival, Avantivardhana did not heed her words and found himself and his wife captured.

As the wailing townspeople looked on, their eyes turned to the sky, the enraged Ipphaka snatched him up and carried him off.*

Angaravati fainted when she heard of her grandson's abduction and the two ministers revived her with words, water and fresh air. In consternation, she told them to hurry to the Dark Mountain and tell Palaka what had happened to his nephew. They went on their way.

After bowing before the ascetics there, who were headed 3.80
by Kashyapa, they greeted Palaka and told him that his nephew had been abducted. He was about to breathe his last when Kashyapa brought him back to life with an ambrosial utterance: "This episode will definitely have a happy ending. If you are doubtful, look up at the sky: learn that good news of your nephew is on its way."

Then the ascetics turned their eyes to the sky and saw a divine being approaching in the heavens, his sword and shield sparkling. He had captured Ipphaka and came down from the sky with the king of Avanti. He greeted Kashyapa and the others. After Surasamanjari had worshipped Palaka's feet and he had come to his senses, the sorcerer told the sages what had happened.

«Naravāhanadattasya vidyādhara|pateḥ priyam
māṃ Divākaradev'|ākhyaṃ jānīta paricārakam.
So 'haṃ Himavato gacchan nabhasā Malay'|ācalam
upariṣṭād Avantīnāṃ caṇḍālaṃ dṛṣṭavān imam,
Apahṛty' âpagacchantaṃ sa|dāraṃ medinī|patim
Ipphakaṃ nāma mātaṅgaṃ vidyādhara|kul'|âdhamam.
‹Muñc' êti› ca may" ôktaḥ san yad" âyaṃ na vimuktavān
tadā yuddhena nirjitya prāpitaś cakravartinam.
3.90 Anuyuktaś ca ten' âyam, ‹ayaṃ rājā hṛtas tvayā
kim ity?› avocad etena, ‹yan me dārā hṛtā iti.›
Atha bhartr" âham ādiṣṭaḥ: ‹saṃyamya prāpyatām ayam
sabhā|sadbhiḥ sabhāṃ sadbhiḥ Kāśyap'|ādyair adhiṣṭhitām.
Vyavahāre vinirjitya labdhā Surasamañjarīm
vardhamānaka|mālāṃ vā nirjito 'yaṃ sa|rāsabhām.
Aham apy āryuṣaṃ draṣṭuṃ Kāśyapaṃ svaṃ ca mātulam
āgantā śvaḥ pratijñātaṃ teṣām āgamanaṃ mayā.›
Tataḥ saṃmānya rājānaṃ divyair ambara|bhūṣaṇaiḥ
āliṅgya ca sa|sauhārdaṃ mayā saha visṛṣṭavān.
Sa c' âyam Ipphako baddhaḥ sa|dāraś c' âiṣa bhū|patiḥ
cakravartī ca vo draṣṭum āgantā s'|âvarodhanaḥ.»

Te Divākaradevasya śrutv" êdam ṛṣayo vacaḥ
harṣ'|âśru|sikta|tanavaḥ kṛcchrād akṣapayan kṣapām.
Atha prāto nabho|vyāpi nir|abhre vyomni garjitam
ākarṇya munayo 'pṛcchan kim etad iti khe|caram.

So 'bravīd «eṣa nirghoṣo dundubhīnāṃ vimāninām
vimāna|garbha|vartitvāc chrūyate garjit'|ākṛtiḥ.

"I am Divakaradeva, a favorite servant of Naravahanadatta, the king of the sorcerers. I was flying from the Himalayas to Mount Malaya when above Avanti I saw this outcaste. A jungly fellow called Ipphaka, the lowliest of the sorcerer clan, he was fleeing after abducting the king and his wife. When I told him to release them and he refused, I defeated him in battle and brought him before the emperor. The 3.90
emperor asked him why he had abducted the king, and he said that the latter had abducted his wife. I was instructed by my master thus: 'Restrain him and bring him before the legal assembly presided over by those good counsellors, Kashyapa and the other saints. If he wins the case, he will get Surasamanjari; if he loses, he will get a necklace of saucers* and a ride on a donkey. And I shall come tomorrow to see the noble* Kashyapa and my maternal uncle*; I have promised them a visit.' Then he honored the king with divine clothes and ornaments, embraced him affectionately, and sent him off with me. This is Ipphaka here, in irons, and here is the king with his wife. The emperor is coming to see you with his harem."

When the sages heard this speech from Divakaradeva, their bodies became wet with tears of joy and they had difficulty getting through the night. In the morning the sages heard in the cloudless sky a rumbling that filled the firmament. They asked Divakaradeva, the sky-ranger, what it was.

He replied, "That is the noise of the drums of the sky-charioteers. It comes from inside the sky-chariots so it sounds like thunder. Here comes our master, the emperor

Ayam āyāti naḥ svāmī vidyādhara|pat'|īśvaraḥ
gārjad|dundubhi|jīmūto nabhasā dṛśyatām iti!»
3.100 Rohit'|êndra|dhanur|vidyud|balākā|dyuti|piñjaram
ambho|dānām iva vyāpta|sakal'|āśā|nabhas|talam,
Nānā|ratna|prabhā|jāla|karālam atha tāpasaiḥ
ārād āyād vimānānāṃ divo vṛndam adṛśyata.

Avatīry' āśrama|dvāri vimānaṃ cakravartinaḥ
sthitam anyāni śailasya kandarā|sānu|mūrdhasu.
Vidyādhar'|âdhirājasya vimānaṃ kamal'|ākṛti
padma|rāga|palāśānāṃ ṣaḍ|viṃśatyā pariṣkṛtam.
Svayaṃ garuḍa|pāṣāṇa|karṇikā|madhyam āsthitaḥ
sthitās tasya palāśeṣu bhāryāś citra|vibhūṣaṇāḥ.
Sa|bhāryā|kariṇī|yūthaḥ sa vidyādhara|kuñjaraḥ
sabhā|kamalinīm āgāt phull'|ānana|saro|ruhām.

Abhivādya tatas tatra Kāśyapa|pramukhān munīn
harṣ'|âtiśaya|niś|ceṣṭaṃ vavande mātulaṃ munim.
Bhartāram anuyāntībhir anujyeṣṭhaṃ tapasvinaḥ
devībhir vanditās tasya śvaśuras tad|anantaram.

Anujñāt'|āsan'|āsīnaṃ Kāśyapaś cakravartinam
prasṛṣṭ'|ānanda|netr'|âmbur abravīd gadgad'|âkṣaram.
«Aprāpt'|êṣṭ'|ârtha|saṃpatti|vāñch" āśīr abhidhīyate
āyuṣmatā tu tat prāptam āśiṣāṃ yad agocaram.
3.110 Kiṃ tu saṃbhāṣitaiḥ kāryaṃ pratisaṃbhāṣaṇaṃ yataḥ
ācāram anugacchadbhir asmābhir idam ucyate:

of all the sorcerer kings, flying through the air amid clouds of thundering drums. Look!"

Like a bank of clouds filling the sky in every direction, 3.100
gleaming gold with the dazzle of *rohita** rainbows, lightning and cranes, the ascetics saw arriving from far off in the heavens a fleet of sky-chariots; the lattice of light from its myriad gems was awe-inspiring.

The emperor's sky-chariot landed at the gate of the hermitage; the others came down in the valleys, and on the ridges and peaks of the mountain. The sky-chariot of the emperor of the sorcerers was in the form of a lotus surrounded by twenty-six petals of ruby. He himself sat in the middle of the emerald pericarp; his wives, wearing fabulous jewels, were in the petals. Like a great tusker and his herd of lady elephants, the sorcerer and his wives arrived at the assembly hall, which, with its beaming lotus-faces, was like a lotus pond.

After saluting the sages there, with Kashyapa at their head, he greeted his saintly maternal uncle, who stood stock-still through a surfeit of bliss. The queens, following their master, paid their respects to the ascetics in order of seniority, and then to his maternal uncle.

In a faltering voice and with his eyes pouring forth tears of joy, Kashyapa addressed the emperor, who had sat in the seat to which he had been directed. "A blessing is uttered in the hope that someone obtains something they want but do not have, but what Your Reverence already has is
beyond the scope of blessings! However, one must reply 3.110
to a greeting, so by way of formality we say this: 'May

‹Anindyam idam aiśvaryaṃ sa|bhāryā|suhṛdas tava
mahā|kalp'|âvasāne 'pi kūṭa|sthaṃ tiṣṭhatām iti!›»
Pālaken' ânuyuktas tu vadhūnāṃ gotra|nāmanī
Gomukhaḥ kathayām āsa preritaś cakravartinā.
Evam|ādi|kath"|ânte ca cakravartī tapasvinaḥ
abravīd: «Ipphakaḥ pūjyā mātaṅgo 'nuyujyatām!
Kaṃ doṣam ayam uddiśya yātrā|vyāpṛta|mānasam
sārdhaṃ Surasamañjaryā rājānaṃ hṛtavān iti?»
Sa pṛṣṭaḥ pratyuvāc' êdaṃ «mahyam Utpalahastakaḥ
dattvā duhitaraṃ paścād etasmai dattavān iti.»
Atha «brūh' îti» pṛṣṭaḥ sann uvāc' Âvantivardhanaḥ
«dattvā na dattavān yo 'smai nanv asau pṛcchyatām» iti.
Ath' ôjjhit'|āsanaḥ sabhyān uvāc' Ôtpalahastakaḥ:
«yath" āh' âyaṃ tath" âiv' êdaṃ viśeṣaṃ tu nibodhata.
Nāradena purā śaptaḥ kruddhen' âhaṃ yathā tathā
pratyakṣam eva pūjyānāṃ divya|locana|cakṣuṣām.
Tadā may" âiṣa dīrgh'|āyur bahukṛtvaḥ prabodhitaḥ,
‹sutā dattā mayā tubhyam upayacchasva tām iti!›
3.120 Uktaś c' âivam uvāc' âyaṃ ‹ninditāṃ kaḥ sa|cetanaḥ
kanyakām upayaccheta śāpa|dagdhāt kulād iti?›
Pratyākhyātā yad" ânena Caṇḍasiṃh'|ādi|saṃnidhau
Avanti|pataye dattā tadā Surasamañjarī.
Saṃdehaś ced amī sarve vidyādhara|gaṇ'|ēśvarāḥ
pṛcchyantām iti» pṛṣṭaiś ca «tat tath" êti» niveditam.
Kāśyapas tam ath' âvocad «avasanno 'si khe|cara
Caṇḍasiṃh'|ādibhir yasmāt pramāṇaiḥ pratipāditaḥ.

this faultless sovereignty of you and your wives and friends remain unchanged, even at the end of the great time-cycle!'"

At Palaka's request and urged on by the emperor, Gomukha called out the family and personal names of the wives. When he had finished, the emperor addressed the ascetics: "Your Reverences, let the outcaste Ipphaka be interrogated! What crime did he have in mind when he abducted Surasamanjari and the king, whose mind was absorbed in the festival?"

On being questioned he replied, "Utpalahastaka promised his daughter to me but then gave her to this man."

When he was asked to speak, Avantivardhana replied, "Surely you should be questioning the man who promised him his daughter and then did not give her to him?"

Utpalahastaka got up from his seat and addressed the assembly: "What this man has said is in fact true, but please understand that there is a qualification. With their divine sight the venerable ones know that I was cursed by the enraged Narada. I told this honorable fellow Ipphaka many times, 'I have promised my daughter to you: marry her!'

He replied, 'What man in his right mind would marry 3.120
an unworthy girl from a family tainted by a curse?'

After he had rejected her in the presence of Chandasimha and others, I promised Surasamanjari to the king of Avanti. If there be any doubt, ask all these lords of the bands of sorcerers." When asked, they confirmed that it was true. Then Kashyapa said to Ipphaka, "Sky-ranger, you have lost the case because of the evidence of Chandasimha and the others. For this crime, you must carry out the following act

Asya c' âvinayasy' êdaṃ prāyaścittaṃ samācara
Vārāṇasyāṃ mṛt'|âṅgāni Gaṅg''|âmbhasi nimajjaya.
Pret'|āvāsa|kṛt'|āvāso vasānaḥ preta|cīvaram
bhaikṣ'|āśanaś ca varṣ'|ânte mukta|śāpo bhaviṣyasi.»

Ath' Ôjjayanyāḥ katham apy upāgatair
jar''|ândha|jāty|andha|jaḍ'|ârbhakair api
didṛkṣubhir Vatsa|nar'|êndra|nandanaṃ
tapo|anaṃ sa|pramadais tad'' āvṛtam.

iti Bṛhatkathāyāṃ Ślokasaṃgrahe
kathā|mukhaṃ tṛtīyam.

of expiation. You will immerse dead bodies in the waters of the Ganga at Varanasi. Living in the cremation-ground, wearing rags from corpses and eating alms, you will be liberated from this curse after one year."

Then the penance grove was filled with people who had somehow managed to reach there from Ujjain, including even men blind through old age or birth, dullards, children and women, all wanting to see the son of the king of Vatsa.

Thus ends the third introductory canto
of the Long Story Abridged into Sanskrit Verse.

CANTO 4
THE STORY OF PIṄGALIKĀ

Atha vidyādhara|patiḥ
Kāśyapen' āryuṣā puraḥ
ṛṣi|mātula|mitrāṇāṃ pṛṣṭo bhāryā|gaṇasya ca,
«Āyuṣman vayam ete ca tapo|vittāḥ sa|Pālakāḥ
tvat|kathā|śravaṇ'|ôtkaṇṭha|niṣ|kampa|manasaḥ sthitāḥ.
Aiśvaryaṃ durlabhaṃ labdham idam āyuṣmatā tathā
svī|kṛtāś ca yathā vadhvas tathā naḥ kathyatām iti!»
Atha vidyādhar'|ēśasya pṛṣṭasy' êti tapasvinā
trāsāt pṛthutar'|âkṣasya jātam acchāyam ānanam.
Acintayac ca «kaṣṭ" êyam āpad āpatitā yataḥ
aty|āsanno 'ti|capalaḥ ko na dahyate vahninā?
‹Iyaṃ mayi bhṛśaṃ raktā prīty" âham anay" āhṛtaḥ›
idaṃ sa|cetanaḥ ko nu kathayed guru|saṃnidhau?
‹Śūro mayā hataḥ śatrur māṃ śūraḥ śaraṇaṃ gataḥ›
iti śūra|kathāṃ śūraḥ kuryāt kaḥ śūra|saṃnidhau?
Anākhyāne muneḥ śāpo mahā|pātakam anyathā
su|labh'|ânto varaṃ śāpo dus|taraṃ na tu pātakam.
Kṛta eva tu Gauryā me prasādo ‹saṃkaṭeṣu mām
smarer iti!› na ca nyāyyaṃ tām api smartum īdṛśi.»
4.10 Iti cintita|mātr" âiva purastāc cakravartinaḥ
abhāsata Mahāgaurī prabh"|ôpahata|bhāskarā.
«Ṛṣi|mātula|bhāryāṇāṃ suhṛdāṃ ca sa|bhū|bhujām
śrotuṃ yad ucitaṃ yasya sa tac chroṣyati n' êtaraḥ.»
Ity uktvā vadane tasya paṭū|bhūtvā Sarasvatī
caritaṃ kathayām āsa sā citraṃ cakravartinaḥ.
«Muni|mātula|mitrāṇi rājāno dayitāś ca ye

THEN THE KING of the sorcerers was asked by the noble Kashyapa in front of the sages, his maternal uncle, his friends, and all their wives, "My lord, we ascetics here, together with Palaka, are transfixed by the desire to hear your tale. Tell us how Your Reverence came by this extraordinary majesty and won these wives!"

When the ascetic asked him this, the king of the sorcerers became wide-eyed with trepidation and the color drained from his face. He said to himself, "I am in dire straits, for who does not get burnt when recklessly sitting too close to the fire? What sensible man would say in front of respected elders, 'This girl was madly in love with me... I was captivated by this one...' What brave warrior would tell brave warriors tales of bravery like, 'I killed a brave enemy warrior... A brave warrior surrendered to me...'? If I do not tell my tale, the sage will curse me; if I do, I shall commit a great sin. A curse is easily ended and is preferable to a sin, which is hard to atone for. Even though Gauri has granted me a boon—'Think of me in times of crisis!' she said—it would be inappropriate to think of her at a time like this."

But merely by being thought of in this way, the great 4.10
goddess Gauri appeared in front of the emperor, her splendor eclipsing the sun. "The sages, your maternal uncle, the wives, the friends, the kings—each of them will hear what is appropriate for them to hear, to the exclusion of anyone else." After she said this, Sarasvati became eloquent in his mouth and told the story of the emperor's wondrous deeds.

"O sages, my maternal uncle, friends, kings, wives, listen

ākhyāyamānaṃ caritaṃ śṛṇvantv acala|cetasaḥ!
Asti Vatseṣu nagarī Kauśāmbī hṛdayaṃ bhuvaḥ
saṃniviṣṭ" ânu|Kālindi tasyām Udayano nṛpaḥ.
Manāg jana|padasy' âsya nagaryāḥ pārthivasya ca
kathayeyaṃ yadi guṇān na kathā kathitā bhavet.
Yo hi sapt'|ârṇava|dvīpāṃ draṣṭum uccalitaḥ kṣitim
ratnāni gaṇayen Meroḥ kadā draṣṭā sa medinīm?
Tasmād alaṃ prasaṅgena kathā|vyāsaṅga|kāriṇā!
kathyamānāṃ kathām eva śṛṇuta prakṛtāṃ mayā.

Mah"|âvarodhanasy' âpi bhāryā|buddhir dvaye sthitā
tasya Vāsavadattāyāṃ Padmāvatyāṃ ca bhū|pateḥ.
Mahā|prabhāvā nṛ|pateḥ śārṅga|pāṇer bhujā iva
sa|kāyā iva c' ôpāyāś catvāro mitra|mantriṇaḥ.
4.20 Ṛṣabhaś ca Rumaṇvāṃś ca tathā Yaugandharāyaṇaḥ
Vasantakaś c' êti sa taiḥ saha kālam ayāpayat.

Kadā cid āsthāna|gataṃ nṛpaṃ vāṇija|dārakau
jānu|spṛṣṭa|mahī|pṛṣṭau saṃvyajñāpayatām idam:
‹Dev' âvayoḥ pitā yātaḥ sa|bhayaṃ makar'|ālayam
saha tena sa potena nāga|lokaṃ praveśitaḥ.
Jyeṣṭhaś ca tanayas tasya pitṛ|bhakty" âiva sāgaram
gatas tatr' âiva ca gataḥ so 'pi tāta|gatāṃ gatim.
Yac ca no draviṇaṃ sāraṃ tad gṛhītvā prajāvatī
sthitā na mṛgyamāṇ" âpi bahu|kṛtvaḥ prayacchati.
Tena deva yadi nyāyyaṃ pitṛ|draviṇam āvayoḥ
bhrātṛ|jāyā tataḥ sā nau vyutthitā dāpyatām iti.›

Atha rāj" âvadat prahvāṃ prātihārīṃ Yaśodharām
‹duṣ|karaṃ kula|nārībhī rāj'|āsthāna|praveśanam.
Tena gatvā gṛhaṃ tasyās tvayā vāṇija|yoṣitaḥ

attentively to the story being told! There is a city in the country of Vatsa called Kaushambi. It is the heart of the world and is situated on the banks of the Yamuna. Its king is Udayana. If I were to relate but a fraction of the virtues of the country, the city, and the king, this story would never end. For if a man sets out to see the earth with its seven oceans and seven continents, but stops to count the gems on Mount Meru, when will he ever get to see the world? So, enough inessentials that keep us from the story! Listen to the tale unfold now that I have started to tell it.

Although he had a large harem, the king regarded only two women as his wives: Vasavadatta and Padmavati. He had four dear ministers, who were like the mighty arms of lord Vishnu and embodiments of the means to success*.
They were Rishabha, Rumanvan, Yaugandharayana and 4.20
Vasantaka; he passed his time with them.

One day the two sons of a merchant knelt before the king in the assembly hall and respectfully said the following: 'Sire, our father went to the cruel ocean and sank with his boat to the underworld. His eldest son went to sea out of devotion to him and suffered his father's fate. Our sister-in-law took all our money, and, despite having been asked many times, she has not returned it. So, Your Majesty, if you deem it right, please make our wayward sister-in-law give us our father's money.'

The king said to the bowing Yashodhara, his lady door-keeper, 'It is not easy for a woman of good family to enter the royal assembly hall, so go to the house of the merchant's wife and report what she says to the assembly.'

sā yad āha sabhāyās tat samakṣaṃ kathyatām iti.›
Atha vijñāpayām āsa yāt"|āyātā Yaśodharā
‹vijñāpayati sā yat tad ākārṇayitum arhatha.
Sā dūrād eva māṃ dṛṣṭvā pratyudgamya sa|saṃbhramā
«svāgataṃ rāja|jihvāyā ity» avocat kṛta|smitā.
Atha vetr'|āsan'|āsīnāṃ prayukt'|ârgh'|ādi|satkriyām
sā mām āh' «āgame kāryam āryayā jñāpyatām iti.»
Dev'|ādeśe tu kathite tay" ôktaṃ paṭu|lajjayā
«ārye sarvam idaṃ satyaṃ devarau me yad āhatuḥ.
Kiṃ tu tasy' ânayor bhrātur vipannaṃ vahanaṃ śrutam
vahanasya punaḥ svāmī vipanna iti na śrutam.
Sāṃyātrikāś ca bahavaḥ śruta|pota|vipattayaḥ
avipannā gṛhān eva śrūyante punar āgatāḥ.
Tathā kadā cid anayoḥ sa bhrātā vahan'|āpadaḥ
vimuktaḥ punar āyāyān mam' âvaidhavya|lakṣaṇaiḥ.
Anyac c' āpanna|sattvāyā māso 'yaṃ daśamo mama
vartate bhrātṛ|putro 'pi kadā cid anayor bhavet.
Putro me yadi jāyate jīvan vā patir āpatet
tataḥ svīkṛta|sarva|svau devarau me kva yāsyataḥ?.
Etan manasi kṛtv" ârthaṃ dravyaṃ devarayor aham
na nikṣiptavatī śeṣam āryayā jñāpyatām iti.»›
Iti śrutvā mahī|pālo vāṇijāv idam abravīt:
‹kuṭumb'|ācāra|caturā yuktam āha kuṭumbinī.
Bhrātrīye bhavator jāte bhrātur āgamane 'tha vā
ubhayor n' ôbhayor v" âpi yuktaṃ bhakṣyāmahe tadā.›
4.40 Ath' âniṣṭhita ev' âsminn ālāpe pūrit'|âmbaraḥ

After she had gone and come back, Yashodhara said, 'Please listen to what she has to say. She saw me from afar and hurriedly came to meet me. With a smile she said, "Welcome, mouthpiece of the king." After seating me on a cane chair and respectfully receiving me with offerings of water and the like, she said, "Pray tell why you have come, madam."

On being told of Your Majesty's instructions, she replied with great humility, "Madam, what my brothers-in-law have said is all true. However, although we have heard that their brother's vessel has been lost, we have not heard that its owner was lost too. Many tales are heard of travellers returning home unharmed after their ships have been reported lost. So, since I have none of the signs of widowhood, perhaps their brother escaped the shipwreck and will return. What's more, I am in the tenth month of pregnancy—perhaps the two brothers will get a nephew. If I have a son, or if my husband should suddenly appear alive, then what will my brothers-in-law do if they have taken all our property? With this in mind, I have not consigned the money to my brothers-in-law. Madam, please make known what was left unsaid."'

When he heard this, the king said to the merchants: 'The lady of the household is well versed in family customs and has spoken correctly. If a nephew is born to you, or if your brother returns, or if both things happen, or neither of them, we shall allot the wealth accordingly.'

Even before this speech was over, a loud hubbub filled the 4.40
air, together with the clamor of musical instruments. Sud-

tūrya|garjita|saṃbhinnas tāraḥ kalakalo 'bhavat.
Sa|hāsayā ca sahasā vāso|vās'|ādi|hastayā
vaṇig|gaṇikayā rājā vyajñāpyata viyātayā:
‹Vardhatāṃ naś ciraṃ devo diṣṭyā prakṛti|saṃpadā!
vaṇijor bhrātṛ|jāyāyā jātaḥ putro 'nayor iti!›
Citrīyamāṇa|cittena cintitaṃ ca mahī|bhujā
‹aho! putrasya māhātmyaṃ pratyakṣam anubhūyate.
Kuṭumbinaḥ putra|nāmni jāte śoṇita|binduke
harṣa|vibhrānta|cittānāṃ vaṇijāṃ paśya ḍambaram!
Vaṇijo draviṇasy' âyam ataḥ pālaka ity amī
samaṃ harṣa|viṣādābhyāṃ mitr'|âmitrāḥ samāgatāḥ.
Asmākaṃ tu dhanasy' âsya medinī|maṇḍalasya ca
avasāne vinā putrāt pālakaḥ ko bhaviṣyati?›
Iti putra|gatāṃ cintām upāsīnasya bhū|pateḥ
dīrgha|śvāsa|sahāyasya divasāḥ kati cid yayuḥ.
Tam ekadā sukh'|āsīnaṃ senā|patir abhāṣata
‹yātrā Mṛg'âjin'|ôdyāne tvad|dṛṣṭyā maṇḍyatām iti.›
Gataś ca dṛṣṭavāṃs tatra tatra tatra niveśitāḥ
viśālāś citra|śālāḥ sa citra|nyasta|nar'|âdhipāḥ.
4.50 Apṛcchac ca Rumaṇvantam «ayaṃ kaḥ kaḥ kṣit'|īśvaraḥ
ye c' âitān anutiṣṭhanti te ke ke puruṣā iti.»
So 'bravīd ‹eṣa Sagaraḥ kīrti|laṅghita|sāgaraḥ
ṣaṣṭyā putra|sahasrāṇāṃ śūrāṇāṃ parivāritaḥ.
Ayaṃ Daśaratho rājā vṛto Rām'|ādibhiḥ sutaiḥ
ayaṃ Pāṇḍur amī c' âsya tanayāḥ pañca Pāṇḍavāḥ.›
Evam|ādīn asau dṛṣṭvā svargiṇaḥ putriṇo nṛpān

denly the merchant's shameless courtesan, holding clothes and scents in her hands, addressed the king with a laugh: 'Long may our noble ruler be blessed with his wealth of subjects! A son has been born to the sister-in-law of these two merchants!'

The king was bowled over and thought, 'Ah! I am experiencing at first hand the importance of a son. Look at the to-do among the merchants! They are beside themselves with joy at the birth to the housewife of this drop of blood called a son! From now on it is he that shall look after the merchant's wealth, and because of this, these friends and enemies that have come together are simultaneously experiencing joy and sorrow. But if I die without a son who shall look after my wealth and my kingdom?'

Many days passed and the king, sighing deeply, remained anxious about having a son.

One day when he was relaxing the commander of the armies said to him, 'There is a festival at the Deer-skin Park. Please grace it with your appearance!'

He went there and saw set up about the place huge picture
halls in which there were portraits of kings. He asked Ru- 4.50
manvan who the various kings and men attending upon them were.

He replied, 'This is Sagara, whose fame has crossed the oceans. He is surrounded by his sixty thousand warrior sons. This is king Dasharatha with Rama and his other sons. This is Pandu and those are his sons, the five Pandavas.'

After seeing these and other kings who had fathered sons and dwell in heaven, he was lost in thought and did not

vi|cintaś cintayām āsa citrāṃ yātrām acintayan,
‹Puṇyavanta ime bhūpāḥ putravanto divaṃ gatāḥ
maṇḍa|puṇyena yātavyaṃ manye puṃ|narakaṃ mayā.›

Sa Mṛg'âjina|yātrāyāḥ parītaḥ putra|cintayā
nivṛty' âpaśyad āvantyāṃ mandir'|ôdyāna|sevinīm.
Sva|kar'|âmbu|ruhac|chāyā|saṃlohitita|pallavam
tāmr'|âśoka|latā|prāntam avalambya vyavasthitām.
Anādarād anahitair mālya|candana|bhūṣaṇaiḥ
udvegam iva śaṃsantīṃ mlān'|ānana|saro|ruham.
Upagamy' âbravīc c' âināṃ ‹kim aśokaḥ sa|śokayā
vandyeta labdha|vijayo rakto? bālo niṣevyate!›

S" âbravīt sahas"|āyāta|bhartṛ|kārita|saṃbhramā
‹mahārāja kutaḥ śoko? nām' âpi tava gṛhyatām.
4.60 Kiṃ tu pārāvatīm enāṃ cañcvā cañcuṣu taṇḍulān
āvapantīṃ sva|śāvānām īkṣe putra|vatīm iti.›

Āsīc ca nṛpateś cintā «yath" âhaṃ putra|cintayā
anantayā saṃtatayā tath" êyam api khidyate.»
Atha tatra kṣaṇaṃ sthitvā gatvā Padmāvatī|gṛham
adṛṣṭvā tatra tāṃ tasyāḥ pṛṣṭavān paricārikām,
‹Kva dev" îty?,› uktay" ākhyātam, ‹udyāne putrakasya sā
mādhavyā sahakārasya vivāham anutiṣṭhati.›

Śrutv" êti Vatsa|rājasya buddhir āsīd ‹aho! mama
bhāryāṇāṃ divasā yānti saha putra|mano|rathaiḥ.
Lokasy' ânicchataḥ putraiḥ kīrṇa†gṛha†karoṭibhiḥ

pay attention to the wonderful festival, thinking, 'These kings must have had great merit to have had sons and gone to heaven; I think I, with my lack of merit, shall have to go to hell.'

When he returned from the Deer-skin festival seized with anxiety about having a son, he saw Vasavadatta in the palace garden. She was holding on to the tip of a twig from a red *aśoka* tree, its blossoms made redder by the reflection of her lotus hand. Through neglect she had not put on garlands, sandal and ornaments, indicating her apparent distress, and her lotus-face was haggard. He went up to her and said, 'Why should an *aśoka** tree be greeted by a grieving lady when it is triumphantly red? It should be tended when a stripling!'

Flustered by her husband's sudden arrival, she replied, 'Great king, how can I be sad? All I need do is utter your
name. But I have been watching that mother pigeon use her 4.60
beak to feed grains of rice into the beaks of her offspring.'

The king then had the worrying thought that, like him, she too was tormented by endless and ever-present anxiety about having a son. He stayed there for a while and then went to Padmavati's house. When he did not see her there he asked her maidservant, 'Where is the queen?' She said, 'She is in the garden, attending the wedding of her adopted son, a mango tree, with a *mādhavī* vine.'

When he heard this, the king of Vatsa thought, 'Oh dear! My wives are spending their days longing for sons. People who do not want them cannot get a break from sons scattering pots and pans about and screaming in their cots. We

phalakeṣu kṛt'|ākrandair avakāśo na labhyate.
Asmākam icchatām ekaḥ kula|jīvita|kāraṇam
na labhyate sutaḥ paśya vaiparītyaṃ vidher iti!›
Niryāya sa tataḥ svasmin mandir'|ôdyāna|maṇḍape
an|āgat'|āgata|suhṛt|parivāra upāviśat.
Apṛcchat suhṛdas tatra ‹bhavatāṃ jīvit'|âuṣadham
mūlaṃ kula|taroḥ kasya kiyantaḥ putrakā iti?›
Teṣu niṣprativākyeṣu kiṃ|cin|namita|mūrdhasu
Vasantakaḥ parihasan praṇayitvād abhāṣata,
4.70 ‹Svāmi|bhaktā vayaṃ deva svāmi|vṛtt'|ânuvartinaḥ
yāvantaḥ svāminaḥ putrās tāvanto 'smākam apy ataḥ.›
Tam avocat samīpa|sthaḥ śanair Yaugandharāyaṇaḥ
‹aprastāve 'pi bhavato mukham etad anāvṛtam.
Putra|cintā|ruj" ârtasya kurvāṇaḥ śalya|ghaṭṭanam
nanv aneka|guṇāṃ bhartur utpādayasi vedanām.
Tasmād evaṃ|vidhe kāle bhṛtya|vṛtta|vidā tvayā
svāmi|citt'|ânukūl" âiva vṛttir āsthīyatām iti.›
So 'bravīt ‹putra|cint" âinaṃ yadi satyena pīḍayet
tataḥ Piṅgalik" êv' êyaṃ devam ārādhayed iti.›
Ath' êdaṃ nīcakair uktaṃ yuktaṃ śrutvā mahī|bhujā
‹y" âsau Piṅgalikā sā naḥ putriṇī kathyatām iti.›
Anantaraṃ ca ḍhaukitvā jaya|śabda|puraḥ|saram
‹putravān bhava dev' êti!› brāhmaṇī tam avardhayat.
Abhivādya mahī|pālas tām apṛcchad ath' ‹āryayā
āgamyate kutaḥ ke vā tav' âmī bālakā iti?›
‹Gṛhād Vāsavadattāyā rājann āgamyate mayā

who want them cannot get a single son to extend the family line. Behold the irony of fate!' He left and sat down in his own bower in the palace garden, surrounded by friends who had come to see what was about to happen.

He asked his friends there, 'Which of you have sons—the elixir of life and the root of the family tree—and how many do you have?'

When they lowered their heads a little and did not answer, Vasantaka, because he was the favorite, said with a laugh, 'Sire, we are devoted to our master and copy our master's 4.70
actions, so we have as many sons as our master.'

Yaugandharayana, who was sitting close by, said quietly, 'That mouth of yours opens even out of turn. Our master is pained by anxiety about having a son. By rubbing salt into his wounds you are undoubtedly multiplying his agony. At a time like this, you, as someone who knows how a servant is to behave, should act in a way befitting our master's disposition.'

He replied, 'If anxiety about a son is truly troubling him, then, like Pingalika here, he should seek a favor from a god.'

The king heard this whisper clearly and said, 'Let this Pingalika, a mother of sons, speak to us herself!'

The brahmin lady immediately came near, hailed him with the word 'Victory!' and honored him by saying, 'May Your Majesty father a son!'

The king greeted her and asked, 'From where have you come, madam, and how are you related to these boys?'

She replied, 'I have come from Vasavadatta's house, sire,

bālakāś ca sutā ete mam' êti› kathitaṃ tayā.
Atha tām abravīd rājā ‹citram etat tvay" ôditam
na hi bhartrā na ca sutair bhavitavyaṃ tav' ēdṛśaiḥ.
4.80 Tvaṃ lekhābhiḥ pati|ghnībhiḥ sakal" âiva karālitā
cira|proṣita|kāntāyā gṛha|bhittir iva striyāḥ.
Na ca patyā vinā putrair bhavitavyaṃ yataḥ striyāḥ
tasmād idaṃ mahac citraṃ sphuṭaṃ naḥ kathyatām iti!›
Ath' âvocad ‹asau deva yath" āttha na tad anyathā
mahatī tu kathā śrotum icchā cec chrūyatām iyam!
Asty Avantiṣu viprāṇām adhivāsaḥ Kapiṣṭhalaḥ
agni|kuṇḍa|citā sīmā sphīta|godhūma|go|kulaḥ.
Uvāsa brāhmaṇas tatra Somadattas trayī|dhanaḥ
yasy' ântevāsibhir vyāptā vasudhā veda|vedibhiḥ.
Patnī Vasiṣṭha|kalpasya Vāsiṣṭhī tasya su|vratā
Vasiṣṭha|patnīm api yā sādhu|vṛttām alajjayat.
Tasya tasyām a|putrasya kāle mahati gacchati
utpann" ôlk" êva saṃdhyāyāṃ sutā locana|durbhagā.
Somadattas tu tāṃ dṛṣṭvā strī|lakṣaṇa|viśāradaḥ
pati|putra|dhanair hīnām ādideśa bhaviṣyatīm.
An|arthānāṃ balīyastvād a|cireṇ' âiva dur|bhagā
dhūma|ketu|śikh" êv' ôccaiḥ paruṣā sā vyavardhata.
Bhikṣām ācchidya śiṣyebhyo bubhukṣā|kṣapita|trapā
a|prakṣālita|hast" âiva tat samakṣam abhakṣayat.
4.90 Dur|bhagatvād virūpatvāt khalīkāritayā ca tām
na kaś cid varayām āsa varaḥ prāpta|varām api.
Na ca tāṃ Somadatto 'pi kasmai cid aśubhām adāt

and these boys are my sons.'

Then the king said to her, 'What you say is strange, for you should have neither a husband nor sons like these. The 4.80 signs of a husband-killer have made you completely repulsive, like the walls of the house of a woman whose beloved has long since departed. Without husbands, women do not have sons, so this is very strange. Explain it to us!'

She replied, 'Your Majesty, what you say is quite true. My story is long. If you wish to hear it, listen!

There is a settlement of brahmins in Avanti called Kapishthala. Its boundary is lined with sacrificial fire-pits, and wheat and herds of cows are abundant. A brahmin called Somadatta lived there. His wealth was the three Vedas and his pupils, versed in the Vedas, spread throughout the world. Vasishthi, the pious wife of that second Vasishtha, put even Vasishtha's virtuous wife to shame. For a long time he did not have a child, and then, like an ill-omened comet appearing in the twilight, an ugly daughter was born to his wife. Somadatta was skilled at interpreting the signs on women's bodies, and when he saw her he predicted that she would never have a husband, nor a son, nor wealth. Inauspicious things are strong, so the coarse, ugly girl grew very quickly, like the tail of a comet. When hunger removed her shame, she would snatch alms from students and eat in front of them without even washing her hands. Because she 4.90 was ugly, misshapen and abusive, no suitor asked for her hand, despite her dowry*. And even Somadatta himself did not offer the accursed girl to anyone, lest they be afflicted by misfortune after accepting the wretch. Just as the rubbish

mā sma yujyata duḥkhena prāpy' âinām ninditām iti.
Grāmy'|âgnin" êva saṃkāra|kūṭikā s" âpy adahyata
sarvaṃ|kaṣa|prabhāveṇa prabalen' âṅga|janmanā.

Kadā cit kaś cid āgatya vācāṭo baṭur uccakaiḥ
mastaka|sth'|ôbhaya|karaḥ Somadattam abhāṣata:
«Upādhyāyasya duhitā mām ākrudhya nirāgasam
iṣṭakā|loṣṭakair hanti ten' âsau vāryatām iti!»

Somadattas tataḥ kruddhaḥ sutāṃ caṇḍam abhartsayat:
«ulke piśācike! gaccha śīghraṃ mama gṛhād iti!»

Sā tu tat paruṣaṃ śrutvā manasvi|jana|duḥ|śravam
smara|pīḍ"|â|sahatvāc ca maraṇāya mano dadhe.
Araṇyānīṃ tato gatvā maraṇ'|ôpāya|kāṅkṣayā
adrākṣīt kva cid uddeśe prāsādaṃ daitya|ghātinaḥ.
Tasy' âdūre ca sarasīṃ kūjat|kurara|sārasām
guñjan|madhu|kara|śreṇīm anumātavya|rodhasam.

Āsīc c' âsya, «mayā tāvan martavyam iti niścitam
upāyeṣu tu saṃdehas tatr' ôpāyo 'yam uttamaḥ.
4.100 Devaṃ Mādhavam arcantī kamal'|êndīvar'|ādibhiḥ
paṅkaj'|âvayav'|āhārāt kṣīṇā tyakṣyāmi jīvitam.
Kṛta|puṇyā mṛtā svargaṃ yāsyāmi nir|upadravam
narakaṃ tu na yāsyāmi strī|mṛtyu|mṛta|saṃkulam.»

S" âkarod iti niścitya yathā|saṃkalpam ādṛtā
rātrau ca baddha|paryaṅkā devaṃ Mādhavam asmarat.
Māsa|mātre gate 'paśyat svapn'|ânte Madhusūdanam
«varaṃ varaya putr' îti!» bhāṣamāṇaṃ mudā|yutam.

S" âtha vyajñāpayat prahvā devaṃ viracit'|âñjaliḥ

heap is burnt by the village bonfire, she was ablaze with a mighty carnal passion whose power was all-consuming.

One day a brahmin student arrived wailing loudly and holding his head in his hands. He said to Somadatta: "Teacher, your daughter is angry with me though I have done nothing wrong and is hitting me with bricks and clods of earth. Stop her!"

The furious Somadatta then fiercely scolded his daughter: "You ill-starred she-devil! Get out of my house at once!"

But those unkind words—so hard for a sensitive person to hear—and her inability to endure the torment of her desire, made her decide to kill herself. She went to the forest in the hope of finding a way to die, and saw in some spot a temple of Vishnu. Not far from it she found a lake whose banks had to be surmised from the calling of ospreys and cranes and the line of buzzing bees.

She thought, "I have decided that I must die, but I am
not sure how. Of all the methods, this is the best: I shall 4.100
worship Vishnu with pink, blue and other lotuses, and live off a diet of parts of lilies, thereby starving myself to death. Having earned merit, when I die I shall go to heaven without mishap; I shall not go to the hell filled with women who have committed suicide."

After making this decision, she diligently did as she had planned. At night she would sit cross-legged and concentrate her mind on Lord Vishnu. After just one month had passed, she saw Krishna in a dream. He was saying joyfully, "My daughter, choose a boon!"

Bowing down before the god with her hands joined, she

«maraṇaṃ me jagan|nātha prasādaḥ kriyatām iti!»

Devas tām avadan «n' êdaṃ devat"|ārādhanāt phalam prāṇi|hatyā|vipāko 'yam ātma|hatyā ca ninditā. Tasmād anyaṃ varaṃ brūhi pati|putra|dhan'|ādikam yena hīn" âsi vairāgyān niryātā sva|gṛhād iti.»

S" âbravīt «kṛta|puṇyābhiḥ paty|ādiḥ strībhir āpyate ahaṃ tv ācarit'|âpuṇyā duḥkhair eva vibhāvitā. Ten' âlaṃ pati|putr'|ādi|cintayā phala|hīnayā mṛtyunā śāntim icchāmi sā me saṃpādyatām iti.»

So 'bravīt «satyam ev' êdaṃ kiṃ tu janm'|ântare tvayā yav'|āḍhakaḥ pitur gṛhe brāhmaṇāy' ôpapāditaḥ.

4.110 Sa ca jātaś catur|vedaḥ sva|puṇyair iha janmani su|rūpaḥ sādhu|vṛttaś ca sa te bhartā bhaviṣyati. Sa ca tvām Urvaśī|rūpām eko drakṣyati n' âparaḥ ‹krīto yav'|āḍhakena tvam iti› yāvan na vakṣyasi. Janm'|ântare ca pūrvasmin bhakṣayantyās tilās tava aṣṭau nipatitā vahnāv añjaler viral'|âṅguleḥ. Te te putrā bhaviṣyanti putri candra|nibh'|ānanāḥ maraṇād dāruṇāt tena cittam āvartyatām iti.»

Ity uktv" ântar|hite deve pratibuddhā dadarśa sā sa|śiṣya|vargaṃ pitaraṃ tad|gaveṣiṇam āgatam. Tapaḥ|kṛśāṃ sa|karuṇaḥ pitā kārita|pāraṇām śrāmyantīm anayad gehaṃ viśrāmyantīṃ tarau tarau.

said, "Be so kind as to let me die, o lord of the universe!"

The god replied, "That is not a reward for worshipping a deity, it is a consequence of killing a living being. Moreover, suicide is sinful. So choose a different boon, such as a husband, a son, wealth or such like, lacking which you left your home in disgust."

She said, "Husbands and so forth are obtained by women who have accumulated merit, but I have performed bad deeds and earnt only sorrows. As a result I have had enough of fruitless anxiety about husbands, sons and the like, and want peace through death. Please grant me that!"

He replied, "What you say is indeed true, but in a previous existence you gave a bag of barley to a brahmin in
your father's house. In his present incarnation, that same 4.110
man has, as a result of his meritorious actions, been born as a brahmin who knows the four Vedas. He is handsome and has a good living. He shall be your husband. He alone and no one else shall see you in the form of the beautiful nymph Urvashi, as long as you do not tell him that he was bought for a bag of barley. In an earlier existence, you were eating sesame seeds and eight fell into the fire from the open fingers of your cupped hand. They, my daughter, shall become your sons and have faces as beautiful as the moon, so turn your thoughts away from a cruel death!"

After saying this the god disappeared. When she awoke she saw that her father had come looking for her with a group of pupils. She was emaciated because of her austerities and her father, taking pity, fed her to break her fast. He

Yā sā Piṅgalikā deva devam ārādhya keśavam
varaṃ labdhavatī tasmāt tāṃ mām eva nibodhatām.
Ekadā tu catur|vedaḥ s' ânte|vāsī yadṛcchayā
gṛham asmākam āyātaḥ kṛt'|ātithyo dadarśa mām.
Mama tātaṃ tu so 'pṛcchad «brahman kasy' êyam ātma|jā
kānti|nindita|candr'|ābhā? yuktaṃ cet kathyatām iti.»
«Mam' êti» kathite pitrā māṃ prārthayata sa dvi|jaḥ
pitrā dattāṃ ca vidhivan muditaḥ pariṇītavān.
4.120 Tataś c' ārabhya divasāt sa siddha iva kiṃkaraḥ
na kāṃ cin na karoti sma mam' ājñāṃ ninditām api.
Amī c' âṣṭau sutās tasmād acireṇ' âiva dur|labhāḥ
labdhā mayā sutā ye 'sya prasādāl loka|dhāriṇaḥ.
Iti kāle gate bhartā māṃ kadā cid abhāṣata,
«pṛṣṭhaṃ duḥkhāyamāṇaṃ me caṇḍi saṃvāhyatām iti.»
Anukta|pūrva|vacanam uktavantam ath' âbruvam
«kim ahaṃ bhavatā krītā pṛṣṭha|saṃvāhik" êti?» tam.
So 'bravīn nīcakais trāsād aṅguṣṭh'|âgreṇa gāṃ likhan
«ahaṃ vā kiṃ tvayā krīto yena preṣyatvam āgataḥ?»
Tato vismṛtya samayaṃ bhartāraṃ roṣa|dūṣitā
«krīto yav'|āḍhaken' âsi may" êty» a|priyam abruvam.
Asāv api ca māṃ dṛṣṭv" âsahaj'|ākāra|vañcitām
saṃnikarṣād apakramya saṃbhrānta idam abravīt:

took the exhausted girl home, and she rested under trees along the way.

Your Majesty, understand that I am that Pingalika who propitiated Vishnu and received a boon from him. One day the brahmin who knew the four Vedas unexpectedly came to our house with his pupils. After he had been received with due hospitality, he noticed me. He asked my father, "O brahmin, who is the father of this girl whose beauty shames that of the moon? If it is appropriate, tell me."

When my father told him that I was his daughter, the brahmin asked for my hand in marriage. My father gave it and the brahmin happily married me with due ceremony.

From that day on he was like the perfect servant and did 4.120
not fail to obey even my most demeaning order. Not long after, by the grace of Vishnu the preserver of the universe, I received these eight dear sons. The time passed thus until one day my husband said, "Darling, my back hurts: please rub it."

He had never said this before and I replied, "What, did you buy me to be a back-rubber?"

Scraping the earth with the tip of his big toe, he replied in an anxious whisper, "Rather, since I have become a slave, did you buy me?"

Then, forgetting the condition of the boon and beside myself with rage, I snapped at my husband, "I bought you for a bag of barley!"

When he saw me as I really am he quickly moved away and said: "Who are you and where have you appeared from? How did you change? I hope you are not Pingalika! And

«Api k" âsi kutaś c' âsi? ken' âsi vikṛtā kṛtā?
kaccit Piṅgalikā n' âsi! kaś ca nāma yav'|āḍhakaḥ?»
Iti ten' ânuyukt" âhaṃ yathā|vṛttam avarṇayam
so 'pi saṃjāta|nir|vedo na jāne kva palāyitaḥ.
Tasmin deś'|ântaraṃ yāte tāte ca tridaś"|ālayam
pitṛ|bhartṛ|vihīn" âham etaṃ deśam upāgatā.
4.130 Sva|deśa|prīti|yogāc ca devyā Vāsavadattayā
sa|putr" ânugṛhīt" âsmi bhakt'|ācchādana|rakṣaṇaiḥ.
Tena devena yat pṛṣṭaṃ «kutas te bālakā iti?»
evam ete mayā labdhās tuṣṭād Nārāyaṇād iti.›
Iti hṛṣṭa|matir niśāmya tasyāś
caritaṃ putra|samūha|lābha|hetum.
sacivaiḥ sahitaś cakāra rājā
suta|samprāpti|phalaṃ kriyā|vicāram.

iti Piṅgalik"|ākhyānaṃ
caturthaḥ sargaḥ.

what is this about a bag of barley?”

In response to his questions, I told him the story. Disillusioned with me, he fled I don’t know where. With him in another country and my father in heaven I came to this country as an orphan and a widow. Because of her love for 4.130
her compatriots, queen Vasavadatta has shown me and my sons kindness, granting us food, clothes and protection. Your Majesty asked where these boys are from. I obtained them like this from a gratified Vishnu.’

The king was pleased when he heard her story of how she had obtained so many sons, and together with his ministers thought up observances that would result in his getting a son.”

Thus ends the fourth canto,
the Story of Pingalika.

CANTO 5
SATISFYING PREGNANCY CRAVINGS

ATHA SAMPREṢIT'|ĀSTHĀNAḤ
sacivān abravīn nṛpaḥ
«yad bravīmi nibodhantu bhavantas tat sa|cetasaḥ.
Ṛṇaiḥ kila samāyuktaḥ puruṣo jāyate tribhiḥ
brahma|cary"|êṣṭi|saṃtānair ṛṣi|deva|svadhā|bhujām.
Tatr' âdhigata|vedo 'ham iṣṭ'|âśeṣa|mahā|kratuḥ
aputratvāt tu pitṛbhir gṛhītaḥ piṇḍa|bhojibhiḥ.
Na ca putr'|âṅga|saṃsparśāt sukha|hetur an|uttaraḥ
sukhibhiḥ sa hi nir|diṣṭaś candanād api śītalaḥ.
Alaṃ c' âti|prasaṅgena sarvathā gṛha|medhinām
dṛṣṭ'|âdṛṣṭa|sukha|prāpteḥ putrād anyan na kāraṇam.
Tad asti yadi vaḥ kāṅkṣā niṣ|prajānāṃ prajāṃ prati
ārabhadhvaṃ mayā sārdhaṃ devat"|ārādhanaṃ tataḥ.»

Te tu sa|pramadāḥ śrutvā rājñaḥ putr'|ârthinaḥ kathām
siddha|kalp'|ātma|saṃkalpāḥ pratyūcur darśita|smitāḥ:
«Putra|janma vaṇig|vadhvā yātrāyāṃ citra|darśanam
Piṅgalī|darśanaṃ c' êti prayogo 'yam anuṣṭhitaḥ
Asmābhiḥ sa ca devena tath" âiva saphalī|kṛtaḥ!
kṛtaḥ kāle prayogo hi n' â|phalo jātu jāyate.
5.10 Tena saṃkalpa|sadṛśīm ārabhadhvaṃ kriyām iti»
sacivair abhyanujñātas «tath" êti» pratipannavān.

Sa puṇye 'hani saṃpūjya devat"|âgni|dvi|janmanaḥ
yayau nāga|van'|ôdyānaṃ sa|dāraḥ saha mantribhiḥ.

THE KING THEN DISMISSED the assembly and said to his ministers, "Listen carefully to what I have to say. A man is said to be born with three debts: the study of the Vedas, the performance of sacrifices and the production of sons, and these are for the benefit of the sages, the gods and the ancestors respectively. Of these, I have studied the Vedas and performed all the major sacrifices, but, because I do not have a son, I am beholden to the ancestors, who live off the offerings of their descendants. Furthermore, there is no greater way to happiness than the touch of a son's body, for it is said by the blissful to be cooler even than sandalwood paste. But enough beating about the bush: in a nutshell, for householders to achieve happiness in this world or the next, there is no means other than a son. So, if you childless men desire children, then join me and start worshipping the gods!"

They and their wives heard this speech from the king: he wanted a son—their aim was as good as accomplished! They smiled openly and replied, "The birth of a son to the merchant's wife, catching sight of the pictures in the festival procession, the appearance of Pingalika: these were all part of a plan put into action by us and, as planned, Your Majesty has made it bear fruit! For a plan executed at the right moment cannot but succeed. Therefore, please 5.10
start carrying out rituals appropriate to your purpose." The king concurred with his ministers' advice.

On an auspicious day, after he had worshipped the gods, the sacred fire and the brahmins, he went to the Snake Forest park with his wives and ministers.

Māgadhī tu kṛt'|ôtsāhā devyā Vāsavadattayā
«alam āli tav' ânena kheden' êti» nivāritā.
Uktā ca «nanu bāl" âsi mṛṇālī|tantu|komalā
anubhūta|sukhā c' âsi bhrātur bhartuś ca veśmani.
Duḥ|sahāni tu duḥkhāni mayā nindita|bhāgyayā
anubhūtāni ten' âhaṃ śaktā duḥkham upāsitum.
Yaś ca me bhavitā putraḥ sa bhavatyā bhaviṣyati
Kṛttikā|garbha|saṃbhūto Bhavānyā iva ṣaṇ|mukhaḥ.»

Iti tasyāṃ nivṛttāyāṃ saha Vāsavadattayā
tapobhir a|cirād rājā rāja|rājam atoṣayat.
Ekadā pratibuddhau tu daṃpatī jāta|saṃbhramau
«hā devi!,» «h" ārya|putr' êti!,» vyāharantau parasparam.

Ath' ôpaspṛśya nṛ|patir namaskṛtya dhan'|âdhipam
puraḥ purohit'|ādīnām ācakhyau svapnam ādṛtaḥ.
«Adya paśyāmy ahaṃ svapne vyomni kām api devatām
prabh"|âmbhaḥ|saṃtati|vyasta|nabho|maṇḍala|nīlatām.
5.20 Sā mām uktavatī vācā gambhīra|sukumārayā
‹tvām āhvayati vitteśas tad|āśāṃ gamyatām ataḥ!›
May" ‹âum iti› pratijñāte saṃdhyā|raktataraṃ karam
āropya prasthitā vyomni diśaṃ vitt'|ēśa|pālitām.
‹Śarveṇ' êha dhṛtā Gaṅgā pariṇīt" âtra Pārvatī›
ity|ādīn darśayantī nau pradeśān Pārvatī|pituḥ.

Nīyamānaḥ krameṇ' êttham ath' âhaṃ dṛṣṭavān puraḥ
candra|pāṣāṇa|nirmāṇa|prākārām Alakā|purīm.
Gaṇānāṃ Pārvatī|bhartur gaṇair a|gaṇitair yutam

Padmavati had been keen to come but was dissuaded by queen Vasavadatta, who said, "My friend, do not trouble yourself with this, for you are a child, as delicate as a lotus fiber, and are accustomed to comforts in the houses of your brother and husband. I have had wretched luck and experienced terrible sorrows, so I can put up with hardship. The son that I bear shall be yours, like Bhavani's six-faced son Karttikeya, who was born to Krittika."

After Padmavati had gone back, the king and Vasavadatta soon satisfied Kubera with their austerities. One day the two of them woke up in a panic. He was saying to her, "Oh, my queen!," and at the same time she was saying to him, "Oh, my husband!"

The king, after sipping water from his hand and worshipping the lord of wealth, carefully told his dream to the chaplain and the other brahmins. "Today I dreamt that I saw in the sky some goddess or other, whose streaming splendor dispersed the darkness of the firmament. In a low 5.20
and tender voice, she said to me, 'The lord of wealth is calling you: go to him!' When I agreed, she put me in her hand, which was redder than the sunset, and set off through the sky for the region ruled by the lord of wealth. On the way she pointed out the territories of Parvati's father, saying things like 'Here Shiva supported Ganga... there he married Parvati.'

While I was being carried along like this, I saw before me the city of Alaka, its ramparts made of moonstone. On its outskirts was a forest of wish-fulfilling trees, whose limits could not be seen, filled with countless bands of

yasyā bāhyam adṛṣṭ'|ântaṃ kalpa|pādapa|kānanam.
Nānā|maṇi|prabhā|jāla|kalmāṣa|śikharāṇy api
śubhrayaty eva harmyāṇi yasyām Rudr'|êndu|candrikā.
Avatārya tu māṃ dvāre guhyak'|ēśvara|veśmanaḥ
vadati ‹kṣaṇam atr' âiva sthīyatām iti› devatā.
Sā praviśya pratīhāryā saha nirgamya bhāṣate
‹anujñāta|praveśo 'si deven' āgamyatām iti.›
  Bhavanān' îva devānāṃ ṣaḍ atikramya saptame
kakṣ'|ântare prakṛṣṭa'|rddhau paśyāmi draviṇ'|ēśvaram.
Atha tatr' âpsarāḥ kā cit kāṃ cid āha nirīkṣya mām
‹sakhi nūnam asāv eṣa yasy' âsau bhavitā sutaḥ?
5.30 Mayā mantrayamāṇānām ṛṣīṇām agrataḥ śrutam
«Bharatānām ayaṃ vaṃśe viśuddhe jāyatām iti!»
Na c' âiṣaḥ kevalaṃ dhanyas tena putreṇa pārthivaḥ
so 'pi sādhūyamānasya putraḥ pātraṃ bhaviṣyati.
Tena tat tādṛśaṃ putraṃ labhatām eṣa bhū|patiḥ
asāv api Śacī|Śakra|caritau pitarāv api!›
  Kārye guruṇi saktatvāt tṛṇī|kṛta|sur'|âṅganaḥ
sa|kiṃkara|gaṇaṃ prahvaḥ praṇamāmi dhan'|âdhipam.
  Manuṣya|dharmā tu bhujaṃ bhujag'|ēśvara|pīvaram
udyamy' āha ‹manuṣy'|êndra svāgataṃ! sthīyatām iti!›
  Āsanne ratna|caraṇe dāpite kanak'|āsane
vyavadhāya tu mām āste devī nīcaistar'|āsanā.
Svananti parivādinyas tāḍitā Nārad'|ādibhiḥ
anek'|ākāra|karaṇaḥ śrūyate puṣkara|dhvaniḥ.
Urvaśī|Menakā|Rambhā|Citralekhā|Kratusthalāḥ
gāyantyaḥ kuṭṭita|talā nartayante Tilottamām.
  Evaṃ|prāye ca vṛtt'|ânte kumāro Nalakūbaraḥ

Shiva's attendants. Even though their towers were dotted with lattices of light from variously colored jewels, the light from Shiva's moon made the great houses of the city look white. The goddess put me down at the gate of Kubera's palace and told me to wait there for a moment. She entered and returned with a gatekeeper, saying, 'You have been given permission to enter. Come, Your Majesty.'

I passed through six halls that were like palaces of the gods, and in the seventh, the most lavish, I saw the lord of wealth. There a sky-nymph noticed me and said to another, 'My friend, is this not he whose son Kubera is to become?
I heard the sages say in front of me that Kubera is to be 5.30
born into the pure lineage of the Bharatas. Not only will the king be enriched by having him as a son, but he also will be the worthy son of a virtuous man. So, may the king have a son like Kubera, and may Kubera get parents who behave like Shachi and Indra!'

Because I was concentrating on an important matter in hand, I paid no heed to the nymphs and bowed down in respect before the lord of wealth and his body of servants.

But Kubera raised his arm, which was as thick as a king cobra, and said, 'Welcome, king among mortals! Stand up!'

A nearby golden seat with jewelled legs was offered and the queen had me sit on it before sitting apart, on a lower seat. Narada and others strummed lutes, and the sound of drums was heard, in various different pitches and rhythms. Tilottama danced to the singing and clapping of Urvashi, Menaka, Rambha, Chitralekha and Kratusthala.

While this was going on, Kubera's son, prince Nalaku-

rāja|rāja|sutaḥ krīḍann āyātaḥ saha bālakaiḥ.
Meru|sāra|mahā|ratna|saṃghāta|kṛta|saṃhatim
krīḍā|śakaṭikāṃ karṣann itaś c' êtaś ca gacchati.
5.40 Atha skhalita|cakrāyās tasyāḥ kusuma|saṃcaye
utplutya patitaṃ ratnaṃ vaiḍūrya|kṣoda|kuṭṭime.
Atha prasārita|karaḥ Kubero Nalakūbaram
‹mahyam etad dadasv' êti!› tad ratnam udayācata.
Nyastaṃ ca rāja|putreṇa rāja|rāja|kar'|ôdare
ratnaṃ paṅkaja|garbha|stha|bandhūkam iva rājate.
Duṣṭa|lakṣaṇa|muktānāṃ muktānāṃ parivāritam
ṣaḍ|viṃśatyā padma|rāgam aṣṭ'|âśri bahala|prabham.
Vitt'|âdhipatinā mahyaṃ dattaṃ devyai ca tan mayā
stanayor antare nyastam anay" âpi sphuran|mudā.
Siṃha|śāvas tato bhūtvā cañcad|vāladhi|keśaraḥ
vidārya dakṣiṇaṃ kukṣim etasyāḥ praviśaty asau.
Tad|avasthām imāṃ dṛṣṭvā ‹hā dev' îti!› vadann aham
pratibuddhaḥ iti» svapnam ācaṣṭe sma nar'|âdhipaḥ.
Atha nakṣatra|śāstra|jñaḥ siddh'|ādeśaḥ sa|saṃmadaḥ
Ādityaśarmā svapnasya dvi|jaḥ phalam avarṇayat:
«Vijayasva mahā|rāja putreṇa dviṣatāṃ gaṇam
samādhin" êva balinā rāg'|ādīnāṃ balīyasām!
Vimāna|ghana|saṃghāta|sthagit'|êndu|divākaraḥ
vidyādhara|samūh'|êndraḥ putras tava bhaviṣyati.
5.50 Yās tā muktāḥ parīvārās tasya ṣaḍ|viṃśati maṇeḥ
mahā|kulā bhaviṣyanti bhāryās tava sutasya tāḥ.
Ye c' âṣṭāv aśrayo ratnaṃ parito lakṣitās tvayā
vidyās tā viddhi putrasya bhaviṣyantī bhaviṣyataḥ.»
Evaṃ ca sthāpite svapne rājakīye dvi|janmanā

bara, arrived, playing with some children. He wandered here and there, pulling a toy cart that contained a heap of
huge gems from inside Mount Meru. Then one of the cart's 5.40
wheels skidded on a heap of flowers, and a jewel bounced out and fell onto the mosaic floor inlaid with pieces of cat's eye. Kubera held out his hand and asked Nalakubara for the jewel, saying, 'Give it to me!'

When the prince put the jewel in Kubera's hand, it looked like a *bandhūka* flower in a lotus. It was an eight-pointed ruby of deep hue, surrounded by twenty-six flawless pearls. The lord of wealth gave it to me, and I gave it to the queen, who, beaming with pleasure, placed it between her breasts. It then turned into a lion cub with a bristling tail and mane, ripped open her right side and entered into her. It was when I saw her like that, that I called out 'Oh queen!' and woke up." The king related his dream thus.

Adityasharma, a brahmin astrologer whose predictions had been proven to be true, said with delight what the dream foretold: "O great king, may you overcome your host of enemies with your son, just as mighty meditation overcomes the mightier host of passion and other vices! You shall have a son who will be the king of all the sorcerers, and he will have a fleet of sky-chariots that conceals the
moon and the sun like a bank of cloud. The twenty-six 5.50
pearls surrounding the jewel shall be your son's noble-born wives. As for the eight points that you saw on the jewel, they are the eight magical sciences* that your future son will possess."

After the king's dream had been explained, queen Vasa-

sva|svapnaḥ kathitas tatra devyā Vāsavadattayā:
«Ārya|putreṇa yo dṛṣṭaḥ sa eva sakalo mayā
kukṣau vidāryamāṇe ca ‹h" ārya|putr' êti› bhāṣitam.»
Iti śrutavataḥ svapnau tulyāv Ādityaśarmaṇaḥ
bhaviṣyad|viṣaye jñāne dṛḍhatāṃ niścayo gataḥ.
Atha vijñāpayām āsa Rumaṇvān medinī|patim:
«dṛṣṭaḥ svapno mayā yaḥ sa śravaṇen' ânugṛhyatām.
Deve sa|niyame jāte Cedi|Vatsa|nivāsinaḥ
devasy' âpatya|lābhāya sarve sa|niyamāḥ sthitāḥ.
Tatr' âham adya paśyāmi svapne Garuḍa|vāhanam
mārgitaś ca mayā ‹dehi svāmine naḥ prajā iti.›
Sa vihasy' ôktavān ‹pūrṇaḥ svāminas te mano|rathaḥ
tav' âpi pūrayām' îti!› mahyaṃ bāṇaṃ vitīrṇavān.
Sa|praṇāmaṃ tam ādāya hṛdaye nidadhāmi ca
a|kāla|kaumudīṃ c' êmāṃ paśyāmi pratibodhitaḥ.»
5.60 Eṣo 'pi sthāpitaḥ svapnaḥ prīteṇ' Âdityaśarmaṇā
«yādṛśo 'sya suto bhāvī tādṛśaḥ śrūyatām! iti.
Sāyako hi guṇen' ârthī tasmād asya bhaviṣyati
putraḥ ṣāḍguṇya|tattva|jño yuktaś c' âyaṃ guṇair guṇī.
Para|tantra|gati|sthānaḥ kha|gāmī ca yataḥ śaraḥ
tena rāja|suta|praiṣyaḥ khe|caraś ca bhaviṣyati.»
Ath' âkathayad ātmīyaṃ svapnam Yaugandharāyaṇaḥ:
«mam' âdy' âik'|ōna|pañcāśan maruto darśanaṃ gatāḥ.
Teṣām ekaḥ sphurad|dyotaḥ kha|dyota|nikara|dyutim
svaṃ vimucya mudā mahyaṃ saṃnāhaṃ dattavān iti.»
«Bhartuḥ saṃnāha|sadṛśaḥ śūro 'dhyavasitaḥ sutaḥ
bhavato bhavit" êty» evaṃ svapnam asthāpayad dvi|jaḥ.
Ṛṣabhen' êti kathitaṃ «dṛṣṭavān asmi go|gaṇam

vadatta related hers: "I saw everything that my husband saw, and, as my side was being ripped open, I called out to him."

When he heard that the two dreams were identical, Adityasharma became convinced of his prognostication.

Then Rumanvan addressed the king: "Please listen to my dream. When Your Majesty undertook his observances, all the inhabitants of Chedi and Vatsa did the same, in order that Your Majesty might have children. As a result of this, today I saw Vishnu in a dream and I begged him to grant children to our master. He laughed and said, 'Your master's wish has been fulfilled and I shall fulfill yours too!' So saying, he gave me an arrow. I bowed, took it and put it next to my heart. When I awoke I saw these impromptu celebrations."

This dream was also interpreted by the happy Aditya- 5.60
sharma: "Hear what his son will be like! An arrow is made effective by a bowstring, so his son will be an expert in the six foreign policies and have many strings to his bow*. And just as an arrow is dependent on something else for its propulsion and goes by way of the sky, so he will be a servant of the king's son and a sky-rover."

Then Yaugandharayana related his dream: "Today I saw the forty-nine gods of the wind. One among them was sparkling with light. His armor shone like a swarm of fireflies; he took it off and joyfully gave it to me."

The brahmin interpreted the dream thus: "Your son shall be like a suit of armor to his master and considered a hero."

Rishabha said, "I saw a herd of cows and one of them

bravīti tatra mām ekā ‹praviś' êmāṃ guhām iti.›
Tatra praviśatā dṛṣṭāś catuḥ|ṣaṣṭir mayā kalāḥ
catasraś ca mahā|vidyā vinyastāś citra|karmaṇi.
Tatra citrīyamāṇo 'haṃ citraṃ citraṃ vilokayan
bodhito jṛmbhaṇair mandrair bherīṇāṃ garjitair iti.»

Sthāpito 'yam iti svapnaḥ: «putras tava bhaviṣyati
a|śeṣa|citra|vinyasta|kalā|kuśala|dhīr iti.»

5.70 Dṛṣṭaṃ Vasantaken' âpi svapnaṃ kathitam ity atha:
«dattavān pāvako mahyaṃ kuṇḍalaṃ rucir'|ôjjvalam.»
[ ].

Iti vyākriyamāṇeṣu svapneṣu ravi|sāratheḥ
bhinnaṃ bhābhis tamo jātaṃ cakora|nayan'|âruṇam.
Komal'|ânila|vikṣipta|nalina|sparśa|bodhitāḥ
resur vivāda|rasitāḥ sarasīṣu śakuntayaḥ.
Gambhīra|pratinirghoṣa|bhīṣit'|êndr'|âvarodhanaḥ
devat"|āgāra|bherīṇām uccair dhvanir ajṛmbhata.
Avandanta ca vṛndāni bandināṃ medinī|patim
«pūrit'|ârthi|samūh'|āśa tav' āśā pūryatām iti!»
«Yuvā dhīraḥ sa te yogyo yajamānasya jāyatām!»
ity|ādibhir dvijāś c' âinaṃ mantra|vādyair avardhayan.
Nimittair evam|ākāraiḥ kārya|saṃsiddhi|śaṃsibhiḥ
Ādityaśarmaṇo jātam aṅgaṃ rom'|âñca|karkaśam.

Padmāvatyās tato harṣād vivāha iva nṛtyati
Vasantake dhvanat|tāle nanarta gaṇikā|gaṇaḥ.
Alaṃ c' âti|prasaṅgena! saṃkṣepād avadhāryatām
vadhū|vṛṇda|parīvārāḥ pranṛttāḥ śvaśurā api!

said to me, 'Come into this cave.' When I went in there I saw the sixty-four arts and the four great sciences* depicted in paintings. As I looked in amazement at the pictures one by one, I was woken by the deep, booming rumblings of the drums."

This dream was interpreted thus: "You shall have a son who is skilled in all the arts portrayed in the paintings."

Vasantaka had also had a dream, which he told thus: 5.70
"The sun god gave me a beautiful gleaming earring."

[ ].*

As the dreams were being interpreted, the darkness was pierced by the light of dawn, the charioteer of the sun, and became red, like the eyes of a chakora bird. The birds were awakened by the touch of lotus flowers blown about in the soft breeze, and the sounds of their various voices echoed around the lakes. The temple drums boomed so loudly that the women of Indra's harem were terrified by their deep echo. Bands of bards praised the king, saying, "May your wishes be fulfilled, you who have fulfilled the wishes of a host of supplicants!" And the brahmins exalted him with verses such as "May you have a brave son worthy of you, the patron of the sacrifice!" Such omens signalled the success of the matter in hand and made Adityasharma's body tingle all over.

Then, while Vasantaka danced and clapped joyfully, like he had done at Padmavati's wedding, the troupe of courtesans took to the floor. But enough of this lengthy digression! Let me put it to you in a nutshell: even the king's fathers-
in-law danced, surrounded by his wives! The Gandharvas 5.80

5.80 Ati|harṣa|parītatvād vitantrī|parivādinīḥ
tāḍayanti sma gandharvāḥ svara|vismṛta|sāraṇāḥ!
Evam|ādau tu vṛtt'|ânte vartamāne mahī|patiḥ
kṛt'|âbhiṣek'|ādi|vidhiḥ sura|viprān apūjayat.
Praviśya stūyamānaś ca vṛndair brāhmaṇa|bandinām
pauram antaḥ|puraṃ c' âiva dān'|ādibhir amānayat.
Māsa|dvaya|parīmāṇe tataḥ kāle 'tigacchati
devyāṃ sattva|samāveśa|varttāṃ prāvartayat kṣitau.
Yena yena śrutā vārttā śabareṇa śukena vā
giriṣṭhaḥ pañjara|stho vā mugdhas tatr' âiva tatra saḥ.
Striyaḥ prasūti|kuśalāḥ kumār'|ādi|cikitsakāḥ
garbha|karma|vidaś c' ânye nityaṃ tāṃ paryacārayan.
Mlāyan|madhūka|vicchāya|kapolaṃ jihma|locanam
śvaśrūs tasyā mukhaṃ dṛṣṭvā bubudhe dohada|vyathām.
Pṛcchati sma ca tāṃ «putri, śīghram ācakṣva dohadam
anākhyāte hi garbhasya vaiphalyam api dṛśyate!»
Lajjamānā yadā n' âsau kathayām āsa dohadam
tadā sva|vṛttaṃ sā vadhvai vyāhartum upacakrame.
«Antarvatnīm apṛcchan mām ekadā śvaśuras tava
‹bādhate dohado yas tvāṃ sa kṣipraṃ kathyatām iti.›
5.90 Mayā tu praṇayiny" âpi prakṛṣṭatara|lajjayā
sakhī|mukhena kathitaṃ bahu|kṛtvo 'nuyuktayā:
‹Iyaṃ māṃ bādhate śraddhā s" āśu saṃpādyatām iti›
sā ca saṃpādit" āmātyaiḥ Śatānīkasya śāsanāt.
Bāla|bhāskara|bimb'|ābhā dadhānāḥ s'|ânulepanāḥ

were so overcome with joy that they forgot to tune their lutes and strummed them discordantly! As this and more was going on, the king was ritually anointed and carried out his other duties before worshipping the gods and brahmins. While being glorified by bands of brahmins and bards, he went into the city and then to his inner apartments, where he honored their inhabitants with presents and so forth.

After two months had gone by, he spread throughout the land the news that the queen was pregnant. Whether hillman on a mountain or parrot in a cage, whoever heard the news was overcome right there and then.

Midwives, pediatricians and gynecologists attended her constantly. When her mother-in-law looked at her face and saw her cheeks as pale as fading *madhūka* flowers and her eyes askance, she diagnosed the cravings of pregnancy.

She begged her, "My daughter, quickly say what you crave, for women who haven't told their cravings have even been known to miscarry!"

When, embarrassed, she did not relate her craving, her mother-in-law started to tell her her own story. "Once when I was pregnant your father-in-law asked me to tell him im-
mediately the craving that was bothering me. Even though 5.90
I was his wife, I was extremely embarrassed, and I was asked many times before telling him through a friend about the craving that was troubling me. I asked him to have it satisfied soon. At my husband Shatanika's command, the ministers arranged for it to be satisfied. Wearing clothes, ornaments, garlands and makeup as red as the orb of the morning sun, crowds of attendants wandered about the

vyacaranta purīṃ raktā ambar'|ābharaṇa|srajaḥ.
Rakt'|ātapatra|vyajanā rakta|kambala|vāhyakāḥ
rakt'|âśoka|van'|ākāra|parivāra|kadambakāḥ.
Suyāmunam ath' āruhya padma|rāga|nag'|âruṇam
dig|dāhād iva raktānām apaśyaṃ maṇḍalaṃ diśām.

Atha pakṣ'|ânila|bhrānta|saṃbhrānta|jana|vīkṣitaḥ
jyeṣṭha|putra iv' āgacchad Garuḍasya vihaṃgamaḥ.
Sa|ras'|āmiṣa|gṛddhaś ca mugdhām ādāya mām asau
agamad gaganaṃ vegāc Chatānīkasya paśyataḥ.
Tataḥ pradeśe kasmiṃś cid avatāritavān sa mām
bhakṣayiṣyan niṣiddhaś ca ken' âpy ākāśam āśrayat.
Paśyāmi sma ca tatra dvau kṛśāv ṛṣi|kumārakau
prabhā|maṇḍala|saṃsarga|piṅgal'|âṅgau jvalaj|jaṭau.

Tau mām avocatāṃ ‹devi mā bhaiṣīr ayam āśramaḥ
Vasiṣṭhasy' āśritaḥ puṇyām Uday'|âdrer upatyakām.
5.100 Āgaccha nanu pāvas tvāṃ tatr' êty› ukte gatā satī
paśyāmi sma jagaj|jyeṣṭhaṃ śreṣṭha|tāpasa|veṣṭitam.

Vanditaś ca mayā dūrād āśiṣā mām avardhayat
‹putri putraṃ vijāyasva yaśaḥ|pātram ajarjaram!
Na c' ôtkaṇṭhā tvayā kāryā sva|jane mat|sa|nāthayā
āditya|vaṃśa|jānāṃ hi saṃniveśaḥ par'|āyaṇaḥ.›

Iti viśvāsya māṃ vākyair madhurair evam|ādibhiḥ
‹āvāsaḥ kriyatāṃ vadhvā iti› śiṣyān samādiśat.
Kṣipram āvasathaṃ kṛtvā te śilā|dāru|veṇubhiḥ

city. With red parasols and fans, with red blankets and vehicles, they looked like a grove of red *aśoka* trees. I climbed the Suyamuna palace, which, like a mountain of rubies, was the color of the dawn, and I saw the curve of the horizon in all directions glow red as if the skies were ablaze.

Then a bird that looked like Garuda's eldest son appeared, watched by the astonished people, who were sent reeling by the wind from its wings. Eager for some tasty flesh, it snatched me, dumbstruck as I was, and soared into the sky before Shatanika's eyes. Then it put me down somewhere. It was about to eat me but someone forbade it and it flew away. I saw two gaunt young sages there, with shining matted hair and bodies that were golden in the glow of their gleaming haloes.

They said to me, 'Madam, do not be afraid. That is Vasishtha's hermitage, nestling in a sacred valley at the foot
of the mountain of the Rising Sun. Come along now. We 5.100
shall look after you there.' After they said this, I went there and saw the most venerable man in the world, surrounded by great ascetics.

I greeted him from afar and he blessed me, saying, 'My daughter, may you give birth to a son of never diminishing glory! Under my protection, there is no need for you to long for your own people, for this place is the ultimate destination for those born into the solar dynasty.'

After thus reassuring me with these and other kind words, he ordered his pupils to make me a place to stay. They quickly built a dwelling out of stone, timber and bamboo, with a moat and a fence around it, and informed Vasishtha.

khāta|śāla|parikṣiptaṃ Vasiṣṭhāya nyavedayan.
Tāpasī|kṛta|sānāthyā tatr' âham avasaṃ sukham
ṛṣibhiḥ kriyamāṇeṣu garbha|saṃskāra|karmasu.
Prasūtā c' âsmi daśame māse putraṃ patiṃ tava
anukūla|savitr|ādi|graha|sūcita|saṃpadam.

Jāta|karma tataḥ kṛtvā sūrya|vaṃśa|guruḥ svayam
divase dvādaśe nāma putrasya kṛtavān mama:
‹Bālo jātaḥ su|jāto 'yaṃ yasmād Udaya|parvate
tasmād Udayano nāma prasiddhim upayātv iti.›

Vede gāndharva|vede ca sakalāsu kalāsu ca
śāstreṣu c' âstra|śastreṣu buddhir asya vyanīyata.
5.110 Gacchatsu divaseṣv evaṃ Vasiṣṭhen' âiṣa vāritaḥ
‹mā kadā cid bhavān asmād dūraṃ gā āśramād iti.›
Nisarga|karkaśatvāt tu kṣatra|jātes tapo|vanāt
niryāya mṛgayām eṣa samakrīḍata kānane.

Ekadā bhrājamāno 'yaṃ divyaiḥ srak|candan'|ādibhiḥ
abhivāditavān bhīto Vasiṣṭhaṃ darśita|smitam.

Vasiṣṭhaḥ pṛṣṭhavān enam ‹api dṛṣṭāḥ kumārakāḥ
nalinyāṃ prastuta|krīḍā bhavatā bhoginām iti?›

‹Āma dṛṣṭā iti› prokte sutena mama nīcakaiḥ
‹ācakṣva vistareṇ' êti› Vasiṣṭhas tam abhāṣata.

Pṛṣṭen' Ôdayanen' ôktam ‹aham ājñāpitas tvayā
«na gantavyaṃ tvayā dūram etasmād āśramād iti.»
Ārabhya ca tataḥ kālāt, «kiṃ punaḥ kāraṇaṃ guruḥ
māṃ nivārayat' îty» āsam ahaṃ kautūhal'|ākulaḥ.
So 'haṃ doṣam asaṃcintya gurv|ājñā|bhaṅga|saṃbhavam
dūram ady' āśramād asmād gacchāmi diśam uttarām.

Helped by the female ascetics, and with the sages carrying out pregnancy rites, I lived there in comfort. In the tenth month, I gave birth to a son, your husband, whose good fortune was indicated by the favorable positions of the sun and other heavenly bodies.

Then, having performed the rites of childbirth himself, on the twelfth day the guru of the solar dynasty named my son: 'Because this noble boy has been born on the mountain of the Rising Sun, let him be known as Udayana*.'

He was instructed in the Veda, music, all the arts, the
law books, archery and swordsmanship. As the days passed 5.110
thus, Vasishtha warned him that he must never stray far from the hermitage. However, being naturally daring because of his warrior birth, he used to leave the penance grove to enjoy himself hunting in the forest.

One day, looking resplendent in divine garlands, sandal paste and so forth, he timidly greeted Vasishtha, who smiled openly.

Vasishtha asked him, 'Have you seen the young snake-boys playing in the lotus pond?'

When my son quietly replied that yes, he had seen them, Vasishtha asked him to tell him the whole story.

Udayana replied, 'You told me not to go far from this hermitage. From that time onward I was intrigued as to why my guru had warned me thus. So, paying no heed to the bad consequences that arise from disobeying one's guru, today I went far to the north of this hermitage. There I came across a lotus pond where there were many different

Tatra paśyāmi nalinīṃ nānā|sarasi|j'|âṇḍa|jām
vana|vāraṇa|saṃkṣobha|saṃghaṭṭita|nad'|âmbhasam.
Tasyām a|mānuṣ'|ākārā mayā dṛṣṭāḥ kumārakāḥ
unmajjanto nimajjantas tarantaś c' âruṇ'|ēkṣaṇāḥ.
5.120 Te māṃ taṭa|stham ālokya puñjī|bhūya sa|saṃbhramāḥ
dīrgha|dīrgha|bhuj'|ākṣepair agādhaṃ jalam āśritāḥ.
Ahaṃ tān uktavān asmi «mā palāyadhvam! āsyatām!
nanv ahaṃ bhavato draṣṭum āśramād ṛṣir āgataḥ!»
Iti mad|vacanaṃ śrutvā teṣām ekena bhāṣitam
«kiṃ te 'smābhir mahā|sattva bhāṣitair? gamyatām iti!»
«Satya|satyaṃ na yakṣo 'smi na piśāco na rākṣasaḥ
tena mā bhaiṣṭa ḍhaukadhvam iti!» tān aham uktavān.
Tais tu saṃjāta|viśrambhaiḥ saṃharan vā muhūrtakam
«āgaccha prārthito mitra gṛhaṃ no gamyatām iti!»
Mayā tad|anurodhena «gacchām' îti» pratiśrute
mām ādāya nimagnās te tasy' âiva saraso 'mbhasi.
Ath' ânudita|candr'|ârka|graha|nakṣatra|tārakam
candra|sūrya|maṇi|dyota|pradhvasta|dhvānta|saṃcayam.
Sthavir'|ātura|nirvṛtta|virūpa|jana|varjitam
ramya|harmy'|âvalī|garbha|jṛmbhit'|ātodya|nisvanam.
A|śeṣair viyutaṃ doṣair a|śeṣaiḥ saṃyutaṃ guṇaiḥ
praveśito 'smi muditair adhiṣṭhānaṃ kumārakaiḥ.
Teṣām ekas tu mām āha «bhogināṃ bhoginām iyam
purī Bhogavatī nāma vasatiḥ kalpa|jīvinām.
5.130 Tanayaḥ Kambalasy' âham ayam Aśvatarasya tu
anye ca sūnavo 'nyeṣāṃ nāga|senā|bhṛtām iti.»

lotuses and birds, and its waters rippled with the splashing of wild elephants.

In it I saw young boys who did not look human. They were jumping, diving and swimming, and had red eyes.
When they saw me on the bank as a group they quickly 5.120
moved away to deep water with long strokes of their long arms. I said to them, "Don't flee! Stay here! I'm a sage and I have come from the hermitage to see you!"

When he heard what I had said one of them replied, "Why should you want to talk to us, noble sir? Please go!"

I replied to them, "I promise I am not a *yakṣa**, nor a *piśāca**, nor a demon, so don't be frightened; come here!"

Emboldened, they huddled together for a moment and said, "Come, friend, you are invited to our home. Let's go!"

When I agreed and said that I would come, they took hold of me, and plunged into the water of that very same pond. Where the moon, the sun, the planets, the constellations and the stars do not rise, but where the dense darkness is destroyed by the light of moonstones and sunstones, where there are no old, sick, indolent nor deformed people, where the sounds of musical instruments pervade the avenues of beautiful houses, where all faults are absent and all virtues are present—such was the place that the happy youths took me to.

One of them said to me, "This city, called Bhogavati, is the home of the snake-people, who are devoted to pleasure
and live to the end of the time-cycle. I am the son of 5.130
Kambala, this is the son of Ashvatara, and the others are sons of other soldiers of the snake-people's army."

Tataḥ Kambala|putreṇa nītv" âhaṃ svaṃ gṛhaṃ mahat
grāhit'|ârgh'|ādi|satkāraḥ kārito veṣam īdṛśam.

Itare netum aicchanta svagṛhān māṃ may" ôditāḥ
«anujānīta mām adya suhṛdo mā sma kupyata.
Guruṇā pratiṣiddho 'ham etāṃ bhūmim upāgataḥ
bhītaś ca kupitāt tasmāt tasmān nayata mām iti.»

Te tu mām āhur «uttiṣṭha! gamyatāṃ! svam idaṃ puram
punar āgacchatā kāryam an|utkaṇṭhaṃ bhujaṃ|gamam.
Tasyām eva ca ramyatvāt krīḍāmaḥ saṃtataṃ vayam
suhṛdo 'pi yad' îcchā syād gacchet tāṃ nalinīm iti.»

Ity uktvā mama tair vaktre paṭ'|ânten' âvaguṇṭhite
uttīrṇam aham ātmānaṃ paśyāmi sarasas tataḥ.
Iti Bhogavatīṃ dṛṣṭvā so 'ham āyāmi saṃprati
mam' âsminn aparādhe ca pramāṇaṃ bhagavān iti!›

Vasiṣṭhas tam ath' âvocad: ‹upāyo 'yaṃ mayā kṛtaḥ
yena nāga|kumārās te dṛṣṭi|gocaratāṃ gatāḥ.
Idānīm api taiḥ sārdhaṃ gatvā Bhogavatīṃ tvayā
gāndharvaṃ hasti|vidyā ca śikṣitavyāḥ sa|vistarāḥ.

5.140 Yadi ca grāhayet kiṃ cit tvāṃ nāg'|âdhipatis tataḥ
sa|nāga|mūrcchanā grāhyā vīṇā Ghoṣavatī tvayā.
Aṅkam āropitāyāṃ ca tantryo yasyām anāhatāḥ
madhuraṃ nisvaneyus tāṃ vidyā Ghoṣavatīm iti›.

Guror Udayanaḥ śrutvā nāga|lokaṃ gatas tataḥ
gate bahu|tithe kāle vīṇā|pāṇir upāgataḥ.

Then Kambala's son led me to his large house and, after welcoming me with offerings of water and so forth, he had me put on these clothes.

The others wanted to take me to their houses but I said to them, "Please excuse me today, my friends, and don't get angry. I came to this place after being forbidden to do so by my guru. I am scared of him when he is angry, so take me back."

They said to me, "Hurry up and be on your way! This city is your city—you must remove the longing of the snake-people by coming here again. We always play in that same lotus pool because it is so beautiful. If the desire takes you too, friend, you should go there."

After they said this, they covered my face with the end of a piece of cloth and I found I had come out of the pool. So it is after visiting Bhogavati that I come to you now like this; you, my lord, are to be the judge of this wrongdoing of mine!'

Vasishtha said to him: 'I used this ploy to make you come across the snake-boys. Now you must return to Bhogavati
with them and learn in detail music and elephant lore. If 5.140
the king of the snake-people lets you ask for something, you must choose the Ghoshavati lute, which plays the snake-people's melody. You will know Ghoshavati because when it is in your lap its strings sound sweetly without being plucked.'

After listening to his guru, Udayana went to the world of the snake-people. Many days later, he came back with the lute in his hand. His guru greeted him and hugged him

Kṛt'|âbhivādo guruṇā pariṣvaktaś ca s'|âśruṇā
tad|viyog'|âgni|tapt'|âṅgīm ambām aṅgair aśītayat.
Ekadā tu sukh'|āsīno Vasiṣṭhas tam abhāṣata
‹tāta Ghoṣavatī|ghoṣa|saṃgītaṃ śrāvyatām iti›.
Tan|nideśāc ca patyau te pragīte saha vīṇayā
jagat|pracalan'|ācāryo nabhasvān api n' âcalat.
Niś|ceṣṭam āśramaṃ dṛṣṭvā mūka|keśari|vāraṇam
raktāṃ Ghoṣavatīṃ muktvā tūṣṇīm āsīt patis tava.
Uktaś c' âiṣa Vasiṣṭhena ‹na tvay" âsmiṃs tapo|ane
vādanīyā punar vīṇā geyaṃ vā śanakair api.
Anye 'pi dhvanayaḥ prāyaś calayanti samāhitān
samādheḥ kiṃ punar yena śākhino 'pi vimohitāḥ?
Tasmād a|vīta|rāgāṇāṃ samādhim a|vihiṃsatā
dūre tapo|vanād asmād vīṇ" êyaṃ vādyatām iti.›
5.150 Tataś c' ārabhya divasād Uday'|âcala|cāriṇaḥ
nāgān Udayano 'gṛhṇād ramyair Ghoṣavatī|rutaiḥ.
Dānta|vyāla|gaj'|ārūḍhaḥ siṃh'|ādi|vyāla|vellitaḥ
kvaṇad|Ghoṣavatī|pāṇir āyāti sma tapo|anam.
Evaṃ yāti kva cit kāle bhagavān mām abhāṣata
‹dārakas taruṇo jātaḥ Kauśāmbīṃ gamyatām iti›.
Mayā tu nir|vacanayā kathite 'smin mano|rathe
guruṇā tīrtha|salilair abhiṣiktaḥ suto mama.
Tac|chiṣyās tu tad|ādiṣṭā mām ādāya sa|putrakām

tearfully. Then he cooled his mother with his embrace—her body was burning with the fire of separation from him.

One day Vasishtha was relaxing and said to him, 'Child, let's hear some music from Ghoshavati.' When your husband obeyed and sang along to the lute, even the wind, the teacher of movement to the world, was motionless. When he saw that nothing was moving in the hermitage and that the lions and elephants were quiet, your husband put down the sweet Ghoshavati and fell silent.

Vasishtha said to him, 'You must never again play the lute or sing, even softly, in the hermitage. Other sounds may also disturb people in meditation, but what is meditation to a sound that bewitches even the trees? Therefore, so that you do not disturb the meditation of those who are yet to rid themselves of desire, you must only play this lute far away from the hermitage.'

From that day on, Udayana would captivate the elephants 5.150
that roamed on the mountain of the Rising Sun with the beautiful sounds of Ghoshavati. He used to ride back to the hermitage on a wild elephant that he had tamed, jostled by lions and other wild animals, with Ghoshavati resonating in his hand.

Time passed like this until one day the venerable sage said to me, 'The boy has become a young man. You must go to Kaushambi.'

Without saying a word I indicated that I felt the same and the guru anointed my son with water from holy places. At his command, his pupils took hold of me and my son, and in an instant they led us through the sky to this city.

ākāśena nayanti sma kṣaṇena nagarīm imām.
Ath' âhaṃ nagar'|ôdyāne ramye tair avatāritā
muhūrtaṃ preritavatī gagan'|āgamana|śramam.
  Avatīrya tu te bhartā krīḍā|puṣkariṇīṃ pituḥ
padma|bhañjikayā krīḍan dṛṣṭa udyāna|pālakaiḥ.
Tair gatvā kathitaṃ rājñe ‹deva deva|kumārakaḥ
adhun" âiv' āgataḥ svargād gāhate nalinīm iti.›
  Rājā tu drutam āgatya dṛṣṭvā deva|samaṃ sutam
‹deva ev' âyam› ity uktvā praṇāmaṃ kartum udyataḥ.
  Tatas tapasvibhiḥ kha|sthaiḥ saṃbhrāntaiḥ sa nivāritaḥ
‹rājann Udayanaṃ putraṃ na namaskartum arhasi!
5.160 Saṃdehaś ced imāṃ pṛccha mahiṣīṃ Mṛgayāvatīm
prema|saṃbhrama|saṃtrāsa|lajjābhiḥ kheditām iti!›
Rājā tu tān ath' ô dṛṣṭvā mām apaśyat sutaṃ tataḥ
muhūrtaṃ cintayitvā tu vihasan prasthito gṛhān.
  Ath' âyam ṛṣibhiḥ proktaḥ puraḥ sthitvā sa|saṃbhramaiḥ
‹na gantavyaṃ! na gantavyaṃ! n' âiṣaḥ svapno! nivartyatām!
Atha vā bhavatu svapnaḥ svapne 'pi na virudhyate
durlabhen' âpi hi svapne vallabhena samāgamaḥ.
Yac ca brūmas tad ākarṇya cetaḥ|karṇa|sukh'|āvaham
tato yāsyasi s'|âpatyām ādāya dayitām iti.›
  Nivṛttāya ca te tasmai bhāruṇḍa|haraṇ'|ādikam
ācakṣate sma vṛtt'|ântam āśram'|ānayanād iti.
  Rājā tu putram āliṅgya harṣa|mūrchā|vicetanaḥ

They put me down in the beautiful city park, and I quickly shook off the fatigue of the aerial journey.

After your husband had landed he was seen by the park wardens playing at plucking lotus leaves in his father's lotus play-pond. They went and said to the king, 'Your Majesty, a divine boy arrived from heaven just now; he is bathing in the lotus pond.'

The king came running and when he saw his godlike son he said, 'He is indeed a god,' and started to bow down in reverence.

The ascetics in the sky were aghast and stopped him, saying, 'O king, this is your son, Udayana—you should not bow down before him! If you do not believe us, ask 5.160
queen Mrigayavati here. See how she is stricken by love, confusion, fear and embarrassment!' The king looked at them, and then at me, and then at his son, and thought for a moment before laughing and setting off for his palace.

The bewildered sages stood in front of him and said, 'Don't go! Don't go! This isn't a dream! Turn back! But even if it were a dream, let it be so, for reunion with a loved one, even one who is out of reach, is not impossible in a dream. Listen to what we have to say—it will delight your ears and heart—and then you will take your wife and child with you!'

He turned back and they told him the story, from my abduction by the bird of prey to our being brought back from the hermitage.

The king embraced his son. In paroxysms of joy, he lost consciousness and as he fell to the ground his son rushed to

nipatan dharaṇī|pṛṣṭhe putreṇ' ālambhitaḥ kṣaṇam.
Māṃ ca dṛṣṭvā ciraṃ dṛṣṭvā deva|dṛṣṭi|viceṣṭayā
niśvāsair akṣipad dīrghair netr'|âmbu|kaṇikā|gaṇam.
Baddh'|âñjalir nara|patir bravīti sma ca tān ṛṣīn
‹avatāreṇa gurubhiḥ prasādaḥ kriyatām iti.›
Tair uktaṃ ‹na samādiṣṭā Vasiṣṭhena vayaṃ tataḥ
gacchāmo n' âvatīry' âiva svasti tubhyaṃ bhavatv iti!›
5.170 Tān ayācata bhūpālo ‹yat kiṃ cit sv'|âṅga|dhāritam
asmat|pāvanam ujjhitvā yath"|êṣṭaṃ gamyatām iti.›
Mṛg'|âjināni te kṣiptvā taḍit|kānti|jaṭā|guṇāḥ
tatr' âiv' ântar|dadhuś caṇḍa|marud|vyastā iv' âmbudāḥ.
Mṛg'|âjināni tu nṛpo daivatān' îva bhaktimān
pūjayitvā tad udyānaṃ nāmn" âvocan Mṛg'âjinam.
Sā Mṛg'âjina|yātr" êyaṃ tataḥ|prabhṛti vāsarāt
pravartitā nṛ|patinā prasiddhim agamad bhuvi.
Tataḥ kṛtvā sutaṃ rājā yuva|rājaṃ Mṛg'âjine
praviṣṭo hṛṣṭa|hṛdayaḥ prahṛṣṭāṃ nagarīm iti.
So 'yaṃ may" ēdṛśo labdhaḥ putraḥ saṃpādya dohadam
tav' âpi dohado yaḥ sa putri saṃpādyatām iti!»
Yadā tu n' âiv' âkathayad lajjayā nṛ|patis tadā
Māgadhīm uktavān «pṛccha dohadaṃ bhaginīm iti.»
Padmāvatī tu tāṃ pṛṣṭvā tad|ākhyātam avarṇayat
«‹duḥ|saṃpādā kila śraddhā mam' êty› āha śanair iyam.»
Atha tām abravīd uccair hasitvā Mṛgayāvatī

catch him. He stared at me for an age with the unblinking gaze of a god, and then, sighing deeply, he poured forth floods of tears.

The king put his palms together and said to the sages, 'Would Your Reverences be so kind as to come down to earth.'

They replied, 'We have had no instruction from Vasishtha to do so, so we shall leave without descending to earth. Best wishes to you!'

The king asked them, 'Please throw down whatever you 5.170
are wearing on your bodies as a means for us to sanctify ourselves, and go as you please.'

Their locks of matted hair shining like lightning, they threw down their deer-skins and disappeared there and then, like clouds scattered by a violent wind. The devoted king worshipped the deer-skins as though they were divine, and he named the park 'Deer-skin.' From that day the king started this Deer-skin festival, and it became world-famous.

The king made his son crown prince in the Deer-skin Park, and entered the joyful city with a happy heart.

It was after thus satisfying a pregnancy craving that I had a son like Udayana. My girl, you too must have your craving satisfied!"

But when, out of embarrassment, Vasavadatta still did not speak, the king told Padmavati to ask her sister what her craving was. After asking her, however, Padmavati reported that she had whispered, "I think my desire will be difficult to satisfy."

Then Mrigayavati laughed loudly and said to her, "O you

«mugdhe! kiṃ nāma duḥ|sādhyam upāya|caturair nṛbhiḥ?
Śrūyatāṃ vā pur" āvṛttaṃ Mathurāyām abhūn nṛpaḥ
Ugraseno mahā|senaḥ śatru|sen"|âmbu|d'|ânilaḥ.
5.180 Tasya strī guṇa|saṃpannā śucy|ācāra|kul'|ôdbhavā
āsīn manoram'|ācārā yā nāmn" âpi Manoramā.
Kadā cid āgate kāle samṛddha|kuṭaj'|ârjune
rasan|mayūra|sāraṅga|megha|maṇḍūka|maṇḍale,
Manoramaṃ gṛh'|ôdyānaṃ praviveśa Manoramā
kadamb'|ânilam āghrātum udbhūta|pratham'|ārtavā.
Tadā ca Drumilo nāma dānavo nabhasā vrajan
udyāna|śobhay" ākṛṣṭa|dṛṣṭis tāṃ tatra dṛṣṭavān.
Kṛt'|ôgrasena|rūpeṇa tena sāpāya|cetasā
samagacchata sadyaś ca sa|sattvā samapadyata.
Strībhiś ca dohadaṃ pṛṣṭā kṛcchrād uktavatī hriyā
‹Viṣṇoḥ śoṇita|māṃs'|ântrair gamayāmi tṛṣām iti.›
Śrutv" êdam Ugrasenena ciraṃ saṃmantrya mantribhiḥ
sṛṣṭaḥ piṣṭa|mayo Viṣṇur meṣ'|āmiṣa|bhṛt'|ôdaraḥ.
Manda|pradīpa|kiraṇe tasyā vasati|mandire
nyastaḥ piṣṭa|mayo Viṣṇuḥ kṣapāyāṃ kṣapitas tayā.
Duḥ|saṃpāde 'pi saṃpanne dohade 'sminn upāyataḥ
vadhyaṃ Yādava|siṃhasya Kaṃsaṃ sutam asūta sā.
Tena bravīmi ‹n' âsty eva duḥ|saṃpādā kriyā nṛbhiḥ›
tasmāt tav' âpi yā śraddhā s" âpi saṃpādyatām iti.»
5.190 Kathitaṃ ca tataḥ śrutvā Padmāvaty" «êyam icchati

silly girl! What is difficult for resourceful men? Listen to an old story. In Mathura, there was a king called Ugrasena. With his large army he was to his enemies' armies as the wind is to clouds. He had a virtuous wife, who lived a pure 5.180
life and was from a noble family. She behaved in a charming fashion so was called Manorama*.

One day, in the season when the *kuṭaja* and *arjuna* trees are in blossom, and all the peacocks, cuckoos, clouds and frogs are in full voice, Manorama, who had just had her first menstruation, entered the delightful palace garden to smell the scented air from the *kadamba* tree. Then a Danava* called Drumila who was flying by had his gaze attracted by the beauty of the garden and saw her there. The malevolent demon assumed the form of Ugrasena and had intercourse with her. She became pregnant.

When the women asked her about her craving, she replied feebly and with embarrassment, 'I am thirsting after the blood, flesh and guts of Vishnu.'

When he heard this, Ugrasena conferred at length with his ministers before making an image of Vishnu out of dough, with mutton inside. In the night, the dough Vishnu was placed in her home in the weak lamplight, and she ate it. Despite being difficult to satisfy, this pregnancy craving was satisfied by a ruse, and she gave birth to a son, Kamsa, who was to fall prey to the lion of the Yadavas*. So, I tell you, there is no task too difficult for men. Therefore, whatever your desire may be, let it too be satisfied."

When she heard this, Padmavati said, "She wants to fly 5.190
in a sky-chariot and see the whole world."

ambara|stha|vimāna|sthā kṛtsnāṃ draṣṭuṃ mahīm iti.»
Ath' ôvāca hasann uccaiḥ krīḍā|śīlo Vasantakaḥ
«devasya dāsa|bhāryāṇām ayam eva mano|rathaḥ.
Mayā tu bhaṇitāḥ sarvā ‹dīrgha|stambh'|âvalambinīm
dolām āruhya nabhasā muhur āyāta yāta ca.
Upāyam anyaṃ patayo bhavatīnāṃ na jānate
ten' ākāśa|gati|śraddhā tathā vaḥ pūryatām iti.›»
Tataḥ prahasitāḥ sarve. Rumaṇvān idam abravīt
«nivartyatāṃ parīhāsaḥ prastutaṃ vartyatām iti.»
Yaugandharāyaṇen' ôktaṃ «kim atra paricintyate?
asādhāraṇa ev' âyaṃ viṣayaḥ śilpinām iti».
Rumaṇvatā tu takṣāṇaḥ saṃnipātya pracoditāḥ
«yantram ākāśa|saṃcāri tvaritaiḥ kriyatām iti.»
Ath' ôtkramya ciraṃ sarve mantrayitvā ca śilpinaḥ
Rumaṇvantam abhāṣanta saṃtrāsa|praskhalad|giraḥ:
«Catur|vidhāni jānīmo vayaṃ yantrāṇi tad yathā
jal'|âśma|pāṃśu|yantrāṇi kāṇḍa|rāśī|kṛtāni ca.
Ākāśa|yantrāṇi punar Yavanāḥ kila jānate
asmākaṃ tu na yātāni gocaraṃ cakṣuṣām iti.»
5.200 Tatra ca brāhmaṇaḥ kaś cid abravīd āgrahārikaḥ
«bhoḥ sabhe śrūyatāṃ tāvad yan may" ākhyānakaṃ śrutam.
Asti Pukvasako nāma Mahāsenasya vardhakī
skandh'|āvāreṇa sārdhaṃ sa Surāṣṭra|viṣayaṃ gataḥ.
Tena tatr' âparo dṛṣṭaḥ surūpaḥ śilpi|dārakaḥ
Viśvilo nāma yaḥ śilpī sadṛśo Viśvakarmaṇā.
Atha Pukvasakas tasya pitaraṃ Mayam abravīt
‹tava putrāya duhitā dattā Ratnāvalī mayā.

Vasantaka, who liked a joke, laughed loudly and said, "The wives of Your Majesty's servants have this same wish! I told them all, 'Sit on a swing hanging from high posts and ride back and forth through the sky! Your husbands know of no other way, so you must satisfy your desire for flight like this.'"

At this everyone burst out laughing. Rumanvan said, "Stop laughing: we must turn to the matter in hand."

Yaugandharayana said, "What is the point of us concerning ourselves with it? This is a most specialized matter, a subject for the artisans."

Rumanvan assembled the engineers and instructed them to build at once a machine for travelling through the air.

All the artisans stood aside and talked at length among themselves before speaking to Rumanvan in voices faltering with fear: "We know of four types of machine*: machines for water, stone, and dust, and those for pressing sugarcane. As for sky-machines, they are apparently known to the Greeks but we have not come across them."

At this, a certain landowning brahmin hailed the assem- 5.200
bly and said, "Please listen for a moment to a short tale that I have heard. Mahasena had a carpenter called Pukvasaka. He accompanied the king's entourage to Saurashtra. There he saw another young craftsman, a handsome man called Vishvila, who was Vishvakarman's equal as an artisan. Then Pukvasaka said to Vishvila's father, Maya, 'I am giving my daughter Ratnavali* to your son. You do not need to ask me what qualities she has, for she is a veritable garland of such precious qualities as respectability, beauty

Praṣṭavyaś ca tvayā n' âhaṃ «kīdṛśī sā guṇair iti?»
kula|rūp'|âbhijāty|ādi|guṇa|ratn'|āvalī hi sā.
Saṃpadyate ca naḥ kiṃ cin Mahāsena|parigrahāt
tasmāt saṃvardha|siddhy|arthaṃ putraṃ prasthāpayer iti!›
Mayena ca pratijñāte gatvā Pukvasako gṛhān
jāmātr|āgaman'|ākāṅkṣī mahāntaṃ kālam akṣipat.
Kṛtvā rāja|kule karma kadā cid gṛham āgatam
bhaṇati sma na taṃ kaś cit ‹snāhi bhuṅkṣv' êti› c' ākulaḥ.
Bhāryayā kathitaṃ tasmai «kim etad iti» pṛṣṭayā
‹āgantukena ken' âpi sarvam ākulitaṃ gṛham.
Ātmīyās taṇḍulās tena randhanāya samarpitāḥ
«mandako 'ham amībhir me maṇḍaḥ saṃpādyatām iti.»
5.210 Kāṣṭha|bhāra|śataṃ dagdhaṃ na ca svidyanti taṇḍulāḥ
ten' âyam ākulo lokas tat kim etad bhaved iti?›
Atha Pukvasaken' ôktaṃ pariṣvajya kuṭumbinīm
‹gṛha|sthe vardhase diṣṭyā! prāptas te duhitur varaḥ!›
‹Kv' âsau? kv' âsau viśva|bhadra iti?› pṛcchati bhartari
śiraḥ pravṛtya bhāry" âsmai karma|śālām adarśayat.
Niṣkramya karma|śālā|taḥ satvaraṃ Viśvilas tataḥ
abhivāditavān prahvaḥ prasārita|bhujaṃ gurum.
Utkṣipya śvaśureṇ' âpi harṣa|netr'|âmbu|varṣiṇā
nirantaraṃ pariṣvaktaś cir'|âdṛṣṭaḥ suhṛd yathā.
Kṛt'|ârgh'|ādi|saparyaś ca pṛṣṭaḥ Pukvasakena saḥ
‹kiṃ|mayās taṇḍulās tāta kathyatām iti?› so 'bravīt,
‹Ete pāṇḍura|kāṣṭhasya mayā kāṣṭhena taṇḍulāḥ
ghaṭitā ghaṭikā|mātrāt kara|ghāṭa|taror iti.›
Atha Pukvasaken' ôktaṃ, ‹karm' êdaṃ Viśvakarmaṇaḥ

and nobility. We earn something from Mahasena's estate, so, to ensure your prosperity, send forth your son!' When Maya agreed, Pukvasaka went home and spent a long time awaiting the arrival of his son-in-law.

One day when he returned home after completing his work in the king's household, everyone was upset and nobody asked him to bathe or eat. He asked his wife what was going on and she said to him, 'The whole house has been thrown into a state of confusion by an uninvited guest. He has given his own rice to be cooked, saying, "I have a weak digestion. Please provide me with the scum produced by boiling these grains." A hundred loads of wood have been 5.210
burnt and the rice has not softened. That is why everyone is in such a state. So what can be going on?'

Pukvasaka hugged his wife and said, 'Congratulations my dear! Your daughter's bridegroom has arrived!'

When he asked, 'Where is he? Where is that wonderful fellow?,' his wife nodded toward the workshop. Then Vishvila emerged from the workshop and immediately bowed down to greet Pukvasaka, who was holding out his arms. With tears of joy raining down, his father-in-law picked him up and hugged him like a long-lost friend.

After he had been received hospitably with water and the like, Pukvasaka asked him, 'Son, tell me what these rice grains are made of.' He replied, 'I made them in just half an hour, out of a length of white wood from a *karaghāṭa* tree.'

Pukvasaka replied, 'Other than Vishvakarman and you —a lion among artisans—no one could produce such work.

tav' âpi śilpi|siṃhasya tṛtīyasya na vidyate.
Ady' âiva ca dinaṃ bhadram ato Ratnāvalī|karaḥ
gṛhyatām iti› ten' ôkte Viśvilen' ôktam ‹om iti.›
Ratnāvalyā sa saṃgamya sphurad|ujjvala|śobhayā
saṃmīyate sma n' âṅgeṣu daridra iva kāmukaḥ.
5.220 Ālekhya|vidyādharayor yathā saṃmukhayos tayoḥ
mahān kālo 'tiyāti sma nimeṣ'|ôjjhita|cakṣuṣoḥ.
Atha Ratnāvalīṃ dṛṣṭvā vicintām iva Viśvilaḥ
‹kim etad iti› saṃdihya ‹kim etad iti› pṛṣṭavān.
Tasyām abhāṣamāṇāyām ek" âbhāṣata dārikā
‹bhartṛ|dāraka yady asti śrotum icchā tataḥ śṛṇu.
Syālakās tava jalpanti «pūrvam ekākinīṃ vayam
adhunā saha jāmātrā puṣṇīmo bhaginīm iti.»›
Iti śrutvā vanaṃ gatvā chittvā dārūṇi kāny api
yantrāṇi ghaṭayām āsa Yāvanāny atha Viśvilaḥ.
Vṛkṣ'|āyur|veda|nir|diṣṭaiḥ pādap'|âṅgaiś cakāra saḥ
āyur|ārogya|kārīṇi pāk'|ôpakaraṇāni ca.
Sahasra|guṇa|mūlyāni tāni vikrīya tad dhanam
śvaśurāya dadāti sma sa ca prītas tad ādade.
Evaṃ dineṣu gacchatsu vidrāṇa iva Pukvasaḥ
Viśvil'|ādīn samāhūya sa|viṣādam abhāṣata,
‹Aham ājñāpito rājñā: «Brahmadattaḥ suhṛn mama
Kāśi|deśa|patis tena praṇayād aham arthitaḥ,
‹Tava Pukvasako nāma takṣ" âsti kuśalaḥ kila
dharm'|âdhikāra|kārāya sa me prasthāpyatām iti.›

Today is an auspicious day, so take Ratnavali's hand in marriage!' Vishvila agreed. When he married the dazzlingly beautiful Ratnavali, he was like a poor suitor finding a dazzlingly beautiful necklace of jewels*, and could not contain himself.

They stared unblinkingly at one another, like two sorcer- 5.220
ers in a painting, and an age went by.

Then Vishvila saw Ratnavali looking lost in thought, and, wondering what was the matter, he asked her.

When she did not reply, a servant girl said, 'If you want to find out, my lord, then listen. Your wife's brothers have been muttering that they used to have to provide for just their sister, but now they have to do so for both her and their brother-in-law.'

When he heard this, Vishvila went to the forest and cut some pieces of wood from which he made machines in the manner of the Greeks. And from parts of trees described in treatises on arboriculture, he made cooking utensils that prolong life and prevent disease. After selling them for a thousand times their original worth, he gave the profit to his father-in-law, who gladly accepted it.

The days passed thus until Pukvasa, seeming flustered, summoned Vishvila and the others, and addressed them sadly, 'The king has instructed me thus: "I have an ally, Brahmadatta, the king of the Kashi region, and he has petitioned me as a friend, saying 'Apparently you have a skilled carpenter called Pukvasaka, please send him to me
to build a place of worship.' Construct a wooden temple* 5.230
in Varanasi whose work is equal to your talent, and you

5.230 Tacca|deva|kulaṃ kṛtvā sva|buddhi|sama|karmakam
Vārāṇasyām avighnena bhavān āvartatām iti.»
Avaśyaṃ ca mayā tatra gantavyam anujīvinā
martavyaṃ c' âsya caṇḍasya rājño vākyam akurvatā.
Dīrgha|kālaṃ ca tat karma daśā c' êyam anuttarā
tasmāt Pukvasakaḥ sarvaiḥ su|dṛṣṭaḥ kriyatām iti.›
Viśvilena tataḥ proktam ‹alaṃ trāsam upāsya! vaḥ
bhṛtyaṃ Vārāṇasīṃ yāntam anujānīta mām iti!›
Śvaśureṇ' âbhyanujñātaḥ prītena ca mahī|bhujā
dūtaiḥ sa pratidūtaiś ca saha Vārāṇasīṃ gataḥ.
Bahu|kāla|prayāte 'pi patyau Ratnāvalī mukham
saṃtat'|âśru|jal'|āsāra|dhautaṃ mlāna|kapolakam,
Āyat'|âśīta|niśvāsaṃ nās'|âgr'|āhita|locanam
dant'|āvaraṇa|saṃskāra|śūnyam āgalit'|âlakam
Visraṃsamāna|raśanaṃ jaghanaṃ malin'|âṃśukam
na dadhāti sma śok'|ândhā bāhū ca skhalad|aṅgadau.
Tasyām ittham|avasthāyām amantrayata Pukvasaḥ
gṛhiṇīṃ cakitaḥ ‹paśya niś|cintāṃ tanayām iti!›
S" âbravīt ‹suṣṭhu paśyāmi lajjamānā ca te mukham
na darśayāmi nanv evaṃ straiṇaṃ kim api cāpalam.
5.240 Yasy' âsamena rūpeṇa guṇaiś c' âgaṇitaiḥ purī
vṛtā na labhate śāntim apaśyantī tam utsukā.
Darśana|sparśan'|ālāpaiś ciraṃ yā tena lālitā
s" êyam evam aśok" êti manda|bhāgyā bhaṇāmi kim?›
Jāyā|patyos tayor itthaṃ mitho mantrayamāṇayoḥ

will be free to return." As his servant I am obliged to go there; the king is fierce—if I don't obey him, I will have to die. The job will take a long time, and there is no stage of life after this one, so you should all take a long last look at Pukvasaka.'

Vishvila said, 'Have no truck with fear! Allow me, your servant, to go to Varanasi!'

With the permission of his father-in-law and the king, who was delighted, he went to Varanasi accompanied by emissaries from both courts.

Even though her husband had been away for a long time, the marks of a woman blinded by grief—a face washed by a constant stream of tears, pale cheeks, long, hot sighs, eyes fixed on the tip of the nose, an absence of lipstick, freely hanging hair, hips which are wrapped in a dirty robe and are so emaciated that the girdle slips off them, bracelets falling from the arms—were not shown by Ratnavali.

Remarking on her condition, a bewildered Pukvasaka said to his wife, 'Look at the girl: she hasn't a care in the world!'

She replied, 'I see it all too clearly. I have been embarrassed to show my face to you. Surely this is some sort of feminine caprice. The city, deprived of the man's unique beauty and 5.240
countless qualities, is yearning for him, and in his absence cannot find peace. But this girl here, who was for a long time indulged by him with his glances, touch and talk, is without sorrow. How was I, unfortunate as I am, to tell you this?'

A few days passed with the husband and wife continuing

dina|stokeṣu yāteṣu garbhaṃ Ratnāvalī dadhau.
Kṛta|krodha|smito bhāryām atha Pukvasako 'bravīt
‹bhoḥ paśya dayit'|âpatye duhituḥ prakriyām iti!›

Bhartṛ|kopa|nimittena tanayā|doṣa|janmanā
jātena ca nṛpāc caṇḍāt prākampata bhayena sā.
Āsīd ayaṃ ca vṛtt'|ânto rāj'|āhutaś ca Pukvasaḥ
sutā|doṣa|vipākaṃ ca paśyan rāja|kulaṃ gataḥ.

Sa vihasya nṛpeṇ' ôkto ‹mā bhaiṣīr: duhitus tava
jāmātr" âiv' āhito garbhas tac c' êdam avadhīyatām.
Ye mayā preṣitā dūtā jāmātrā bhavataḥ saha
nivṛtta|mātrais tair evaṃ mahyam āveditaṃ yathā,
Ārabhya prathamād eva prayāṇād eṣa Viśvilaḥ
yantra|kukkuṭam āsthāya pradeśe kv' âpi yātavān.
Rātrau ca yāma|śeṣāyāṃ prāvṛty' āgatya mastakam
avijñātaḥ kil' âsmābhir adhyaśeta sva|saṃstare.
5.250 Kadā cit pratibuddheṣu dūteṣu sa parāgataḥ
pādeṣu patitas teṣām ayācata viṣaṇṇakaḥ,
«N' êdaṃ kasya cid ākhyeyaṃ śilpikasy' êtarasya vā
ākāśa|yantra|vijñānaṃ dur|vijñānam a|Yāvanaiḥ.
Khaṭvā|ghaṭana|vijñānam iv' êdaṃ pracurī|bhavet
lokena paribhūyeta kṣaṇa|rāgā hi mānuṣāḥ.
Nindite vandanīye 'sminn āstāṃ tāvac ca pātakam
dṛṣṭa eva mahān doṣo jīvanasy' âpahāraṇam.
Ahaṃ hi bhāryayā sārdham uṣitvā rajanīṃ divā
kurvan nara|pater ājñāṃ neṣyāmi divasān iti.»

Tacca|deva|kulaṃ tena ghaṭitaṃ kila tādṛśam

to deliberate thus with one another, and then Ratnavali fell pregnant. With a sneer Pukvasaka said to his wife, 'Oh, devoted mother, look what your daughter has done!'

She trembled with a fear brought about by her husband's anger, her daughter's sin, and the ferocity of the king. The story turned out as follows. Pukvasaka was summoned by the king. Imagining that this was the consequence of his daughter's wrongdoing, he went to the palace.

The king laughed and said to him, 'Have no fear: it is your son-in-law that has made your daughter pregnant. Listen to this. As soon as they returned, the messengers that I sent with your son-in-law said to me, "From the very first halt, this man Vishvila would get on an artificial bird and go somewhere. When there was one watch left in the night, he would, it seems, come back with his head covered and, unnoticed by us, go to sleep in his own bed. One day he 5.250
came back when the messengers from Brahmadatta's court were awake. Distraught, he fell at their feet and pleaded, 'This science of flying machines, which is hard for those who are not Greek to understand, must not be told to anyone, whether artisan or otherwise. Should it become widespread, like the science of making bedsteads, it might be derided by everyone, for men's passions are fleeting. If this praiseworthy science is scorned, first of all sin will be incurred and, when it is witnessed, there will be a terrible consequence: the loss of my way of life. For I want to spend my nights in the company of my wife and my days carrying out the king's orders.'

Apparently the wooden temple he has built is such that

draṣṭum icchā samutpannā yena duś|cakṣuṣām api.
Brahmadattena dattaṃ ca dhana|rāśim anuttamam
na gṛhṇāti sma vakti sma ‹gurur me labhatām iti.›»

Evam uktvā Mahāseno mahatā dhana|rāśinā
sarva|sva|haraṇāt trastaṃ toṣayām āsa Pukvasam.
Viśvilo ’pi muhūrtena Vārāṇasyāḥ parāgataḥ
ākāśa|yantram āsthāya praviṣṭaś ca gṛhān niśi.

Atīte māsa|mātre ca Viśvilaṃ Pukvaso ’bravīt
‹adya mām āha nṛpatiḥ śanair utsārya sa|smitam:
5.260 «Ākāśa|yantra|vijñānaṃ jāmātre kathitaṃ tvayā
yan mahyam api tat sarvam arthine kathyatām iti!»

Mayā tu kathitaṃ tasmai «na tasmai kathitaṃ mayā
tasmai tu kathitaṃ prītaiḥ śilpibhir yāvanair iti.»

Rājñā tu kupiten’ ôktaṃ «n’ êdaṃ loka|vaco mṛṣā
‹śilpinaḥ saha śāṭhyena jāyanta iti!› ghuṣyate.
Tad idaṃ śāṭhyam ujjhitvā man|nideśaṃ samācara
anyathā jīva|loko ’yaṃ su|dṛṣṭaḥ kriyatām iti!»
Tad rakṣatā mama prāṇān sa|putrān anujīvinaḥ
rājñe tad yantra|vijñānam arthine kathyatām iti.›

Viśvilas tu pratijñāya śvaśurāya ‹tath” âstv iti›
rātrau Ratnāvalīṃ suptāṃ pratibodhy’ êdam abravīt:
‹Āmantraye ’haṃ bhavatīṃ gacchāmi sva|gṛhān prati
upāyais tava pitr” âham asmāt sthānād vivāsitaḥ.
Ākāśa|yantra|vijñānaṃ prāptuṃ mattaḥ sa vāñchati
pracchādyaṃ ca tad asmābhir nidhānaṃ kṛpaṇair iva.
Tad āstāṃ tāvad ātmā me tava vā dayitaḥ pitā

even the evil-eyed want to see it. And when Brahmadatta gave him unsurpassed riches, he refused them, saying that his guru should have them."

After he said this, Mahasena gratified Pukvasaka, who had been scared that all his property would be taken away, by giving him great riches. Vishvila returned from Varanasi in an instant, mounted on a flying machine, and went into his house that night.

After just one month had passed, Pukvasaka said to Vishvila, 'Today the king dismissed the court and, with a smile, said quietly to me: "You have told your son-in-law 5.260
the science of flying machines. Tell me all about it too: I am keen to find out!"

But I said to him, "I did not tell him about it; he was told about it as a reward by Greek artisans."

The enraged king replied, "It's not for nothing that they say that artisans are born liars! Very well, stop lying and carry out my orders, or take a look at the world of the living for the last time!" So, please teach the science of flying machines to the greedy king, and thereby safeguard my life and my dependents and their children.'

Vishvila agreed, saying 'So be it,' to his father-in-law, but in the night he woke the sleeping Ratnavali and said, 'I bid you farewell: I am going home. Your father has contrived to have me banished from this place. He wants to learn the science of flying machines from me but we must keep it hidden as misers do treasure. So be it. Never mind myself or your beloved father, I would abandon even you in order to safeguard that science.'

vijñānasy' âsya rakṣāyai tyajeyaṃ bhavatīm api.›
Iti Ratnāvalī śrutvā bhartāram idam abravīt
‹kiṃ c' âhaṃ dur|bhagā yena bhaktāṃ tyajasi mām iti?›
5.270 Yānaṃ kukkuṭa|saṃsthānam āsthāya saha bhāryayā
rātrāv ākāśam utpatya sva|sthānaṃ Viśvilo yayau.
‹te c' âivam aurasān bandhūn śilpa|guptyai tyajanti ye
te śilpaṃ darśayant' îti› kasy' êyam asatī matiḥ?
Tasmād amī śaṭhā baddhāḥ pīḍyantāṃ tāḍan'|ādibhiḥ
asādhyāḥ sāma|dānābhyāṃ nīcā hi vadha|sādhanāḥ.»
Iti senā|patiḥ śrutvā sarvān saṃyamya śilpinaḥ
atāḍayad avocac ca «yantram āyojyatām iti!»
Etasminn eva vṛtt'|ânte kaś cid āgantuko 'bravīt
«ahaṃ karomi vo yantraṃ mā sma tāḍyanta śilpinaḥ.
Yantr'|ôpakaraṇaṃ c' êdam idānīṃ dīyatām iti»
tac ca saṃpāditaṃ sarvam acireṇa Rumaṇvatā.
Teṣu c' ânyatamaḥ śilpī tam āgantum abhāṣata:
«ārohaka|parīmāṇaṃ senā|nīr anuyujyatām.
Ajñāta|vāhya|saṃkhyābhir bahavaḥ śilpino nṛpaiḥ
vipanna|yantraiḥ śrūyante mathitāḥ kupitair iti.»
Atha ten' ôktam «anye te varākā grāmya|śilpikāḥ
kiṃ vā vacobhir bahubhiḥ kṣaṇam āsthīyatām iti.»
Ity uktvā Garuḍ'|ākāram acireṇa cakāra saḥ
vimānam ambar'|ôpetaṃ mandāra|kusum'|ârcitam.

When Ratnavali heard this, she said to her husband, 'Am I, your devoted wife, so repugnant that you are abandoning me?'

Vishvila and his wife mounted a cockerel-shaped vehicle 5.270
and, flying off into the night, went home.

Who could be so mistaken as to think that those who would thus abandon their own relatives to protect their craft would ever reveal it? Therefore, have these rogues bound and tortured with floggings and so forth, for lowly people cannot be won over by negotiation or gifts, only by corporal punishment."

When he heard this, the commander of the armies bound all the artisans and had them flogged. Then he told them to build the machine.

Just as this was happening, a stranger arrived and said, "I shall make the machine for you; stop flogging the artisans. Give me what I need to make the machine right away." Rumanvan quickly provided everything.

One of the artisans addressed the stranger: "You must ask the commander of the armies how many people are to ride in it. We have heard several stories of artisans being punished by angry kings whose vehicles crashed when the number of passengers had not been specified."

He replied, "Those others were lowly village artisans. But there is no point in talking too much— just wait a moment."

After saying this, he quickly had made a sky-chariot shaped like Garuda*, which had an awning and was decorated with *mandāra* flowers.

5.280 Sa c' âbhāṣata rājānaṃ «rājan rāja|Janārdana
ākramya Garuḍaṃ krāma krānta|pūrvāṃ mahīm imām!»
Atha rāj" âvadad devīṃ: «devi kiṃ sthīyate 'dhunā?
vimānam idam āruhya yath"|êṣṭaṃ gamyatām iti!»
Avocat sā ca rājānam «āryaputra tvayā vinā
n' ôdyānam api gacchāmi kuto 'nālambanāṃ divam!»
Evaṃ devī bravīt' îti rājñ" ôkte śilpin" ôditam
«nanu voḍhum idaṃ śaktaṃ sakalāṃ nagarīm iti!»
S'|ântaḥ|pura|parīvāraḥ sa|dāra|sacivas tataḥ
sa|paura|śreṇi|vargaś ca yānam adhyāsta bhū|patiḥ.
Tena ketu|patāk'|ādi|chāyā|vicchurit'|âmbarām
puṇyam ākāśam āviśya prāk prācīm agamad diśam.
Dadarśa darśakas tatra yānaṃ yān nagar'|ôpari
«devo vidyādharo v" âpi bhoḥ ko 'yam iti?» c' âbravīt.
Padmāvatī|dvitīyena sa ca rājñ" âbhivāditaḥ
anujñātaś ca khaṃ yātaḥ nṛpaḥ pavana|vartmanā.
Iti pradakṣiṇīkṛtya sa bhuvaṃ sāgar'|âmbarām
Avanti|nagarīṃ prāyāt pravṛtt'|ôdaka|dānakām.
Yātr"|ânubhavan'|ôtkaṇṭhaṃ jñātvā śilpī mahī|patim
stambhayām āsa tad yantram ath' âtuṣyan nar'|âdhipaḥ.
5.290 Pradyotasya tad ālokya ratna|pradyota|piñjaram
«kim etad iti» saṃdeha|dolādolam abhūn manaḥ.

He said to the king, "O king, o Vishnu among kings, step onto Garuda and cross this land that Vishnu crossed in the past!" 5.280

Then the king spoke to the queen: "Good lady, now what are you waiting for now? Climb aboard this sky-chariot and go wherever you want!"

She replied to the king, "My husband, without you I do not go even to the garden, let alone into the unsupported sky!"

When the king told the artisan what the queen had said, he replied, "But this vehicle could support the entire city!"

Then the king, together with his harem, his wives, his ministers, and groups of guilds from the city, mounted the sky-chariot. He went into the sacred sky, and at first flew toward the east where the sky was strewn with colored flags, banners and other decorations.

A watchman there saw the chariot flying above the city, and said, "Oh! Who can this be? A god or a sorcerer?"

The king and Padmavati greeted him, and with his permission they journeyed on through the sky by the path of the wind. When he had thus flown around the world with its mantle of oceans, he went to the city of Avanti where the festival of offering water to the ancestors was in full swing. Knowing that the king was keen to see the festival, the artisan brought the machine to a standstill. The king was delighted.

When Pradyota saw it gleaming with the light from the 5.290
gems, his mind wavered in doubt as to what it was. "If it signifies a great disaster then why is it beautiful? If it

«Mahāṃś ced ayam utpāto ramaṇīyam ataḥ katham?
iṣṭa|saṃprāpti|lambhaś cen n' âsmābhiḥ śrutam īdṛśam.»
Saṃdihan mānasasy' êti Pradyotasya puraḥ śaram
pātayām āsa Vats'|ēśaḥ śanakair lekhit'|âkṣaram.
Mahāsenas tam ādāya citram etad avācayat
«rājann Udayanaś cauraḥ sa|dāras tvāṃ namasyati.»
Iti śrutvā Mahāseno jāmātaram abhāṣata
«caurāya dattam abhayaṃ tasmād avataratv iti.»
Āloky' Âvanti|Kauśāmbyāṃ vimān'|ôdaka|dānake
draṣṭavyeṣu tanū|bhūtam adbhuteṣu kutūhalam!
Kāṃ cid velām upāsy' âivam āmantrya śvaśurau tataḥ
lok'|ālokita|yānaś ca Kauśāmbyām avarūḍhavān.
Pūjit'|âmara|vipr'|âgni|guru|paur'|ânujīvinā
ājñāpitaṃ nṛpatinā «śilpī saṃmānyatām iti.»
Ath' âbhibhūya prabhayā su|prabhām acira|prabhām
tiṣṭhantīm ambare 'paśyad devatām avan"|īśvaraḥ.
Tataś citrīyamāṇaṃ sā tam abhāṣata pārthivam,
«pūjit" âiva tvayā yat tvāṃ pūjyaṃ pūjitavaty aham.
5.300 Vijñāpyaṃ śrūyatāṃ c' êdam asmy ahaṃ guhyak'|âṅganā
guhyak'|âdhipater āptā Bhadr" êti paricārikā.
Kadā cin nabhasā yāntī satī dṛṣṭavatī saraḥ
kandarāyāṃ nag'|êndrasya Mahendrasya nabhaḥ|prabham.
Tatra saṃkrīḍamānaṃ ca kareṇu|kara|dhāritaiḥ

signifies the attainment of something desirable, we have not heard of its like before."

As Pradyota was wondering thus the king of Vatsa gently threw down before him an arrow on which characters were inscribed.

Mahasena picked it up and read out the following strange message: "O king, the thief* Udayana and his wives pay their respects to you."

When he heard this, Mahasena said to his son-in-law, "I grant the thief safety, so he may land."

Having seen the sky-chariot and the festival of offering water to the ancestors, the curiosity of the people of Avanti and Kaushambi for fantastic spectacles had worn thin! Udayana stayed for a few hours and then bid his parents-in-law farewell. He landed in Kaushambi as the people looked on at the vehicle. The king worshipped the gods, the brahmins, the sacred fire, the elders, the townspeople and his dependents, and gave an order for the artisan to be honored.

Then the king saw standing in the sky a goddess who shone brighter than a brilliant bolt of lightning.

She said to the amazed king, "Because you honored me,
you deserve to be honored and I have honored you. Listen 5.300
to what I have to say: I am a Guhyaka* lady called Bhadra, a trusted handmaiden of Kubera. One day as I was flying along I saw a sky-blue lake in the valley of Mount Mahendra. The chief of a herd of wild elephants was there, playing about and being fanned with lotuses held in the trunks of the she-elephants. When I saw him stroking the face of

vījyamānaṃ sarasi|jaiḥ kāntāra|kari|yūtha|pam.
Āsīc ca mama taṃ dṛṣṭvā kar'|āmṛṣṭa|vaśā|mukham
kartāro hasti|śikṣāyāṃ satyam āhur idaṃ yadā
Deva|dānava|gandharva|piśāc'|ôraga|rakṣasām
kanyāsu jātā diṅ|nāgair nānā|sattvās tato gatāḥ.

Tataḥ sapadi nirmāya hastinī|rūpam ātmanā
mad'|āmoda|vibhinn'|âmbhas tad ev' âvātaraṃ saraḥ.
S'|āmarṣa|kariṇī|yūtha|kaṭ'|âkṣ'|ēkṣita|rūpayā
prītena yūtha|patinā ciram ākrīḍitaṃ mayā.
Ath' êndu|kiraṇ'|ākāra|kiraṇe 'ruṇa|sārathau
sa gajaḥ kṣālita|kaṭaḥ kaṭakaṃ prāviśad gireḥ.
Ahaṃ tu vyasanaṃ sevā|phalam utprekṣya dāruṇam
sadyaḥ kṛta|nij'|ākārā rāja|rāja|sabhām agām.
Dhana|dasy' ôrum ālambya tasya yūtha|pateḥ karam
smarantī tāḍayāmi sma cāmareṇa dhan'|âdhipam.
5.310 Sa kaṭ'|âkṣeṇa māṃ dṛṣṭvā krodha|visphurit'|âdharaḥ
trās'|ôtkampita|dik|cakraḥ kṛtavāñ śāpa|bhājanam:
‹Dhyāyantyā hastinaṃ yasmāc cāmareṇ' âham āhataḥ
tvam Avanti|pates tasmād abhavye hastinī bhava!›

Tatr' ôktaṃ Pūrṇabhadreṇa yakṣeṇ': ‹āgasi tucchake
prabhunā deva|devena muktaḥ śāpo mahān iti.›
Śrutv" êdaṃ Pūrṇabhadro 'pi śapto: ‹yasmāt tvam etayā
śaptayā pīḍitas tasmād bhava hastī mahān iti!›

a she-elephant with his trunk, I realized that the practitioners of elephant lore were right when they said that the elephants of the directions fathered various creatures by the daughters of the gods, the Danavas, the Gandharvas, the goblins, the snake-people and the demons, from whom the lineages continued.

I immediately transformed myself into a she-elephant and went down to the lake, whose water was permeated with the strong smell of the fluid of rut. I played at length with the delighted chief of the herd, while the angry she-elephants cast side glances at my beautiful form. When the sun's rays became like those of the moon, the bull-elephant, his temples washed, went to the mountainside. I, however, imagining that the consequence of my service would be terrible misfortune, quickly assumed my natural form and went to Kubera's court. When I leant upon Kubera's thigh, I thought of the trunk of the elephant-chief, and I struck the lord of wealth with a fly whisk.

He looked at me out of the corner of his eye and his lower 5.310
lip trembled with rage. The whole world quaked with fear. Then he put a curse on me: 'You struck me with a fly whisk because you were thinking of an elephant, so you shall become the she-elephant of the king of Avanti, you unseemly woman!'

At this, a *yakṣa* called Purnabhadra said that his master, the god of gods, had delivered a severe curse for such a trifling misdemeanor. When he heard this, Kubera cursed Purnabhadra too: 'Because you were aggrieved by this woman being cursed, you shall become a great bull-elephant!'

Śoka|dīna|mukhāv āvāṃ dṛṣṭvā vitta|pater abhūt
karuṇ"|ôtkhāta|kopasya nava|nīta|nibhaṃ manaḥ.
Abravīc ca, ‹yad" âhaṃ vāṃ smariṣyāmi kva cit tadā
śāpād asmād vimokṣyethe bibhītaṃ mā sma putrakau.›
S" âhaṃ Bhadravatī jātā Mahāsenasya hastinī
Pūrṇabhadro 'pi tasy' âiva nāgo vyālo Nalāgiriḥ.
Mahāsenasya bhavane para|tantrasya tiṣṭhataḥ
āvayoś caritaṃ yat tat sarvaṃ pratyakṣam eva te.
Tadā c' âpaharantī tvāṃ dhan'|âdhipatinā smṛtā
aham aprāpya Kauśāmbīṃ vipannā gahane vane.
Na tathā vyasanen' âsi pīḍitas tena tādṛśā
yathā mayi vipannāyāṃ priya|dāraḥ striyām iva.
5.320 Yakṣa|yonim avāpy' âhaṃ tiryag|yonim iv' âpsarāḥ
tvām eva śocitavatī s" êva śaptaṃ śata|kratum.
Āsīc ca me, ‹kadā nāma kathaṃ nāma ca bhū|pateḥ
kaṃ nāma ca kariṣye 'ham upakāraṃ manāg iti.›
Nītaś c' âsi mayā svapne tadā dhana|pateḥ sabhām
bhrāmitaś ca vimānena sa|garbha|stha|suto mahīm.
Bhaviṣyantaṃ ca te putraṃ magnaṃ kasyāṃ cid āpadi
vidyādhar'|êndram uddhartā sukham āstāṃ bhavān iti.»
Prākārasya tataḥ khaṇḍam apanīya jagāma sā
yat tad Bhadravatī|dvāram Kauśāmbyāṃ prathitaṃ bhuvi.
Ath' âśrūyanta paurāṇāṃ jalpitāni gṛhe gṛhe
«siddh'|ādeśa|vacaḥ satyaṃ kṛtaṃ vyoma|carair iti.»
Sīmant'|ônnayan'|ânta|karma|viratāv autsukya|garbhā purī

When he saw our downcast faces, the lord of wealth's anger was destroyed by compassion, and his heart melted like fresh butter. He said, 'My children, have no fear: whenever I next think of you, you shall be freed from this curse.'

I was born as Bhadravati, Mahasena's she-elephant, and Purnabhadra became Nalagiri, his powerful tusker. You witnessed everything that we two did when you were staying as a prisoner in Mahasena's palace. Then, as I was taking you away, the lord of wealth remembered me, and before I reached Kaushambi I fell down dead in the dense jungle. You were not as pained by your predicament as you were by my demise, at which you were like a loving husband at the death of his wife.

When I was born as a Yakshi*, I longed for you alone, 5.320
just as the Apsaras* born as a lowly animal longed for Indra after he had been cursed. I wondered how and when I might assist you in some way, however small.

Then in a dream you were led by me to the lord of wealth's assembly, and taken around the world with your son in your wife's womb. If he meets with any calamity, I shall rescue your son, the future emperor of the sorcerers; you may rest assured."

She went on her way, after removing a piece of the city walls, where now there is Kaushambi's world-famous Bhadravati Gate.

In all the citizens' houses people were heard to say that the predictions of the accomplished soothsayer had been confirmed by the sky-rovers.

Once the rite of parting the hair* was over, the city was

pratyāsanna|kara|grah" êva taruṇī kṛcchrān nināya kṣapām.
śuddh'|ânte ca śuk'|ādi|pañjara|vayaḥ|kolāhale 'pi śrute
rājā dāraka|janma|saṃpad|aghana|prahlādam utpraikṣata.

iti dohada|saṃpādano nāma
pañcamaḥ sargaḥ.

filled with expectation and, like a girl whose wedding day is at hand, passed the nights with difficulty. When he heard even the cries of the parrots and other caged birds in his harem, the king fancied that they were shrill cries of joy at the successful birth of his son.

Thus ends the fifth canto,
called Satisfying Pregnancy Cravings.

CANTO 6
THE BIRTH OF THE PRINCE

TATAḤ SMARA|SAKHE KĀLE
Puṣya|yukte niśākare
divākare mṛdu|kare devī putraṃ vyajāyata.
Putra|janma nar'|êndrasya jagataḥ sukha|janma ca
śaṅkā|janma ca śatrūṇāṃ samaṃ samabhavat trayam.
Atha saṃbhūya gaṇakair uktaṃ gaṇita|jātakaiḥ
«cakra|varti|pitā lokāv ubhau vijayatām iti!»
Tataḥ saciva|bhāryāṇāṃ tasminn eva dine sutāḥ
alpa|kāl'|ântare jātāḥ kanīyāṃso nṛp'|ātma|jāt.
«Kim utsavaḥ? kiṃ vyasanaṃ?
kiṃ prāṇāḥ prāṇayantu? kim
āgataṃ?» Cedi|Vatsānām
iti n' âsīd viniścayaḥ.
Jāta|karmaṇi nivṛtte prāpte ca dvādaśe 'hani
anvartha|nāmnas tanayān akurvan rāja|mantriṇaḥ.
«Vāhanena nareṇ' âiva Kubero nara|vāhanaḥ
Naravāhanadatto 'stu dattas tena yatas tataḥ.»
Iti nāma kṛtaṃ rājñā putrasya sa|purodhasā
bhūmi|hema|gaj'|âśv'|ādi|dāna|prīta|dvi|janmanā.
Nāmnā Hariśikhaṃ cakre Rumaṇvān ātmajaṃ yataḥ
tasmai vitīrṇavān svapne deva|devaḥ śaraṃ Hariḥ.
6.10 Yaugandharāyaṇaḥ putraṃ cakāra Marubhūtikam
saṃnāha|chadmanā tasmai yatas taṃ Maruto daduḥ.
Cakāra Gomukhaṃ putram Ṛṣabhaḥ saṃjñayā yataḥ

THEN, IN THE TIME OF SPRING, Love's companion, when the moon was in the constellation Pushya and the sun's rays were gentle, the queen gave birth to a son. Three things came about all at once: the birth of a son to the king, the birth of happiness to his people, and the birth of fear to his enemies. The astrologers calculated the baby's horoscope and unanimously declared: "May the father of the future emperor conquer both heaven and earth!"

Then very shortly afterward on that very same day, the wives of the ministers gave birth to sons, younger than the king's son.

The people of Chedi and Vatsa were unable to determine what had happened. Should they celebrate or had something gone wrong? Was the breath of life animating the newborn? What had happened? On the twelfth day, when the birth rites were over, the king and the ministers gave their sons suitable names. "Because men are his vehicle, Kubera is called Naravahana; because this child has been given by him, let him be called Naravahanadatta!" The king, with his chaplain, after gratifying the brahmins with gifts such as land, gold, elephants and horses, named his son thus. Rumanvan called his son Harishikha, because in a dream Hari, the god of gods, had given him an arrow.
Yaugandharayana called his son Marubhutika because he 6.10
had been given to him by the Maruts in the form of a suit of armor. Rishabha called his son Gomukha because kindly cows had shown him the paintings of their own accord. Vasantaka called his son Tapantaka because he had been

svayaṃ gobhiḥ prasannābhiś citraṃ tasmai pradarśitam.
Putraṃ Tapantakaṃ nāmnā karoti sma Vasantakaḥ
yasmāt taṃ Tapanas tasmai kuṇḍala|chadmanā dadau.

Evaṃ labdhaś ca jātaś ca yaḥ kṛtaṃ nāma yasya ca
aham eva sa te c' âite sarve Hariśikh'|ādayaḥ.
Te vayaṃ tu yathā|kālaṃ kṛt'|ânna|prāśan'|ādayaḥ
avardhāmahi laghv eva sanāthāḥ pādapā iva.
Tataḥ kumāra|vaṭakām upādhyāyair adhiṣṭhitām
sa|brahma|caryakaiś chāttrair dhātrībhīś c' āśrayāmahi.

A|vratair eva c' âsmābhir abhyastāḥ sakalāḥ kalāḥ
sa|vratais tu catasro 'pi vidyāḥ sarvaṃ ca vāṅ|mayam.
Gacchatsu divaseṣv evam ekadā Marubhūtikaḥ
bāla|bhāvād anadhyāye krīḍati sma sa|kandukaḥ.
Taṃ tu bāla|svabhāvena tasmād ācchidya kandukam
ahaṃ javena mahatā prayātaḥ pitur antikam.
Ath' ânubadhnan māṃ vegāt paṭu|śvasita|saṃtatiḥ
baddha|muṣṭi|karaḥ krodhād āgato Marubhūtikaḥ,
6.20 «Kiṃ? kiṃ tāt' êti?» tātena sa pṛṣṭa idam uktavān
«kanduko me hṛto 'nena tam ayaṃ dāpyatām iti!»
Tato rājñā pariṣvajya dāpit'|âpara|kandukaḥ
tarjanī|tarjitaḥ pitrā kumāra|vaṭakāṃ gataḥ.

Aham apy aṅkam āropya tātena paribhāṣitaḥ
«mā sma tāta punar bhrātṝn kopayeḥ kopanān iti!»
Tath" âpi pratiṣiddho 'haṃ keli|śīlatayā śiśoḥ
yath" âinān kopayāmi sma tath" âite mām akopayan.
Abhyāsam ekadā kurvan nārācaṃ Marubhūtikaḥ
icchati sma ca visraṣṭuṃ mayā ca calitaṃ dhanuḥ.
Asāv api ca nārācaś calitāc cāpataś cyutaḥ

given to him in the form of an earring by Tapana, the sun god.

I, Naravahanadatta, am the one who was obtained, born and named thus, and these men are Harishikha and all the others. Ceremonies such as our first feeding with solid food were performed at the appropriate junctures and we grew quickly, like well-tended trees. Then we lived in a princes' cloister, which was overseen by teachers together with religious students and nurses.

Before we had our Vedic initiation we learned all the arts, and once we were initiated we learned the four Vedas and the whole of literature. The days passed like this. One day when we didn't have to study, Marubhutika was playing with a ball, as children will. I childishly snatched the ball from him and sprinted over to my father. Marubhutika chased after me and appeared, panting heavily, his fist clenched with rage. My father asked him, "What is it? 6.20
What's happened, child?," and he replied, "He's taken my ball; make him give it back!" At this the king hugged him and had him given another ball. When his father wagged his finger at him he went to the princes' cloister.

My father sat me in his lap and said, "Don't make your hot-headed brothers angry again, my child!" Despite being forbidden like this, I used to annoy them in the playful way that young boys will, and they in turn annoyed me. One day when Marubhutika was practicing archery, he was about to let loose an arrow when I jogged his bow. The arrow was released from the jogged bow and just missed its target, the bud of a *mālatī* flower. Enraged, he threw

mālatī|mukulaṃ lakṣaṃ tanmātreṇ' âiva n' âspṛśat.
Utsṛjya kupitaś cāpaṃ dhāvamānaḥ sa mām anu
āsthāna|stha|mahī|pāla|samīpam agamat tataḥ.
Yaugandharāyaṇo dṛṣṭvā kupitaṃ Marubhūtikam
kupito bhartsayitv" êdam abhāṣata mahī|patim:
«Veditā sarva|vidyānām āsanna|nava|yauvanaḥ
rāja|putro mahārāja yauva|rājye 'bhiṣicyatām.
Yāvad yāvadd hi śāstra|jñāḥ śāstr'|ârthān na prayuñjate
tāvat tāvad bhavanty eṣāṃ kuṇṭhāḥ kāryeṣu buddhayaḥ.
6.30 Amī Rumaṇvad|ādīnāṃ putrā Hariśikh'|ādayaḥ
vijānanto 'pi śāstrāṇi sutarām andha|buddhayaḥ.
Vastuny alpe 'py an|ātma|jñāḥ saṃrabdh'|ālohit'|ānanāḥ
prabhum eva jighāṃsanti mṛg'|êndraṃ markaṭā iva!
Tad ete 'pi niyojyantām adhikāreṣu keṣu cit
vijñāpanā madīy" êyaṃ saphalī|kriyatām iti!»
Yaugandharāyaṇa|vacaḥ su|bhagaṃ niśamya
prītyā nar'|êndra|sabham ucchrayit'|âgra|hastam,
«bhoḥ sādhu sādhu nara|kuñjara! sādhu mantrin!»
ity ujjhit'|āsanam abhāṣata nirvyavastham.

iti kumāra|janma
ṣaṣṭhamaḥ sargaḥ.

down the bow and chased me as far as the king, who was sitting in his assembly. When Yaugandharayana saw the enraged Marubhutika he became angry himself and told him off. He then addressed the king: "O great king, the prince knows all the sciences and has reached manhood. Have him anointed crown prince. As long as the educated do not use their learning, their minds remain blunted in the
exercise of their duties. Look at the sons of Rumanvan and 6.30
the other ministers—Harishikha and his friends. Despite being educated, they have very blinkered minds. Even in a trifling matter, these boys, having no self-awareness, become red in the face with rage and virtually attack their very master, like monkeys attacking a lion! So have these boys employed in some positions of responsibility and make this request of mine bear fruit!"

When they heard this judicious speech from Yaugandharayana, the king's assembly threw up their hands in delight and, out of keeping with usual practice, abandoned their seats, saying, "Oh, well done, well done, you elephant among men! Well done, minister!"

Thus ends the sixth canto,
called the Birth of the Prince.

CANTO 7
CONSECRATION AS CROWN PRINCE

Tatas tātaḥ sabhāṃ dṛṣṭvā
tathā|saṃjāta|saṃpadam
yathā|pradhānam ābhāṣya vinītavad abhāṣata,
«Kim atra pṛcchyate yatra kṣipt' âṅgirasa|buddhayaḥ
apṛṣṭā eva bhāṣadhve prīti|nirvāsita|trapāḥ?
Tena yad rocate sādhu pūjyebhyaḥ pūjitaṃ dinam
tatr' âyaṃ sva|suta|prītyā bālaḥ saṃskriyatām iti!»
Atha prastāva etasminn anujñāta|praveśayā
Kaliṅgasenayā rājā dūrād eva namaskṛtaḥ.
«Eh' îti» sā nṛpeṇ' ôktā n' âtimanthara|vikramā
upagamy' ôpaparyaṅkam adhyāst' ādiṣṭam āsanam.
Āyukta|mauktika|stoka|bhūṣaṇā vimal'|âmbarā
śarad|vimala|haṃs" êva cakāśat|kāśa|cāmarā.
Kandharā|mūla|visrasta|ślatha|bandha|śiro|ruhā
paścim'|âcala|kūṭa|stha|timirā dyaur iv' ôṣasi.
Yauvan'|ântam anuprāptā prāvṛḍ|antam iv' âpagā
calac|caṭulat"|ākārā bhṛt" âpi nibhṛt'|ākṛtiḥ.
Vinīt" âpi pragalbh" êva sthavir" êva taruṇy api
mita|vāg api vācāl"|âvyākhyātavyā hi tan|matiḥ.
7.10 Upaviṣṭā puras tasyā daśa|varṣ" êva bālikā
tayā me dṛṣṭir ākṛṣṭā guṇair naur iva mantharā.
Acira|sthāpita|sphīta|bhaṅgura|snigdha|mūrdhajā
nilīna|kokila|kulā tanvī cūta|lat" êva sā.
Nimeṣ'|ônmeṣa|śūnyena sahaj'|āyāma|śobhinā

When my father saw that the assembly was thus agreed, he consulted them in order of rank and then humbly said, "What is to be questioned in this matter when you whose intellects exceed that of Brihaspati speak without being asked, your timidity dispelled by affection? Therefore, on an auspicious day approved of by your worthy selves, with the happiness due one's own son, the boy is to be consecrated!"

At that moment Kalingasena was given permission to enter and she hailed the king from afar. The king told her to approach, and she hurried over and sat on a low chair that was offered to her. Adorned with brooches made from small pearls, wearing spotless white clothes, and carrying a fly whisk that resembled shining *kāśa* grass, she was like a pure white swan in autumn. With her hair loose and falling about at the base of her neck, she looked like the dawn sky, with darkness on the peak of the western mountain. Having reached the end of youth, she was like a river at the end of the rainy season, flirtatiously fluid in form, and timidly gentle though full.

Though demure, she seemed brazen; though young, she seemed old; though softly-spoken, she was garrulous: her disposition could not be discerned. Sat in front of her was 7.10
a young girl of about ten years of age; she drew my gaze like ropes pulling a barge. Her thick, curly, glossy hair had just been dressed, and she looked like a tender creeper from a mango tree on which was sitting a family of black *koyal* birds. Looking at me with unblinking eyes whose innate width made them beautiful, she made me like Indra with

cakṣuṣā vīkṣamāṇā māṃ sahasr'|âkṣam iv' âkarot.
Rūḍha|dāḍima|garbh'|ābha|daśan'|ôdbhāsit'|ānanā
dāḍimī|mukul'|ākāra|vibhakta|daśana|chadā.
Sita|sārasan'|ônnaddha|mahā|rajana|kañcukā
rakt'|êndīvara|māl" êva mṛṇāla|dala|bandhanā.
unnīyante sma bālāyāś cihnair aṅgāni komalaiḥ
latāyāḥ sahakārasya phalāni mukulair iva.

Ath' âpṛcchan mahī|pālaḥ, «kasy' êyaṃ rūpiṇī Ratiḥ
duhitṛtvam anuprāptā? nām' âsyāḥ kathyatām iti!»

Kaliṅgasenay" ākhyātaṃ, «śocy" êyaṃ tanayā mama
yām eva pṛcchati svāmī bhṛtyāṃ Madanamañjukām.»

Tataḥ sa|sneham āhūya, «mātar eh' îti!» bhū|patiḥ
ūrum āropayad bālām āc" êmāṃ vāma|locanām.

Drutam Ādityaśarmā ca gṛhītvā lagnam abravīt
«aho citram iti!» smeram abhūc ca nṛpater mukham.

7.20 Yudhyamāna|rajan|meṣa|viṣāṇ'|ônmeṣa|janmanā
dhvanin" âpi na tac|cakṣur ākṣiptaṃ nihitaṃ mayi.
Rājā tu vastr'|ābharaṇam analpam apakalmaṣam
s'|âmbāyai dāpayitv" âsyai tad āsthānaṃ vyasarjayat.

Antaḥ|puraṃ mahī|pālaḥ kumāra|vaṭakām aham
dīrgham uṣṇaṃ ca niśvasya bālā svaṃ bhavanaṃ yayau.
Atha puṇye dine rājā dvi|ja|rāja|jan'|āvṛtaḥ
svayaṃ bhadr'|āsana|sthaṃ māṃ yauva|rājye 'bhiṣiktavān.
Tathā Hariśikhaṃ rājā mud" ājñāpitavān iti
«yatra prasthāpyate bhartā gantavyaṃ tava nirvyatham.

his thousand eyes. Her face with its shining teeth looked like the inside of a ripe pomegranate, and her parted lips were like pomegranate buds. Wearing a bodice the color of safflower tied with a white girdle, she looked like a garland of red lotuses tied with a strand of lotus stalk. The limbs of the girl revealed themselves through delicate impressions, like the fruits of a mango-creeper from its buds.

Then the king asked, "When Rati* took on this beautiful form, whose daughter did she become? Tell me her name!"

Kalingasena replied, "This poor girl that you are asking about is my daughter, your servant Madanamanjuka."

Then the king fondly called her over, saying, "Come here, young lady!" My father sat me and the fair-eyed young girl on his lap*.

Adityasharma immediately grasped the significance of the moment, saying, "Oh, how wonderful!," and a smile crossed the face of the king.

Her gaze was fixed on me, and not even the sound of 7.20
the fiercely fighting rams and the blowing of the horns could shift it. The king gave her and her mother many beautiful clothes and pieces of jewelry, and then dismissed the assembly.

The king went to his apartments, I went to the princes' cloister and the girl, with long, hot sighs, went to her house. On an auspicious day, I sat upon a throne and the king himself, surrounded by brahmins, kings and subjects, anointed me crown prince. The king then joyfully commanded Harishikha, "You must not hesitate to go wherever your master is sent.* You shall be zealous both as commander-in-chief

Senā|patiś ca mantrī ca bhavān bhavatu s'|ôdyamaḥ,»
ity ājñāpitavān rājā prahvaṃ Hariśikhaṃ tataḥ.
«Khaḍga|carma|dharo rakṣed
apramattaḥ prabhuṃ bhavān»
ity ājñayā pramuditaṃ
kṛtavān Marubhūtikam.
Ādiśad Gomukhaṃ, «bhartū ramaṇīyaṃ manas tvayā
ramaṇīyaiḥ kriy"|ālāpair apavād'|ôjjhitair iti.»
Tapantakam ath' âvocat, «karṇa|kuṇḍala|vṛttinā
na tyājyo bhavatā svāmī kadā cid iti» pārthivaḥ.
Tair ahaṃ saṃvṛto 'nyaiś ca gṛhīta|chattra|cāmaraiḥ
maṅgal'|âlaṃkṛt'|âṅgaś ca sura|viprān avandiṣi.
7.30 Pitur mātaram āsīnāṃ pitaraṃ ca sa|mantriṇam
ambā|dvaya|pradhānaṃ ca sphītaṃ rāj'|âvarodhanam.
Tataḥ puṣpa|rath'|ārūḍhaḥ prasarpan|maṅgala|dhvanim
puṣpa|pallava|lāj'|āḍhyām ākrāmaṃ paritaḥ purīm.
Tataḥ prāpt'|âbhiṣeko 'haṃ sārdhaṃ Hariśikh'|ādibhiḥ
sv'|âdhikāra|paraiḥ krīḍan saṃvatsaram ayāpayam.
Varṣ'|âbhiṣeke nivṛtte pūrveṇa sama|ḍambare
āvṛttyā sarva|vidyānāṃ sthiratām udapādayam.
Evaṃ me samatīteṣu keṣu cid divaseṣv aham
prātarbhojana|velāyāṃ na paśyāmi sma Gomukham.
Na c' ânena vinā mahyaṃ nirvāṇam api rocate
ten' ânena vin" âsmābhir abhuktair gamitaṃ dinam.

and minister." The king ordered the prostrate Harishikha thus.

Marubhutika was overjoyed when he was told, "Carrying a sword and a shield, you shall vigilantly protect your master."

Gomukha was told, "You must delight your master's mind with charming actions and conversation, and no harsh words."

Then the king said to Tapantaka, "Like an earring, you must never desert your master."

Surrounded by them and others holding parasols and fly whisks, and with my body adorned with auspicious
decorations, I paid homage to the gods, the brahmins, my 7.30
seated paternal grandmother, my father with his ministers, and the extensive royal harem, headed by the two queens. Then I mounted a float and rode around the city. There were flowers, blossoms and grains of rice everywhere, and shouts of good luck were ringing out all around.

After my consecration, I spent a year amusing myself in the company of Harishikha and the others, who were intent on their respective duties. By the time that the anniversary of the consecration—which was celebrated with similar pomp—had passed, I had, through regular practice, become competent in all the sciences.

A few days later, Gomukha did not show up at breakfast time. Without him, not even *nirvāṇa* held any interest for me. He was absent all day and we ate nothing. When I said, "Find out where Gomukha is!," Marubhutika went off and returned saying that he had gone mad. "If Your Highness

«Jñāyatāṃ Gomukhaḥ kv' êti!» may" ôkte Marubhūtikaḥ
«unmattakaḥ sa saṃvṛtta ity» avocad gat'|āgataḥ.
«Yadi c' âtr' āryaputrasya n' âsti saṃpratyayas tataḥ
gatvā Tapantakas tasya vikārān prekṣatām iti.»
Tatas Tapantako gatvā punar āgatya c' ôktavān
«āryaputra na tan mithyā yad āha Marubhūtikaḥ.
Vimal'|ādarśa|saṃkrāntaṃ mukham ālokya Gomukhaḥ
kampayitvā śiraḥ krodhān nirdārayati locane.
7.40 Kadā cic ca smitaṃ kṛtvā prasanne netra|tārake
saṃcārayati karṇ'|ântaṃ kadā cin nāsik"|ântaram.
Madh'|ûcchiṣṭa|nighṛṣṭau ca tāmbūla|drava|lohitau
vivṛtya dūram adharau dant'|ânten' âpi niśyati.
vikārān evam|ākārān dṛṣṭvā tasy' âham āgataḥ
ten' āryaputra tvaritaṃ kriy" âsya kriyatām iti!»
Ath' ânantaram āgatya saṃbhoga|mṛdit'|âmbaraḥ
prāgalbhyān mṛdu|vailakṣyo mām avandata Gomukhaḥ.
«Kaccit sva|stho 'si bhadr' êti»
may" ôktaḥ sann abhāṣata
«kim arthaṃ c' âham a|svastho?
na hy ahaṃ Marubhūtikaḥ.
Yo hi nāgarakaṃ|manyo manyate mām anāmayam
unmattakaṃ sa unmattaḥ prakṛti|bhraṣṭa|mānasaḥ.
Atha śāstr'|ôpaniṣadas tāta Yaugandharāyaṇāt
ahaṃ śikṣitum ārabdhaḥ sa c' âpi vyāpṛtaḥ sadā.
vyācaṣṭe ca tadā mahyam antaraṃ labhate yadā
tena māṃ mā pratīkṣadhvaṃ bhojanāy' ôdyatā iti.»
Tataś c' ārabhya divasāt sāyam āyātavān ayam
kadā cid divase 'nyasmin dvayos triṣu gateṣu ca.
Ekadā bhojanasy' ânte kuto 'py āgatya s'|ādaraḥ

does not believe it, then have Tapantaka go and see how deranged he is."

Tapantaka left and when he came back he said, "Your Highness, what Marubhutika has said is true. When Gomukha looks at his face in the mirror, he shakes his head and angrily stares agog. Sometimes he smiles and turns his 7.40
bright eyes toward his ears, sometimes to the space between his nostrils. He opens his mouth wide, his lips rubbed with beeswax and red with betel juice, and bites his lips. When I saw how disturbed he was I came back. My lord, something must be done for him immediately!"

Soon afterward, Gomukha came and greeted me; his clothes were crumpled from use, but he was so full of himself that he was hardly embarrassed at all.

I said that I hoped he was well and he replied, "Why should I not be well? I am not Marubhutika. He thinks that he is a man-about-town and I am mad, when I am healthy and it is he who is mad: his mind is deranged. Dear friend, I have started to study scholarly treatises and Upanishads under Yaugandharayana. He is always busy; he instructs me when he gets the chance, so don't wait for me when you're about to eat."

From that day onward, he would come over in the evenings, but sometimes not for two or three days. One day at the end of a meal he arrived from who knows where. He politely praised the sweets, saying, "Oh, how beautiful

«aho śobhanta ity!» uccaiḥ prāśaṃsat khaṇḍa|modakān.
7.50 Mayā tu dāpitān anyān krudhyann iva vihāya saḥ
balād ākṛṣya gatavān svayam ucchiṣṭa|modakān.
«Āryaputra sphuṭī|bhūtam unmattatvaṃ priyasya vaḥ
acikitsyaś ca saṃvṛtta ity!» avocat Tapantakaḥ.

Evam ābharaṇaṃ vāsas tāmbūlaṃ candan'|ādi ca
labdhaṃ labdhaṃ gacchati sma gṛhītvā kv' âpi Gomukhaḥ.
Evaṃ|prāye ca vṛtt'|ânte kumāra|vaṭakāṃ gataḥ
nivedit'|âbhyāgamano Rumaṇvān mām avandata.
Taṃ tātam iva dṛṣṭv" âham upakrāntaś ca vanditum
tena c' ôddhata|hastena, «tāta mā m" êti!» vāritaḥ.
Uktaṃ ca, «na tvayā tāta bālen' êv' âsmad|ādayaḥ
vandyās tvam adhunā prāpto loke 'smiĩ loka|pālatām.
Anyac ca rāja|saṃdeśam ākhyātum aham āgataḥ
yat tvām āha mahā|rājaḥ sa|bhṛtyaṃ tan nibodhyatām.

‹Puryām atra śarat|kāle yātrā citrā pravartitā
yā Nāga|vana|yātr" êti na kva cin na vikathyate.
Etāvantaṃ ca sā kālaṃ yuṣmabhyaṃ na prakāśitā
mā bhūd vidyā|vighāto vas tad|vyākṣipta|dhiyām iti.
Citt'|âpahāriṇī yātrā hārya|cittā ca bālatā
citta|vidyā ca vidy" êti durghaṭas trika|saṃgamaḥ.
7.60 Uktaṃ c' âjāgarūkasya manda|buddheḥ sukh'|ātmanaḥ
grantha|bhīroś ca sidhyanti na śāstrāṇi tapāṃsi ca.
Adhunā buddha|bodhavyāḥ prāpta|komala|yauvanāḥ
bhavanto niḥ|sukhāḥ santaḥ saṃtapant' îva me manaḥ.

they are!" When I had some more produced for him, he 7.50
seemed angry and cast them aside before grabbing the left-over sweets and going on his way. Tapantaka said, "Your Highness, your friend's madness is obvious, and he has become incurable!"

In a similar fashion Gomukha took an ornament, some clothes, betel, sandalwood and other items, and carried them away somewhere. During the period when this was going on, Rumanvan came to the princes' cloister. His arrival was announced and he greeted me respectfully. He was like a father to me, and when I saw him I started to salute him, but he raised his hand and stopped me, saying, "Don't! Don't, sir!" He continued, "Sir, you must not salute people like me as though you were a child: you are now the protector of the world. Besides, I have come to give you a message from the king. Listen to what His Highness has to say to you and your servants.

'In autumn a wonderful festival is held in the city. It is called the Snake Forest Festival, and is renowned everywhere. You have not been told about it until now for fear that it might distract you and your studies would be interrupted. A festival captivates the mind, in childhood the mind is readily captivated, and studies are dependent on the mind. The simultaneous occurrence of these three—a
procession, childhood and studies—is dangerous. It is said 7.60
that neither learning nor asceticism can be mastered by someone who is lazy, dimwitted, self-indulgent or afraid of books. Now that you have learned what there is to be learned and are in the flush of youth, it troubles my mind

Tad asti yadi vaḥ kāṅkṣā taṃ yātr"|ôtsavam īkṣitum
tato yāta nir|āśaṅkā n' âsti ced āsyatām iti!›»

May" ôktaṃ, «suhṛdaḥ pṛṣṭvā yan no niṣpadyate hitam
tad vo vijñāpayiṣyāmi tāvat pṛcchāmi tān iti.»

Rumaṇvatā tataḥ proktaṃ kapol'|āgalit'|âśruṇā
«Haihayānāṃ kulaṃ tuṅgaṃ ciraṃ vijayatāṃ jagat!
Bhavatā sādhu|vṛttena gotra|dāsāḥ kṛtā vayam
yan naḥ saṃbhāvitāḥ putrāḥ praśna|prativacaḥ|kṣamā!»

Ity uktvā nirgate tasmin suhṛdaḥ pṛṣṭavān aham
«yasya yad vaḥ sthitaṃ buddhau tena tat kathyatām iti.»

Tato Hariśikhen' ôktaṃ, «na me gamanam īpsitam
yataḥ śūnyāni durgāṇi gṛhyante 'n|antarair nṛpaiḥ.
Śrutam ev' āryaputreṇa proṣite jagatī|patau
vijñāya nagarīṃ śūnyāṃ yat tad Āruṇinā kṛtam.
Durgasya ca kṛtā rakṣā rājā ca paritoṣitaḥ
khyāpitaṃ dhīra|citta|tvam ātmanaś ca bhaved iti.»

7.70 «Tvaṃ kim ātth' êti» pṛṣṭaḥ sann avocan Marubhūtikaḥ
«yuktaṃ!» Hariśikhen' ôktam ity etac ca Tapantakaḥ.

Ath' ôktavān smita|mukhaḥ sāsūya iva Gomukhaḥ
«kim atra bhaṇyate? ko 'nyaḥ mantrī Hariśikhād varaḥ?
Idaṃ tv ācakṣva ken' âyaṃ niyukto durga|rakṣaṇe?
rakṣataś c' â|niyuktasya doṣam andha na paśyasi?
Yuva|rājo yuvā vidvān kṛt'|âstro manda|kautukaḥ
bhavad|ādi|sahāyaś ca kathaṃ yāyād a|cittatām?
Yac ca rāj'|ôditaṃ vakṣye, ‹n' âsti ced āsyatām iti›

that you have no diversions. So, if you would like to see the festival celebrations, then don't hesitate to go; if not, stay!'"

I replied, "I shall consult my friends as to what is best for us and let you know. Let me just ask them."

With tears trickling down his cheeks, Rumanvan said, "Long may the noble race of the Haihayas reign victorious over the world! You have been kind enough to make us servants of your family, and you have honored our sons by considering them worthy of answering your questions!"

After saying this he left, and I asked my friends to say what each of them thought.

Harishikha said, "I am reluctant to go because neighboring kings have been capturing empty citadels. Your Majesty must have heard what Aruni did when the king was away and he found out that the city was empty. If you stay, then the citadel will be protected, the king will be pleased and you will be shown to be strong-willed."

When I asked Marubhutika what he thought, he replied 7.70
that what Harishikha had said was right, and Tapantaka said the same.

Then Gomukha smiled and somewhat disdainfully said, "What is the point of talking now? Who is a better counsellor than Harishikha? But tell me this: who has asked the prince to defend the fortress? Are you blind that you cannot see that it is wrong to defend it without being asked? The crown prince is a young man, he is educated, skilled with weapons, temperate, and has you and the others as assistants. How could he become so stupid? And I shall

tad|āśaya|parīkṣ"|ârtham api cet tan na duṣyati.
Ataḥ pustaka|vinyasta|grantha|baddh'|ârtha|buddhayaḥ
praśn'|ânugraham arhanti n' ēdṛśaḥ kūṭa|mantriṇaḥ.
Ahaṃ punar guṇ'|ôpāya|prayoga|kuśalo yataḥ
cetasyaiḥ saha saṃparkaḥ prayoga|kuśalair mama.
Sukhaṃ naḥ sevituṃ kālo na ṣāḍguṇya|kadarthanām!
yac c' ôktaṃ dharma|śāstreṇa tat tāvad avadhīyatām:
‹Vayasaḥ karmaṇo 'rthasya śrutasy' âbhijanasya ca
veṣa|vāg|buddhi|sārūpyam ācaran vicared iha.›
Ten' ôttiṣṭhata! gacchāmo yātrām adbhuta|darśanām
krīḍiṣyāmaś ca kāntāsu sthalīṣu mṛgayām iti!»
tac ca me Gomukhen' ôktaṃ praviṣṭaṃ hṛdayaṃ yataḥ
yukti|mac c' ânukūlaṃ ca vacaḥ kasmai na rocate?
Punaś ca Gomukhen' ôktaṃ: «yātrāṃ lokasya gacchataḥ
prāsāda|talam āruhya samṛddhir dṛśyatām iti!»
Ath' âham abhraṃ|liha|śṛṅga|cakraṃ
dhvaja|prabhā|pīḍita|śakra|cāpam.
prāsādam āroham udāra|śobhaṃ
śaś" îva pūrv'|âcala|rāja|kūṭam.

iti yauva|rājy'|âbhiṣekaḥ
saptamaḥ sargaḥ.

remind you that the king has said that if we do not want
to go we should stay. He wants to find out our intentions.
Either way we will not be doing wrong. Furthermore, men
who understand the principles contained in treatises laid
down in books should be graced with this question, not
fake counsellors like these. I, on the other hand, am skilled
in the use of political means and methods because I am
in touch with mindful* men who are proficient in their
use. Now is the time for us to indulge in pleasure, not
pointless politics! Turn your minds for a moment to what
is said in the law books: 'One should live one's life with
the dress, speech and attitude appropriate to one's age, des-
tiny, wealth, education and birth.' So, get up! Let's go to
the festival with its wonderful sights: we shall enjoy some
sport in beautiful places!" What Gomukha said went to my 7.80
heart: who does not like words that are both reasoned and
agreeable?

Gomukha continued: "The people are on their way to the festival. Let's go up to the roof terrace and see how splendid they look!"

Then, like the moon climbing the magisterial peak of the eastern mountain, I climbed onto the magnificent roof terrace, where the ring of turrets kissed the sky and the beauty of the banners eclipsed that of the rainbow.

Thus ends the seventh canto,
the Consecration as Crown Prince.

CANTO 8
THE SPORT OF HUNTING

TATR' ÂPAŚYAM PURA|DVĀRĀN
niryāntīm janatām aham
citr'|âlaṃkāra|saṃskārāṃ vācaṃ kavi|mukhād iva.
Turaṃga|ratha|mātaṅga|kareṇu|śibik'|ādibhiḥ
kuṭumbi|parivāro 'pi yatr' âgacchad a|maṇḍanaḥ.
Iti saṃpaśyamāno 'ham apaśyaṃ hastinī|gatam
niṣkrāmantaṃ Rumaṇvantam ārya|veṣa|sahāyakam.
Adhyāsita|vaśā|yūtham ambā|dvaya|puraḥ|saram
kañcuky|ādi|parīvāram antaḥ|puram ataḥ param.
Sārdhaṃ makara|yaṣṭyā ca cañcad|rakta|patākayā
gaṇikā|gaṇam ākṛṣṭa|pramatta|jana|mānasam.

Atha māṃ Gomukho 'vocad, «aryaputra kim āsyate?
ayaṃ vaḥ samayo gantum!» ity ath' âham avātaram.
Saṃcāri|Meru|kūṭ'|ābham āruhya sa|suhṛd ratham
nadan|nandi|mṛdaṅg'|ādi|tūrya|pracala|madhya|gam.
Turaṃga|heṣitais tārair mandaiś ca gaja|garjitaiḥ
śikhaṇḍi|ghana|saṃghāta|nirghoṣa iva jṛmbhitam.
Jana|saṃghaṭṭa|niṣpiṣṭa|tulā|koṭika|mekhalam
rāja|mārgam atikramya rāja|dvāram ayāsiṣam.
8.10 Suyāmuna|sthas tatra|stham anujñ"|âbhinayena mām
«gaccha! gacch' êti!» bhū|pālaḥ kṣipta|pāṇir acodayat.
Ahaṃ tu taṃ namaskṛtya harṣam asy' âbhivardhayan
pratiṣṭhe bandi|saṃghāta|prayukta|jaya|ghoṣaṇaḥ.
Prāg|dvāreṇa ca niryāya jana|saṃpad|didṛkṣayā

FROM THERE I WATCHED the people coming out of the city gate adorned with wonderful decorations, like language adorned with imagery and figures of speech coming out of a great poet's mouth. A retinue of simply dressed servants followed, with horses, carriages, male and female elephants, palanquins and so forth. While I was watching, I saw Rumanvan riding forth on an elephant, his attendants dressed like noblemen. Then I saw the king's harem riding on a herd of elephants. The two queens were at the front, followed by the chamberlain and the rest of their attendants. And, with a crocodile flagstaff from which fluttered a red flag, I saw the troupe of courtesans, who drew the attention of the excited crowd.

Gomukha said to me, "Your Highness, what are you waiting for? You should go now!," and I went down. I and my friends mounted a carriage in the middle of the road. It moved along to the sound of the tabour and other celebratory instruments, and looked like a peak of Mount Meru in motion. The shrill whinnying of horses and the deep trumpeting of elephants filled the air, like the sounds of peacocks and thunderclouds combined. I crossed the main street, where ankle bracelets and girdles lay trampled and crushed by the crowd, and approached the palace gate.
From the Suyamuna Palace the king indicated his approval 8.10
to me as I stood there by saying "Go! Go!" and urging me onward, waving his hand. I bowed to him and added to his joy by setting forth to the sound of cries of victory from the mass of bards. I went out by way of the eastern gate and, wanting to see the pomp of the crowd, stopped on the royal

rāja|mārgam adhiṣṭhāya mandaraṃ gantum ārabhe.
ath' âṣṭābhiḥ śaśāṅk'|ābhaiḥ kuṅkuma|sthāsak'|âṅkitaiḥ
hema|bhāṇḍaiḥ pravahaṇaṃ yuktam ukṣa|kumārakaiḥ.
dhaval'|âmbara|saṃvītaṃ sa|jyotsnam iva mandiram
gṛhīta|manda|saṃcāraṃ paśyāmi sma samīpagam.
Tatra pravahaṇ'|ācchāda|cchann'|ârdham aham ānanam
apaśyaṃ megha|ruddh'|ârdham iva prāleya|dīpitam.
Lalāṭa|taṭa|vinyasta|mṛdu|tāmr'|âṅguli|dvayam
nibaddham añjaliṃ cāru|saroja|mukul'|ākṛtim.
Kām'|ôpacāra|vijñāna|śūnyo yasmād ahaṃ tataḥ
na jānāmi sma ken' âpi taṃ baddhaṃ vandan'|âñjalim.
Atha māṃ Gomukho 'vocat, «srastena mukuṭena vaḥ
lalāṭam āvṛtaṃ tena tat samādhīyatām iti!»
Ath' āmṛṣṭe lalāṭ'|ânte mayā dakṣiṇa|pāṇinā
yāne kanyābhir unmuktas tasmin kalakalaḥ paṭuḥ.
8.20 Anyataś ca mukhaṃ kṛtvā pārśva|spandana|sūcitam
Gomukhena smitaṃ sadya upakṣiptaṃ kath"|ântaram.
Krīḍā|sthānāni paśyantaḥ kāritāni Rumaṇvatā
samāsīdāma Kālindīṃ taraj|jana|nirantarām.
Yat tat pravahaṇaṃ pūrvaṃ dṛṣṭaṃ dṛṣṭaṃ ca tan mayā
uttāryamāṇaṃ Yamunāṃ sādareṇa Rumaṇvatā.
Utsāhita|niṣādena, «siddha|yātr' êti» vādinā
nāvaḥ saṃcaratā nāvaṃ ten' âiv' ôttāritā vayam.
Susaṃvihita|saṃbhāre nadī|taṭa|niveśite
sthitvā krīḍā|gṛhe rātrim utthitāḥ prasthitās tataḥ.
N' âtidūram atikramya kṛcchrāl labdh'|ântarāḥ pathi
prāptā Nāga|van'|ôdyānaṃ śobhā|nindita|nandanam.

highway. Then I started to move slowly along. To my side I noticed a carriage yoked to eight moon-white young bulls adorned with saffron paste and wearing golden harnesses. It was moving at a gentle pace and, with its covering of white cloth, resembled a temple bathed in moonlight. Inside I saw a face half-hidden by the carriage's awning, like the moon half-hidden by a cloud. Two delicate, copper-red fingers were touching a forehead; the palms were joined and looked like a lovely lotus flower. Ignorant of the ways of love, I did not realize that whoever it was had joined their hands as a gesture of greeting.

Gomukha said to me, "Your crown has slipped and is covering your forehead. Put it right!" When I brushed my brow with my right hand, the girls in the carriage gave
a shrill titter. Gomukha looked away and the shaking of 8.20
his sides showed that he was laughing. He then quickly changed the subject.

While looking at the playgrounds that Rumanvan had set up, we reached the river Yamuna. A crowd was streaming across it. I noticed the carriage that I had seen earlier being helped across the Yamuna by the considerate Rumanvan. He had encouraged the forest-dwellers to assist him and was running the ferries back and forth, wishing everyone a successful trip. He took us across himself.

We spent the night in a well-equipped house of fun on the riverbank, and set off when we rose. After we had gone just a short distance, having had difficulty finding any space on the road, we reached the Snake Forest park, the beauty of which put Indra's paradise to shame. As I moved along,

Saṃtat'|ânanta|vṛtt'|ântāṃ nitānt'|āhita|kautukaḥ
yātrāṃ paśyan prayāmi sma janat"|âṅguli|darśitaḥ.
Senā|patis tu māṃ nītvā prāṃśu kāñcana|toraṇam
kḷpta|nānā|vidhā|krīḍaṃ yātrā|gṛham aveśayat.
Tatr' âhaṃ sa|suhṛd|vargaḥ krīḍā|snān'|âśan'|ādikāḥ
kriyāḥ kurvan nayāmi sma netr'|ônmeṣa|samaṃ divam.

Atha pradoṣe senā|nīr āgaty' âsmān abhāṣata
«śvaḥ saṃpādayitā krīḍā yā vaḥ sā kathyatām iti.»
8.30 «Mṛgay" êti,» may" ākhyāte yāte senā|patau vayam
abhinīya niśāṃ prātaḥ pratiṣṭhāmahi kānanam.
Anye 'pi mad|anujñātāḥ prītāḥ paura|kumārakāḥ
kareṇu|karabh'|āśv'|ādi|vāhanāḥ saṃghaśo 'vrajan.
Atha duṣ|parisaṃkhyānam apaśyaṃ vana|randhra|gam
pluṣṭa|sthāṇu|van'|ākāra|pulinda|balam agrataḥ.
Tato niryāya pīn'|âṅgaḥ nikharvas tāmra|locanaḥ
senā|patiḥ Siṃha|śatruḥ senā|patim avandata

Ten' ôktaṃ, «bhrātṛ|jāyā me kīdṛśī Cintyamekhalā?
tau vā Śāmbara|Sāraṅgau putrau kuśalināv iti?»

Siṃhaśatrur avocat taṃ, «śivaṃ naḥ sakale kule
yad|arthaṃ vayam āhūtās tat samājñāpyatām iti.»

Rumaṇvān abravīd, «eṣa kumāraḥ sa|suhṛt tava
nyāsas tena sa|sainyena prayatnāt pālyatām iti.»

Naila|hāridra|kausumbha|vāso|rāśim adāpayat
taila|kumbha|sahasraṃ ca Rumaṇvān Siṃhaśatrave.
Susaṃvihita|rakṣaṃ māṃ anujñāpya Rumaṇvati
nivṛtte Gomukhen' ôktam, «aho! tātena śobhitam!

looking with unstinting curiosity at the festival and its endless succession of sights, I was pointed out by the people. The general of the armies led me through a tall golden arch and put me up in a rest house that had been equipped with various types of entertainments. There my friends and I passed the day in the blink of an eye, doing things like playing, washing and eating.

In the evening the general arrived and asked what amusements were to be arranged for us the following day. After I 8.30
replied that we would be going hunting, the general left.

The next morning we waited in the forest. Happy groups of other young townsmen that I had invited arrived, riding elephants, camels, horses and other animals. I saw ahead in a clearing an army of Pulindas, looking like a forest of burnt trees, their numbers impossible to estimate. From among them emerged a fat, dwarfish, red-eyed commander called Sinhashatru. He greeted our general.

The latter said, "How is my sister-in-law Chintyamekhala? Are the two boys Shambara and Saranga well?"

Sinhashatru replied, "All our family is well. Tell us why we have been summoned."

Rumanvan said, "The prince and his friends here have been entrusted to you, so guard them carefully with your army!"

Rumanvan gave Sinhashatru a pile of clothes dyed with indigo, turmeric and safflower, and a thousand pots of sesame oil. Having put me in good hands, Rumanvan took my leave and went back. Gomukha said, "Ah! How splendid of uncle Rumanvan! If he had failed to realize what we

Vijñāt'|âsmad|abhiprāyo na nivarteta yady ayam
kumāra|vaṭak" êv' êyaṃ bhaved dāruṇa|yantraṇā!»
8.40 Tato dhār"|ādi|mṛgayā|prakārair bahubhir mṛgān
nighnanto ghātayantaś ca na tṛptim alabhāmahi.
Atha nātham araṇyānyā dviṣantaṃ vāji|kuñjarān
Yamāya prahiṇoti sma mahiṣaṃ Marubhūtikaḥ.
Ratna|budbuda|citr'|âṅgās tato 'dṛśyanta saṃghaśaḥ
carantaḥ saṃcarantaś ca tatra vātamajā mṛgāḥ.
Tān hantuṃ darśit'|ôtsāhāś ciraṃ Hariśikh'|ādayaḥ
bhagn'|ôtsāhā nyavartanta vīrebhya iva bhīravaḥ.
Tais tu senā|patiḥ pṛṣṭo, «na dṛṣṭāḥ kaiś cid īdṛśāḥ
mṛgā yadi ca jānāsi tato naḥ kathyatām iti.»
Ten' ôktam, «aham apy etān na jānāmi pitā tu me
prastāve kva cid ācaṣṭa yāṃ vārttāṃ kathayāmi tām,
‹Utpadyate yadā loke cakravartī tadā kila
evaṃ|rūpa|jav'|ākārā dṛśyante mṛga|jātayaḥ.
Na c' ēśvara|śareṇ' âpi tri|pur'|êndhana|dāhinā
samāsādayituṃ śakyāḥ kuta ev' ânya|sāyakaiḥ.
Etān pradakṣiṇīkṛtya yena kṣiptaḥ śaraḥ kila
tūṇam āyāti tasy' âiva vitta taṃ cakravartinam›.»
Tān ahaṃ baddha|saṃrambhaḥ prasthitaś ca vihiṃsitum
te ca māṃ dūram ākṛṣya divaṃ haṃsā iv' āsthitāḥ.
8.50 Ath' âvatīrya turagād gṛhīta|prabala|śramaḥ
ramaṇīya|saras|tīra|taru|chāyām upāśrayam.
Cirān mṛgayamāṇā māṃ turaṃga|pada|vartmanā
sen"|ânubaddha|vartmānaḥ prāptā Hariśikh'|ādayaḥ.
Tataḥ kurvan parīhāsaṃ mām abhāṣata Gomukhaḥ

intend to get up to and not gone back, then this place would have been as severely restrictive as the princes' cloister!"

We could not get enough of attacking and killing game, 8.40
and used several methods of hunting, including the rain* of arrows. Marubhutika dispatched to the god of death a buffalo, the lord of the jungle, which had been attacking the horses and elephants. Then we noticed, grazing and moving about together, a herd of antelopes that were as swift as the wind, their bodies speckled with jewel-like spots. For a long time Harishikha and the others showed their determination to kill them, but they turned back with their determination dashed, like cowards before brave warriors. They asked the general, "None of us has seen deer like these: if you know what they are please tell us!"

He replied, "I too do not recognize them, but my father once said that when an emperor is born into the world, species of deer are seen whose beauty, speed and appearance are like theirs. Not even Shiva's arrow, which burnt down the three cities, can hit them, let alone the arrows of anyone else. Know him to be the emperor whose arrow when shot flies in a circle around them and returns to his quiver."

With great excitement I set out to hunt them, and they drew me far away before rising up into the sky like swans.
I got down from my horse, and, exhausted, rested in the 8.50
shade of a tree on the bank of a beautiful lake. After a long time searching for me by following my horse's hoofprints, Harishikha and the others arrived, with the army close behind. Then Gomukha jokingly said to me, "How many wind-antelopes have you killed?" I replied, "I did not kill a

«kiyanto vāta|hariṇā yuṣmābhir nihatā iti?»
May" ôktaṃ, «na may" âiko 'pi hataḥ kṣiptas tu yaḥ śaraḥ
pradakṣiṇīkṛtya sa tān eṣa tūṇaṃ mam' āgataḥ.»
Atha ten' ôktaṃ, «tasya śara|rājasya pūjanam
yaś cakra|varti|cihnānāṃ sphuṭānām agraṇīr iti!»
Siṃha|śatrur atha tām iṣuṃ mudā
Gomukh'|ādibhir apūjayat saha
siddha|sārtha|vadha|jāta|saṃmado
datta|kāṅkṣita|varām iv' Âmbikām.

iti mṛgayā|vihāra|sargaḥ.

single one, but the arrow that I fired made a circle around them and here it is, returned to my quiver."

Then he said, "This king among arrows is to be worshipped: of the signs denoting an emperor that have appeared so far, it is the clearest!" Simhashatru joined Gomukha and the others in joyfully worshipping the arrow, in the same way that when pleased with the successful ambush of a caravan he would worship the mother goddess for giving him what he wanted.

Thus ends the Sport of Hunting canto.

CANTO 9
THE MEETING ON THE RIVERBANK

TATO MAD'|ÂNDHA|VANITĀ|
kapola|sthala|komalam
saroja|pattraṃ kara|jaiś chettum ārabdha Gomukhaḥ.
Pattra|chedyaṃ tatas tasyāḥ saritas tarad|ambhasi
sa|jīvam iva saṃpannaṃ calatvāt paṭu|raṃhasaḥ.
Anukūlaṃ prasarpantaṃ praśaṃsantaś ca Gomukham
pattra|chedyam apaśyāma mukt'|âvayava|saṃkaram.
Asmābhir anuyuktaś ca, «kathay' êti» sa|vistaram
Gomukho vyākaroti sma pattra|chedasya lakṣaṇam.
«Ih' ârya|putra vijñeyaṃ pattra|chedyaṃ samāsataḥ
try|asraṃ ca catur|asraṃ ca dīrghaṃ vṛttaṃ ca bhedataḥ.
Try|asraiś catuṣ|padaṃ śailā niṣpadyante gṛh'|ādi ca
catur|asraiḥ sa|śālāni purāṇi puruṣ'|ādi ca.
Dīrghair nada|nadī|mārga|pratāna|bhuja|g'|ādayaḥ
vṛttair bhūṣaṇa|saṃyoga|śakunta|mithun'|ādayaḥ.»
Gomukhe kathayaty evam āgatya Marubhūtikaḥ
«aho nu mahad āścaryam ārya|putr' êty!» abhāṣata.
asau Hariśikhen' ôktaḥ, «sarvam eva bhavā|dṛśām
kūpa|kacchapa|kalpānām āścaryaṃ sthūla|cakṣuṣām!»
9.10 «Paśya duḥ|śraddadhān' êti!» tam uktvā Marubhūtikaḥ
«idam āścaryam!» ity uccaiḥ pulinaṃ no vyadarśayat.
Tato Hariśikhen' ôktaṃ kṛtvā hasitam ulbaṇam
«āścaryaṃ pulinaṃ paśya! namas tasmai sa|cakṣuṣe!
Nimnena salilaṃ yāti pulinaṃ sikatā|sthalam
āścaryaṃ yadi tan mūḍha dveṣaḥ kaḥ salile tava?»
So 'bravīt, «kena ‹pulinam āścaryam iti› bhāṣitam?

THEN, USING HIS FINGERNAILS, Gomukha started to make cuts in a lotus leaf that was as soft as the cheek of a lovelorn lady*. In the flowing water the leaf-figure seemed to come to life with the movement of the impetuous river. Singing Gomukha's praises, we watched the leaf-figure floating downstream; it had become more than the sum of its parts.

When we asked him to tell us, Gomukha described in detail the defining characteristics of a leaf-figure. "On this matter, my lord, one should know that leaf-figures are, briefly, divided into the following categories: triangular, square, rectangular and round. With triangular ones are made things like quadrupeds, mountains and houses; with square ones, cities, houses, people and so forth; with rectangular ones, rivers, roads, creepers, snakes and such like; with round ones, things like ornaments and pairs of birds."

As Gomukha was saying this, Marubhutika arrived and said, "My lord, a great miracle has happened!"

Harishikha said to him, "Everything is miraculous for people like you who are as blinkered as tortoises in a well!"

9.10 "Take a look, you incredulous fellow!" replied Marubhutika, and he showed us the riverbank, exclaiming, "This is the miracle!"

At this Harishikha laughed loudly and said, "Behold the miraculous riverbank! Homage to this visionary! Water is flowing along the riverbed: if the sandy bank is miraculous then what, fool, have you got against the water?"

Marubhutika replied, "Who said the riverbank was miraculous? It's what's on it that's miraculous: have a look!"

puline yat tad āścaryam atha vā dṛśyatām iti!»

Ten' ôktaṃ «puline santi sikatāḥ kiṃ tad adbhutam?»

«n' êty» ukte tena dṛṣṭvā tu pulinaṃ Gomukho 'bravīt,

«mā mā bhadra|mukhaṃ kaś cit paribhūd Marubhūtikam

mayā hi puline dṛṣṭaṃ saṃniviṣṭaṃ pada|dvayam.»

Uktaṃ Hariśikhen' âpi, «yady āścaryaṃ pada|dvayam

aty|āścaryam idaṃ paśya pada|koṭīś catur|daśa!»

Ten' ôktaṃ, «s'|ânubandhāsu n' āścaryaṃ pada|koṭiṣu

idaṃ vicchinna|saṃtānaṃ ten' āścaryaṃ pada|dvayam.»

Ten' ôktaṃ, «yadi śeṣāṇi parāmṛṣṭāni pāṇinā

bhaveyur iti?» ten' ôktaṃ, «tataḥ syād eva vālukā.»

«Y" êyaṃ tīra|taroḥ śākhā pulinaṃ yāvad āgatā

tayā gatv" âvatīrṇaḥ syāt kaś cin nāgarako yadi.

9.20 Etām eva samālambya dūram ālamba|pallavām

nivartet' êti» ten' ôkte, «parṇ'|ākīrṇā mahī bhavet.»

«Kasya tarh' îti?» ten' ôkte, «divyasy' êty» abravīt sa tam

«divyānāṃ katamasy' êti» sa vidyā|dharam ādiśat:

«Na spṛśanti bhuvaṃ devāḥ sthūlatvād yakṣa|rakṣasām

dūraṃ padāni majjanti pulineṣu viśeṣataḥ.

Tapaḥ|kṣāma|śarīratvāt siddhānām ṛṣibhiḥ saha

a|vyakt'|âṅguli|pārṣṇy|ādi|nikṣepaṃ jāyate padam.

Anyeṣāṃ ca manuṣyāṇām upapattyā niyujyate

Harishikha replied, "There are grains of sand on the bank. Is that amazing?"

When Marubhutika said it was not, Gomukha looked at the riverbank and said, "Don't be rude to goodly Marubhutika, for I can see a pair of footprints on the bank".

Harishikha said, "If a pair of footprints is a miracle, then this is beyond miraculous—look: one hundred and forty million pairs of footprints!"

Gomukha replied, "There is nothing miraculous in tens of millions of footprints in succession; what makes this pair of footprints a miracle is that it is alone."

Harishikha answered, "What if the rest have been rubbed out by hand?"

"Then there would be loose sand," replied Gomukha.

Harishikha said, "There's a tree on the other side of the river. Do you see the branch that reaches this bank? What if some clever fellow* climbed along it and got down here?
He might have returned by grabbing hold of the same 9.20
branch—its shoots hang down a long way." Gomukha replied, "The ground would be strewn with leaves."

When Harishikha asked, "Then to whom do the footprints belong?," Gomukha replied, "To a divine being." When asked what sort of divine being, he specified that it was a sorcerer: "Gods do not touch the ground. Because they are heavy, the footprints of *yakṣas* and demons make deep indentations, especially on riverbanks. The bodies of perfected saints and sages are emaciated because of their asceticism, so their feet leave indistinct imprints of their toes, heels and other parts. Those of other human beings

avagāḍhaṃ bhavaty agre viparītaṃ tu yoṣitaḥ.
Bhār'|ākrāntaḥ sa c' êty» ukte bhūyo Hariśikho 'bravīt.
«Śilā|pāda|pa|śatrūṇāṃ ko 'sya bhāro bhaved iti?»
«Śilāyām avagāḍhaṃ syāt parṇa|kīrṇaṃ ca pāda|pe
śatrau na śatruṃ puline ramaṇīye 'vatārayet.
Tasmād a|siddha|vidy" âsya bhāro vidyā|dharī yataḥ
na vidyā|siddhim āptv" âpi jāyante paṅgu|vṛttayaḥ.
Āropitaṃ ca ten' âsyā jaghanaṃ dakṣiṇaṃ bhujam
nimagnaṃ yena tasy' êdaṃ dakṣiṇaṃ kāminaḥ padam.
Patitair uttam'|âṅgāc ca keśa|dhūp'|âdhivāsitaiḥ
mālatī|kusumair vāsam avakīrṇaṃ na paśyasi?
9.30 Ramaṇīyatarāṃ c' êmāṃ na tyakṣyati sa nimna|gām
ten' ânyatr' âpi dṛśyantāṃ padāni nipuṇair iti».
Tataḥ paurair madīyaiś ca vicinvadbhir itas tataḥ
strī|puṃsayor adṛśyanta padāni salil'|ântike.
Sah' âsmābhis tam uddeśaṃ gatvā dṛṣṭvā ca Gomukhaḥ
«tena nāgarakeṇ' âpi bhāvyam» ity etad uktavān.
«Kathaṃ vetth' êti» pṛṣṭaś ca sa vihasy' êdam uktavān
«jñeyaṃ kim atra dur|jñānam? atha vā kathayāmi vaḥ.
Para|citt'|ânuvṛttiś ca sva|cittasya ca nigrahaḥ
y" êyaṃ nāgarakair uktā sā nāgarakatā matā.
Mantharaṃ parisarpantīṃ kāminīm anugacchati
ayaṃ nāgarako yasmād atikramya na gacchati.
Idānīm eva tau yātau padavī dṛśyatām iyam
tathā hi caraṇ'|ākrānti|natam ady' âpi śādvalam.»
Iti tām anugacchanto navāṃ caraṇa|paddhatim
sapta|parṇam apaśyāma pravṛtta|bhramar'|ôtsavam.

depend on how they are made. A man's is deep at the front, a woman's is the opposite. This man has a heavy load."

Harishikha asked: "What might his load be: a rock, a tree or a foe?" "If it were a rock it would be deeper; if it were a tree there would be leaves scattered about; if it were a foe, he would not have put him down on this lovely riverbank. Therefore this fellow's burden is a sorceress who has not mastered magic: those who have mastered magic do not become lame. The suitor's right footprint is deeper, so he sat her on his right arm. Do you not notice the smell given off by the jasmine flowers that fell from her head and are
scented with her pomade? This river is most agreeable; he 9.30
will not have strayed from it, so let's carefully look elsewhere for footprints."

The townspeople and my retinue searched about the place and found the footprints of a man and a woman near the water. Gomukha accompanied us there. He looked at them and said that that same gentleman must have made them too. When he was asked how he knew, he laughed and replied, "What in this is hard to work out? All right, I shall tell you. Carrying out the wishes of another and suppressing one's own: that's what gentlemen consider gentlemanly conduct. His lover is walking slowly and he is following her. He is a gentleman because he does not go in front of her. They passed just now: look at the path, the grass is still bent over from being pressed down by their feet."

Following those fresh footprints, we came across a *saptaparṇa* tree. It was a riot of busy bees. Gomukha described what had passed in secret between the two sport-

Tan|mūle yāni vṛttāni raho viharamāṇayoḥ
svayam ācaritān' îva Gomukhas tāny avarṇayat:
«Iha sā kupitā tasmai tena c' êha prasāditā
ayaṃ sa|kusumaś c' âtra kḷptaḥ pallava|saṃstaraḥ.
9.40 Śrāntā c' âtr' ôpaviṣṭā sā tathā c' êdaṃ nirūpyatām
āsanaṃ jaghan'|ākrānti|jāta|jarjara|pallavam.
Nidhāya jaghane hastau vinamayya guru trikam
iyaṃ vijṛmbhamāṇāyā magn'|âgra|caraṇā mahī.»
Evaṃ nirūpayantaś ca sapta|parṇa|talād vayam
niryāntīm anvagacchāma tayoś caraṇa|paddhatim.
Ath' âgamyam apaśyāma candra|sūry'|ânal'|ânilaiḥ
mādhavī|gahanaṃ veśma kāminām a|nivāritam.
Vāruṇī|pāna|saṃjāta|mada|bhṛṅga|viluptayā
puṣpavatyā pariṣvaktaṃ śyāmayā tan nir|antaram.
Dṛṣṭvā ca Gomukhen' ôktam, «atr' âiv' āste sa kāmukaḥ!
pracchannaṃ ramaṇīyaṃ ca na h' îdaṃ tyāgam arhati.
Na c' âpi darśanaṃ yuktam āsīnasya yathā|sukham
tasmān muhūrtam anyatra kva cid viśramyatām iti.»
Nīla|śītala|mūlasya dūrvayā vaṭa|śākhinaḥ
chāyayā ca palāśānām atiṣṭhāma tale tataḥ.
Gomukhas tu tad ālokya latā|gṛhakam unmukhaḥ
«n' âsty asāv atra kām" îti» sa|śiras|kampam uktavān.
Tato Hariśikhen' ôktaṃ, «pūrvam, ‹ast' îti!› bhāṣase
idānīm api, ‹n' âst' îti!› sarvath" ônmattako bhavān!»
9.50 Ten' ôktam, «idam a|trastaṃ niṣkrāntaṃ mādhavī|gṛhāt
śikhaṇḍi|mithunaṃ kasmān mūkam andha na paśyasi?
Yadi kaś cid bhaved atra trastam etat tatas tataḥ
mukt'|ārta|kekam uḍḍīya vṛkṣa|durgaṃ viśed iti.»
Tataḥ prasthāpayāmi sma vicetuṃ parivārakān

ing lovers at the foot of that tree as though he himself had been involved: "She was angry with him here... here he won her over... here they made this bed of twigs and
flowers... tired, she sat down here. Look, this is where she 9.40
sat: the twigs are broken from being pressed down by her bottom. Placing her hands on her buttocks, she lowered her heavy behind; the earth here has been pressed down by her toes as she stretched."

Investigating like this, we followed their footprints away from the foot of the *saptaparṇa* tree. Then we noticed a dense thicket of *mādhavī* bushes, impervious to the moon, the sun, fire and wind, but no obstruction to lovers. It was tightly enclosed by blossoming *priyaṅgu* creepers which were being ravished by drunken bees. When he saw it Gomukha said, "Our beau is right here! This spot is hidden and lovely: he wouldn't have left it. It would not be right to see him relaxing and enjoying himself, so let's retire somewhere else for a while." We waited under a banyan tree, in the shade of its leaves, its foot dark and cool with *dūrvā* grass. Gomukha looked toward the creeper bower, shook his head and said that the lover was not there.

Then Harishikha said, "At first you say he's there but now you say he isn't. You are completely mad!"

Gomukha answered, "Why is this pair of peacocks com- 9.50
ing out of the *mādhavī* thicket unruffled and silent? Are you blind? Can't you see them? If there was anyone in there, they would have cried out in alarm and flown up to the safety of a tree."

I dispatched some attendants to investigate. Waving their

calayantas tu hastāṃs te śūnyam ākhyal̃ latā|gṛham.
Svayaṃ tatr' âpy apaśyāma racitaṃ prastaraṃ mahat
prakīrṇa|pallava|nyāsaṃ kiśora|luṭhitair iva.
Taru|śākh"|âvasaktaṃ ca hāra|nūpura|mekhalam
anyatr' ânyatra ca kṣaumam ambho|ruha|dal'|âruṇam.
Patit'|ârka|nikāśaṃ ca vidyā|dhara|dhanaṃ kva cit
varma|ratnaṃ sphurad|ratna|prabhā|kuñcita|locanam.
Sarvaṃ tad grāhayāmi sma puruṣair bhūṣaṇ'|ādikam.
Tasmai niryātayiṣyāmi dṛṣṭāy' êty
atha Gomukhaḥ
Abravīd, «vairiṇā nūnaṃ sa nītaḥ saha kāntayā
tābhyāṃ hi para|tantrābhyāṃ bhūṣaṇ'|ād' îdam ujjhitam.
Dīrgh'|āyuṣkaṃ ca taṃ vitta snigdhās tasya śiro|ruhāḥ
lagnāḥ pāda|pa|śākhāyām ady' âpi hi su|gandhayaḥ.»
Evaṃ nirūpayantaś ca samantād|datta|dṛṣṭayaḥ
n' âti|dūram atikramya kva cit tuṅga|tarau vane.
9.60 Baddhaṃ skandhe kadambasya pañcabhir loha|śaṅkubhiḥ
vidyā|dharam apaśyāma lepa|vidyā|dhar'|â|calam.
Ath', «âvatāryatām eṣa skandhād ity» abhidhāya tān
apasṛtya tataś chāyām āśrayāmi sma śākhinaḥ.
Gomukhas tv abravīn, «n' âite kena cid loha|śaṅkavaḥ.
śakyāḥ kraṣṭum upāyena sarvair api surair iti.»
Ath' âham abruvaṃ smṛtvā, «rāj" âjalpan mayā śrutam
etā oṣadhayaḥ pañca sad" āsthāḥ kila varmaṇi.
Viśalya|karaṇī kā cit kā cin māṃsa|vivardhanī

hands about, they signalled that the creeper bower was empty. We went there ourselves and saw that a large bed had been made, on which twigs were scattered as though by the rolling about of a colt. We saw a garland, some ankle bracelets and a girdle hanging from the branch of a tree, and fine linen clothes strewn about the place, as red as the petals of a lotus. And in another spot we saw precious armor, the prized possession of a sorcerer. It looked like a fallen sun and made us squint with the brilliance of its sparkling jewels. I had all those ornaments and other things gathered together by the men so that I might return them to the fellow when we found him.

Then Gomukha said, “He and his beloved must have been abducted by an enemy: they have abandoned their jewelry and so forth because they have been captured. The fellow shall have a long life. Some of his hair got caught in the branch of a tree: it is glossy and still fragrant.”

Investigating like this, we searched all around and had
not gone far when, in a grove of tall trees, we saw a sorcerer 9.60
attached to the trunk of a *kadamba* tree by five iron spikes, as still as if he were a waxwork. I told the men to get him down from the tree trunk, and moved away to shelter in the shade of a tree. However Gomukha said, “There is no way that these spikes can be pulled out, not even by all the gods.”

Then I remembered something and said, “I heard the king mention that the following five herbs are apparently always found in a suit of armor: one that heals arrow wounds, one that makes flesh grow, one that remedies cuts, one that

vraṇa|saṃrohaṇī kā cit kā cid varṇa|prasādanī.
Mṛta|saṃjīvanī c' āsāṃ pañcamī param'|âuṣadhiḥ
yadi varmaṇi tāḥ santi tābhiḥ saṃjīvyatām iti.»
Muhūrtād iva c' āgatya vismito Gomukho 'bravīt
«prasādād arya|putrasya jīvitaḥ sa nabhaś|caraḥ.
Tā mah"|âuṣadhayo dṛṣṭā nihitās tasya varmaṇi
śalya|prote ca hariṇe prayuktāḥ kramaśas tataḥ.
Tatra dṛṣṭa|prabhāvābhiḥ sa vidyā|dhara|sundaraḥ
a|kṛt'|âṅgaḥ kṛtaḥ sadyaḥ samāśvasy' êti bhāṣate.
‹Jīvitaḥ kena baddho 'ham?› ity ath' âhaṃ tam uktavān
‹asmākam arya|putreṇa prakāraiś caturair iti.›
9.70 Ten' ôktaṃ, ‹kiṃ ca yuṣmākam arya|putro 'pi vidyate?›
‹ām' êti› ca mayā prokte ten' ôktaṃ, ‹na sa mānuṣaḥ.
Asmākam arya|putro 'pi devo vidyā|dharo 'pi vā
prasīdatu tam ākhyāta prasādaṃ cakṣuṣām iti.›
May" ôktam, ‹arya|putreṇa vayam ājñāpitā, «yathā
jīvayitv" âbhyanujñeyo mā sma paśyat sa mām iti».
Kṛt'|ôpakāras tvāṃ draṣṭuṃ n' âyam icchati lajjayā
punaḥ|saṃdarśanāy' âtas tāta prasthīyatām iti.›
Atha visrasta|hastena dattvā jānu|nipātanam
viniśvasya ca ten' ôktaṃ dainya|gadgadayā girā,
‹Idānīm asmi su|mṛtaḥ prāṇa|dān'|ôpakāriṇam
svāminaṃ yan na paśyāmi bhaviṣyaṃ cakra|vartinam.
Pradāya yadi me prāṇān paścāt|tāpena khedyate
evaṃ muñcāmi bhūyas tān na cet paśyatu mām iti!›»
Mayā datte 'bhyanujñāne, «paśyatv evaṃ karotv iti»
gāṃ spṛśañ jānu|śirasā sa mām idam abhāṣata,
«Vidyā|dharo 'mitagatiḥ Kauśikasya muneḥ sutaḥ

restores the complexion, and the fifth, the ultimate herb, which brings the dead back to life. If they are in the suit of armor then use them to bring him back to life."

Not long after Gomukha returned, and said with a smile, "By the grace of Your Highness, the sky-rover has been revived! We found those potent herbs in his suit of armor, and tried them one by one on a deer that had been pierced by an arrow. When we had established their effects, we used them to restore the body of the handsome sorcerer. On being revived, he said, 'Who brought me back to life after I had been impaled?,' and I replied, 'Our master, using clever means.' He said, 'Is he your master too?,' and when 9.70
I replied that he was, he said, 'He is not human. He is also my master, and a god or a sorcerer. Please ask him to be so gracious as to favor me with his presence.'

I replied, 'Our prince told us that after we revived you, you should be sent on your way and not be allowed to see him. Out of modesty he does not want to see you after assisting you. So, sir, please be on your way. We shall meet again.' Then, with his hands hanging down, he dropped to his knees, sighed, and in a voice choked with misery said, 'Now I might as well be dead, because I cannot see my master, the future emperor, who has favored me with the gift of life. If he is regretting having given me life, I shall give it up again. If not, let him see me!'"

When I gave my consent and said that he could do what he wanted and see me, he knelt down, touched the ground with his head, and said to me, "May the ruler of all the sorcerers look upon the humble sorcerer Amitagati, son of

sarva|vidyā|dhar'|ēśena praṇaman dṛśyatām iti».
«Eh' îha!» ca may" āhūya spṛṣṭaḥ pṛṣṭhe nir|āmayaḥ
suhṛd|dṛṣṭyā ca dṛṣṭaḥ san prahṛṣṭaḥ samupāviśat.
9.80 Tato Hariśikhen' ôktam, «uktaṃ vṛṣa|sutena yat
satyaṃ tat priya|saṃbhāṣaḥ mahā|nāgarako hy ayam.»
Idaṃ śrutv" Âmitagatir idam asmān abhāṣata
«n' êdaṃ nāgarakatvaṃ me śrūyatāṃ ca kathā yathā.
Asti Prāleya|śailasya mano|nayana|hāriṇi
śikhare Kauśiko nāma munis tuly'|âśma|kāñcanaḥ.
Taṃ ca Bindumatī nāma tyakta|Nandana|kānanā
ārādhitavatī yatnāt su|dīrghaṃ kālam apsarāḥ.
Ekadā Kauśiken' ôktā, ‹varaṃ brūh' îti› s" âbravīt,
‹yadi me bhagavān prītas tato 'patyaṃ dadātv iti.›
Tena c' ôtpāditaṃ tasyām apatya|yugalaṃ kramāt
ahaṃ ca putraḥ putrī ca mat svasā mat sa|nāmikā.
So 'haṃ saṃvardhitas tena n' âsti tad yan na śikṣitam
dhārayāmi ca tad|vidyās tena vidyā|dharo 'bhavam.
Ekadā pitaraṃ dṛṣṭvā rudantam aham abruvam
‹mā|dṛśaṃ putram utpādya kiṃ roditi bhavān iti?›
Ten' ôktaṃ, ‹cakra|vartitvaṃ na te paśyāmi putraka
aṅgād aṅgān madīyāt tu vṛthā jāto bhavān iti.›
May" ôktaṃ, ‹mama yaḥ svāmī
sa mahyaṃ kathyatām iti,›
ten' ôktaṃ, ‹cakra|vartī yaḥ
sa c' âpy anviṣyatām iti!›
9.90 May" ôktaṃ, ‹cakra|vartitvaṃ yaiś cihnair avagamyate
dṛṣṭvā tāni dhiyā mahyam ācaṣṭāṃ bhagavān iti.›
Ten' ôktaṃ, ‹śatruṇā baddhaṃ

the sage Kaushika."

I called him over, saying, "Come here!," and touched him on the back—he had been healed. Under the gaze of my friends he sat down near me, overjoyed.

Harishikha said, "What Gomukha said is true: this fellow, 9.80
with his agreeable conversation, is indeed a most courteous gentleman."

When he heard this, Amitagati said to us, "I am not just being courteous: listen to my story.

On the charming and beautiful peak of Snow mountain there is a sage called Kaushika to whom stone and gold are as one. An Apsaras called Bindumati left Indra's paradise and served him zealously for a very long time. One day Kaushika told her to ask for a boon and she replied, 'If Your Holiness is pleased with me, then let him give me children.' He had two children in succession by her: a son, me, and a daughter, my sister, who has the same name as me. It was he who made me what I am—he taught me everything. I bear his magical sciences, so I have become a sorcerer*. One day I saw my father crying and said to him, 'You have fathered a son like me: how can you cry?'

He replied, 'My son, I have realized that you will not be an emperor: you were born from my body in vain.'

I asked him to tell me who would be my master and he replied, 'Whoever is the emperor. You must seek him out!'
I said, 'Your Holiness, use your wisdom to ascertain the 9.90
signs by which the emperor is to be recognized, and tell me them.'

He replied, 'You are to recognize as your master the man

yas tvāṃ śaṅkubhir āyasaiḥ
jīvayiṣyati jānīyāt
svāminaṃ taṃ bhavān iti.›

Mama tv Aṅgārako nāma Vyālakaś c' âbhavat suhṛt
saudaryo gamayāmi sma tābhyāṃ kālaṃ sukhaṃ saha.
Atha Vāyupatho nāma rājā tena sah' âgamam
Kāśyapasthalakaṃ nāma puraṃ mānasa|lobhanam.
Tatr' âikadā vicaratā may" ôpavana|cāriṇī
dṛṣṭā kanyā|parīvārā kanyakā Kusumālikā.
Praśasya|varṇa|saṃsthānā sā me buddhau sthirā sthitā
praśastir iva vinyastā bhittau Vindhya|śilā|bhṛtaḥ.

Tām ādāya tayā sārdhaṃ suhṛdbhyāṃ ca mano|harāḥ
rataye saṃcarāmi sma sarid|giri|taru|sthalīḥ.
Aṅgārakam ath' âpaśyaṃ paśyantam Kusumālikām
rāgād apatrapā|trāsaṃ vakra|grīvā|nirīkṣitam.
‹Lakṣito 'ham anen' êti› lakṣayitvā sah'|ânu|jaḥ
an|āmantry' âiva māṃ nīco nīcair utthāya yātavān.
Ahaṃ tu jāta|vailakṣyāt saṃraktāc ca tatas trasan
na jānāmi, ‹kva yām' îti› cakitaḥ saha kāntayā.
9.100 Adya c' êmāṃ samāsādya ramaṇīyāṃ nag'|âpagām
avatīrṇo 'smi puline komal'|â|mala|vāluke.
Surat'|ânubhave yogyaṃ dṛṣṭvā tac ca su|saṃvṛtam
latā|gṛham ahaṃ prāptaḥ phulla|śyāmā|lat"|āvṛtam.
Yac ca śeṣam a|śeṣaṃ tat kathitaṃ Gomukhena vaḥ
tasmād āpt'|ôpadeśo 'yaṃ na nāgarakatā mama.
Ko hi vidyā|dharair baddham a|vidyā|dhara|sainya|paḥ

who brings you back to life after an enemy has impaled you with iron spikes.'

Two men called Angaraka and Vyalaka became my friends, and I passed the time happily in their company, like a brother. There was a king called Vayupatha whom I accompanied to a charming city called Kashyapasthalaka. One day I was wandering about the city when I saw a young girl called Kusumalika walking in a garden with a group of other girls. With her laudable complexion and beauty she became firmly fixed in my mind, like a laudatory inscription written on a rock-face in the Vindhya mountains.

I won her, and with her and my two friends I wandered about beautiful rivers, mountains and forests in pursuit of pleasure. One day I saw Angaraka looking lustfully at Kusumalika. Nervously twisting his neck he cast her a sideways glance. He noticed that I had seen him, and without saying a word to me the wretch quietly stood up and left with his younger brother. He was in love and had been thwarted in his aims; I was scared of him. I became alarmed
and did not know where to go with my beloved. Today I 9.100
arrived at this beautiful mountain river and landed on the riverbank with its fine white sand. When I saw the creeper bower, fit for lovemaking, well hidden and covered with blossoming *priyaṅgu* creepers, I went inside. Gomukha has told you all that happened afterward. Thus my behavior is not because of my courtesy, but of what I learned from a trusted source. For when someone like me has been captured by sorcerers, who other than a sorcerer general could free him? So what the sage said was true.

mocayen mā|dṛśaṃ? tasmāt tath" êdam ṛṣi|bhāṣitam.
Sevante sevakāḥ sevyān prajñā|prāṇa|dhan'|ādibhiḥ
yena ten' ātma|rakṣ"|ârthaṃ mad|vidyā gṛhyatām iti.»
Sadyaḥ kṛt'|ôpakāreṇa mayā mand'|ādareṇa ca
na gṛhīt" âbruvaṃ c' âinam, «anugaccha priyām iti!»
Abravīc ca, «dinād asmāt pareṇ' âham ahar|niśam
a|pramatto bhaviṣyāmi bhavatāṃ deha|rakṣaṇe.
Smartavyaḥ saṃkaṭe c' âham!» ity uktvā naḥ praṇamya ca
vegen' ākāśam utpatya prāgād Aṅgārakaṃ prati.

9.108 Ādityaśarma|vacanaṃ vacanaṃ ca yakṣyā
yānaṃ pradakṣiṇam iṣoś ca marun|mṛgāṇām
prahlādin" âmita|gateḥ kathitena jātam
utkhāta|saṃśaya|kalaṅkatayā viśuddham.

iti pulina|darśana|sargaḥ.

Servants serve their masters with, among other things, their wisdom, their lives and their wealth, so, in order to protect yourself, accept my *vidyā*."

Because I had just helped him* and because I was not interested, I refused it. I said to him, "Go after your beloved!"

He replied, "From this day forth I shall be ready day and night to protect you. Think of me in times of trouble!" After saying this he bowed to us, flew quickly up into the sky and went after Angaraka.

The words of Adityasharma, the words of the *yakṣī* and 9.108
the arrow's circuit around the wind-deer were confirmed by Amitagati's delightful speech and the resultant removal of the stain of doubt.

Thus ends the Meeting on the Riverbank canto.

CANTO 10
THE CONVERSATION ON THE ROAD

ATHA SAṂPĀDITAṂ TATRA
yātrā|sthena Rumaṇvatā
aśitv" ôdāram āhāraṃ yātrāyai gantum ārabhe.
Ukṣa|vṛndārakair yuktam āsthāya syandanaṃ sukham
haṃsair iva śaś'|âṅk'|ābhair vimānaṃ yādasāṃ patiḥ.
A|khaṇḍa|śaśi|bimb'|ābhaṃ Gomukhaś chatram agrahīt
mṛṣṭa|hāṭaka|daṇḍaṃ ca cāmaraṃ Marubhūtikaḥ.
Rath'|âgr'|âvasthito raśmīn ālambata Tapantakaḥ
ātata|jya|dhanuṣ|pāṇiḥ pārśvaṃ Hariśikho 'bhavat.

Āśitaṃ mṛdu|ghāsānāṃ śeṣaṃ snāpita|pāyitam
manda|mandaṃ ca naḥ sainyaṃ syandanaṃ parito 'gamat.
Evaṃ|prāye ca vṛtt'|ânte cāmaraṃ calayan manāk
dṛṣṭvā Hariśikhaṃ vākyam avocan Marubhūtikaḥ,
«Caratā mṛgayā|krīḍām arya|putreṇa pāpikām
pradāya prāṇinaḥ prāṇān dharmaḥ prāpto mahān iti!»

Ten' ôktaṃ, «kim ih' āścaryam an|upāsita|sādhunā
śrama|vyāyāma|sāreṇa bhāṣitaṃ yat tvay" ēdṛśam.
Bhūmi|mitra|hiraṇyānāṃ mitram ev' âtiricyate
tan|mūlatvād itarayos tasmān mitram upārjitam.»

10.10 Tayoḥ saṃjalpator evam aham Gomukham abruvam
«dharm'|ādīnāṃ pradhānaṃ yat tad ācaṣṭāṃ bhavān iti.»

Ten' ôktaṃ, «dharma|mitr'|ârthā yataḥ kāma|prayojanāḥ
prādhānyaṃ tena kāmasya kāmaś c' êcchā|sukh'|ātmakaḥ.

THEN, AFTER EATING the delicious food prepared at the festival by Rumanvan, I started out for the celebrations. I climbed aboard a comfortable carriage drawn by the finest oxen, like the lord of the waters mounting a sky-chariot drawn by swans as white as the moon. Gomukha carried a parasol that looked like the disc of the full moon, and Marubhutika held a fly whisk with a handle of pure gold. Tapantaka was sitting at the front of the carriage and held the reins; Harishikha was at the side, a strung bow in his hand.

The remainder of our troop moved slowly along beside the carriage, having bathed and watered their horses and fed them with soft grass. As we moved along like this, Marubhutika gently swung the fly whisk, looked at Harishikha and said, "While sinfully enjoying himself hunting, the prince has achieved great merit by giving life to a living being!"

Harishikha replied, "It is no surprise that you, who have not served virtuous men and for whom hard work and exercise are all that matters, should say such a thing. Out of land, friends and gold, friends are the most important because they are the basis of the other two. That is why he made a friend."

While they were talking like this, I said to Gomukha, 10.10
"Tell me which is the most important of religious merit and the other aims of life."

He replied, "Because religious merit, friends and wealth are all acquired for the sake of pleasure, pleasure is the most important aim. Pleasure consists of desire and happiness.

Puline hi padaṃ dṛṣṭvā pūrvam icchā prabhor abhūt
‹yen' êdam iha vinyastaṃ taṃ paśyeyaṃ kathaṃ nv iti.›
Taṃ ca dṛṣṭv" ârya|putreṇa sukham āsāditaṃ yataḥ
tan na mitraṃ na dharm'|ârthau kiṃ tu kāmo 'yam arjitaḥ.
Anyo 'py asti mahā|kāmaḥ sa yuṣmākaṃ na go|caraḥ
yūyaṃ hi sarva|kāmibhyo bāhyā dāru|manuṣyakāḥ.
Nirdiṣṭāḥ kāma|śāstra|jñaiḥ puruṣās tu catur|vidhāḥ
uttamā madhyamā hīnāś caturthās tu na ke cana.
Uttamo Gomukhas teṣām ārya|putras tu madhyamaḥ
adhamān kathayiṣyāmi bhavantas tu na ke cana.»

Tataḥ krodhād vihasy' êdam avocan Marubhūtikaḥ
«aho! nāgarakatvaṃ te niṣpannam anujīvinaḥ!
Api bāla|balīvarda! satyam ev' âsi Gomukhaḥ
ko nāma mānuṣa|mukhaḥ sann a|śuddham udāharet?
Uttamo Gomukhas teṣām arya|putras tu madhyamaḥ!
prabhor adhikam ātmānam itthaṃ kaḥ kathayed iti?»

10.20 Ten' ôktaṃ, «dṛḍha|mūḍho 'si! na kiṃ cid api budhyase
na hi prabhutva|mātreṇa bhavaty uttama|kāmukaḥ.
Yaḥ kāmyate ca kāmī ca sa pradhānam ahaṃ yathā
a|kāmī kāmyate yas tu madhyo 'sāv arya|putra|vat.
Yas tu kāmayate kāṃ cid a|kāmāṃ so 'dhamaḥ smṛtaḥ
te na ke cana bhaṇyante ye na kāmyā na kāminaḥ.
It' îdaṃ lakṣaṇaṃ yeṣāṃ tān vijānīta kāminaḥ
na ke cana bhavantas tu yena nir|lakṣaṇā iti.»

When you saw the footprint on the riverbank, sire, there first arose in you a desire to see the person who had made it there. When you saw him, my lord, you became happy. Thus you acquired neither a friend, nor religious merit, nor wealth, but pleasure. There is also another, great, pleasure. It is not within reach of any of you, for you are like wooden men, the opposite of pleasure-seekers. Those who know the science of pleasure have described four types of people: highest, middling, lowest, and the fourth, the nobodies. Of these, I, Gomukha, am of the highest order, and his lordship is middling. I shall come to those of the low category. As for you fellows, you are nobodies."

At this Marubhutika laughed scornfully and said, "What a consummately courteous servant you are! You childish ox! You really are cow-faced*. Who with the face of a man would say such rubbish? 'Gomukha is of the highest order and his lordship is middling'! Who would thus declare himself better than his master?"

Gomukha replied, "You are quite the idiot! You know 10.20
nothing: one does not become a pleasure-seeker of the highest order simply by being a lord. A man who is both loved and loves is of the highest order, and I am thus. A man like his lordship who does not love but is loved is middle-ranking. A man who loves a woman who does not love him is said to be of the lowliest order. Men who are neither loved nor love are called nobodies. You should recognize as lovers those who have one of the attributes of the first three. Because you have none of those attributes, you are nobodies."

Atha cāmaram ujjhitvā sphuṭann iva kutūhalāt
apṛcchad garjita|mukhaṃ Gomukhaṃ Marubhūtikaḥ.,
«Yoṣin madhu|karī y" âsāv upabhoktuṃ vyavasyati
svāmino yauvana|madhu kv' âsau? kathaya tām iti!»
Ten' ôktam, «arya|putrāya bravīmi yadi pṛcchati
na tubhyaṃ sthala|maṇḍūka na hi bhasmani hūyate!»
Atha baddh'|âñjaliḥ prahvo m" âvocan Marubhūtikaḥ
«pṛcchyatāṃ sthira|garvo 'yaṃ prasādaḥ kriyatām iti.»
Icchat" âpi tam ālāpaṃ lajjāṃ bhāvayatā mayā
a|pratyākhyāta|kathitaṃ, «kathay' êty» anumoditam.
Ath' ānand'|âśru|timire netre saṃmṛjya Gomukhaḥ
saṃkāsya śuddha|kaṇṭhaś ca ramyām akathayat kathām:
10.30 «Ath' âham arya|putreṇa yauva|rājye vibhūṣite
abhivādayituṃ devyau nar'|êndr'|ântaḥ|puraṃ gataḥ.
Tatra citraṃ mayā dṛṣṭam a|dṛṣṭaṃ divya|mānuṣaiḥ
varṇa|krama|viśuddhyā yad rājyam asy' êva bhū|pateḥ.
Padmāvatyā ca pṛṣṭo 'haṃ, ‹kim asmin putra Gomukha
paśyas' îti?› tato, ‹devi trayam› ity aham uktavān.
‹kiṃ punas trayam› ity ukte devyai kathitavān aham,
‹ṛddhiṃ vaḥ śilpināṃ śilpaṃ bahu|ratnāṃ ca gām iti.›
Atha devyā vihasy' ôktaṃ, ‹cetasyaḥ khalu Gomukhaḥ
a|cetasyo hi puruṣaḥ katham evaṃ vaded iti?›
Āsīc ca mama tac chrutvā saṃdeh'|âdhyāsitaṃ manaḥ
‹cetasyaḥ kiṃ nu guṇavān āho svid doṣavān iti?›
Na ca pṛṣṭā mayā devī sa|saṃdehe 'pi cetasi
mā sma budhyata sā bālam a|cetasyaṃ ca mām iti.
‹A|pṛṣṭaḥ ko nu kathayec cetasyam iti?› cintayan

Marubhutika put down his fly whisk, and, almost bursting with curiosity, asked the boastful Gomukha, "This bee of a girl that seeks to enjoy the honey of our master's manhood—where is she? Describe her!"

He replied, "I shall tell the prince if he asks, not you, you grounded frog: one doesn't pour sacrificial offerings into ash!"

Then Marubhutika put his palms together, bowed and said to me, "Please be so kind as to ask the stubborn fellow."

Although I wanted to hear what he had to say, I was embarrassed and allowed him to speak only by not forbidding him from doing so. Gomukha wiped his eyes, which were clouded with tears of joy, cleared his throat, and told a charming story: "When the prince had adorned the office 10.30
of crown prince, I went to the king's inner apartments to greet the two queens. I saw there a painting not seen before by gods or men, in which the purity of the range of colors was like the purity of the social order* in the king's realm. Padmavati asked me, 'Gomukha, my boy, what do you notice in here?,' and I replied, 'Three things, Your Highness.' When she asked me what they were, I said, 'Your wealth, the work of the craftsmen, and how much treasure there is in the world.'

The queen laughed and said, 'You really are a mindful man*, for how could an unmindful man speak thus?' When I heard this I was confused: was a mindful man good or bad? Despite my confusion, I did not question the queen for fear that she might think me foolish and unmindful.

I left the palace and headed for my house wondering who,

saṃcaran mandiram ahaṃ nirgato rāja|veśmanaḥ.
Paśyāmi sma rathaṃ yuktaṃ citra|cāmara|maṇḍanaiḥ
nir|antara|khura|nyāsaiḥ pārasīkais turaṃ|gamaiḥ.
Rathasya prājitā tasya puruṣo māṃ vinītavat
pratoda|garbham ādhāya mūrdhany añjalim abravīt,
10.40 ‹Bhartṛ|dāraka vijñāpyam asmin rāja|kule vayam
kula|kram'|āgatā bhṛtyā ratha|vāhana|jīvinaḥ.
So 'ham ājñāpito rājñā, ‹yath" âite pṛṣṭha|vāhinaḥ
a|cirād bhavatā rathyāḥ kriyantāṃ tura|gā iti.›
Mayā c' âite yathā|śakti skandha|dāntās tvarāvatā
na tu saṃbhāvayāmy etān kuśalair a|parīkṣitān.
Tad evaṃ ratham āruhya parīkṣyantām amī tvayā
pada|vākya|pramāṇ'|ârtha|catureṇ' āgamā iva.›
Idam|ādi tataḥ śrutvā kṣaṇam ānamit'|ānanaḥ
‹upacāro bhaved eṣa satyam ev' êty› acintayam.
Lamba|karṇam ath' âpaśyaṃ vinītaṃ lamba|śāṭakam
kāya|sthaṃ sa|maṣī|pātraṃ lekhanī|karṇa|pūrvakam.
So 'bravīd, ‹mahati kleśe pātitāḥ prabhuṇā vayam!
sarvathā dhig imāṃ kṣudrāṃ śva|vṛttim anujīvinaḥ!
Pṛthivyāṃ santi yāvantaś cetasyāḥ puruṣottamāḥ
a|cetasyāś ca kartavyaṃ teṣāṃ lekhyaṃ mayā kila.
Na c' âikam api paśyāmi yuktaṃ cetasya|lakṣaṇaiḥ
a|cetasyās tu sa|kalāṃ kṣobhayanti mahīm iti.›
Pustaka|dvaya|hastena tatra c' âikena bhāṣitam
prasārit'|âṅgulīkena mām uddiśya sa|kautukam,
10.50 ‹Āgaty' ây'|ākṛtim amuṃ nir|dākṣiṇyaṃ na paśyasi

without being asked, might explain what a mindful man was. I saw a carriage yoked to Arab horses decorated with colored fly whisks and trotting in unison. The man who was driving the carriage politely put his whip in his joined
hands, touched them to his head and said to me, 'Noble sir, 10.40
I would like you to know that I am a hereditary servant in the royal household and earn my living as a carriage-driver. The king has instructed me to make these horses, which are used to carrying riders, fit for pulling a carriage as soon as possible. I have quickly, and as best I can, tamed them to take a yoke, but I do not consider them ready because they have not been checked by experts. So, please climb aboard the carriage and check them, just as a man versed in words, sentences, meters and meanings checks the scriptures.'

When I heard all this, I lowered my head for a moment and said to myself, 'If truth be known, he's just being polite.'

Then I saw a long-eared, educated scribe in a long gown who was carrying an inkpot and had a pen behind his ear. He said, 'Our master has landed us in big trouble! I've really had enough of this pathetic dog-like existence as a servant! Apparently I have to make a list of all those fine men in the world who are mindful, and all those who are unmindful. I cannot find even one man who has the qualities of a mindful man; the unmindful are infesting the entire earth!'

A man there with two books in his hand pointed at me
with curiosity and said, 'Why don't you come and have a 10.50
look at this fellow: noble in appearance but awkward, he is like someone who practices medicine for a living but

ājīv'|ârtha|cikitsākaṃ cikitsakam iv' â|dhanam.
Ayaṃ tāvad a|cetasya|pustak'|ādau niveśyatām
ya evam anunīto 'pi rathaṃ n' āroḍhum icchati.
A|prārthito 'pi yaḥ kaś cid ārohati sa likhyatām
cetasya|pustakasy' ādau namas|kārād an|antaram.›
Tataś cetasyatā|lobhād dūram utplutya sa|tvaraḥ
mā sm' ânyaḥ kaś cid ārohad ity āroham ahaṃ ratham.
Tena vegavatā gacchann apaśyaṃ gajam agrataḥ
sukhāyamānaṃ madhurair ālāpaiḥ parikarmiṇām.
Hasty|ārohaṃ rath'|āroho vidhārya ratham uktavān
‹anyato naya mātaṅgaṃ mā cetasya|rathaṃ rudhaḥ!›
Ten' ôktam, ‹anyato yātu cetasy'|âdhyāsito rathaḥ
vihantum aham etasya n' êcchām icchāmi dantinaḥ.
A|pravṛtta|madasy' âsya madaḥ sāntvaiḥ pravartate
icchāyāś c' â|vighātena tena naḥ kṣamyatām iti!›
Avocam atha yantāraṃ, ‹na nāma yadi n' êcchati
ādhoraṇaḥ path'|ânyena rathaḥ prasthāpyatām iti.›
‹Evaṃ nām' êti› c' ôktvā sa parivartitavān ratham
‹cetasy'|āvāsa|madhyena tvāṃ nayām' îti› c' ôktavān.
10.60 Āsīc ca mama, ‹dīrgh'|āyur ayaṃ bhavatu kuñjaraḥ
rundhatā yena me mārgaṃ cetasyā darśitā iti!›
Paśyāmi sma ca vistīrṇa|śilā|tala|dharā|talam
mālya|bhūṣaṇa|dhūp'|ādi|prāya|paṇyaṃ vaṇik|patham.
Tam atikramya ramy'|âgrā harmya|mālāḥ sa|niṣkuṭāḥ
sa|śarīrā iva nyastā vāstu|vidyā|kṛtāṃ dhiyaḥ.

is a penniless quack. He should be placed at the top of the list of unmindful men: despite being asked politely, he won't get on the carriage. If anyone gets on it without even being asked, they should be written at the top of the list of mindful men, straight after the introductory benediction.'

Then, because I wanted to be mindful, I quickly—in case someone else should get on—made a big leap and boarded the carriage. It moved swiftly. I saw ahead an elephant being indulged by the kind words of its attendants. The carriage-driver pulled up the carriage and said to the mahout, 'Move the elephant out of the way: you mustn't obstruct the carriage of a mindful man!'

He replied, 'Please move the mindful man's carriage out of the way: I don't want to obstruct the wishes of this tusker. He has not started rutting, and he comes into rut through gentle coaxing and his wishes not being obstructed, so please bear with us!' I said to the carriage-driver that if the mahout was unwilling to move, he should take the carriage by a different route. He agreed and turned the carriage around. Then he said, 'I shall take you through the district
where the mindful people live.' I said to myself, 'May that 10.60
splendid elephant have a long life: by blocking my way it has shown me the mindful people!'

I saw a market street where the ground was covered in paving stones, and the shops were full of things like garlands, ornaments and incense.

Further on I saw rows of mansions with beautiful façades and pleasure gardens; they were like physical manifestations of the geniuses of the inventors of architecture. In another

Utkaṭ'|ākāra|caritāḥ sa|madāḥ pramadāḥ kva cit
tādṛśān eva puruṣān sevamānāḥ parāṅ|mukhān.

Pṛṣṭhato 'nunayantaṃ ca yuvānaṃ yuvatiṃ kva cit
tayā nirbhartsyamānaṃ ca vākyair madhura|dāruṇaiḥ:
‹Ayi ballavak' âpehi! kiṃ mā chupasi dur|bhagām?
bahu|ballavaka|cchuptāṃ chupa ballavikām iti!›

Calayantīṃ kva cit kāṃ cid vipañcīm añcit'|âṅgulim
kāṃ cit koṇa|parāmarśa|śiñjāna|parivādinīm.

Iti saṃcaramāṇo 'haṃ rathena mṛdu|gāminā
paṭhantīḥ paṭṭikā vyagrāḥ paśyāmi sma kumārikāḥ.
‹Kaḥ punaḥ syād ayaṃ grantha iti?,› śrotuṃ may" êcchatā
dūrāt prahita|karṇena sphuṭam ākarṇitaṃ yathā:
‹Sametya pūrvaṃ na svapyāt suptaṃ ca na parityajet
prāṇ'|âpānau ca yatnena samaṃ saṃdhārayed iti.›

10.70 Āsīc ca mama, ‹kā etā? viṭa|śāstram adhīyate!
manye sārathin" ôpāyair ahaṃ veśaṃ praveśitaḥ.›

Kāma|dev'|ālayaṃ c' ânyaḥ kurvan ko 'pi pradakṣiṇam
abhāṣata, ‹kṛt'|ârtho 'haṃ nidrāṃ prāpsyāmi saṃprati!
Yo 'sau vinaya|garveṇa duḥkham āste sa Gomukhaḥ!
a|vandhyaṃ yauvanaṃ kartum eṣa veśaṃ vigāhate!›

Avocam atha yantāram, ‹a|śobhanam anuṣṭhitam!

place I saw some excited young women of brazen aspect and demeanor. They were flirting with similar men who were turning their faces away.

In another place I saw a young man wooing a young lady. She was scolding him with sweetly harsh words: 'Hey, cowboy, go away! Why are you pestering an ugly girl like me? Go and grope a cowgirl who's already been touched up by lots of cowboys!

Elsewhere I saw a girl playing the lute with arched fingers, and another playing a seven-stringed lute by plucking it with a plectrum.

Travelling along like this in the now slow-moving carriage, I saw young girls busy studying writing tablets. Wanting to hear what the text might be, I cocked my ear and from afar clearly heard the following: 'After intercourse a girl should not be the first to go to sleep, and she should not leave a sleeping man. She should strive to synchronize her breathing with his.' I said to myself, 'Who are 10.70
these women? They are studying a text about debauchees! I think the carriage-driver has contrived to take me into the prostitutes' quarter.'

Some other fellow was circumambulating a temple to the god of love. He said, 'Now I've had my fill and can get some sleep! Look at that man, uncomfortable because of his pride in his propriety. It's Gomukha! He's going into the prostitutes' quarter to make something of his barren manhood!'

I said to the driver, 'You have behaved disgracefully! Turn the carriage around immediately!'

adhunā tu rathaḥ kṣipraṃ pratīpaṃ nīyatām iti!›
Ten' ôktaṃ, ‹mā trasīr veśān n' êdaṃ mātaṅga|pakkaṇam
na ca darśana|mātreṇa kaś cid bhavati doṣavān!
Atītaś ca mahān adhvā śiṣyate stokam antaram
rathaḥ kiṃ pṛṣṭhato yātu kiṃ puraḥ preryatām iti?›
Mayā tu, ‹pura ity› ukte tvaritaḥ sārathī ratham
prairayat tatra c' âpaśyaṃ mandiraṃ Mandar'|ônnatam.
Rāj'|âvarodhan'|ākāraṃ dvāḥ|sth'|âdhyāsita|toraṇam
yoṣid|varṣavara|prāyaṃ vinīta|jana|saṃkulam.
Tasmāt kanyā viniryāya hāri|hār'|ādi|bhūṣaṇāḥ
kānti|bādhita|padminyaḥ parivārya rathaṃ sthitāḥ.
Tāsām ek" âbravīt prauḍhā śiro|viracit'|âñjaliḥ
‹bhartṛ|dāraka vijñāpyam āgacchata kil' êti› mām.
10.80 Mama tv āsīd, ‹aho śaktir bata puṇyasya karmaṇaḥ
jagataḥ prabhur apy eṣā yena praiṣy" êva bhāṣate!
A|cetanair alaṃ puṇyaiḥ kila|śabdaḥ pralīyatām
yaiḥ kṛtā para|tantr" êyaṃ lakṣmīr yena ca sūcitā!›
Kiṃ tu, ‹yāni na yān' îti› saṃśayāne kṣaṇaṃ mayi
dainya|mlāna|mukh'|âmbhojās tā niraikṣanta pṛṣṭhataḥ.
Anuyātā ca tad|dṛṣṭiṃ dṛṣṭam udghāṭitaṃ mayā
vāt'|āyanaṃ kavāṭa|stha|maṇi|jāl'|âṃśu|bhāsuram.
Tena śṛṅgāra|saṃcāraṃ tāla|vṛnta|trayaṃ calat
vibhrānta|grāhiṇī|pāṇi|kara|prakara|piñjaram.
Tāla|vṛnt'|ântar'|ālīnaṃ mukham unnata|kaṇṭhakam

He replied, 'Don't be frightened of the prostitutes' quarter. It's not a settlement of outcastes and no one gets in trouble just by having a look! We have travelled the greater part of the road: a short distance remains. Should the carriage go back or be taken forward?'

When I told him to carry on, the carriage-driver quickly drove the carriage ahead. Then I saw a mansion as high as Mount Mandara. It looked like the king's harem, with gatekeepers at the arched doorway, lots of women and eunuchs, and crowds of sophisticated people. Young girls wearing beautiful garlands and other ornaments came out and stood around the carriage, putting lotuses to shame with their beauty.

A voluptuous girl among them put her joined palms to her head and said to me, 'Noble sir, I must inform you that
you are to come this way.' I said to myself, 'Shame on the 10.80
power of meritorious action, because of which this woman, despite being capable of controlling the universe, speaks as if she were a servant! Down with insentient merits, which have made this girl subservient! Damn the word "must," with its implication of royal authority!'

But, as I deliberated for a moment over whether or not to go, the girls, their lotus-like faces withered with sadness, looked behind them. I followed their gaze and saw an open window, the myriad gems in the frame of which made it sparkle with their rays. Through it I saw an elegantly moving fan made from three palm leaves; like the spread fingers of the girl waving it, it was golden. Between the

saras|taraṃga|randhra|stham unnālam iva paṅka|jam.
Cañcat|pradeśinīkaṃ ca pāṇim uccaiḥ prasāritam
su|kumāra|marut|prāptam iva vidruma|pallavam.
‹K" êyam āhvayat' îty?› etad a|vicāry' âiva yānataḥ
bhuvam āgatam ātmānam āśu cetitavān aham.

Uktaḥ sārathinā c' âsmi, ‹praṇayaṃ praṇayī|janaḥ
karotu sa|phalaṃ tena bhartṛ|putra praviśyatām.
Yāvatīṃ ca bhavān velām ih' āste tāvatīm aham
dhuryān viśramayann āse jāta|tīvra|śramān iti.›

10.90 Gaṇikābhis tv ahaṃ tābhir āraṇyaka iva dvipaḥ
vārīm iva dṛḍha|dvārām ādyāṃ kakṣyāṃ praveśitaḥ.
Praśastair anvitāṃ tatra pradeśaiḥ puṣkar'|ādibhiḥ
adhīyamāna|vinayām apaśyaṃ nāga|kanyakām.
Dvitīyāyāṃ tu kakṣyāyāṃ śilpi|kauśala|śaṃsinī
karṇī|ratha|pravahaṇe śibikāṃ ca śiv'|ākṛtim.
Praśasta|lakṣaṇa|gaṇān raṇad|ābharaṇa|srajaḥ
nānā|deśāṃs tṛtīyāyāṃ vājinaḥ sādhu|vāhinaḥ.
Caturthyāṃ viruvat|keka|cakora|śuka|śārikam
sarāva|kukkuṭa|vrātaṃ vayaḥ|pañjara|maṇḍalam.
Kalā|vinyāsa|kuśalair nān"|ākārāṇi śilpibhiḥ
su|varṇa|tāra|tāmrāṇi kalpitāni tataḥ param.
Ṣaṣṭhyāṃ tu yojyamānāni gandha|śāstra|viśāradaiḥ
dhūp'|ânulepana|mlāna|vāsanāni tatas tataḥ.
Saptamyāṃ racyamānāni raṅga|dhūpana|vāsanaiḥ

leaves of the fan I saw a face atop a long neck, like a long-stemmed lotus in a trough in the waves of a lake. And I saw an outstretched hand with a waving forefinger, like a blossom fallen from a tree floating in a gentle breeze. Before I knew it, I had got down from the carriage without even stopping to question who the girl that was summoning me might be.

The carriage-driver said to me, 'My lord, please go in so that the friendliness of these friendly people might be rewarded. While you are inside I shall wait and rest the exhausted horses.'

The first chamber had solid doors and I was taken into 10.90
it by some courtesans like a wild tusker being led to water by she-elephants. Inside I saw being schooled a young she-elephant whose features—trunk-tip and so on—were first-class. In the second chamber I saw a litter and a carriage that sang the praises of their craftsmen's skill, and a beautiful palanquin. In the third I saw fine horses from various countries. They had many excellent markings and wore tinkling ornaments and garlands. In the fourth I saw a collection of birdcages in which there were noisy partridges, parrots and mynahs, and lots of crowing cocks. In the next I saw gold, silver and copper images of various shapes made by artisans expert in the performance of their art. In the sixth chamber I saw people skilled in the science of perfumes impregnating clothes with incense and oils. In the seventh chamber I saw garments made of fine cloth like cotton, silk and linen being embellished with dyes, incense and scents. In the eighth chamber I saw techniques like

vāsāṃsi paṭṭa|kauśeya|dukūla|prabhṛtīni tu.
Aṣṭamyāṃ maṇi|muktasya prakīrṇa|bahala|tviṣaḥ
saṃskārān dṛṣṭavān asmi niśāna|vyadhan'|ādikān.
Aṣṭasv api ca kakṣyāsu mahā|mātr'|ādayaś ciram
sva|kauśalāni śaṃsanto vighnanti sma gatiṃ mama.
10.100 Āgaty' āgatya tāḥ kanyāḥ kānta|rūpa|vibhūṣaṇāḥ
abruvan, ‹kāraṇī|mūlyād bhavanto mūḍha|buddhayaḥ.
Ayaṃ ken' âpi kāryeṇa praviśan bhartṛ|dārakaḥ
dur|bhagair dhāryate kasmāt sva|śilpa|kathitair iti?›
Hema|kuṇḍala|dhāriṇyaḥ pāṇḍar'|âmbara|mūrdha|jāḥ
prayukta|ratna|puṣp'|ârgham avocan mām atha striyaḥ,
‹Dīrgh'|āyuṣā gṛham idaṃ cintā|maṇi|sa|dharmaṇā
alaṃ|kṛtaṃ ca guptaṃ ca gamitaṃ ca pavitratām.
Tataḥ saṃgatya cetasyaiś cetasya|grāma|ṇīr bhava
guṇi|saṅga|nimittā hi guṇā guṇavatām iti!›
Sūrya|kānta|śilā|kānti|nirasta|timirāṃ tataḥ
kanyā|yūtha|parīvāraḥ prāptaḥ sopāna|paddhatim.
Tayā prāsādam āruhya vāk|praspandana|varjite
prasupta iva saṃsāre citre dṛṣṭiṃ nyaveśayam.
Kalābhir atha citrābhir buddhiṃ sarva|vidām iva
a|prameya|guṇ'|ākārāṃ kanyāṃ kanyābhir āvṛtām.
Anumān'|ôpamā|śabdau su|dūre tāv upāsatām
pratyakṣeṇ' âpi tad|rūpaṃ dur|nirūpaṃ nirūpakaiḥ.
Cakṣur nirīkṣya tasyāṃ hi mūrchā|muṣita|cetanaḥ
pāṣāṇa|puruṣ'|ākāraḥ pratyakṣeṇa kim īkṣyate?
10.110 N' ēśvareṇa na dharmeṇa na pradhānena n' âṇubhiḥ

polishing and piercing being used on brilliantly sparkling gems and pearls. In all the eight chambers the master craftsmen and other artisans boasted at length about their skills and blocked my way.

The beautiful girls with their lovely accoutrements kept 10.100
coming and saying, 'The money you earn for your work has made you lot boring! This nobleman is on his way in for a reason: why do you wretches detain him with talk of your crafts?'

Then some women wearing gold earrings and white coverings over their hair offered me jewels and flowers in welcome and said, 'Like the wish-fulfilling jewel, Your Reverence has adorned, protected and sanctified this house. Please mix with the mindful and become a paragon of mindfulness, for the virtues of virtuous people are caused by contact with the virtuous!'

Escorted by a group of girls, I came to a staircase where the darkness was dispelled by the light of sunstones. I went up it to the terrace and cast my gaze upon a wonderful world that was so still and silent it seemed asleep. I saw a girl of immeasurable beauty surrounded by other girls, like the genius of the omniscient gods surrounded by the various arts. Her beauty would be impossible for observers to describe when perceiving her directly, let alone from afar through inference and analogy or verbal testimony. For after looking at her, one loses consciousness and becomes like a stone statue, so what is there to be seen by means of
direct perception? Such natural beauty cannot be created 10.110
by the supreme being, nor by the Law, nor by the original

na ca kāla|sva|bhāv'|ādyais tādṛśī su|kar'|ākṛtiḥ.
Alaṃ tad|rūpa|kathayā tad|guṇ'|ākhyāna|dīrghayā
kariṣyatha svayaṃ tasyā guṇa|rūpa|vicāraṇām!
Tad ahaṃ tāṃ namas|kartum uttam'|âṅg'|āhit'|âñjaliḥ
tad|rūpaṃ vismitaḥ paśyat tūṣṇīm āsaṃ muhūrtakam.
Unnamayya mukhaṃ s" âpi vikasal|locan'|ôtpalam
‹ciram Gomukha jīv' êti!› māṃ pūrvaṃ samabhāṣata.
Mama tv āsīd, ‹aho dhūrtā mugdh'|ābhā c' âpi khalv iyam
evaṃ nir|abhimānā ca yay" âhaṃ samay'|ârthitaḥ!
Ninditā ca may" ātmīyā buddhir vāk ca pramādinī!
hastau praśastau tābhyāṃ hi pūrvam eva kṛt" âñjaliḥ!
Sarvato hasta|mātro 'ham a|cetana|mukh'|ādikaḥ!
a|pramattā hi jīvanti mṛtā eva pramādinaḥ.›
Iti cintayate mahyaṃ tayā dāpitam āsanam
nikharva|danta|caraṇaṃ tatra c' âham upāviśam.
Sā ha māṃ kṣaṇam āsīnam apṛcchad: ‹Gomukhaḥ kutaḥ
āgacchat' îti› kathitaṃ mayā, ‹rāja|kulād iti.›
Tay" ôktaṃ, ‹kuśalī rājā devyau c' ântaḥ|purāṇi ca
Rumaṇvad|ādayo v" âpi mantriṇaḥ sa|parigrahāḥ.
10.120 Kumār— iti› tataḥ kiṃ cid ullāpy' â|sphuṭa|rephakam
tūṣṇīṃ|bhūtā kṣaṇaṃ dṛṣṭiṃ nās'|âgre niś|calām adhāt.
Pṛṣṭe Hariśikh'|ādīnāṃ krameṇa kuśale tayā
mayā, ‹kuśalam› ity uktaṃ mām apṛcchad asau punaḥ,
‹Jānāmy eva yathā buddhiḥ sarvaiḥ sarvāsu kheditā
prakarṣo yasya yasyāṃ vo vidyāṃ kathaya tām iti.›

substance, nor by atoms, nor by time, nor by innate nature, nor by any other fundamental principle of the universe.

But enough of this talk of her beauty, which would be even longer with a description of her virtues. You shall make up your own mind about both her virtues and her beauty! I joined my palms and bowed my head to greet her; as I beheld her beauty I was astonished and fell speechless for a moment. She raised her face, her wide eyes like lotuses, and spoke first, saying, 'Long live Gomukha!' I said to myself, 'What a crafty woman she is, despite her air of innocence! And shameless too, to have invited me in like this! Curses on my mind and tongue for their negligence! Well done my hands for coming together in greeting! I'm all hands—I have no mind, no mouth, nor anything else! Only alert people are alive: those who aren't are as good as dead!'

While I was thinking this, she offered me a seat with legs made from short elephant tusks and I sat down on it. A short while after I had sat down she asked me where I had come from and I replied that I had come from the palace. She said, 'How are the king and the two queens and the harem and Rumanvan and the other ministers and their
families and the pr—' whereupon she faltered slightly and 10.120
pronounced the 'r' indistinctly. Then she fell silent for a moment and stared at the tip of her nose.

When she asked one by one how Harishikha and the others were I replied that they were well, and then she asked me, 'I know, of course, that you have all applied your intellects to every science, but please tell me which of you excels in what.'

May" ôktam, ‹arya|putrasya prāvīṇyaṃ gaja|nītiṣu
mānuṣair a|vigāhye ca gāndharva|jñāna|sāgare.
Daṇḍa|nītau Hariśikhaḥ śāstreṣu Marubhūtikaḥ
rath'|ādi|yāna|vidyāsu niṣṭhā|yātas Tapantakaḥ.
Mayā tu karabheṇ' êva śamīnām agra|pallavāḥ
gṛhītāḥ sarva|vidyānām eka|deśā manīṣitāḥ.›

S" âbravīd, ‹atha vidyānām āsām āsevanasya kaḥ
bhavatām ucitaḥ kālaḥ katamad vā vinodanam?›

May" ôditaṃ, ‹tri|yām'|ânte prabuddhāḥ stuta|devatāḥ
maṅgal'|âlaṃ|kṛtāḥ paścād itihāsam adhīmahe.
Anujñātās tato vaidyaiḥ su|gandhi|sneha|dhāriṇaḥ
abhyasyāmaḥ sa|yānāni niyuddhāny āyudhāni ca.
Tataḥ snātvā ca bhuktvā ca muhūrtaṃ yāpita|śramāḥ
artha|śāstrāṇi śaṃsantaḥ mahā|kāvyāni c' āsmahe.
10.130 Niśā|mukhe tataḥ saudhe sāndra|candra|prabhā|jiti
ramāmahe sukhaṃ kāntair veṇu|tantrī|rutair iti.›

Atha sā nayan'|ântena śravaṇ'|ânta|visāriṇā
bālikām antik'|āsīnāṃ dṛṣṭv" âpaśyan mad|antikam.
Tataḥ kṛcchrād iv' ôtthāya nitamba|bhara|mantharam
may" āsanne niviṣṭā sā manāg api na lakṣitā.
Evam any" âpi gaṇikā tṛṇavad gaṇitā mayā
yad" âparā tad" āyātā rūpiṇī rūpa|devatā.

S" âbravīt, ‹kaṣṭam āyātam ito guru guror vacaḥ
itaś c' âtithi|sat|kāraḥ kim atra kriyatām iti?›

I replied, 'Our noble lord is skilled in elephant lore and the ocean of the science of music, unfathomable by ordinary men. Harishikha has mastered political science, Marubhutika scholarship, and Tapantaka has excelled in the study of chariots and other vehicles. I, however, like a young camel taking the endmost buds of the *śamī* tree, have taken appetizing parts from each of the sciences.'

She asked, 'When do you usually apply yourselves to these sciences, and how do you amuse yourselves?'

I replied, 'We wake at the end of the night. After worshipping the gods and adorning ourselves with auspicious markings we study the epics. Then, with the permission of the doctors, we put on scented oils and practice mounted, armed and unarmed combat. Then, after bathing and eating, we rest for a while before sitting down to read political
treatises and classical poetry. At nightfall, in a whitewashed 10.130
hall whose brilliance surpasses that of the full moon, we relax and enjoy the lovely sounds of the flute and the lute.'

Then, after looking out of the corner of her eye (which reached up to her ear) at a girl sitting nearby, she looked in my direction. The girl got up with some difficulty and, moving slowly because of the weight of her behind, sat next to me. I did not take even the slightest notice of her. After I had ignored a second courtesan in similar fashion, another one approached, a beautiful girl, a goddess of beauty.

She said, 'My coming over here is fraught with difficulty: on the one hand, there is the weighty command of my mistress, and on the other, the deference due to a guest; what am I to do?'

May" ôktaṃ, ‹devatābhyo 'pi guravo guravo yataḥ
tasmād gurur guror ājñā s" âiva saṃpādyatām iti.›

S" âbravīd, ‹na tvay" ôtkaṇṭhā kāryā mitrāṇy a|paśyatā
kariṣyati nir|utkaṇṭham iyaṃ tvā Padmadevikā.›

Mam' âbhiprāyam ūhitvā lajjamān" êva s" âbravīt
‹na yuktam an|anujñātaiḥ preṣyair āsannam āsitum.
Idaṃ tv āstīrṇa|paryaṅkaṃ śaraṇaṃ bhartṛ|dārakaḥ
praviśya ratha|saṃkṣobha|khedaṃ vinayatām iti.›

Tat praviśya tad|ādeśād vikasad|ramaṇīyakam
śayanaṃ hema|ratn'|âṅgaṃ s'|âpāśrayam apāśrayam.
10.140 Pāda|sthāne tataḥ sthitvā s" âbravīt, ‹kaḥ karotu vaḥ
manda|puṇyair a|saṃbhāvyāṃ pāda|saṃvāhanām iti?›

‹Pāda|saṃvāhanaṃ kāryaṃ bhadraṃ syād yena kena cit
saṃvāhaka|viśeṣeṇa kim atr' êti?› may" ôditam.
Tayā tv ālambite pāde pāṇibhyām abhavan mama
‹nir|doṣe mayi ken' êyaṃ prayuktā viṣa|kanyakā?
Karaṇāny a|sva|tantrāṇi na jāne kī|dṛśaṃ manaḥ
viceṣṭāni ca me 'ṅgāni! dhig an|āryām imām iti!›

Sā tu saṃvāhya caraṇau muhūrtam idam abravīt
‹kathaṃ dāsa|jano vakṣaḥ śrāntaṃ vaḥ sevatām iti?›

Mama tv āsīt, ‹pragalbh" êyam an|ācārā ca yā mama
spṛṣṭa|pāda|talau hastāv urasy ādhātum icchati.›

Mam' âbhiprāyam ūhitvā s" âbravīd darśita|smitā
‹uraḥ spṛśati vaḥ ko vā karābhyāṃ mūḍha|dhīr iti?›

Āsīc ca mama, ‹k" âpy eṣā devatā brahma|vādinī?

I replied, 'Teachers are more important even than gods, so you must obey your mistress's weighty command.'

The mistress said, 'Do not be anxious that you aren't with your friends: Padmadevika here will put you at ease.'

Guessing my thoughts, Padmadevika blushed slightly and said, 'It is not right for servants to sit close without being invited. My lord, a bed has been made in this room. Go in and rid yourself of the fatigue caused by bumping about in the carriage.'

At her instruction I went in there and lay down on a big beautiful bed made from gold and gems and furnished with pillows. She stood at the foot of the bed and said, 'Who is 10.140
to massage your feet? It cannot be done by those of little merit.'

I replied, 'A foot massage by anyone would be good. What need is there here for a special masseur?' As she held my feet in her hands, I said to myself, 'I haven't done anything wrong, so why has this poison-maiden* been set on me? I have lost control of my faculties, I do not know what has become of my mind and my limbs are paralyzed! Curse this vulgar girl!'

She massaged my feet for a while and then said, 'How is a servant girl to tend to your weary chest?'

I said to myself, 'This arrogant girl has no manners: after touching the soles of my feet with her hands she wants to put them on my chest!

Guessing my thoughts, she smiled and said, 'Who could be so foolish as to touch your chest with their hands?'

I wondered whether the girl might be an omniscient

para|citta|jñatā yasmān n' âsti rāgavatām iti.›
Tay" ôktaṃ, ‹ratha|saṃkṣobha|jāta|khedasya vakṣasaḥ
stan'|ôtpīḍitakaṃ nāma saṃvāhanam a|ninditam.
Yadi v" âham anugrāhyā vakṣo vā prabala|śramam
tato mām anujānīta bhartṛ|tantrā hi yoṣitaḥ.›
10.150 Āsīc ca mama, ‹dhīr" êyaṃ nirasta|karuṇā ca yā
anujñāṃ labhate yāvat tāvad āste nir|ākulā.›
Ath' âinām abruvaṃ, ‹bāle par'|āyattaṃ nibodha mām
yaḥ saṃvāhana|śāstra|jñaḥ sa sva|tantraḥ pravartatām.›
Urasā stana|sāreṇa sā madīyam uras tataḥ
saṃvāhayitum ārabdhā sa|kampena sa|vepathu.
Sarvath" âlaṃ visarpantyā prasaṅga|kathay" ânayā
saṃkṣipta|vastu ramye 'rthe na kadā cid virajyate.
Tataḥ krīḍā|gṛhāt tasmād bāhyāṃ tām eva vīthikām
upāgacchaṃ muhūrtāc ca tām ev' ārya|sut" āgatā.
Vanditvā prasthitaṃ sā māṃ kṣaṇam ālokya vismitā
ālapan madhur'|ālāpā smita|pracchādit'|âratiḥ,
‹Idaṃ bhavanam ātmīyaṃ pratyavekṣyaṃ sadā tvayā
dṛśyamāno bhujaṃ|go 'pi kālena paricīyate!›
Atha vastr'|ântam ālambya madīyaṃ Padmadevikā
‹vijñāpyam asti me kiṃ cit tac ca n' âdy' êty› abhāṣata.
Tato hṛdaya|vāsinyā Padmadevikayā saha
tam eva ratham āruhya kumār'|āgāram āgamam.
Tatra yuṣmān a|bhuñjānān paśyāmi sma mayā vinā
upahāsaṃ ca kurvantaṃ taṃ tathā Marubhūtikam.
10.160 Dine 'nyatra ca sevitvā kṣaṇaṃ yuṣmān ahaṃ punaḥ

goddess, for the ability to read minds is not found in those who are lustful.

She said, 'On a chest exhausted from bumping about in a carriage the massage known as the "breast press" is excellent. If I am to be given the privilege, or rather, if your chest is very tired, then allow me. Women only do what their masters tell them.'

I said to myself, 'This girl is strong-willed and pitiless. 10.150
She will wait calmly until I give her permission.' So, I said to her, 'Young lady, consider me to be under another's control. Let one who knows the science of massage take charge.' At this she started to massage my chest with her exquisite breasts. They heaved, my chest quivered. . . .

But enough of this rambling digression! A succinct tale about agreeable things never becomes boring.

Later I went from that house of fun up to the outer terrace. After a while the lady of the house appeared there. I greeted her and was about to be on my way when she looked at me in dismay for a moment before hiding her anxiety with a smile and saying in a sweet voice, 'You must always consider this house as your own. Even a snake, when watched, becomes familiar in time!'

Then Padmadevika grasped the hem of my robe and said, 'I have something to tell you, but not today.' With Padmadevika having taken up residence in my heart I boarded the carriage and went to the prince's house. There I found you, abstaining from food in my absence, and Marubhutika, making jokes.

Another day, after briefly waiting upon you, I went again 10.160

gatv" ârya|duhitur mūlam āseve Padmadevikām.
Uktaś c' ârya|duhitr" âham, ‹a|dhīrāḥ suhṛdas tava
vṛtt'|ânto 'yam atas teṣāṃ mā gamat karṇa|go|caram.›
Tataḥ pratiṣṭhamānaṃ mām avocat Padmadevikā
‹tad vaḥ kiṃ vismṛtaṃ kāryam iti?,› ‹m" êti!,› may" ôditam.
Tay" ôktaṃ, ‹kathayiṣyāmi punar apy āgatāya te
dhatte saṃdhriyamāṇaṃ hi rahasyaṃ ramyatām iti.›
Ath' âparasmin divase gatv" ârya|duhitur gṛham
śoka|mūka|pravṛddh'|âsram apaśyam a|balā|janam.
Kara|dvay'|āvṛta|mukhī stambhe lagnā parāṅ|mukhī
manda|śabdaṃ mayā dṛṣṭā krandantī Padmadevikā.
Tām apṛccham, ‹mahā|rājye Vatsa|rāje su|rājani
jaṅgamasya kutaḥ śoko yuva|rāje ca rājati?›
Na kiṃ cid api s" âvocan mayā pṛṣṭ" â|sakṛd yadā
tadā kila viṣaṇṇo 'haṃ mumoha ca papāta ca.
Tatra c' âikā pramṛjy' âsraṃ mām avocat sa|cetanam
‹tvan|nāth" âślāghanīy" êyam a|śocyā Padmadevikā.
Asyās tu svāminīṃ paśya yuva|rāje virājati
yasyāḥ śok'|ôpataptāyā yato rakṣas tato bhayam.
10.170 Atha vā paśya tām eva paśyatām eva pīḍyate
tvā|dṛśāṃ suhṛdāṃ yasyāḥ sama|duḥkha|sa|jīvanam.›
Tad|āvedita|mārgeṇa gatvā pramada|kānanam
dṛṣṭā kamalinī|kūle tatr' ârya|duhitā mayā.
Mṛṇāla|śaival'|âmbhoja|nalinī|dala|saṃstaram
śoṣayantī sa|niśvāsair muhur viparivartanaiḥ.
Mudrikālatikā nāma dārikā hārikā dṛśaḥ
tad|aṅka|nyasta|caraṇā dhyāyantī puruṣ'|ôttamam.

to the noble lady's establishment and sported with Padmadevika. The noble lady said to me, 'Your friends are excitable, so do not let this episode reach their ears.'

Then Padmadevika said to me as I was on my way out, 'Have you forgotten what was to be done?,' and I replied that I had not. She said, 'I will tell you when you next come. A well-kept secret is a lovely thing.'

The next day that I went to the noble lady's house I found the women tearful and dumbstruck with grief. I saw Padmadevika sobbing gently, leaning on a pillar, both her hands covering her averted face. I asked her, 'How can people in the kingdom be sad when the king of Vatsa is reigning benignly and there is an illustrious crown prince?' When she said nothing despite my repeated requests, I was upset and collapsed in a faint.

One of the girls wiped her tears and spoke to me when I came to: 'Padmadevika has you as her master, so the shameful girl is not to be pitied. But look at her mistress: there is an illustrious crown prince, but she is stricken with grief and troubled by that which protects her! Just take a 10.170
look at the girl, on seeing whom, her friends, such as you, simultaneously suffer a sympathetic sadness!'

She showed me the way to a pleasure garden where I found the noble lady on the banks of a lotuspond. She was drying out the bed of lily stems, duckweed and lotus leaves with her sighs and relentless rolling about. There was a beautiful girl there called Mudrikalatika, on whose lap she had put her feet as she fixed her thoughts on her perfect man. I quickly went up to her, joined my palms in

Ath' ôpagamya saṃbhrāntas tāṃ kṛt'|âñjalir abravam
‹devī duḥkh'|âṅga|dānena saṃbhāvayatu mām iti.›
S" âbravīd, ‹alam ākarṇya pravṛddha|sukha|bhāginaḥ
tathā mam' â|pratīkārāṃ lajjā|śoka|karīṃ kathām?
Ko hi Nandana|saṃcāri|kāminī|jana|kāmukaḥ
taran makara|gambhīrāṃ viśed Vaitaraṇīm iti?›
Tataḥ prasādayantī tāṃ Mudrikālatik" âbravīt
‹bhartṛ|dārikayā kaś cit smaryate na vimānitaḥ!
Yadi ca svayam ākhyātum a|śaktā bhartṛ|dārikā
tato mām anujānātu dhṛṣṭo hi gaṇikā|janaḥ.›
Evam ukt" âbravīd evam, ‹evaṃ nāma nigadyatām!
a|kṛtvā sāhasaṃ kair vā mahāl̃ labdho mano|rathaḥ?
10.180 Na c' êmaṃ Gomukhād anyaḥ śrotum ālāpam arhati
bheda|saṃdhāna|dakṣo hi dūtaḥ kārye niyujyate.›
Ath' ôtsārya tato deśān Mudrikālatikā kathām
mahyam ākhyātum ārabdhā: ‹kṣaṇam adhīyatāṃ manaḥ.
Bharato nāma rāj" āsīt tri|varg'|ânta|parāyaṇaḥ
sa samāhṛtavān kāntāḥ kumārīr ā mah'|ôdadheḥ.
«Yuga|pat pariṇīy' âham etāḥ sarvā rahogatāḥ
sukhāny anubhaviṣyāmi saṃtatān' îty» acintayat.
Yasyāś ca prathamaṃ tena gṛhītaḥ kampanaḥ karaḥ
tasyām eva sa saṃtuṣṭaḥ śuddha|puṇy'|ârjit'|ākṛtau.
Pariśeṣās tu yās tāsāṃ mano|nayana|hāriṇaḥ
mano|ruha|kar'|ākārān aṣṭau prākalpayad gaṇān.
Gaṇe gaṇe ca pramukhāṃ mukhar'|ābharaṇ'|āvṛtām

greeting and said, 'Noble lady, please honor me by sharing your sorrow.'

She said, 'Why listen to my tale, which brings shame and grief and has no remedy, when you are blessed with great happiness? What lover of the amorous damsels that roam Indra's paradise would enter the deep monster-infested Vaitarani*?'

Then Mudrikalatika calmed her down by saying, 'It is not as if the man that your ladyship dreams of has been slighted! If your ladyship is unable to tell the tale herself, then allow me: courtesans are a daring lot.'

She replied, 'All right, tell it as it is! Who has ever realized a great ambition without being bold? And no one is more 10.180
suited to hearing it than Gomukha, for when employing a go-between one should use someone skilled in breaking and making alliances.'

Mudrikalatika took me aside and started to tell the story: 'Pay attention for a moment. There was a king called Bharata who was completely devoted to the three ends of man*. He gathered together lovely girls from as far as the great ocean. He thought that he would secretly marry them all at the same time and experience a constant stream of pleasures. However, he was satisfied by the very first girl whose trembling hand he took: her beauty had been earned through pure meritorious acts. Out of the rest of those girls, who were charming to both the mind and the eyes and whose beauty inspired passion, he made eight troupes. The king had the foremost girl in each troupe wear tinkling ornaments and he allowed her to have a throne, a parasol

anujñāt'|āsana|chattra|cāmarām akaron nṛpaḥ.
Tā gaṇ'|ântar|gatā yasmād anyāsāṃ ca mahattamāḥ
taṃ mahā|gaṇikā|śabdam alabhanta nar'|âdhipāt.
Mahā|guṇās tataś c' ânyās tato 'py anyās tataḥ parāḥ
yāvad ghaṭaka|saṃghaṭṭa|kaṭhora|kaṭayaḥ khalāḥ.
Ya eṣa gaṇikā|bheda idānīm api dṛśyate
tataḥ kālāt prabhṛty eva Bharatena pravartitaḥ.
10.190 Gaṇa|mukhyās tu yās tāsām ekasyāṃ kila saṃtatau
jātā Kaliṅgasen" êyaṃ sarasyām iva padminī.
Sur'|âsur'|ôraga|strīṇāṃ nindantī rūpa|saṃpadam
anayā tanayā labdhā s" êyaṃ Madanamañjukā.
Eṣā rāja|kulaṃ yāntīṃ dṛṣṭvā mātaram ekadā
«aham apy āci yām' îti» punaḥ punar abhāṣata.
Jñātvā tu dṛḍha|nirbandhāṃ s" ācī duhitaraṃ priyām
gṛhīta|bāl'|ābharaṇām anayan nṛpa|saṃsadam.
Atha rāja|kulād eṣā nivṛttā lakṣitā mayā
sa|vikāsaiḥ sa|toṣ" êva kapola|nayan'|âdharaiḥ.
Sthitā saṃprasthit" āsīnā niṣīdantī ca saṃtatāḥ
karoti sma sakhī|madhye rāj'|āsthāna|gatāḥ kathāḥ.
Dina|śeṣam atiprerya kṣaṇa|dāṃ ca sa|jāgarā.
Prātaḥ sādaram ādatta citraṃ maṇḍanam ātmanaḥ.
Prasthitā prasthitāṃ dṛṣṭvā rāj'|āsthānāya mātaram
tayā pṛṣṭā, «kva yās' îti?,» «yatra tvam iti!,» c' âbravīt.
Tay" ôktam «an|anujñātaiḥ putri gantuṃ na labhyate
rāj'|āsthānaṃ tanu|snehāḥ paruṣā hi nar'|âdhipāḥ.
Tena māto nivartasva labdh'|ânujñā gamiṣyasi
dhṛṣṭā hi dveṣyatāṃ yānti praṇayinyo 'pi yoṣitaḥ.»

and a fly whisk. Because they were from the troupes and were greater than the others, the king called them "great courtesans"*. Then there were other distinguished courtesans, followed by others graded in rank down to wenches whose hips were calloused from being rubbed by the water pots they carried. This division of courtesans established by Bharata has been in use since then and is still seen today.

Our Kalingasena was born into one of the great courte- 10.190
sans' lineages, like a lotus in a pond. She had a daughter who puts to shame the perfect beauty of the women of the gods, demons and snake-people. This is her, Madanamanjuka. One day she saw her mother going to the palace and insisted, "Mother*! I'm coming too!"

When she realized how determined her dear daughter was, she had her wear some jewelry suitable for a child, and took her to the palace. On her return from the palace I saw from her blossoming cheeks, eyes and lips that she appeared happy. Standing up, walking about, sitting and lying down, she continuously spoke to her friends of the king's assembly. She passed the rest of the day and the night without sleeping.

In the morning she carefully put on various ornaments. When she saw her mother set out for the king's assembly she set forth too. On being asked by her mother where she was going, she replied, "Where you're going!" Her mother said, "My girl, one can't go to the king's assembly without being invited, for kings are small-hearted and cruel. So, young lady, go back; you can go when you are invited. No one likes pushy women, even if they are affectionate."

10.200 Madhurāś c' ôpapannāś ca śrutvā mātur imā giraḥ
kaṭukā dur|ghaṭāś c' êyaṃ manyamānā nyavartata.
Dṛṣṭa|naṣṭa|nidhān" êva daridra|vaṇig|aṅganā
mukta|nidr"|āśan'|ālāpā śayy"|âika|śaraṇ" âbhavat.
Ekadā prastuta|kathāḥ sakhīr iyam abhāṣata
«svaptum icchāmy ahaṃ sakhyas tāvan nirgamyatām iti.»
Yātāsu tāsu manasā yat satyaṃ mama śaṅkitam
etāḥ prasthāpitāḥ sakhyaḥ kim a|kāraṇam etayā.
Yā sakhībhir vinā nidrāṃ n' âiva labdhavatī purā
tasyās tā eva nighnanti nidrām iti na badhyate.
Cintayitv" êti tiṣṭhantī jāla|vāt'|āyan'|āvṛtā
maṇḍana|vyāpṛtām etāṃ paśyāmi sma sa|darpaṇām.
Abhi|rāja|kulaṃ sthitvā baddh'|âñjalir abhāṣata
«janm'|ântare 'pi bhūyāsam ahaṃ tasmin vadhūr iti!»
Dukūla|pāśam āsajya kaṃdharāyām an|antaram
udalambayad ātmānaṃ sa|tvarā nāga|dantake.
Vegād iṣur iv' āgatya prāṇ'|âpaharaṇ'|ôdyatam
kaṇṭha|pāśaṃ tam etasyāḥ kāla|pāśam iv' âkṣipam.
Śayanīyam ath' ānīya sa|jalair vyajan'|ânilaiḥ
balāt pratyānayaṃ saṃjñāṃ preta|rāja|kulād aham.
10.210 Kramen' ônmīlya nayane mantharā tāmra|tārake
ninīya mayi mattaś ca pratyāhṛty' êdam abravīt,
«Tan mitram ati|kaṣṭād yad vyasanāt kila rakṣati
vyasane praharantyā tu śatrutvaṃ darśitaṃ tvayā.
Ahaṃ hi sarva|duḥkhānām idam utpannam ālayam
tvayā jīvitam ujjhantī vidhṛtā kim a|kāraṇam?
Ānukūlyena nirvāhya kālam eka|pade tvayā

When she heard her mother's kind and pertinent words, 10.200
she turned back, thinking them sharp and cruel. Like a merchant's wife who has found a treasure and then lost it, she did not sleep, eat or talk, and her bed was her only refuge.

One day, in the middle of a conversation, she said to her friends, "I want to sleep, friends, so please leave." After they had left I was very worried indeed about why she had sent her friends away with no explanation. It was inconceivable that the friends without whom in the past she had been unable to sleep now prevented her from sleeping.

When I realized this, I hid behind a latticed window and saw her with her mirror busy making herself up. Then she stood facing the palace, joined her palms and said, "Let me be a bride there in my next life!" Straight away she put a noose of fine cloth around her neck and quickly hanged herself from a peg. As quickly as an arrow I rushed over and removed the noose, which was about to strangle her as though it were the noose of Yama*. Then I put her to bed and wrenched her consciousness back from Yama's palace by sprinkling her with water and fanning her.

She gradually opened her bloodshot eyes. When she fo- 10.210
cussed on me she turned away and said, "A friend protects one from a terrible predicament; by bringing me back to my predicament you have shown yourself to be an enemy. My life has become home to every kind of sorrow. Why have you pointlessly prevented me from abandoning it? After spending so much time as my friend, by obstructing my wishes you have suddenly shown that you don't like

vighnantyā mama saṃkalpaṃ darśitā pratikūlatā.
Yad etad ucyate loke sarvathā na tad anyathā
a|śeṣ'|ôpāya|duḥ|sādhyo mitram śatrur mahān iti.»
Bruvāṇām ity a|saṃbaddham ity enām aham abravam
«svāmini prabhur ity asmān upālambhena takṣasi.
Idaṃ kathaya nas tāvad vyasane 'bhyudaye 'pi vā
svāminyā vayam āyāte kasmin n' âbhyantarī|kṛtāḥ?
Jāt" âsi kṛpaṇ" êdānīṃ dāsa|vargam apāsya yā
tanum ekākinī tyaktvā sukham āsitum icchasi.
Duḥkha|hetum ataḥ śaṃsa yadi sādhyaṃ bhaviṣyati
jīviṣyāmas tataḥ sarvā mariṣyāmo viparyaye.»
Atha sthitvā kṣaṇaṃ tūṣṇīṃ śanakair idam abravīt
eka|jīva|śarīrāyai kiṃ tubhyam api kathyate?
10.220 Atha jānanty api tvaṃ māṃ nirlajjayitum icchasi
idam ākhyāya te ko vā strībhyaḥ sāhasikaḥ paraḥ?
Ahaṃ rāja|kulaṃ yātā deven' āhūya sādaram
dakṣiṇaṃ parigh'|ākāram ūrum āropitā tadā.
Upaviṣṭas tu nṛ|pater ūrau vāme nṛ|p'|ātma|jaḥ
mayā dṛṣṭaḥ praviṣṭaś ca hṛdayaṃ me '|nivāritaḥ.
Dahano 'pi vasann antar na dahaty araṇīṃ sa tu
saumyo 'pi puṇyavān asmān nir|dhūmaṃ dagdhum icchati!
Sa hetur asya duḥkhasya sakṛd|darśanam āgataḥ
adhunā śrūyamāṇo 'pi kiṃ vā vilapitair iti?»
Śrutv" êdam aham asyās tu jātā yat satyam ākulā
upāyam etam āśaṅkya samudr'|ôtseka|duṣ|karam.
«Hā h" êti» hasiten' ôccair gūhamānā viṣaṇṇatām

me. People are absolutely right when they say that a friend is a mighty foe and hard to defeat by any means."

While she was going on in this unreasonable fashion, I said to her, "My lady, because you are my mistress you are hurting me with your abuse. But just tell me this: in what situation, good or bad, did your ladyship ever not take me into your confidence? Now you have become niggardly: you disregard your servants and want to find happiness by abandoning your body in solitude. So tell me the reason for your unhappiness. If there is a way to overcome it then we shall all live. Otherwise we shall die."

She stayed silent for a moment and then said quietly, "Do you need to be told, even though you share my body and
soul? Despite knowing already, you want to embarrass me 10.220
by having me tell you. There is no one more inconsiderate than a woman!

When I went to the palace, His Majesty fondly called me over and sat me on his right thigh, which was like an iron bar. The king's son sat on his left thigh and when I saw him he went straight to my heart. Fire, even though it lives in the kindling stick, does not burn it; he, on the other hand, despite being as cool as the moon and virtuous, wants to incinerate me! He is the cause of my sorrow. I have seen him once and now I am hearing about him as well. But that's enough complaining!"

When I heard this from her I became very upset indeed, and was worried that remedying the situation would be as difficult as making the ocean overflow. Hiding my anxiety by laughing loudly, I comforted her with platitudes. "My

etām āśvāsayāmi sma niḥ|sārair vacanair iti.
«Muñca svāmini saṃtāpam! api vidyā|dhar'|ēśvaram
vaśayeyaṃ tava prītyai kiṃ punaḥ puruṣ'|ēśvaram!
Kiṃ tu tvarāvatā śakyaṃ na labdhaṃ phalam īpsitam
rājāno 'pi hi sām'|ādīn krameṇ' âiva prayuñjate.
Tena dhairya|prakarṣeṇa manaḥ saṃdhṛtya cañcalam
loken' âlakṣitā kāṃś cit sahasva divasān iti.»
10.230 Taṃ c' êyaṃ siddham ev' ârtham arthi|bhāvād abudhyata
antaś c' âkathayat toṣaṃ vikasan|mukha|paṅka|jā.
Divase divase c' âitāṃ vacobhir madhur'|ân|ṛtaiḥ
kārya|saṃsiddha|saṃbaddhair darśit'|āśām ayāpayam.
Vandhy'|ôttarair yad" ātmānaṃ vañcyamānām amanyata
moktu|kāmā tadā prāṇān punar utprekṣitā mayā.
Tataḥ saṃbhrāntayā gatvā may" âsyā mātur antikam
saṃpradhārya tayā sārdham upāyo 'yam anuṣṭhitaḥ.
Śarīraṃ rāja|putrasya dvitīyam iva Gomukhaḥ
sa kena cid upāyena veśam āśu praveśyatām.
Sa eva saha|cāritvād āneṣyati nṛ|p'|ātma|jam
manaḥ|śrotra|har'|ālāpo vasantam iva kokilaḥ.
Kaliṅgasenayā c' âyaṃ vṛtt'|ântaḥ kathitas tadā
Padmāvatyai tayā c', «âsi cetasy' êti» bhāṣitaḥ.
Tataḥ sārathi|kāya|stha|hasty|āroh'|ādibhis tathā
dhūrtair asmat|prayuktais tvaṃ veśam etaṃ praveśitaḥ.
Tisṛṇāṃ ca prayuktānām abhavad bhavataḥ priyā
tantrīṇāṃ varṇa|tantr" îva madhurā Padmadevikā.
Sā tu nirvartita|sv'|ârthā suhṛd|artha|parāṅ|mukhī
na nivedayate tubhyaṃ sv'|ârtha|bhraṃśa|viśaṅkayā.

lady, don't be anxious! To make you happy, I would subjugate the emperor of the sorcerers, let alone a human king! But those who hurry do not get what they want: even kings only use the methods of diplomacy and so forth in gradual succession. So with great patience restrain your flighty
mind, and suffer for a few days out of the public eye." In the 10.230
way that those who want something will, she thought that her desire had been fulfilled, and her blossoming lotus-face told of her inner happiness.

Every day I kept her hopes up with sweet untruths about my successes in the affair. When she realized that she was being deceived with empty words I saw that she was again suicidal. In a panic I went to her mother and after conferring with her the following scheme was put into action: "Gomukha is like a second body to the prince. Somehow he must soon be made to enter the courtesans' district. Because they are always together, he will bring the prince, just as the *koyal*, whose chatter charms the mind and the ears, brings spring."

Kalingasena then told Padmavati about the plan and she called you mindful. After that we used tricksters like the charioteer, the writer and the mahout to make you enter the prostitutes' quarter. You became fond of one of the three women that we used, sweet Padmadevika; it was as though she was the lute string in harmony with you. But after achieving her aim she neglected that of her friend: worrying that her desires might be frustrated, she did not tell you
what to do. When our mistress realized that no further steps 10.240
were being taken, her long sighs became unstoppable. She is

10.240 N' ôpāyam a|paraṃ dṛṣṭvā prayuktaṃ bhartṛ|dārikā
a|sādhy'|āyata|niśvāsā nir|āśā dṛśyatām! iti.
Tad idaṃ duḥ|sahaṃ duḥkhaṃ yasmād asmākam āgatam
tvad|āyattaḥ sa śeṣaś ca saṃvidhattāṃ bhavān iti.›
Ath' âham abruvaṃ, ‹kasmān nakha|chedyam upekṣayā
kuṭhāra|chedyatāṃ nītaṃ bhavatībhir idaṃ tṛṇam?›
Svayam eva tato gatvā devī vijñāpitā mayā
‹mucyatām eṣa saṃtāpaḥ! siddhaṃ viddhi prayojanam!
Yuva|rāj'|ârthinī devī sa ca' rta|guṇa|vatsalaḥ
saṃdhātā Gomukhaś c' êti dhanyas trika|samāgamaḥ!
N' âsty eva ca mam' āyāsaḥ śarat|kānty|unmanā yataḥ
rāja|haṃso hi nalinīṃ svayam ev' ôpasarpati!
Alaṃ c' ālāpa|jālena sarvath" âhaṃ nṛ|p'|ātma|jam
svāminyai kārayiṣyāmi praṇāmam a|cirād iti!›
S" âbravīd, ‹na na saṃbhāvyam idaṃ nāgarake tvayi
kiṃ tu prastāvam āsādya yatethāḥ kārya|siddhaye.
A|prastāva|prayuktā hi yānti niṣ|phalatāṃ kriyāḥ
an|iṣṭa|phalatāṃ v" âpi kopayitvā prabhūn iti.›
Tatas tasyai namas|kṛtya kumāra|vaṭakām agām
ucchiṣṭān āgataś c' âsmi gṛhītvā modak'|ādikān.
10.250 Tāṃ ca vijñāpayāmi sma, ‹rāja|putreṇa modakāḥ
svayam ārabhya hastābhyāṃ yuṣmabhyaṃ prahitā iti.›
S" âbravīj, ‹jālam apy etad āśvāsayati mā|dṛśam
āśvasanti kṣaṇaṃ dṛṣṭvā mṛgā hi mṛga|tṛṣṇikām.
Mālya|candana|tāmbūla|vāso|bhūṣaṇa|dhūpanaiḥ
yuṣmābhiḥ preṣitān' îti tām āśvāsitavān aham.

desperate: look at her! This, then, is the unbearable sorrow that has befallen us. The rest is in your hands: you must make suitable arrangements!'

I replied, 'Why did you ladies carelessly let this trifling grass-like affair, which could have been cut with fingernails, become so that it has to be cut with an axe?' Then I went and spoke to the lady myself: 'Stop torturing yourself! Consider your goal achieved! This is a lucky conjunction of three things: your ladyship longs for the prince, he is fond of truth and virtue, and Gomukha is the matchmaker! And I don't even have to make an effort, because the royal swan longs for the beauty of autumn and will go of his own accord to the lotus pond! But enough of all this verbal trickery: I shall have the prince pay his respects to your ladyship before long!'

She replied, 'You are a clever fellow, so it is not impossible. However, for success in the matter you should make your attempt at an opportune moment, for actions undertaken at inopportune moments do not bear fruit and, by angering the powerful, can even have unwanted results.'

I paid her my respects, went to the princes' cloister and returned after taking the leftover sweets. I said to her, 'The 10.250
prince has sent you these sweets after shaping them with his own hands.'

She replied, 'Even if this is a trick it is cheering to a woman in my condition: deer are temporarily consoled by the sight of a mirage.' I kept her spirits up with garlands, sandal, betel, scents, ornaments and incense, saying that you had sent them.

‹Eṣa vijñāpayāmy adya, śvo vijñāpayit" êti› ca
a|labdh'|âvasaraḥ kālam etāvantam ayāpayam.
Atha mām abravīd devyāḥ purato Mudrikālatā
‹aho saṃbhāvanā kāryā mahā|nāgarako bhavān!
«Praṇāmaṃ kārayām' îti» visphūrjya bhavatā tathā
kim iyaṃ vañcyate mugdhā pattra|puṣpa|phal'|ādibhiḥ?
Atha vā tiṣṭha tāvat tvam! aham ev' ānayāmi tam
viraktam api saṃdhātum alaṃ kauśalam asti naḥ!›
Evam uttejjitas tasyā gurubhir vacanair aham
‹phalena jñāsyas' îty!› uktvā prastāv'|âvahito 'bhavam.
Yātrāyāṃ tu pravṛttāyām abhyāse 'tra yad eva me
tan mayā kāritā yūyaṃ kṣiptvā Hariśikh'|ādikān.
Yat tat pravahaṇaṃ gacchat pathi yuṣmābhir īkṣitam
tad arya|duhit" âdhyāsta vidyud abhram iva dhvanat.
10.260 Tatra yat tan|mukhasy' ârddhaṃ lalāṭa|nihit'|âṅguli
yuṣmabhyaṃ darśitaṃ vandyaṃ tat tayā vandamānayā.
Yac ca vijñāpitā yūyam, ‹ānataṃ mukuṭaṃ manāk
unnamyatām iti› mayā tatr' âp' îdaṃ prayojanam.
Āsīd āsāṃ, ‹praṇāmo 'yam arya|putreṇa nāgaraḥ
kṛtas toṣayatā kāntām asmākaṃ svāminīm iti›.
S" êyaṃ kāmayate devaṃ devī Madanamañjukā
prajñā|parākrama|prāṇaṃ lakṣmīr iva nar'|âdhipam.
A|yatn'|ôpanatā c' êyaṃ na pratyākhyātum arhati

I thought, 'I shall tell him today. I'll tell him tomorrow,' but I never got an opportune moment and whiled away all this time.

Then Mudrikalatika said to me in front of the noble lady, 'Oh! We must congratulate you, you great man-about-town! "I shall have him pay his respects," you boasted. So why have you been deceiving this innocent lady with leaves, flowers, fruits and so forth? Now, you just wait! I shall bring him myself: I have wiles enough to matchmake even a passionless man!'

Spurred on by these ominous words, I replied, 'You'll understand when you see how it all turns out!' and awaited my chance.

During the festival, I contrived to have you next to me by moving Harishikha and the others out of the way. Her ladyship was sitting in the carriage that you saw travelling along the road, like lightning in a rumbling cloud. The 10.260
half-concealed face inside with the fingers touching the forehead—it was hers and she showed it to you as a greeting. And when I told you to adjust your crown because it had slipped a little, that too had a purpose. The ladies thought that it was a polite greeting by Your Majesty, done to gratify your beloved, their mistress. This lady Madanamanjuka loves you like the goddess of wealth loves a king who holds wisdom and bravery as dear as life. She has come to you unbidden and does not deserve to be rebuffed. She is like a fresh garland of *mālatī* flowers: her virtues and beauty are most alluring! She has been bitten by the snake of love, and must be treated immediately, for those whose insides

nav" êva mālatī|mālā lobhanīya|guṇ'|ākṛtiḥ!
Daṣṭ" ân|aṅga|bhujaṃgena laghu saṃbhāvyatām asau
na hy āśīr|viṣa|dagdh'|ântrāḥ kṣamante divasān iti!»
Iti Gomukhataḥ śrutvā kathāṃ nava|daśa|priyām
tat|kath"|âpahṛta|vrīḍaḥ prakāśam aham abravam:
«Tad" âiva hṛdaye 'smākaṃ rāj'|ôtsaṅga|niṣaṇṇayā
a|śīrṇaṃ manmatha|taroḥ prakīrṇaṃ bījam etayā.
Tad|guṇa|śravaṇ'|âmbhobhiḥ sicyamānaṃ tadā tadā
bādhamānaṃ mano jātam ucchvasat|karkaś'|âṅkuram.
Tad dohadam iv' āsādya priyāṃ pravahaṇe sthitām
kampa|niḥ|śvāsa|jananān amuñcat pallavān iva.
10.270 Samāpt'|âvayavo yāvan mano|bhava|mahā|taruḥ
na samākramya mṛdnāti tāvad darśaya tām iti.»
Ten' ôktaṃ, «nartan'|ācāryāv aspardhetāṃ parasparam
‹tvat|pravīṇo 'ham› ity uktau tau ca bhū|patinā kila,
‹Alaṃ vāṃ kalahaṃ kṛtvā karma|śāstra|vidau yuvām
yasya yā kuśalā śiṣyā sa nartayatu tām iti.›
Śvaḥ Suyāmunadantāṃ ca tasmād ārya|sutāṃ ca naḥ
nṛtyantīṃ nṛ|patir draṣṭā tatra draṣṭā stha tām iti.»
Yā svābhāvika|rūpa|khaṇḍita|jagad|rūp'|âbhimānā priyā
śṛṅgār'|ādi|rasa|prayoga|su|bhagā jāyeta sā kīdṛśī
ity adhyāsita|cetasā katham api prakrāntayā cintayā
paryaṅk'|âṅka|vivartin" ārta|tanunā nītā tri|yāmā mayā.

iti Rathyā|saṃlāpo nāma sargaḥ.

are inflamed by snake venom cannot survive the passing of the days!"

Gomukha's story was delightful to a nineteen-year-old, and when I heard it from him it removed my shyness and I announced: "The moment the girl sat in the king's lap she sowed the seed of the evergreen tree of love in my heart. Being sprinkled over and over again with the water of tales of her qualities, it became a blossoming *karkaśa* sprout, and my mind became troubled. When it came across my sweetheart in the carriage, it was as if its craving had been satisfied, and it put forth buds that made me tremble and sigh. It has reached maturity, so before I am outgrown and 10.270
crushed by the great tree of desire, show her to me!"

Gomukha replied, "The two dancing teachers have been vying with one another over who is the more skilled, and the king has said to them, 'Enough of your arguing. You both know the rules. Let each of you have his best pupil dance!' So tomorrow the king is going to watch Suyamunadanta and our good lady dance: you will see her there!"

My beloved's natural beauty shattered the pride of all those in the world who were beautiful, and as I thought of how she would look when delightfully engaged in portraying the dramatic sentiments of love and the like, I struggled to get through the night, tossing and turning my stricken body about the bed with increasing anxiety.

Thus ends the Conversation on the Road.

CANTO 11
THE WINNING OF MADANAMAÑJUKĀ

Atha nāgarak'|ākāras
tad|ākāra|suhṛd|vṛtaḥ
saṃprasthāpya manaḥ pūrvaṃ nṛ|p'|āsthānam agām aham.
Tatra puṣpaka|saṃsthāna|mañca|sthānaṃ mahī|patim
praṇamya tad|anujñātaṃ mañc'|ântaram aseviṣi.
Raṅg'|âṅgaṇam ath' ālokya kuśala|prekṣak'|ākulam
nṛty'|ācāryau namas|kṛtya mahī|pālam avocatām:
«Rājann upānta|nepathye bhṛtye vaḥ samupāgate
draṣṭum icchatha yāṃ pūrvam ājñāpayata tām iti.»
So 'bravīd, «nṛtya|gīt"|ādi|kalā|śāstra|viśāradaḥ
Gomukhaḥ sa ca yām āha sā pūrvaṃ nṛtyatām iti.»
Tābhyām āgatya pṛṣṭaś ca, «kā pūrvaṃ nṛtyatām iti»
sa, «Suyāmunadant" êti» tad|upādhyāyam ādiśat.
Tatas tasyāṃ pranṛttāyāṃ pranṛttā nṛtya|vedinaḥ
raṅga|śeṣas tu niśceṣṭaḥ suṣupt'|âvasthāṃ gataḥ.
Pratyāhṛtya tataś ceto hriyamāṇaṃ balāt tayā
mano|netr'|âṅga|saṃcārair an|āhāryair acintayam,
«N' ânugantum alaṃ Rambhā nṛttam asyāḥ sa|Menakā
kuta eva parājetum a|balā bālikā priyā?
11.10 Rāja|haṃsaḥ pipās"|ândhaḥ prāptaḥ paṅka|jinīṃ yathā
paṅk'|āvila|jalāṃ paśyet tath" âdhyāsam ahaṃ priyām.»
Avocaṃ Gomukhaṃ c' êdaṃ, «jīyamānāṃ priyām aham
a|śaktaḥ prekṣituṃ tena raṅgān nirgamyatām iti!»
Ten' ôktam, «icchayā gantum āgantuṃ vā na labhyate
Vatsa|rāja|kulāt tena muhūrtaṃ sthīyatām iti!»
Viratāyāṃ tatas tasyāṃ purāṇ'|ârka|rucāv iva

DRESSED LIKE A GENTLEMAN and surrounded by similarly attired friends, I went to the palace—having sent my mind ahead. The king was sitting on a throne shaped like Kubera's chariot. I bowed to him and he invited me to sit on another throne. The two dance teachers saw that the theatre hall was filled with expert observers and after bowing to the king they said: "Sire, your two servants have arrived backstage. Please tell us whom you would like to see first."

He replied, "Gomukha knows the treatises on arts such as dancing and singing. He shall decide who is to dance first." They went and asked him who should dance first and he told Suyamunadanta's teacher that it was to be her. When she danced those who knew how to dance danced too, while the rest of the audience was motionless and went into a trance. As she stole my mind with her apparently uncontrived emotions, eye movements and gestures, I pulled it back and thought, "Rambha* and Menaka* could not follow the dance of this lady: how on earth is my weak and childlike sweetheart going to win? Just as a royal swan, 11.10
blinded by thirst, might go to a lotus pond and find the water clouded with mud, so have I been mistaken about my beloved."

I said to Gomukha, "I can't watch my sweetheart being beaten; let's leave the theatre!"

He replied, "One cannot come and go at will from the palace of the king of Vatsa; wait a moment!"

When Suyamunadanta had finished, my beloved brightened up the theatre like moonlight brightening up the

jīva|lokam iva jyotsnā priyā raṅgam arañjayat.
Apṛccham Gomukhaṃ, «c' āsāṃ katamā Padmadevikā
Mudrikālatikā c' êti» sa vihasy' êdam abravīt,
«Kīrti|Kāntyor iyaṃ madhye yā Lakṣmīr iva rājate
eṣā naḥ svāminī devī vāmato Mudrikālatā.
Na c' êyaṃ śakyate jetum alaṃ vaḥ śaṅkayā yataḥ!
dṛṣṭā kena śaraj|jyotsnā kha|dyota|prabhayā jitā?
Mayā vijayamān" êyam an|ekaṃ nartakī|śatam
dṛṣṭā saṃbhāvayāmy asyās tena nṛtta|guṇān iti.»
Gomukh'|âbhimukho yāvat s'|âvadhānaṃ śṛṇomy aham
tāvaj, «jaya jay' êty» uccair vimuktaḥ prekṣakair dhvaniḥ.
Raṅgād dṛṣṭā ca niryāntī bādhyamān" êva sā mayā
dainya|vepathu|vaivarṇya|viṣādaiḥ saha|jair iva.
11.20 Tato visarjit'|āsthānaṃ namas|kṛtya mahī|patim
svam āvāsaṃ vrajāmi sma kāntā|cintā|puraḥ|saraḥ.
Gomukhaṃ c' âbravaṃ, «kasmān mām idānīm upekṣase?
na hy ādeśam upekṣante tvā|dṛśā mā|dṛśām iti!»
Ten' ôktam, «aparaḥ kaś cit pratyay'|ârthaṃ visarjyatām
śraddhāsyati na me vākyaṃ vipralabdhā hi sā mayā.»
«Eṣām anyatamaṃ yāhi gṛhītv" êti» may" ôdite
«Marubhūtika ev' âtra yogya ity» ayam uktavān:
«Ayaṃ Hariśikhas tāvan nītyā vakra|gatiḥ kṛtaḥ
apāya|śatam ālokya kadā cij jālam ālikhet,
‹Kathaṃ kaṣṭatame bālo vyasanānāṃ catuṣṭaye
yat|pradhānaṃ striyas tatra rāja|putraḥ pravartyate?›
Evam aṅguli|bhaṅgena vicāry' âlīka|paṇḍitaḥ

world after the light of the dying sun has gone out. I asked Gomukha which of them was Padmadevika and which Mudrikalatika. He laughed and said, "The one who looks like Lakshmi* between Kirti* and Kanti* is our lady mistress; Mudrikalatika is on the left. And don't you worry, she can't be beaten! Who has seen the light of the autumn moon surpassed by that of a firefly? I have seen her beat hundreds of dancing girls so I have a high regard for her dancing skills."

While I was turned toward Gomukha and listening attentively, the audience shouted out cries of victory, and I saw her leaving the theatre as though afflicted by depression, trembling, pallor and disappointment, and they appeared
not to be put on. The king dismissed the assembly and I 11.20
bowed to him before heading for home worried about my sweetheart*.

I said to Gomukha, "Why are you now disregarding me? Your sort do not disregard the orders of people like me!"

He replied, "You must send someone else to win her confidence. She has been deceived by me and will not believe what I say." When I told him to take someone else from among my retinue, he replied that only Marubhutika was suitable: "Political science has made Harishikha here unable to get straight to the heart of the matter. He will consider a hundred possible calamities and might portray the situation as a trap, saying, 'Why should the young prince get involved in the perilous tetrad of vices, the worst of which is women?' Wagging his finger and deliberating thus, the bogus scholar might even ruin our chances, so he should

vihanyād api naḥ kāryaṃ tasmād eṣa na yujyate.
Tapantako 'pi bālatvān mūḍhaḥ śūnya|mukho yataḥ
tasmād evaṃ|vidhe kārye niyogaṃ n' âyam arhati.
Vikram'|âika|rasatvāc ca samartho Marubhūtikaḥ
abhyasta|sāhasas tasmād eṣa prasthāpyatām iti.»

Tatas tau sahitau yātau cirāt tu Marubhūtikam
prāptaṃ Hariśikho 'pṛcchat, «kiṃ vṛttaṃ bhavator iti.»

11.30 Ten' ôktam, «āvayos tāvad veśa|madhyena gacchatoḥ
āyāty abhimukhī y" âiva s" âiva yāti parāṅ|mukhī.
Bhañjantī c' âṅgulīḥ krodhād vadaty ārakta|locanā
‹na spraṣṭavyo na saṃbhāṣyo Gomukhaḥ pāpavān iti.›

Kruddha|dauvārik'|ākrānta|hāṭaka|stambha|toraṇaiḥ
kakṣyā|dvāraiḥ praviṣṭau svaḥ sthānam arya|sut"|āsthitam.
Tatr' âikā dārik" âvocad, ‹dārikāḥ paśyat' âdbhutam!
dhūrten' ânena cāturyād gomayaṃ pāyasī|kṛtam!
Aparādho 'yam etāvat sarpaḥ prāṇa|haraḥ kṛtaḥ
tam eva paśyat' ânena vācālena guṇī|kṛtam.›

Vandamāno yadā kopāt svāminyā n' âbhinanditaḥ
saṃbhrāntaś ca vilakṣaś ca tadā tām āha Gomukhaḥ,
‹Manye niṣ|kāraṇaṃ kopaṃ devyāḥ ko nāma mā|dṛśaḥ
sevakaḥ paracitta|jñaḥ svāminaṃ kopayed iti?›

Tath" ânyatamayā kopāt tāla|vṛnta|bhṛt" ôditam
‹kathaṃ niṣ|kāraṇo nāma? kim idaṃ laghu kāraṇam?
Utkaṇṭh" ādarśam icchantī kasy' âpi cira|kāṅkṣitam
tvayā nartayatā kāntā kim iyaṃ sukham āsitā?

not be used. And, because of his youthfulness, Tapantaka is foolish and empty-headed, so he should not be employed in a task like this. Marubhutika is intent on valor alone, is capable and has exercised his courage: he should be sent."

Those two left together. It was a long time before Marubhutika returned. Harishikha asked him what had happened to the pair of them. He replied, "As we went through 11.30
the courtesans' district every woman that we met would turn her head and walk away. Angrily wagging their fingers and red-eyed, they would say, 'Gomukha is not to be touched nor spoken to. He is a wicked man.'

Through the doors to the inner apartments, whose arches had golden columns on which were leaning angry doorkeepers, we entered the room where the noble lady was. One of the ladies there said, 'Girls, behold a miracle! With his cunning this rogue has turned cow dung into rice pudding! Let's say his crime is a poisonous snake. He tells you to look at it, and the smooth-tongued fellow will have turned it into a rope—a virtue*!'

When, in her anger, the noble lady did not return his greeting, Gomukha was both upset and disappointed. He said to her, 'I don't think you have any due cause to be angry, madam: what servant like me, who understands the minds of others, would anger his master?'

Then another girl, fan in hand, said angrily, 'How can you say she has no due cause? Is this cause trivial? She has long been hankering after a glimpse of a certain fellow, so why, when you were arranging the dancing, did you leave her sitting pretty? But that aside, why did you then

Atha vā tad gataṃ nāma svāmī kiṃ kāraṇaṃ tvayā
paśyann abhimukhaṃ prītyā sa tathā vi|mukhī|kṛtaḥ?
11.40 Bhavān paśyatu vā mā vā tvad|vidheyo yuvā janaḥ
tvam icchasi jayaṃ yasyāḥ kim asau na parājitā?›
Tato bhiy" âvanamitaṃ mukham unnamya Gomukhaḥ
uktavān, ‹paśyat' ân|arthaṃ doṣo bhūto guṇo 'pi naḥ!
Yadi prāk svāminī nṛtyet tayā rājā su|toṣitaḥ
kadā cid itarāṃ n' âiva paśyed vṛtta|kutūhalaḥ.
Tadā ca guṇa|vidveṣī jano vaktā bhaved yathā
«pakṣa|pātān nar'|êndreṇa dṛṣṭā Madanamañjukā.»
Itarā yadi nṛtyantī tena dṛṣṭā bhavet tadā
n' Ôrvaśīm api paśyet sa kuto Madanamañjukām!
Prītyā yaś c' ônmukhaḥ paśyan kṛtaḥ svāmī parāṅ|mukhaḥ
may" ôpāyaḥ prayukto 'sau, «katham?» ity avadhīyatām!
Na Suyāmunadantāyāḥ śakyaḥ kartuṃ parā|bhavaḥ
kṛt'|ânukaraṇaiḥ sākṣād Bharaten' âpi nṛtyatā.
Arya|putre tu vimukhe yuṣmābhiḥ sā parājitā
sahajair iva vaivarṇya|viṣāda|sveda|vepanaiḥ.
Tena bravīmi sev" âpi yāti yady aparādhatām
bhakty|ārādhita|bhartāraḥ sevakā hanta duḥ|sthitāḥ!
Atha vā s'|âparādho 'pi dūtaḥ saṃmānam arhati
saṃdeśa|śravaṇāt tena saṃmānayata mām iti›.
11.50 Atha s" âtra parāvṛtya prasāda|viśad'|ānanā
īṣad|vihasita|jyotsnā|salila|snapit'|âdharā,
‹Ayi candra|mukhaṃ mā sma Gomukhaṃ paruṣaṃ vada!
na hi Vats'|ēśvar'|āsannāḥ śrūyante strī|suhṛd|druhaḥ.
An|ālāpena yac c' âsi kṣaṇam āyāsito mayā

distract your master when he was looking lovingly in her direction? Whether you realize it or not, the young man 11.40
is under your influence. Did she not lose, the girl whose victory you desired?'

Gomukha's head had been hanging down in trepidation. He raised it and said, 'Look at this injustice! Even my good offices have become a vice! If your mistress were to have danced first the king might have been completely satisfied by her and, having lost interest, he would not have watched the other girl. Then the cynical people would have said that the king was biased toward Madanamanjuka. After seeing the other girl dance he would not have watched even Urvashi, let alone Madanamanjuka! So when I distracted my master while he looked on lovingly, I was being crafty. How? Listen! Suyamunadanta could not have been beaten, even if Bharata himself had copied her dance. But when the prince had his face turned away, you defeated her with your apparently unaffected pallor, depression, perspiration and trembling. That is why I say pity the poor servants who wait on their masters with devotion if their good offices are taken for offenses! Moreover, even a messenger who is at fault deserves respect, so please show me respect by listening to my message.'

At this she turned around. Her face was glowing with 11.50
happiness and her lips were bathed in the moonlight of the flicker of a smile, as she said, 'Oh, don't speak harshly to moon-faced Gomukha! One never hears of those in the inner circle of the king of Vatsa acting maliciously toward ladies or friends. Forgive me for briefly troubling you by

tat kṣamasva na hi svasthā bādhante tvā|dṛśām iti.›
  Tataḥ sā Gomukhen' ôktā, ‹draṣṭum icchati vaḥ priyaḥ
saṃdehaś ced iyaṃ mudrā tadīyā dṛśyatām iti.›
  Tay" ôktaṃ, ‹kumbha|kārāṇāṃ koṭir vasati vaḥ pure
koṭiḥ kim iti n' ānītā na hi te kṣīṇa|mṛttikā?›
  Ten' ôktaṃ, ‹kena v" ānītā mudrā vā mṛttikā|mayī?
na hy ārabdha|mahā|kāryāḥ pramādyanti sa|cetasaḥ!
Yaugandharāyaṇa|sutaḥ priyaṃ mitraṃ priyasya vaḥ
svāminā preṣitaḥ prītyā dṛśyatāṃ Marubhūtikaḥ!›
  Atha devī namas|kṛtya prītā vijñāpitā mayā
‹yat saṃdiśati naḥ svāmī yuṣmabhyaṃ tan niśāmyatām.
Preritas tvām ahaṃ draṣṭuṃ yena Lakṣmīm iv' âlasaḥ
krīḍat" âsmad|vidhair eṣa vilakṣaḥ kriyatām iti.›
  Prasthitāyāṃ tato devyām āha māṃ Padmadevikā
‹iyaṃ prasādhyate yāvat tāvad āstāṃ bhavān iti.›
11.60 Devyā saha praviśy' ântar muhūrtād iva sā tataḥ
āha prakṛṣṭa|pramudā praphulla|nayan'|ôtpalā,
‹Mayā Kaliṅgasenāyai tayā gatvā Rumaṇvate
ten' âpi bhūmi|pataye vṛtt'|ânto 'yaṃ niveditaḥ.
Ten' ôktaṃ, «kim ih' ākhyeyaṃ? taruṇo nanu dārakaḥ?
jīva|loka|sukhāny eṣa tasmād anubhavatv iti.»
S" êyaṃ rājñ" âbhyanujñātā guruṇā manmathena ca
iyam āyāti te paścād yātu tāvad bhavān iti?›
  Atha praviśya saṃbhrāntā pratīhārī nyavedayat

not speaking: people at ease with themselves don't trouble people like you.'

Gomukha replied, 'Your beloved wants to see you; if you don't believe it then take a look at this, his seal.'

She replied, 'Tens of millions of potters live in your city: why didn't you bring that many seals, for there is no shortage of clay?'

He answered, 'Who has brought a seal made of clay? When they undertake an important task, intelligent people do not do things by halves! The son of Yaugandharayana is a dear friend of your beloved and has been sent with affection by my master. Behold Marubhutika!'

I bowed before the delighted lady and said to her, 'Pay heed to our master's message! Like a lazy man being sent to see the goddess of wealth, I have been sent by him to see you. Please disconcert him by enjoying a joke with a man like me!'*

Then her ladyship went out and Padmadevika said to me, 'Please wait while she does her makeup.'

After an hour or so Padmadevika returned with her la- 11.60
dyship. Her lotus eyes blossomed wide with delight as she said, 'I told the news to Kalingasena, she went to Rumanvan and told him, and he told it to the king. The king said, "What is there for me to say on the matter? Is my son not a young man—let him experience life's worldly pleasures!" The lady has the permission of the king, her mistress and the god of love. She will follow you: please go ahead!'"

Then the lady gatekeeper hurried in and said, "Gomukha is here with a carriage and has asked to be given an

«sa|yāno Gomukhaḥ prāha laghu śrāvaya mām iti.»
May" ôktaṃ, «Gomukhas tāvad ekākī praviśatv iti.»
Sa praviśy' ôktavān, «dvāre devī kiṃ vidhṛt" êti?» mām.
«A|jñāta|pramadā|saṅgam ākulī|bhūta|mānasam
kuru nāgarakaṃ tāvat tvaṃ mām» ity aham uktavān.
Ten' ôktaṃ, «yuddha|velāyāṃ damyante tura|gā iti,
yad etad ghuṣyate loke tad etat tathyatāṃ gatam.
Na nāgarakatāṃ prāptum upadeśena śakyate
iyaṃ hi mokṣa|vidy" êva prayog'|āvṛtti|sādhanā.
Saṃkṣepatas tu vakṣyāmi yad yad devī kariṣyati
tat tad ev' ânukuryās tvaṃ dakṣo hi labhate śriyam.»
11.70 Anuśiṣya sa māṃ evaṃ niryāy' ānīya ca priyām
«sukhaṃ supyāstam» ity uktvā yathā|svaṃ sa|suhṛd gataḥ.
Tataḥ praviśya dayitā mām ardh'|âkṣṇā niraikṣata
kṛtaṃ tath" âiva ca mayā vanditena ca vanditā.
Sarvathā yad yad ev' âham anayā kāritas tadā
tad ev' ânukaromi sma nartan'|ācārya|śiṣya|vat.
Atha buddhv" ânukūlaṃ mām iyam anv|artha|vedinam
smitvā s'|ôtkampa|romāñcaṃ gāḍham aṅgam apīḍayat.
Tato 'ham an|apekṣy' âiva tat|kṛt'|ânukṛta|kramam
a|śarīrasya kasy' âpi gato bhūtasya vaśyatām.
Strī|puṃsatām āgatayor an|abhipreta|nidrayoḥ
pradoṣa eva kṣaṇadā kṣīṇā kṣaṇavad āvayoḥ.
Prātaḥ pravahaṇen' âiva priyām ādāya Gomukhaḥ
mātur ev' ānayad gehaṃ man|mānasa|puraḥ|sarām.

immediate audience."

I replied, "For the time being, have only Gomukha come in."

He entered and said to me, "Why has her ladyship been kept back at the gate?" I answered, "I'm worried because I do not know how to interact with young women—quickly, turn me into a man-about-town!"

He replied, "The saying that horses are tamed in the hour of battle has been proved true! One cannot become a man-about-town by instruction. It is like the science of liberation—mastered through repeated practice. But I'll give you a hint: copy whatever the noble lady does. He who is dexterous wins the prize!"

After instructing me thus he went out and fetched my 11.70
sweetheart. He said "Sleep well!" to us both and then he and his friends went to their homes. My sweetheart came in and gave me a sideways glance; I did the same. She greeted me; I greeted her. I copied everything that she did, like a pupil copying a dance instructor. When she realized that I was favorably inclined and felt the same way as her, she smiled and pressed tightly against my tingling and trembling body. I forgot the plan of copying her actions and fell under the power of some incorporeal spirit of love. She became a woman, I became a man, and we had no desire for sleep. The night was over in an instant for us; it felt like it was still evening!

In the morning Gomukha put my beloved in a carriage and took her to her mother's house, accompanied by my heart. A few days passed like this and my love continued

Vardhamāna|rater evam atiyāteṣu keṣu cit
dineṣu mama saṃprāptaḥ senā|nīr idam abravīt,
«Ady' âṣṭāsu prayāteṣu muhūrteṣu pravakṣyati
mauhūrt'|ânumato rājā rātreḥ śānti|puraḥ|saram.
Tārayiṣyāmi Yamunām ahaṃ yātrā|gataṃ janam
yuṣmābhir api kartavyaṃ yat tad ājñāpyatām iti».
11.80 May" ôktaṃ, «Gomukho gatvā yuṣmān vijñāpayiṣyati»
iti tasmin gate mahyaṃ Gomukhena niveditam,
«Adha sa|kāmuka|gaṇaḥ śvo gantā gaṇikā|gaṇaḥ
ten' âiva sahitā yūyaṃ gantāraḥ śanakair iti.»
Gomukhena tu vṛtt'|ânte kathite 'smin Rumaṇvate
pratiṣṭhe sa|suhṛt prātaḥ pṛṣṭhato jana|saṃhateḥ.
Tac ca krīḍā|gṛhaṃ prāpya kalpitaṃ Yamunā|taṭe
divasaṃ gamayāmi sma taṃ tri|yāmā|mukh'|ôtsukaḥ.
Gomukh'|ānītayā sārdham āsitvā kāntayā saha
niśāyāṃ yāta|kalpāyām apaśyaṃ rudatīm imām.
«Kim etad iti» pṛṣṭā ca mayā saṃbhrānta|cetasā
yadā n' ôktavatī kiṃ cit tad" ânyā dārik" âbravīt,
«Apaiti guṇavat saṅgād doṣo doṣavatāṃ kila
gaṇikā|śabda|doṣas tu n' âinām ady' âpi muñcati.
Kāśī|rājasya yā kanyā vṛtā tubhyaṃ purodhasā
tasyāś cāmara|dhāriṇyā bhavitavyaṃ kil' ânayā!
S" êyam utprekṣya tad duḥkhaṃ dāruṇaṃ maraṇād api
viṣa|pāna|kṛt'|ôtsāhā hātum icchaty asūn iti!»
May" ôktam, «aham apy aṅgaṃ tvad|viyoga|ruj" āturam
nity'|ôtkṣapitam a|kṣībaṃ tyaktvā sthāsyāmy a|vedanaḥ!»
11.90 Ity asminn eva samaye prāptā Hariśikh'|ādayaḥ
vṛtt'|ântam evam ākarṇya bhīṣaṇaṃ sa|bhiyo 'bhavan.

to grow stronger. One day the leader of the armies came to me and said, "Today, after eight *muhūrtas** have passed, the king, as advised by the astrologers, will set forth in the calm of the night. I shall take the festival-goers across the Yamuna. Please tell me what you intend to do."

I replied that Gomukha would come and tell him. When 11.80
he had gone Gomukha said to me, "The troupe of courtesans is leaving tomorrow, together with that of their lovers. You should accompany them, without any ceremony." Gomukha told Rumanvan this turn of events and I set out with my friends in the morning, after the crowds.

I reached the house of fun that had been built on the bank of the Yamuna, and passed the day there eager for nightfall. Gomukha fetched my beloved and I spent the night with her. When it was almost over I saw her crying. I anxiously asked her what was the matter. When she didn't say anything another girl said, "Even though it is said that the faults of the wicked disappear in the company of the virtuous, the stain of the word 'courtesan' does not leave her even now. The chief priest has chosen the daughter of the king of Kashi to be your wife. Perhaps this lady will have to carry her fly whisk! She would consider that a tragedy more dreadful even than death, and has made up her mind to drink poison—she wants to kill herself!"

I replied, "I too shall solemnly abandon my body, which will be stricken by the sickness of separation from you and emaciated from fasting. Then I shall be free of sorrow!" At 11.90
that very moment Harishikha and the others arrived. When they heard the terrible news they became frightened. After

Tataḥ saṃbhāṣya suhṛdāv avocan Marubhūtikaḥ
«vayam eva viṣaṃ pūrvaṃ pibāmaḥ kalpyatām iti.»
Tato Hariśikhen' ôktaṃ, «kv' âsau saṃprati Gomukhaḥ?
yo hi mūlam an|arthasya sa tāvat pāyyatām iti!»
Tena Gomukham āhvātuṃ prahit" āgatya dārikā
abravīd, «Gomukho vakti, ‹kiṃ may" âtaḥ prayojanam?
Dīrghajīvita|nāmānam adhyāyaṃ cira|vismṛtam
aham adhyetum ārabhdo vaidyāt prāṇa|pradād iti.›»
Tato Hariśikhen' ôktaḥ kruddhena Marubhūtikaḥ
«preryamāṇaṃ gal"|āṣṭrābhiḥ śīghram ānaya taṃ śaṭham!»
«Yas tvayā ghaṭito 'n|arthaḥ svāmino jīvataḥ sukham
svāminyā saha saṃyogaḥ so 'yam evaṃ vijṛmbhate!»
So 'bravīt, «so 'yam āyāto vādaḥ saṃprati satyatām
‹jvariṣyām' îti› saṃcintya maṇḍaṃ pibati muṇḍitaḥ!
Sa kālas tāvad āyātu svāminī yad viśaṅkitā
tatr' âiva vidyāma nyañcaḥ pāsyāmas tyajyatāṃ tvarā.
11.100 Atha v" âlaṃ pralāpena mahī|pālaṃ Tapantakaḥ
vijñāpayatu ten' âsya dattaḥ pūrvam ayaṃ varaḥ,
‹A|prasaṅge 'pi bhavatā kāryā vijñāpanā mayi›
siddhiṃ yāsyati c' â|vaśyaṃ mā sma śaṅkāṃ karod iti!»
It' îmām anukūlābhir vāgbhir āśvāsya Gomukhaḥ
mātur ev' ānayan mūlaṃ prāviśāma tataḥ purīm.
Kumāra|vaṭakā|sthena may" ânūktas Tapantakaḥ
«Gomukhena yad ākhyātaṃ tat kāryaṃ sādhyatām iti.»
Tapantakas tu s'|āsphoṭam, «idaṃ siddham iti» bruvan

talking to his two friends, Marubhutika said, "We shall drink the poison first: let's prepare it."

Then Harishikha said, "Where is Gomukha now? He is the cause of this disaster. Have him drink the poison first!" He sent a girl to summon Gomukha. She returned and reported that Gomukha had said, "Why should I care? I have started studying a long-forgotten treatise called 'Longevity' with a doctor who can give the gift of life."

Harishikha was furious at this and said to Marubhutika, "Go at once and get the rogue, and drag him here with a cattle goad around his neck!*"

"The union that you arranged between our master—who was living happily—and the noble lady has turned out to be a disaster. Look what has happened now!"

He replied, "The saying that the hermit drinks rice scum when he thinks he is about to get a fever has now come true! Let the time come that the noble lady is worried about; then we shall see what happens and perhaps drink poison like wretches. Don't be rash! Anyway, that's enough 11.100
chatter for now. Tapantaka, go and speak to the king. He gave you that privilege in the past, when he said, "You can make a request to me at any time and it will definitely be fulfilled—do not worry!" After cheering the girl up with these felicitous words, Gomukha took her to her mother and then we entered the city.

At the princes' cloister I reminded Tapantaka to do what Gomukha had said should be done. Tapantaka clapped his hands, said "Consider it done," and went to the palace. On his return he said, "When His Majesty the king asked

gatvā rāja|kulaṃ tasmād āgaty' êdam abhāṣata,
«Rāja|pādair ahaṃ pṛṣṭas, ‹tāta kiṃ kriyatām iti›
śālīnena may" âpy uktaṃ, ‹modako dīyatām› iti.»
Evaṃ mālā|phal'|ādīni niḥ|sārāṇi Tapantakaḥ
yācate sma prahīṇatvād gatvā gatvā mahī|patim.

11.107 Iti sa|śarīrayā kṣaṇam iva kṣaṇadāḥ kṣapayan
saha vi|śarīrayā dayitayā vi|rasān divasān.
dina|rajanī|vihāra|viparītam aham caritai
ratha|caraṇ'|āhvayasya caritāni viḍambitavān.

iti Ślokasaṃgrahe
Madanamañjukā|lābhaḥ.

what he could do for me I was embarrassed and asked him to give me some sweets." Tapantaka repeatedly went to the king and, because he was inadequate, would ask him like this for trifles such as flower garlands and fruits.

Passing nights with my sweetheart as though they were 11.107
but moments, and dull days without her, I mocked the behaviour of the *cakravāka** goose by reversing its daily and nightly behavior.

Thus ends the Winning of Madanamanjuka
in the Abridgement into Sanskrit Verse.

CANTO 12
THE WINNING OF VEGAVATĪ:
THE SUBSTITUTION IN THE GARDEN

Atha māṃ kṛta|kartavyaṃ
sukh'|āsīnam ahar|mukhe
vādī jita iv' â|chāyas trapayā Gomukho 'bravīt:
«Aham arya|sutāṃ nītvā gṛhaṃ sva|gṛham āgataḥ
tato 'pi vandituṃ devyau nar'|êndr'|ântaḥ|puraṃ gataḥ.
Vanditā ca vihasy' āha devī Padmāvatī yathā
‹kiṃ|kāraṇaṃ vadhūr adya n' âsmān āyāti vanditum?
Bhrātrā te kiṃ na mukt" âiva? na v" âdy' âpi vibudhyate?
kopitā vā bhaved bhartrā śiṣṭā duś|caritair iti?›
Ath' āgatā hat'|ôras|kā krandantī Padmadevikā
‹n' âsti naḥ svāmin" îty!› uktvā devyor nipatitā puraḥ.
Tato devyau tataḥ śeṣam a|śeṣam avarodhanam
rājā ca śruta|vṛtt'|ântaḥ s'|āsthāno dhairyam atyajat.
Tataḥ prāpy' â|cirāt saṃjñāṃ Māgadhyā Padmadevikā
›kathaṃ jānāsi n' âst' îti› pṛṣṭ" ācaṣṭa, ‹niśāmyatām.
Yath" âiva Gomukhen' âsau svam āvāsaṃ praveśitā
tath" âiva jhagiti ghrāto gandho 'smābhir a|mānuṣaḥ.
A|kasmāc ca kṣaṇaṃ nidrāṃ gacchāmaḥ pratibudhya ca
śūnyām īkṣāmahe śayyām a|śrīkāṃ nalinīm iva.
12.10 Tato, «hā h" êti» vikruṣya sa|mūrchāḥ kṣaṇam āsmahe
na kva cic ca vicinvatyaḥ paśyāmaḥ svāminīm iti.›
Kaliṅgasenayā tv atra śoka|gadgaday" ôditam
idaṃ tad āgataṃ manye dur|vidyā|dhara|ceṣṭitam.
Bālikām aham ādāya pūrvaṃ Madanamañjukām
harmy'|âgre krīḍayāmi sma candrik"|āsaṅga|śītale.
«Ehi vidyā|dharā3 ehi gṛhāṇ' êmāṃ su|rūpikām

One morning, when I had completed my duties and was relaxing, Gomukha, looking as pale as a defeated disputant, spoke to me with embarrassment: "After I had taken the noble lady to her house and been home, I went to the king's harem to pay my respects to the two queens. On being greeted, Padmavati smiled and said, 'Why has the young lady not come to pay us her respects today? Has your brother Naravahanadatta not let her go out? Or is she yet to wake up? Or might your brother have angered the cultured girl with his misbehavior?' Then Padmadevika arrived, beating her breast and crying. She said, 'Our mistress has disappeared!,' and collapsed in front of the two queens. At this the two queens and all the rest of the harem were beside themselves, as were the king and his court when they heard the news.

Before long Padmavati came to her senses and asked Padmadevika how she knew that Madanamanjuka had disappeared. She replied, 'Listen! As soon as Gomukha had taken her home we suddenly smelt an unearthly smell. For no apparent reason, we fell asleep for a short while. When we awoke we saw that the bed was empty, like a lotus without Lakshmi*. We cried out and fell into a faint for a moment. 12.10
When we searched for her we could not find our mistress anywhere.'

At this, Kalingasena, her voice choked with grief, said, 'I think this is the doing of a wicked sorcerer. Once, when Madanamanjuka was a child, I took her to play on the roof terrace, where it was cool in the moonlight.

"Come sorcerer! Come sorcerer! Come sorcerer! Come!

ekām eva mayā labdhāṃ sutāṃ dur|labhikām iti.»
Tataś carm'|âsi|keyūra|hār'|ādi|kara|bhāsuraḥ
avātarad divaḥ ko 'pi divya|gandha|srag|ambaraḥ.
Dūrād eva ca māṃ bhītāṃ, «mā bhaiṣīr iti» sāntvayan
gambhīra|dhvani|vitrasta|tanayām idam abravīt,
«Yadi mahyam iyaṃ dattā satyena tanayā tvayā
tato muñca nayāmy enāṃ nyāsa|bhūtā hi kanyakā!
Nāmnā Mānasavego 'haṃ vidyā|dhara|gaṇ'|âdhipaḥ
sarva|vijñeya|vijñāna|mano|jvalita|dhīr iti!»

An|icchantī tatas tasya saṃnidhau ciram āsitum
prayatnād dhairyam ādhāya pragalbh" êva tam abravam,
«Arhaty a|vaśyam ev' êyam īdṛśī tvādṛśaṃ patim
na punar dīyate tāvad bālikā śaiśavād iti.»
12.20 Atha māṃ abhivādy' âsāv ulkā|saṃghāta|bhāsuraḥ
dṛśyamāno mahā|vegaḥ kṣaṇen' ântar|hito 'bhavat.
Tena bravīmi ten' âdya tat smṛtvā kṣudra|buddhinā
vidyā|dhar'|âdhamen' âsau nītā yadi bhaved iti.›
Sarvathā dṛśyate n' êha devī Madanamañjukā
yad atr' ân|antaraṃ nyāyyaṃ tad anuṣṭhīyatām iti.»

Tataḥ samutpatann eva śokaḥ krodhena māmakaḥ
preritaḥ pavanen' êva prabalena balāhakaḥ.
«Strī|taskara! dur|ācāra! mūḍha! Mānasavegaka!
tiṣṭha! tiṣṭha! kva yās' îti?» prālapaṃ gagan'|ônmukhaḥ.
Yuga|pat krodha|śokābhyāṃ śoṣito 'haṃ krameṇa ca

Take this beautiful girl, my one and only precious daughter!" When I sang this, a being came down from the sky, sparkling with the light from his shield, sword, armlets, necklaces and other accoutrements, and wearing heavenly scents, garlands and clothes. I was scared; from a distance he reassured me by saying, "Do not be afraid," but my daughter was terrified by his deep voice. He continued, "If you really are giving your daughter to me, then let go of her and I shall take her: a little girl is an investment for the future! My name is Manasavega; I am the king of all the sorcerers. My mind is ablaze with a genius that knows all there is to be known!"

Not wanting to stay for long in his presence, I struggled to pull myself together and, pretending to be brave, I said to him, "A girl like this does indeed deserve a husband like you. However, I will not hand the youngster over yet—
she is still a child." He then took his leave of me and I 12.20
watched him vanish in an instant, moving with great speed and shining like a shower of meteors. That's why I think that today the mean-minded wretch of a sorcerer might have remembered this incident and taken her away.' Lady Madanamanjuka is nowhere to be found around here: we must do at once whatever is appropriate in this situation."

My burgeoning sorrow was driven away by rage, like a cloud being driven away by a strong wind. Looking up at the sky, I shouted "Woman-stealer! Brute! Idiot! You wretch, Manasavega! Stop! Stop! Where are you going?" Anger and grief combined to gradually dry me out, just as a clump of lotuses is withered in winter by wind and frost.

yath" ânila|tuṣārābhyāṃ śiśire kamal'|ākaraḥ.

Gomukhas tu nṛ|p'|āhutaḥ pratyāgaty' êdam abravīt
«‹kim etad iti?› pṛṣṭena vṛtt'|ânto 'yaṃ may" ôditaḥ.
Tataḥ saṃbhrama|visrastam ākarṣann uttar'|âmbaram
viṣād'|ākulito rājā prasthito yuṣmad|antikam.
Antare ca Rumaṇvantam āha, ‹k" êyaṃ pramāditā
sarvathā khyāpitaṃ lokair bhavatāṃ nīti|kauśalam.
Yuktaṃ tadā yad" ālocya mahat sīdat prayojanam
vipralabdho 'smi yuṣmābhir devyā Vāsavadattayā.
12.30 Adhunā dhriyamāṇe 'pi samartha|sacive mayi
apanītā vadhūḥ kasmād bālān mama sutād iti?›

Sa tam āha, ‹nivartadhvam alaṃ tatra gatena vaḥ
yuṣmān dṛṣṭvā hi sa śiśuḥ prāṇān api parityajet.
Ājñāpayatha māṃ yac ca yac ca vijñāpayāmi vaḥ
āsīnān āsane tena nivṛtya sthīyatām iti.›

Upaviṣṭāya c' ācaṣṭa, ‹sphuṭaṃ divyena sā hṛtā
a|nāth" âpi na vaḥ kā cit kena cit paribhūyate.
Yāvad antaḥ|pur'|âṭavyau yāvac ca gṛha|pakkaṇāḥ
n' âsty asau yo na c' âsmābhir īkṣitaś cāra|cakṣuṣā.
Ākāśe tu na me prajñā kramate divya|gaś|care
tena vidyā|dhareṇ' âsau hṛt" êti hṛdaye mama.
Atha vā bhavat' ûdyāne yuva|rājaḥ parīkṣatām
kadā cit kupitā bhartre tatr' āsīta vadhūr iti.
Kupitānāṃ hi bhartṛbhyaḥ śrūyante kula|yoṣitām
sādhubhiḥ kathyamānāni pañca sthānāni tad yathā.
Śvaśrū|bhrātṛ|nanāndṝṇāṃ bhartṛ|mitrasya vā gṛham
duṣṭa|saṃcāra|śūnyāni mandir'|ôpavanāni vā.›»

Gomukha was summoned by the king. On his return he said, "When he asked me what was going on I told him the news, at which the king was overcome with despair and in his consternation his cloak fell off. Pulling it on he set off to see you. In the meantime he said to Rumanvan, 'What carelessness this is! Everyone holds your skill in political science in the highest regard. It was all very well when, realizing that an important plan was at stake, you deprived
me of queen Vasavadatta*. But now that I am ruling and 12.30
have capable ministers, how is it that the girl has been taken away from my young son?'

Rumanvan said to him, 'Please turn around. Do not go there: if the boy sees you he may even take his own life. You can give me orders and listen to my reports while sitting on your throne, so please go back and stay where you were.'

He sat down and Rumanvan said to him, 'It is clear that she has been abducted by a divine being. In your realm, no woman, even if she has no parents or husband, is ever harrassed by any man. From the harem to the jungle, from the houses to the forest settlements, there is no one who is not watched by us with our spies. However, my intelligence does not reach as far as the sky, which is the realm of divine beings, so I believe she has been abducted by a sorcerer. But perhaps the prince should take a look in the garden. Women who are angry with their husbands are sometimes to be found there. The sages speak of five places for women of respectable families who are angry with their husbands, namely: the houses of their mothers-in-law, their brothers,

Atr' ântare kathitavān ākhyānaṃ Marubhūtikaḥ
«prastāve yan mayā pūrvaṃ śrutaṃ tad avadhīyatām.
12.40 Aṣṭāvakrasya duhitā Sāvitrī nāma kanyakā
āsīd yā carit'|ākāraiḥ sāvitrīm atiricyate.
Aṣṭāvakram ayāciṣṭa kadā cid ṛṣir Aṅgirāḥ
‹brahmann a|kṛta|dāro 'smi sutā me dīyatām iti.›
So 'bravīd, ‹bhavataḥ ko 'nyas trailokye 'pi varo varaḥ?
kiṃ tu datt" êyam anyasmai kṣamatāṃ bhagavān iti.›
Tasya bhrātā Vṛṣo nāma sa c' Âṅgirasam abravīt
‹Amṛtā nāma duhitā mama sā gṛhyatām iti.›
Pariṇīya tu tāṃ kanyām Amṛtām a|mṛt'|ôpamām
ātmānam Aṅgirā mene pīt'|â|mṛtam iv' â|mṛtam.
Sā kadā cit kathaṃ cit taṃ kāraṇe 'lpe 'pi pīḍitā
upālabdhavatī nātham ṛṣi|putrasya vallabhā:
‹Cakṣū|raktena bhavatā Sāvitrī svayam arthitā
ahaṃ tv an|icchate tubhyaṃ pitrā dattā balād iti.›
Nānā|vidhaiḥ sa śapathair Amṛtāṃ parisantvayan
kaṃ cid abhyanayat kālam.
ekad" âstaṃ|gate ravau
Paścāt sandhyām upāsīnam āsīnaṃ mauna|dhāriṇam
apṛcchad Amṛt" āgatya, ‹kiṃ dhyāyati bhavān iti.›
Tena vandita|saṃdhyena cirād uktaṃ, ‹nanu priye
devīṃ vihāya Sāvitrīṃ kim anyac cintayāmy aham?›
12.50 Atha sā, ‹śrutam› ity uktvā svasminn āśrama|pāda|pe
devatābhyo namas|kṛtya śarīram udalambayat.

their sisters-in-law, and their husband's friends, or private gardens where there are no bad elements.'"

At this juncture Marubhutika told a story: "Listen to
something I've heard on this subject. Ashtavakra had a 12.40
daughter called Savitri who surpassed the original Savitri* with her conduct and beauty.

One day the sage Angiras said to Ashtavakra, 'Brahmin, I do not have a wife: give me your daughter.'

He replied, 'Who in the three worlds would make a better groom than you? However, she is betrothed to someone else. Forgive me, Your Reverence.'

Ashtavakra had a brother called Vrisha who said to Angiras, 'I have a daughter called Amrita; take her.' Amrita was like the nectar of immortality, and after he had married her Angiras considered himself to be an immortal, as if he had drunk the nectar of immortality.

One day the sage's sweetheart had been peeved by some trifling matter and she chided her lord: 'You fell in love with Savitri at first sight and wanted her, but my father imposed me upon you.' For a while he reassured Amrita with various promises.

One day when the sun had set and he was sitting in silence doing his evening worship, Amrita went and asked him what he was meditating upon. He finished his worship and after a long pause said, 'But my dear, upon what other than Lady Savitri would I be meditating?'

She replied, 'I see,' bowed to the gods and went to hang 12.50
herself from one of the trees in her hermitage. When she put the noose around her neck she saw before her a goddess

Ākṛṣṭa|kaṇṭha|pāśā ca puraḥ praikṣata devatām
vidyut|piṅga|jaṭ'|ābhārāṃ s'|âkṣa|mālā|kamaṇḍalum.
Tato danta|prabhā|jāla|prabhāsita|tapo|anā
devat" âvocad Amṛtām a|mṛten' êva siñcatī.
‹putri mā sma tyaja prāṇān dus|tyajān dharma|sādhanān
straiṇam a|jñānam āśritya saṃtuṣṭo hi patis tvayā.
N' Âṣṭāvakrasya duhitā Sāvitrī tena cintitā
kiṃ tv ahaṃ Brahma|Rudr'|ādi|sapta|loka|namas|kṛtā.
Sarvathā mat|prasādāt te putri putro bhaviṣyati
balena tapasā yasya na samāno bhaviṣyati.›
Iti dattvā varaṃ tasyai Sāvitrī divam āśrayat
Amṛt" âpi gat'|āśaṅkā bhartrā saha sameyuṣī.
Tena bravīmi kupitā kadā cid Amṛt" êva sā
udyānaṃ praviśet tatra svayam anviṣyatām iti!»
Ath' âhaṃ śibik"|ārūḍhaḥ prasthito veśam a|smṛtiḥ
cakṣuś|ceto|har'|ākārāḥ paśyan veśyāḥ samūhaśaḥ.
Āsīc ca mama, «devībhyāṃ prayogo 'yam anuṣṭhitaḥ:
‹api nām' âsya kasyāṃ cit striyāṃ bhāvo bhaved iti.›»
12.60 Tad" âyaṃ moha|saṃkalpo na hi saṃkalpa|janmanaḥ
Rater anyāsu saṃkalpaḥ pramadāsu pravartate.
Tataḥ saṃkalpayann evam a|candrikam iv' âmbaram
kāntā|mātur gṛhaṃ kāntaṃ kāntā|śūnyam upāgamam.
Prakāśān a|prakāśāṃś ca pradeśān bahuśo bahūn
anviṣyanto bhramāma sma na c' âpaśyāma tatra tām.

with a mass of matted hair as yellow as lightning, a rosary of *rudrākṣa* beads and an ascetic's water pot. Illuminating the penance grove with the lattice of light from her teeth, the goddess spoke to Amrita and it was as though she was sprinkling her with the nectar of immortality.

'My girl, suicide is bad and life is a means to merit; do not kill yourself in womanly ignorance, for your husband is happy with you. It was not Ashtavakra's daughter Savitri that he was thinking about, but me, to whom homage is paid in the seven worlds by Brahma, Rudra and the other gods. My girl, I guarantee that through my grace you shall have a son whose might and asceticism will be unequalled.' After granting her this boon Savitri flew into the sky. Amrita's worries were gone and she rejoined her husband. This is why I think that, like Amrita, Madana-manjuka might have become angry and gone to the garden. You should look for her there yourself!"

I set out on a palanquin for the courtesans' district. I saw
large numbers of beautiful and charming courtesans, but
did not pay them any attention. I told myself that the two
queens had planned to make me fall for some other woman.
But that was fanciful: Kama, the god of love, does not have 12.60
eyes for any maiden other than Rati. As I was thinking this I
arrived at my lover's mother's lovely house, which, without
my lover, was like the sky without moonlight. I searched
many times, in many places, both obvious and hidden,
but did not find her there. With Gomukha showing the
way, I went into the garden and asked the witnesses—the
monkeys and the birds—for news of my beloved. Like an

Gomukh'|ôddiṣṭa|mārgaś ca praviśya gṛha|kānanam
pṛcchāmi sma priyā|vārttāṃ s'|âkṣi|śākhā|mṛg'|âṇḍa|jān.
Kebhyaś cit kupitaḥ śāpān kebhyaś cid vitaran karān
viḍambayann a|śāstra|jñam ity utkaṭa|rasaṃ naṭam.
Ath' ôpagamya tvaritaḥ prahṛṣṭo Marubhūtikaḥ
«arya|putr' ârya|duhitā mayā dṛṣṭ" êty!» abhāṣata.
Tatas tasya parāmṛjya pāṇinā vikasan mukham
«api satyam idaṃ saumya syāt krīḍ" êty?» aham abravam.
So 'bravīt, «satyam apy etat! krīḍā y" âiṣ" âti|harṣa|jā!
a|satye hy atra yā krīḍā tad unmatta|vijṛmbhitam.
Atha v" âlaṃ vimarśena mah"|âbhyudaya|vairiṇā!
tvaritaṃ gamyatāṃ! yasmān n' ārtaḥ kālam udīkṣate!»
Paśyāmi sma tato gacchann aśoka|śiśum agrataḥ
raktaṃ kusuma|saṃghāta|mayam ā|bhūmi|pallavam.
12.70 «A|kāle kim aśokasya kusumān' îti» cintayan
tasya skandhe hriy" ālīnam apaśyaṃ prāṇa|dāyinīm.
Āsīc ca mama, «kiṃ citraṃ yat pāda|sparśa|dohadaḥ
sadyaḥ kusumito 'śokaḥ prāpya sarv'|âṅga|saṃgatim.
Idam atra mahac citraṃ yad" ālokitam etayā
vana|devatay" ôdyānaṃ sakalaṃ na vijṛmbhitam!
Sarvath" â|cetanā vṛkṣāḥ kāntāyā darśane sati
su|bhage nir|vikāratvād aṅgāra|tuṣa|bhasmavat!»
Ath' āliṅgitum ārabdhaḥ s'|ânurāgam ahaṃ ca tām
tayā c' âṅgāni saṃhṛtya, «mā tāvad iti!» vāritaḥ.
Tataḥ prasara|bhaṅgena vilakṣam upalakṣya mām
s" âbravīd, «aparodho 'yam arya|putreṇa mṛṣyatām.
Ārādhitavatī yakṣam ahaṃ kanyā satī yathā
arya|putrasya bhūyāsaṃ dayitā paricārikā.
‹Tubhyaṃ kārye ca saṃsiddhe śamī|lāja|su|gandhinā

ignorant actor overacting, I angrily cursed some of them and held out my hands to others.

Then a delighted Marubhutika came running up and said, "Your Majesty, I have found her ladyship!"

I stroked his beaming face and said, "Is this true, kind sir, or might you perhaps be joking?"

He replied, "It is true! I'm jolly because I'm so happy! If it were untrue, to make a joke of it would be the mark of a madman! But that's enough discussion, the great enemy of success! Hurry along! A man in trouble doesn't dither!"

On the way I saw ahead a young *aśoka* tree. Red and
thick with flowers, its blossoms reached the ground. While 12.70
wondering how an *aśoka* tree had flowered out of season, I saw my reason for living leaning bashfully against its trunk.

I said to myself, "No wonder the *aśoka* tree, which craves the touch of a foot, has suddenly flowered on coming into contact with an entire body! The big surprise here is that the whole garden has not come into flower under the gaze of this forest goddess! The trees must be as unconscious as charcoal, chaff and ash, to have remained unchanged after having a blessed vision of my beloved!"

I was about to give her a passionate embrace when she drew back and stopped me, saying, "Don't!"

Then, seeing that I was disappointed at having my advance rebuffed, she said, "My husband, please forgive my refusal. When I was a girl I prayed to a *yakṣa* that I might become your beloved servant. I told him that when my wish was fulfilled I would repay him by offering him a drink from a hand scented with *śamī* wood and puffed

pānaṃ hastena dāsyāmi prasīdatu bhavān iti.›
Sa ca tasya prasādān me yātaḥ siddhiṃ mano|rathaḥ
āyācitaṃ tu yakṣāya na mayā pratiyācitam.
Ten' âhaṃ pāna|śauṇḍena nītā dhana|pateḥ sabhām
vṛtt'|ântaḥ kathitaś c' âyam ath' ôkto dhana|dena saḥ,
12.80 ‹Āyācitam iyaṃ tubhyam a|cireṇ' âiva dāsyati
nītvā samarpaya kṣipraṃ dārakāya vadhūm iti!›
Tena c' âham ih' ānītā gagan'|āgamanāc ca me
śarīraṃ paruṣī|bhūtaṃ vāritāḥ stha tato mayā.
Tasmai yakṣāya yuṣmābhiḥ sa me saṃpādyatām iti.»
Ath' âsyai gaṇik"|âdhyakṣo rāj'|ādeśaṃ nyavedayat
«ady' ārabhya kula|strītvaṃ bhavatīnāṃ bhavatv iti.»
Taṃ c' ākarṇya mahā|mano|ratham idaṃ
pūrṇaṃ cirāt kāṅkṣitaṃ
n' âiva prīti|vikāsi|hāri|hasitaṃ
dhatte sma kāntā|mukham
yācñā|vṛtti|kad|arthitair bahubhir apy
āptair na hi prārthakāḥ
prītiṃ yānti tathā yathā tanubhir apy
arthaiḥ sukh'|âbhyāgataiḥ.

iti Vegavatī|lābhe Udyāna|nimayo nāma
dvādaśaḥ sargaḥ

rice.* Thanks to the *yakṣa* my wish has been fulfilled, but I have not repaid him. That sottish *yakṣa* took me to Kubera's
assembly and told the story. Kubera said to him, 'She will 12.80
give you what you want before long. Take her and hand her over immediately to the young man as his bride!' He brought me here. My body is dirty from the flight, so I turned you away. Please have me fulfill my promise to the *yakṣa*."*

Then the officer in charge of the courtesans told her that the king had decreed that from that day forth she had the status of a noblewoman. When she heard that her long-cherished heartfelt desire had been fulfilled, the face of my beloved did not beam with a sweet smile of satisfaction. Repeated requests demean even the most valuable of prizes; those who ask for them are given greater pleasure by meager gains easily come by.

Thus ends the twelfth canto, called
the Substitution in the Garden
in the Winning of Vegavatī.

CANTO 13
VEGAVATĪ

Tato divasam āsitvā
kāntā|mātur ahaṃ gṛhe
priyāṃ nava|vadhū|veṣāṃ pradoṣe pariṇītavān.
Prasādād arya|pādānāṃ kula|strītvam upāgatām
tām ādāya svam āvāsaṃ pravṛtt'|ôtsavam āgamam.
Tatra sā sa|dhan'|âdhyakṣaṃ taṃ yakṣaṃ kusum'|ādibhiḥ
abhyarcya pāna|dānena su|dus|toṣam atoṣayat.
Padma|rāga|mayīṃ śuktiṃ padma|rāga|drava|tviṣaḥ
ādāya madhunaḥ pūrṇāṃ tato mām abravīt priyā,
«Maṅgalānāṃ pradhānatvāt kārya|saṃsiddhi|dāyinī
eṣā dhana|pateḥ śeṣā svādur! āsvādyatām iti!»
May" ôktam, «an|anujñātas tāta|pādair guṇān api
n' âhaṃ sevitum icchāmi kiṃ punar vyasanaṃ mahat.»
Tataḥ sā dṛḍha|saṃrambhā śapathair a|vyatikramaiḥ
cirān nir|uttarī|kṛtya mām an|icchum apāyayat.
Pīt'|âika|madhu|śuktiṃ ca māṃ s" âpṛcchat kṛta|smitā
«kim āsvādam idaṃ pānam iti» pratyabravaṃ tataḥ,
«Āpāne madhur'|āsvādam anusvāde tu tiktakam
kṣaye kaṣāyaṃ kaṭukam avacchede manāg iti.»
13.10 S" âbravīd, «vyaktam ady' âpi na jānītha rasaṃ punaḥ
pīyatām iti!» pītaṃ ca punaḥ tad|vacanān mayā.
«Idaṃ kīdṛśam» ity asyai pṛcchatyai kathitaṃ mayā
«kim artham api me cittaṃ gatam a|sva|sthatām iti?»
Tay" ôktam, «apar" âpy ekā śuktir āsvādyatāṃ tataḥ
gamiṣyaty a|cirād eva cittaṃ te sva|sthatām iti».
Tasyām api ca pītāyām apaśyaṃ vegavad|bhramān

I SPENT THE DAY in the house of my sweetheart's mother. In the evening my beloved dressed as a bride and I married her. Through the grace of the king she had attained the status of a noblewoman, and I took her to my house, where the celebrations were taking place. Once there she used flowers and other offerings to worship the god of wealth and that insatiable *yakṣa*, and she satisfied the latter by offering him a drink. Holding a cup made of ruby and filled with a ruby-red sparkling liquid, my darling said to me, "This is the remains of what was offered to Kubera. It is the best of all lucky charms, so it will bring you success in whatever you do, and it is delicious! Have a taste!"

I replied, "Without the permission of my worthy father I do not like to indulge even in virtues, let alone a great vice." She was very insistent; with lengthy irrefutable protestations she left me with no response but to drink reluctantly.

When I had drunk one cup of wine she smiled and asked me how it tasted, to which I replied, "When I first drank it it tasted sweet, but then it tasted bitter and finally it was astringent. There was a slightly acidic aftertaste."

She said, "Clearly you do not yet appreciate the flavor. 13.10
Have another drink!" I obeyed her and drank again.

When she asked how that drink was, I said, "Why does my head feel unwell?"

She said, "Try just one more cup and your head will soon feel better."

After I had drunk that one I saw everything whirling around—trees, palaces, mountains! Immobile things were

taru|prāsāda|śail'|ādīn sthāvarān api jaṅgamān!
Yathā c' âhaṃ tay" ôpāyair a|grāmyaiḥ śapath'|ādibhiḥ
an|icchan pāyitaḥ pānaṃ tathā tām apy apāyayam.
Balavadbhyām ath' ākramya madena madanena ca
yad eva rucitaṃ tābhyāṃ tatr' âiv' âsmi pravartitaḥ.
Yaḥ saṃtoṣayituṃ yakṣaṃ vivāhaḥ kṛtrimaḥ kṛtaḥ
tena kṛtrimam ev' âsau kanyātvaṃ pratipāditā.

Tataḥ prāta upāgamya madhu|gandh'|âdhivāsitam
ghrātvā Hariśikho veśma saṃbhrānta|matir uktavān,
«A|pūrva iva gandho 'yam arya|putra vibhāvyate
manye 'rya|putrayā yūyam an|icchāḥ pāyitā iti.»

Sa may" ôktaḥ, «sakhe sakhyā tav' âhaṃ pāyito balāt
bhavat" âpi rucau satyāṃ sthīyatāṃ pīyatām iti.»

13.20 So 'bravīd, «vyasana|grāma|grāmaṇyaṃ bhavatām api
pānaṃ sādhu na paśyāmi kiṃ punar mantriṇām iti.»

May" ôktam, «arya|pādeṣu sa|mitreṣu samā|śatam
pālayatsu kim asmākam ātmabhir vañcitair iti?»

Ten' ôktaṃ, «mantri|sacivair vijñāpyaṃ kāryam āgatam
anuṣṭhāne punaḥ tasya svātantryaṃ svāminām iti!»
Taṃ pibantaṃ sah' āvābhyām ālokya Marubhūtikaḥ
niḥ|śaṅkaḥ pātum ārabdha taṃ ca dṛṣṭvā Tapantakaḥ.

Rājamānas tato raktair aṅga|rāga|srag|ambaraiḥ
punar|ukta|priy'|ālāpo mām avandata Gomukhaḥ.
Tam atyāsannam āsīnam ati|mātra|priyaṃ|vadam
pādau saṃvāhayantaṃ me kruddho Hariśikho 'bravīt:

«Unmatta! kim a|saṃbaddhaṃ

moving! In the same way that she had used imprecations and other cunning methods to make me drink when I did not want to, I made her drink too. Then the two mighty forces of drunkenness and passion came forth and had their way with me. The contrived wedding that was carried out to appease the *yakṣa* made the girl contrive virginity too!

In the morning Harishikha came and found the apartment smelling of wine. Surprised, he said, "Prince, this is the first time that I have noticed this smell here: the princess must have made you drink against your will."

I told him, "My friend, she is a friend of yours, the lady who forced me to drink! If you want to, stay and have a drink yourself!"

He replied, "Drinking is the worst of vices, and I don't 13.20
think it is right for you, let alone for your ministers."

I said, "Why deprive ourselves when the king and his friends will be ruling over us for the next hundred years?"

He replied, "It is up to ministers and counsellors to advise on what is to be done; when it comes to what is actually done, rulers are free to do what they want!" He drank with us and when Marubhutika saw him, he had no qualms about starting to drink. When Tapantaka saw him, he did the same.

Then Gomukha greeted me, resplendent in red makeup, garlands and clothes, and flattered me repeatedly. He sat right next to me, pouring out pleasantries and massaging my feet. Harishikha was livid and said to him: "You drunkard! Why are you irritating our master by babbling incoherently in front of him? Sit away from him!"

bhāṣamāṇaḥ puraḥ prabhoḥ
udvejayasi bhartāram? apasṛty' āsyatām iti!»
Ten' ôktaṃ, «mūrkha! n' âiv' êdaṃ
mada|sāmarthya|jṛmbhitam
svāmino niḥ|sa|patnau tu pādāv icchāmi sevitum.
Yadā t' ûbhaya|Vaitarddha|bhartṛ|mūrdhabhir arcitau
bhaviṣyatas tad" âsmākaṃ sa|sa|patnau bhaviṣyataḥ.»
Vaitarddha|nāma|grahaṇāt tato Madanamañjukā
smita|saṃdarśita|prītir abravīt s'|âśru|locanā,
13.30 «Aho cāturya|mādhurya|pradhāna|guṇa|bhūṣaṇāḥ
ālāpā nirgatāḥ saumyād Gomukhasya mukhād iti!»
May" ôktaṃ, «bhaṇa paśyāmas tvayā kasmāc ciraṃ sthitam
ko vā tav' êdam ākāram ujjvalaṃ kṛtavān iti?»
Ten' ôktaṃ, «vayam āhūya Māgadhyā rāja|saṃnidhau
ājñāpitās, ‹tava bhrātrā pānam āsevitaṃ niśi.
Tena pāna|gṛhāt pānaṃ svādyamānaṃ svadeta yat
svayam āsvādya tad bhrātre tvayā prasthāpyatām iti.›
So 'haṃ devī|dvayen' âpi maṇḍayitvā sva|pāṇibhiḥ
pān'|āgārāya gamitaḥ pān'|âdhyakṣa|puraḥ|saraḥ.
Tatra c' āsvādayann eva tat tat pānaṃ manāṅ manāk
matto 'haṃ preṣayāmi sma yuṣmabhyam api saṃtatam.
Tasmāt pibata niḥ|śaṅkāḥ kāpiśāyanam āsavam!
anujñātāḥ sah'|āmātyair gurubhir muditair iti!»
Sevamānas tataḥ pānaṃ sa|kāntā|mitra|maṇḍalaḥ
divasān gamayāmi sma prahṛṣṭa|paricārakaḥ.
Kadā cid eka|paryaṅka|sthitā Madanamañjukā
«yuṣmābhiḥ sukha|supt" âhaṃ na draṣṭavy" êty» abhāṣata.
Mama tv āsīt, «kim ity eṣā nivārayati mām iti»
yat satyaṃ su|tarāṃ cetaḥ kutūhala|taraṅgitam.
13.40 Kadā cid ardha|rātre 'haṃ sthāvar'|ākāra|jaṅgame

He replied, "Fool! This is no manifestation of the power of intoxication. I want to serve my master's feet while I have no rival. For when they are worshipped by the bowed heads of the kings of both the countries of Vaitarddha,* we will have rivals in serving them."

When she heard the name Vaitarddha, Madanamanjuka's smile betrayed her happiness, and she said with tears in her eyes, "O what skill and charm—the greatest of qualities— 13.30
adorn the words that have come out of Gomukha's lovely mouth!"

I said, "Let's see... tell us, why have you taken so long, and who has made you look so splendid?"

He replied, "Padmavati summoned me and in front of the king she said, 'Your brother has taken to drinking at night, so you must taste the drink from our cellar and send that which you like to your master.'

The two queens dressed me up like this with their own hands, and sent me to the cellar accompanied by the officer in charge of drinking. I gradually became drunk as I sampled the various drinks there, and kept sending them on to you. So drink the wine without worrying: your parents and the ministers have gladly given their permission!"

I spent my days drinking with my beloved and my circle of friends, and my attendants were overjoyed. One time when I was in bed with Madanamanjuka she told me that I must not look at her when she was fast asleep. I wondered why she had forbidden me like that; in fact, my mind was extremely agitated by my curiosity.

Once, in the middle of the night, when everything that 13.40

pāne pariṇatiṃ yāti pratibuddhaḥ pipāsitaḥ.
Tataḥ parijanaṃ dṛṣṭvā prasuptam abhavan mama
«na yuktaṃ sukha|suptasya śatror api nibodhanam.
Bhāryā punaḥ śarīr'|ârdham ato Madanamañjukām
pratibodhya jalaṃ yāce tadd hi me na virūpyate.»
Iti nirdhārya tasyāṃ ca mayā dṛṣṭir nipātitā
yāvad any" âiva sā k" âpi nārī|rūp" êva candrikā!
Āsīc ca mama, «kiṃ yakṣī? kiṃ gandharvī? kim apsarā?
mānuṣī syāt kula|strī syād gaṇikā syād iyaṃ na hi.
Yasmād anyatam" âpy āsāṃ lakṣaṇair n' ôpapadyate
tasmād vidyā|dharī prāptā k" âpi ken' âpi hetunā.»
  Iti nirṇīya nipuṇaṃ kariṇī|tālu|komalau
gāḍhaṃ saṃvāhayāmi sma tasyāś caraṇa|pallavau.
Sā tu saṃtyājitā nidrāṃ sadyaś caraṇa|pīḍayā
mām ālokya tathā|bhūtaṃ bhītā bhūmāv upāviśat.
Abravīc ca, «na kartavyam arya|putreṇa sāhasam!
tvā|dṛśām anukampyo hi balināṃ pramadā|janaḥ!»
  Tataḥ śrūtv" êti yat satyam ātmany ev' âsmi lajjitaḥ
evaṃ|kāriṇam apy eṣā saṃbhāvayati mām iti.
13.50 Sā māṃ lajjitam ālokya jānu|saṃnihit'|ānanam
lajjām apaharant" îva tvarit" êdam abhāṣata,
«Śrūyatāṃ c' â|priyaṃ sā te priyā Madanamañjukā
tvad|guṇa|smaraṇa|vyagrā nayate divasān iti.»
  Āsīn me manasi, «hṛtā na sā mṛtā sā
  yā dṛṣṭer vrajati na gocaraṃ priyā me.

moves was still, I woke up thirsty, having digested the wine that I had drunk. When I saw the servants fast asleep, I thought, "It is not right to wake anyone who is fast asleep, even an enemy. But a wife is one half of one's body so it won't be improper of me if I wake Madanamanjuka and ask her for water." After I had thought this through I cast my gaze on her and saw straight away that she was someone else: it was as though the moonlight had taken on the form of a woman! I thought, "Is this a *yakṣī*? A *gandharvī*? An *apsaras*? For she cannot be a mortal lady, whether a noblewoman or a courtesan. But her features indicate that she is not one of those divine beings, so she must be a sorceress who has come here for some reason."

After I had come to this clever conclusion, I squeezed her bud-like feet, which were as tender as a lady elephant's palate. The pressure in her feet woke her up immediately, and when she saw what I was doing she sat up, terrified. She said, "My lord, you must not be violent! Strong men like you should treat young ladies with tenderness!"

On hearing these words from her I was truly ashamed of myself, for she was treating me respectfully even though I had behaved as I did. When she saw that I was ashamed and 13.50
had buried my face in my knees, she removed my shame by saying quickly, "Listen to some disagreeable news: that sweetheart of yours, Madanamanjuka, passes her days lost in the recollection of your virtues."

I told myself that my beloved, who had disappeared from my view, was not captured but dead. To the blind the bright white light of the autumn full moon may as well be deeply

jyotsnā hi sphuṭa|dhaval" âpi kaumud"|îndor
andhānāṃ bahala|tamo|malīmas" âiva.»

iti Vegavatīdarśano nāma
trayodaśaḥ sargaḥ.

dark and dirty.

Thus ends the thirteenth canto,
called Vegavati Revealed.

CANTO 14
VEGAVATĪ REVEALED

TATAS TĀM ABRAVAṂ, «BHĪRU,
tvam eva hi mama priyā.
tath" âpi tu vinodena tiṣṭhāmaḥ kathyatām iti!»
Grahītavyāni nāmāni guru|deva|dvi|janmanām
yasmāt tena viśuddhy|arthaṃ snānam ācaritaṃ tayā.
«Asti Meru|giri|prāṃśur Āṣāḍho nāma parvataḥ
śūra|paṇḍita|vitt'|āḍhya|vidyā|dhara|kul'|ālayaḥ.
Tatra vidyā|dhara|svāmī vedavān Vegavān iti
yaḥ Kuber'|âdhika|svo 'pi niḥ|sva eva din'|âtyaye.
Tasy' âpi Pṛthivī nāma mahiṣī prāṃśu|vaṃśa|jā
tṛṇāya manyate sthairyād yā devī pṛthivīm api.
Tau ca putram a|vindantau ciraṃ duḥkham atiṣṭhatām
prauḍhāyā iva kanyāyāḥ pitarau sa|dṛśaṃ varam.
Tau Manaḥputrikā nāma kula|vidyāṃ sut'|ârthinau
ārādhayitum ārabdhau tayā c' ôktaṃ prasannayā,
‹Sarva|vidyā|dhar'|ôtkṛṣṭa|vidyā|dhara|parākramaḥ
bhavitā bhavatoḥ putraḥ putrakau duḥkham ujjhatam!
Ekā ca duhitā yasyāḥ kalā|śālī bhaviṣyati
śūraḥ s'|âṅga iv' ân|aṅgo vidyā|dhara|patiḥ patiḥ.›
14.10 Kāle kva cid atīte ca prasūtā Pṛthivī sutam
tri|vargam a|kṣataṃ devī pṛthiv" îva su|rakṣitā.
Manaḥputrikayā dattaḥ sa yasmāt kula|vidyayā
tasmān Mānasaveg'|ākhyaḥ putraḥ pitrā prasādhitaḥ.
Saṃvatsara|traye 'tīte jātāyā duhituḥ kṛtam

THEN I SAID TO HER, "Sweet lady, it is you and you alone that I love. Nevertheless, let's amuse ourselves: tell the story!"

Because she would have to say the names of her parents, gods and brahmins she took a ritual bath to purify herself.

"There is a mountain called Ashadha, which is as high as Mount Meru, and home to a clan of sorcerers who are brave, learned and rich. The king of the sorcerers there knows the Vedas and is called Vegavan. Even though he is richer than Kubera, at the end of each day he has no riches left. His chief queen is called Prithivi and comes from a noble family. In comparison with her own fortitude, the queen thinks nothing of even the earth.*

For a long time they were unhappy because they did not have a son, like the parents of a girl of marriageable age who cannot find a suitable groom. In their quest for a son they started to worship the clan wisdom goddess, Manahputrika. She was pleased and said to them, 'My children, give up your grief! You shall have a son and he will be the bravest of all the sorcerers. And you shall have a daughter; her husband will be the king of the sorcerers, skilled in the arts, brave, and like an embodiment of the bodiless god of love.'

Some time passed and Prithivi gave birth to a son, just 14.10
as a well-protected kingdom produces all three aims of man. Because he had been given by the clan wisdom goddess, Manahputrika, his father called the boy Manasavega. When a daughter was born three years later, Vegavan named her Vegavati after himself. Having obtained their

nāma Vegavat" ātmīyam asau Vegavatī tataḥ.
Labdh'|êṣṭa|tanayau tau ca modamānāv ahar|niśam
nītavantau ciraṃ kālam ek'|âhar|niśa|saṃmitam.
Vegavān ekadā snātaḥ prīṇit'|âgni|sura|dvi|jaḥ
bhadr'|āsana|stham ātmānaṃ dadarśa ādarśa|maṇḍale.
Atha haṃsam iv' āsīnam Añjan'|â|cala|mūrdhani
mṛṇāla|dhavalaṃ keśaṃ dṛṣṭavān ātma|mūrdhani.
Tato bhadr'|āsanaṃ tyaktvā vasu|dhā|sthaṇḍile sthitaḥ
pṛṣṭo Mānasavegena, ‹kim etad iti› Vegavān.
Ten' ôktaṃ, ‹palitaṃ dṛṣṭvā Manaḥputrika|vaṃśa|jāḥ
tapāṃsi vā niṣevante ved'|ânta|vihitāni vā.
Tat prajāḥ pālayeḥ putra prajās tvāṃ pālayantu ca!
pālitair hi mṛg'|êndro 'pi kānanair eva pālyate.›
Atha mānasa|vegena krośantīṣu prajāsu ca
rājā manda|sukh'|ôtkaṇṭhaḥ pratiyātas tapo|anam.
14.20 Bhartrā nivartyamān" âpi vacobhiḥ s'|ôpapattibhiḥ
na nivṛttā yadā devī tad" ôpāyaṃ prayuktavān.
‹Ady' âiv' âhaṃ cyuto rājyād ady' âiv' êyaṃ pati|vratā
na me saṃpādayaty ājñām aho dharmaḥ satām iti.›
Tato hrītā ca bhītā ca s'|âśru|śreṇiḥ sa|vepathuḥ
pādayoḥ patitā patyur vyajñāpayad asau śanaiḥ,
‹Yadā tarhi mayā yūyaṃ pāvayantas tapo|anam
upāsyāḥ pāvanatamaṃ sa kālaḥ kathyatām iti.›
So 'bravīd, ‹dur|labhaṃ putraṃ sthira|siṃh'|āsan'|āsthitam

desired offspring the two parents rejoiced day and night, and passed an age as though it were but a day and a night.

One day Vegavan took a ritual bath, made offerings to the sacred fire, the gods and the brahmins, and then, in the mirror, saw himself sitting on the throne. On his head he saw hair as white as a lotus stem, like a swan sitting on top of Mount Anjana. He quit the throne and stood on the bare earth. Manasavega asked Vegavan what was the matter.

He replied, 'When those born into the lineage of Manahputrika see that their hair has turned gray, they either become ascetics or follow the teachings of the Upanishads. Therefore, my son, you must take care of the people and may the people take care of you! For the lion, too, is cared for by the very same jungle that he takes care of.' The king's desire for worldly pleasures had dimmed and, no sooner said than done, he left for the penance grove while his subjects wept.

When the queen would not turn back despite being sent 14.20
away by her husband with reasoned arguments, he resorted to cunning. He said, 'It was only today that I gave up my throne and here is my wife already disobeying me! Oh, the conduct of the virtuous!'

At this she was both ashamed and scared. Pouring forth tears and trembling, she fell at her husband's feet and said to him softly, 'Then tell me when I might come near to you while you sanctify the already sacrosanct penance grove.'

He replied, 'When you have seen both our dear son sitting firmly on the throne and a husband for Vegavati, you will

bhartāraṃ Vegavatyāś ca dṛṣṭvā draṣṭ" âsi mām iti.›
‹Evaṃ c' âivaṃ ca kalyāṇi pitā vijñāpyatām iti›
uktā Vegavatī mātrā pitaraṃ praṇat" âbravīt:
‹Tāta tvayi vanaṃ yāte ko me dāsyati modakān
kalpa|vṛkṣa|prasūtāni phalāni kusumāni vā?›
Ten' ôktaṃ, ‹yena yen' ārtho dur|labhen' âpi kena cit
tat tan Mānasavegas te bhrātā dāt" āsyatām iti.›
Iti rājya|kalatra|mitra|putrān
gṛha|dhāmaṃ ca tṛṇāya manyamānaḥ,
guru|sattva|rajas|tamaḥ|kalaṅkāṃ
prakṛtiṃ hātum agād vanaṃ nar'|êndraḥ.
Śriyaṃ Mānasavego 'pi kadalī|dala|cañcalām
śakti|traya|prayoga|jñaḥ kṛtavān a|cal'|â|calām.
14.30 Atha yāte kva cit kāle Mātaṅg'|âdhipateḥ sutā
Āṣāḍhaṃ Vāyumukt" êti sakhī|parivṛt" âgamat.
Sā sma Vegavatīm āha, ‹rāja|putri kim āsyate?
uttiṣṭh' ākāśa|mārgeṇa gacchāmo Malay'|â|calam!
Śṛṅga|kuñja|nitambeṣu tasya ramyeṣu ramyatām
netr'|âpidhānik'|ākhyāna|putrikā|kandukair iti!›
Tay" ôktaṃ, ‹n' âsti me śaktir gantum ākāśa|vartmanā
a|labdha|kula|vidyāyāḥ sakhi tan mṛṣyatām iti.›
Upahasya tatas tās tām uccais tāḍita|pāṇayaḥ
ādhūt'|âmbara|pakṣāḥ khaṃ haṃsa|kanyā iv' āsthitāḥ.
Bhrātur antikam āyātā s'|āvegā Vegavaty api
tena c' ôkt" âṅkam āropya, ‹mātaḥ kiṃ dīyatām iti?›
Tay" ôktaṃ, ‹dehi me vidyāṃ mahā|rāja sa|sādhanām
siddha|vidyābhir ady' âhaṃ sakhībhir hāsitā yataḥ!›

see me.'

Vegavati's mother told her various things to ask her father. She bowed her head and said to him: 'Father, with you gone to the forest, who will give me sweets, or fruits and flowers from the wish-fulfilling tree?'

He answered, 'Rest assured that your brother Manasavega will give you whatever you want, even if it is hard to come by.'

So, deeming his kingdom, his wife, his friends, his children, his family and his house as worthless, the king went to the forest to conquer nature and its stubborn stains of existence, activity and inertia. The fortunes of a kingdom are as fickle as a banana leaf, but Manasavega knew how to use the three powers* and made them as firm as a mountain.

After some time had passed, Vayumukta, the daughter 14.30
of the king of Matanga, came to Ashadha with a group of friends. She said to Vegavati, 'Princess, what are you waiting for? Jump up! Let's fly to Mount Malaya! We'll have fun among its beautiful peaks, bowers and valleys with games of hide-and-seek, storytelling, dolls and balls!'

She replied, 'Friend, forgive me: I do not have my family's *vidyā* and am unable to fly.' Then they laughed loudly at her, clapped their hands, flapped their wing-like cloaks, and flew into the sky like young female swans.

She rushed over to her brother, who put her on his lap and said, 'What can I give you, young lady?'

She replied, 'My friends have mastered the *vidyā* of flight and today they laughed at me, so give me the *vidyā* and the means of mastering it, great king!'

‹A|cireṇ' âiva dāsyāmi māta ity› abhidhāya sā
bhrātā visarjit" â|sāra|bāl'|âlaṅkāra|vañcitā.

Ekadā Gaurimuṇḍasya bhaginī Gaurimadyaśāḥ
gatā Vegavatīṃ draṣṭum Āṣāḍhaṃ sa|sakhī sakhīm.
Upahasya ca tāṃ s" âpi vi|pakṣām iva sārasīm
sa|pakṣā rāja|haṃs" îva gatā prati Himācalam.
14.40 Vegavaty api s'|āsthānaṃ gatvā bhrātaram abravīt
‹kim ayaṃ kṣipyate kālo? vidyā me dīyatām iti!›

Ten' ôktam, ‹api dāsyāmi! tvarase kim a|kāraṇam?
guru|kārya|kriyā|vyagraṃ kiṃ na paśyasi mām iti?›

Sā gatvā manyu|bhāreṇa sphurant" îva tvarāvatī
apatan mātur utsaṅge saṃtapt" êva vaśā hrade.
Pṛthivī tu samāhūya sacivau bhartur abravīt
‹a|cireṇa pitur mūlaṃ dārikāṃ nayataṃ yuvām.
Antar|aṅgo hi saṃbandhaḥ putraiḥ pitror a|kṛtrimaḥ
bhrātaras tu dviṣanty eva bhrātṝn ek'|ôdarān api.›

Tau tām ākāśa|mārgeṇa nītavantau tapo|anam
mārg'|āyatana|mārgeṣu s'|âmbhaḥsu gamita|śramām.
Ath' âsthi|maya|kāyānāṃ taḍid|babhru|jaṭā|bṛtām
te 'paśyat tatra vṛndāni tāpasānāṃ tapasyatām.
Pṛcchanti sma ca tatr' âikam abhivādya tapasvinam
‹brahman brūhi tam uddeśaṃ yatr' āste Vegavān iti.›

So 'bravīt, ‹parvat'|âgre 'sāv aṅguṣṭh'|âgreṇa tiṣṭhati
anugacchati gacchantam aṃśumantaṃ ca cakṣuṣā.

'Young lady, I shall give it to you before long,' said her brother, before distracting her with a worthless child's bauble and sending her away.

One day Gaurimunda's sister Gaurimadyasha went with some friends to Ashadha to see her friend Vegavati. She too laughed at Vegavati, like a winged royal swan laughing at a flightless crane, and departed for the Himalayas. Then Ve- 14.40
gavati went to the assembly and said to her brother, 'Why are you wasting time? Give me the *vidyā*!'

He replied, 'Of course I shall give it to you! Why are you in such a pointless rush? Can't you see that I am busy with important affairs?'

Shaking with indignation, she hurried away and fell into her mother's lap like an overheated lady elephant falling into a lake. Prithivi summoned two of her husband's ministers and said, 'Take the girl to her father at once. There is a natural bond between parents and their children, but siblings can hate one another even though they are from the same womb.'

They took her through the air to the penance grove, and she refreshed herself at well-watered resting places along the way. At the penance grove they saw large numbers of ascetics practicing austerities, their bodies like skeletons and their matted hair ruddy like lightning. They respectfully greeted one of the ascetics and asked him to point them in the direction of Vegavan.

He answered, 'He is standing on tiptoe at the top of the mountain and is following the course of the sun with his gaze. This is his leaf-hut. In its yard a lion and an

Parṇa|śālā ca tasy' êyaṃ yasyāḥ siṃha|mataṅga|jau
aṅgaṇe krīḍataḥ prītāv imau ca śikhi|pannagau.
14.50 Āsann'|āgamanaś c' âsau dagdhaṃ hi kaṭhinaiḥ karaiḥ
tasy' āhlādayituṃ cakṣur eṣa mandāyate raviḥ.›
Tapas|tāntaṃ tataḥ kāyaṃ sa|kāyam iva Vegavān
kāya|kleśaṃ vahann āgād vaikhānasa|mṛg'|āvṛtaḥ.
Atha Vegavatī dṛṣṭvā Vegavantaṃ tathā|vidham
abravīn mantriṇaṃ, ‹n' âyaṃ mama tātaḥ! sa Vegavān!
Tasya candra|prabha|chattra|prabhāḥ sa|mukuṭa|prabhāḥ
prabhāsayanti dhāvantīṃ puraḥ sāmanta|santatim.
Ayaṃ tu siṃha|mātaṅga|śārdūla|mṛga|tāpasaiḥ
tyakta|vairaiḥ sah' āyāti nūnaṃ ko 'p' îndra|jālikaḥ.›
Tābhyām uktaṃ, ‹sa ev' âyaṃ tathā c' êtthaṃ ca dṛśyate
tādṛśā eva dṛśyante tathā c' êtthaṃ ca sādhavaḥ!
Vandyatāṃ ca pit'' êty!› uktā vandamān'' ârdra|cakṣuṣā
aṅkam āropitā pitrā rūḍha|darbh'|âṅkura|vraṇam.
Mantriṇāv api bhartāram ucit'|ântara|vartinau
śiro|vāgbhir avandetām atha Vegavat'' ôditau,
‹Āgacchataṃ mam' âbhyāśam alaṃ sthitv'' âti|dūrataḥ
jana|rañjana|mātraṃ hi gataṃ tad rājya|nāṭakam.›
Āsanna|sthaṇḍila|sthau tau pṛṣṭavān atha Vegavān,
‹rājño Mānasavegasya rājyaṃ no varṇyatām iti.›
14.60 Tābhyām uktam, ‹a|śakyaṃ tad Guṇāḍhyen' âpi śaṃsitum!
tam apekṣya tu rājānaḥ śeṣāś chattra|viḍambakāḥ.›
‹Iyaṃ māṇavikā kasmād ānīt'' êti› ca pṛcchate

elephant are playing happily, as are a peacock and a snake.
He will come soon. The sun's harsh rays have burnt his 14.50
eyes; it is becoming weaker now and will bring them relief.' Then Vegavan arrived surrounded by hermits and wild beasts, carrying his penance-weary body as though it was the embodiment of self-mortification.

When Vegavati saw Vegavan in this state she said to the two ministers, 'That's not my father! Vegavan is my father! The brilliant rays from my father's moon-like parasol and crown illuminate the column of vassals that run before him. But this man—who is coming with lions, elephants, tigers, deer and ascetics that have given up their hatred for one another—must be a magician of sorts.'

The two ministers replied, 'It is him. He used to look like that but looks like this now. Only men as saintly as him are seen both as he used to be and as he is now!' They told her to greet her father and, as she did so, he, with tears in his eyes, sat her in his lap, which was covered in scars from blades of *kuśa* grass.*

Staying a respectful distance away, the two ministers bowed and greeted Vegavan. He said to them, 'Come near me! Don't stand so far off! That charade of sovereignty was merely to keep the people happy and is over now.' They stood on a nearby patch of ground and Vegavan asked them to tell him about the reign of king Manasavega.

'Not even Gunadhya could praise it enough! In com- 14.60
parison with Manasavega, other kings bring derision upon their thrones.' When he asked them why they had brought the girl, they said it was to obtain the *vidyā* and told him

‹vidyā|lābh'|ârtham› ity uktaṃ tasmai tābhyāṃ sa|vistaram.
Ten' ôktam, ‹a|cirād eṣā labdha|vidyā gamiṣyati
yuvābhyāṃ nīti|pannābhyāṃ sa bālaḥ pālyatām iti!›
Vegavaty api s'|ôtsāhā karoti sma mahat tapaḥ
kalpit'|āhāra|kartavyā phala|mūla|jal'|ânilaiḥ.
Jal'|āharaṇa|saṃmārga|kusuma|pracay'|ādibhiḥ
ārādhayad dur|ārādhān asau vaikhānasān api.
Uccinvantī kadā cit sā phullāṃ kānana|mallikām
‹hā sarpeṇ' âsmi daṣṭ" êti!› s'|ākrand" âgamad āśramam.
Yathā|saṃnihitais tatra vaikhānasa|kumārakaiḥ
‹mā rāja|dārike bhaiṣīr ity!› uktvā parivāritā.
‹Kv' âsau kv' âsau khalaḥ sarpa iti?› pṛṣṭā kumārakaiḥ
‹amuṣmin mallikā|gulma iti› tebhyo nyavedayat.
Te tv ālokya tam uddeśam avocann uccakais|tarām
‹rāja|putri! na sarpo 'yam ayaṃ sarp'|ântakaḥ sikhī!
Dṛṣṭvā prasāritāṃ grīvām utphaṇ'|āśīviṣ'|ôpamām
tvayā, ‹sarpa iti› jñātaṃ tasmād āśvasyatām iti!›
14.70 Uṭaj'|âṅgaṇam ānītaḥ sa mayūraḥ kumārakaiḥ
vicitrair nartito mārgais tayā kuṭṭita|tālayā.
Prekṣaṇīyaṃ ca tad draṣṭum a|dṛṣṭaṃ vana|vāsibhiḥ
militāḥ sarva ev' âsthus tapo|ana|nivāsinaḥ.
Etasminn eva vṛtt'|ânte Vegavantam upāgatam
viśrāntam upagamy' êdam avocat taṃ tapasvinaḥ,
‹Rāja|dārikayā rājat tapas taptaṃ su|dus|tapam
vayam ārādhitāḥ prītās tad vidyāṃ labhatām iti!›
Ten' ôktaṃ, ‹yadi ca prītā no bhavanto 'nujānate

the story in detail.

He said, 'She will return with the *vidyā* before long. You two are skilled in political science and must look after the boy!' Vegavati enthusiastically undertook great austerities and restricted her diet to fruits, roots, water and air. The hermits were hard to please but she ingratiated herself with them by doing things like fetching water, sweeping and collecting flowers.

One day when she was picking wild jasmine flowers she came to the hermitage screaming, 'I've been bitten by a snake!'

The young ascetics who were nearby gathered around her and said, 'Princess, do not be scared!' The boys asked her, 'Where is it? Where is that wicked snake?' and she told them that it was in the jasmine thicket. But when they looked there they called out, 'Princess! It's not a snake, it's a snake-killer: a peacock! You saw its neck sticking out. It looked like a hooded cobra so you thought it was a snake. You can breathe freely now!'

The boys brought the peacock to the courtyard of the 14.70
leaf-hut and she made it dance in various ways by clapping her hands. All the hermits living in the penance grove came to watch this unique spectacle.

While this was going on Vegavan arrived. After he had rested the ascetics went up to him and said, 'Sire, the princess has completed very difficult austerities. She has propitiated us and we are happy. Let her have the *vidyā*!'

He replied, 'If you are happy and grant me permission, I shall give her numerous *vidyās*, together with their five

tato gṛhṇātv iyaṃ vidyāḥ pañc'|âṅga|parivāritāḥ.
Anayā yat tapas taptam asmābhiś c' êdam īdṛśam
tad asyāḥ kula|vidyānām alaṃ bhavatu siddhaye.
Yac ca Mānasavegasya vidyā|siddhi|prabhāvitam
balaṃ catur|guṇaṃ tasmād bāl" êyaṃ pratipadyatām.
Yaś c' âsyāḥ ko 'pi dīrgh'|āyur grahīṣyati varaḥ karam
rājyasya daśamaṃ bhāgaṃ sa madīyasya bhokṣyati.›
Evam uktvā tatas tasyās tat sarvaṃ kṛtavān pitā
s" âpi labdh'|âbhyanujñānā vegen' ôdapatan nabhaḥ.
Tataḥ kanaka|lekh" êva bhāsā kaṣa|śilām asau
piśaṅga|bhavatī yāntī śyāmalām ambara|sthalīm.
14.80 Dṛṣṭā Mānasavegena saṃbhrama|bhrānta|cakṣuṣā
avātarat tad|āsthāne haṃs" îv' âmbhoja|kānane.
Kathaṃ cit pratyabhijñāya lajjiten' êva tena sā
āliṅgy' ôtsaṅgam āropya gamitā mātur antikam.
Māt" âpi duhitṛ|sneham an|ādṛty' âiva sa|tvarā
apṛcchad, ‹api kalyāṇi kuśalī Vegavān iti.›
Kiṃ v" â|phala|pralāpena? sāram ev' âvadhīyatām
y" âsau Vegavatī s" âhaṃ tasya Vegavataḥ sutā!
Atīte tu kva cit kāle sa|śarīr" êva cārutā
nītā Mānasavegena k" âpi bhūmau var'|âṅganā.
Sā ca tad|guṇa|bhūyiṣṭhāṃ dṛḍhaṃ dveṣṭi kathām api
kṣīṇa|doṣa|guṇā sādhvī kāma|stuti|kathām iva.
Sa kadā cit kva cit kāṃ cid dṛṣṭvā tāpasa|kanyakām
balād bhoktum upakrāntas tayā c' ôktaṃ sphurad|ruṣā,
‹Yuktaṃ śāp'|âgninā dagdhuṃ tvā|dṛśaṃ pāpa|cetasam
kiṃ tu Vegavataḥ sādhoḥ putras tvaṃ tena mucyase.
Sarvathā śāpa|nāmānaṃ pratīcchatu varaṃ bhavān
a|dhīra|hṛdayāḥ prāyas trāsa|gamyā bhavā|dṛśāḥ.

ancillaries.* The austerities completed by her and me are enough to ensure her mastery of the clan's *vidyās*. She shall receive four times the power commanded by Manasavega after he mastered the *vidyās*, and whatever lucky suitor wins her hand will enjoy one tenth of my kingdom.'

After saying this her father did all that he had said. She took his leave and flew quickly up into the sky. Brilliantly yellow, she crossed the deep blue sky like a line of gold
across a touchstone. When Manasavega saw her he could 14.80
not believe his eyes. She landed in his assembly like a swan in a forest of lotuses. He only just recognized her and seemed embarrassed as he embraced her and sat her in his lap. He then sent her to her mother. Her mother, however, neglected to show her love for her daughter and hurriedly asked whether Vegavan was well.

But why bother with pointless prattling? Let's get to the point: I am that same Vegavati, the daughter of Vegavan!

After some time Manasavega brought to Ashadha a lovely lady who was like beauty incarnate. She took a strong dislike to any story full of his praises, just as a worthy lady of faultless virtue dislikes a story in praise of sensuality. He had once come across some ascetic's daughter somewhere and tried to rape her. Shaking with rage, she had said to him, 'Scoundrels like you should be burnt up by a fiery curse! However, as you are the son of the virtuous Vegavan you shall be spared. Take this curse which in all respects but name is a blessing! Men like you are generally weak-willed and won over by fear. If you try to force yourself on any unwilling woman, your brain will burn up and your head will explode into a hundred pieces!'

Balāt kāmayamānasya niṣ|kāmāṃ kāṃ cid aṅganām
bhavataḥ śatadhā mūrdhā dagdha|buddheḥ sphuṭed iti›.
14.90 Tatas trastas tataḥ śāpād a|kāmāṃ kāminīm asau
api n' ôtsahate draṣṭuṃ kuta eva niṣevitum.
Sa tu mām abravīd, ‹mātas tathā Madanamañjukā
protsāhyatāṃ yathā kṣipram upasarpati mām iti!›
Atha bāla|sva|bhāvena sa|kutūhalayā mayā
aśoka|vanikā|madhye dṛṣṭā Madanamañjukā.
Saṃkṣiptam adhitiṣṭhantī rūḍha|parṇa|lat"|ôṭajam
mlāna|campaka|māl" êva purāṇa|kadalī|puṭam.
Parṇa|śayyā|śiro|bhāge nihitaḥ saṃpidhānakaḥ
uṭaj'|âbhyantare nyastaḥ sa|jalaḥ kalaśas tayā.
Atha lambhita|viśrambhāṃ
Mañjukām aham abravam
‹kas te mānuṣakeṇ' ârthaḥ?
kuru vidyā|dharaṃ patim!
Mugdhe mānuṣakās tāvad bahu|rog'|ādy|upadravāḥ
vidyā|dharās tu vidyānāṃ prabhāvān nir|upadravāḥ.
Rājā Mānasavegas tu bhartā te varṇyatāṃ katham
yo vidyā|dhara|rājānāṃ rājā sphīta|śriyām iti?›
Doṣān api manuṣyāṇāṃ gṛhṇāmi sma yathā yathā
tathā tath" âbhavat tasyāḥ prīti|sphīt'|âkṣam ānanam.
Guṇān vidyā|dharāṇāṃ tu gṛhṇāmi sma yathā yathā
tathā tath" âbhavat tasyāḥ krodha|jihm'|âkṣam ānanam.
14.100 Āgantukau yadā c' âināṃ prīti|krodhāv amuñcatām
gṛhṇāti sma tadā śokaḥ sa|niśvās'|âsra|vepathuḥ.
Ath' âsyāḥ parimṛjy' âsram a|śīta|sparśam abravam
‹alaṃ bhagini saṃtapya jīvitaṃ rakṣyatām iti!›
Tayā t' ûktaa, ‹mayā n' êdam ātma|duḥkhena rudyate
a|śakyaṃ tu bhayaṃ bhīmam āhṛtaṃ mandayā mayā.

Since then, fearing that curse, he does not want even to see a desirous woman that has no desire for him, let alone make love to her. 14.90

He said to me, 'Dear girl, persuade Madanamanjuka to fall for me soon!' Then, with the natural inquisitiveness of a child, I had a look at Madanamanjuka in the *aśoka* grove. She was staying in a small hut made of leaves and creepers, and resembled a garland of wilted *campaka* flowers in an old banana leaf cup. She had put her cloak at the head of the leaf bed, and a pot containing water inside the hut.

When I had gained her confidence, I said to her: 'What do you want with men? Take a sorcerer for a husband! Silly girl! Myriad misfortunes befall men, such as diseases and so forth, while because of the power of their *vidyā*s nothing untoward happens to sorcerers. How is one to describe king Manasavega, your prospective husband and the king of the munificent sorcerer kings?'

But the more I mentioned even the faults of men, the more her eyes widened with pleasure, while the more I mentioned the virtues of sorcerers, the more her eyes narrowed with anger.

When these incidental feelings of pleasure and anger left her, grief seized her, accompanied by sighs, tears and trembling. I wiped her warm tears and said, 'Sister, stop tormenting yourself and safeguard your life!' 14.100

She replied, 'It is not out of self-pity that I am crying; I have foolishly brought about an insurmountable and awful calamity. He who knows all the sciences and arts, who is

Sarva|vidyā|kal"|âbhijñaḥ sarva|rūpavatāṃ tulā
kula|vidyā|dhanair yaś ca tuṅgair api na mādyati.
Sa mad|vṛtt'|ântam a|jñātvā daśāṃ yāsyati kām api
tataḥ s'|ântaḥ|pur'|āmātya|rāṣṭraḥ som'|ânvayo nṛpaḥ.
Kiṃ tu pratyāśayā prāṇān ekayā dhārayāmy aham
yad ādiṣṭaḥ sphuṭ'|ādeśair asau vidyā|dhar'|ādibhiḥ.
Vidyā|lava|viṣ'|ādhmātān vidyā|dhara|bhujaṅgakān
vidyā|dhara|nar'|êndro 'yaṃ kartā vānta|viṣān iti.›
Tataḥ śrutv" êti yat satyaṃ jāt" âhaṃ jāta|saṃśayā
‹vidyā|dhara|nar'|êndraḥ syād uta na syād asāv' iti.›
‹Kiṃ kā cid dūtikā yātu? s" âpy a|śaktā parīkṣitum
dūtikā mat|samā n' âsti svayam eva vrajāmy ataḥ.›
Tataḥ sv'|ârth'|āhit'|ôtsāhā pṛcchāmi sma tava priyām
‹tava priyāya kiṃ vārttā tvadīyā dīyatām iti?›
14.110 Atha kṣaṇam iva dhyātvā tay" ôktaṃ smayamānayā
‹tulyam ev' āvayoḥ kāryaṃ śaktau satyāṃ kim āsyate?
Idaṃ hi guru kartavyaṃ kṣipta|kālaṃ ca sīdati
īdṛśaṃ tvā|dṛśī karma kāryate katham anyathā.
Iyaṃ maṇḍalitā veṇī mayā sakhi tav' âgrataḥ
daṣṭu|kām" êva capalā bhīṣaṇ" āśīviṣ'|âṅganā!
Dāhyā vā dahanen' êyaṃ mocyā vā gṛdhra|jambukaiḥ
arya|putreṇa v" â|dagdha|dāruṇā gati|dāruṇā!
Gatvā c' āgaccha dol" êva! na sthātavyaṃ kva cic ciram

a match for anyone in beauty and who, even though he is exceptionally noble, learned and rich, is not arrogant, will, because he does not know what has happened to me, fall into a terrible state, as will the king of the lunar race*, together with his harem, his ministers and his country. However, there is one hope making me cling on to my life: the sorcerers and others have clearly foretold that he, as the king of the human sorcerers, will make the serpent sorcerers, who are puffed up with the poison of their fragmented of *vidyās*, puke up that poison.'

When I heard this I became uncertain as to whether or not this man really was going to be the human king of the sorcerers. I said to myself, 'Should some lady envoy go? But she would not be able to tell. There is no envoy like oneself, so I shall go in person.'

Then, my enthusiasm compounded by self-interest, I asked your beloved, 'Is news of you to be given to your sweetheart?'

After thinking for a while, she said with a smile, 'We 14.110
both want the same thing. If you can do it then why delay? This task is important and wasting time will endanger it. It is a job for someone like you—it is not going to happen otherwise. I have braided this lock of hair in front of you, my friend; it is like a terrifying slippery she-snake about to bite! It is hard to untie and its destiny is dire: it will either be burnt by fire, or loosened by vultures and jackals or by my husband, if his funeral pyre has not already burnt! Go and come back like a swing! Do not stay anywhere for long:

a|saṅgā hi gatiḥ sakhyāḥ kāntaṃ yāntyāḥ smṛter iva!›

Ity ukt" âjjukayā kṣipraṃ nabhas" âham ih' āgatā
apaśyam arya|putraṃ ca, ‹hā! kv' âs' îti?› pravādinam.
A|ninditam upāyaṃ ca vicinty' ātma|samarpaṇe
ajjukā|rūpayā tubhyam ātmā saṃdarśito mayā.
Nivāritāś ca yad yūyaṃ tad|āliṅgana|lālasāḥ
sa doṣaḥ kanyakātvasya viśuddha|kula|janmanaḥ.
Yac c' āyācita|dānāya vivāhaḥ kārito mayā
sa ca saṃskartum ātmānaṃ kv' âtra yakṣaḥ kva c' âjjukā.
Yac ca pātum an|icchantaḥ pāyitāḥ stha balān madhu
tatra yat kāraṇaṃ tac ca prāyaḥ pratyakṣam eva ca.
14.120 ‹Na draṣṭavy" âsmi supt" êti!› pratiṣiddhāḥ stha yan mayā
tat kutūhala|vṛddhy|arthaṃ vāma|śīlā hi bālatā!
Sarvathā vistareṇ' âlam! ajjukā Madamañjukā
nītā Mānasavegena lakṣmīr iva dur|ātmanā.

Tad ājñāpaya māṃ kṣipram imāṃ Madanamañjukām
ānayāmi parair nītāṃ śuddhā nītir iva śriyam.«

Āsīc ca mama, «na nyāyyaṃ praiṣaṇīya|jan'|ôcitam
bhartuḥ kārayituṃ karma bhāryāṃ tuṅga|kul'|ôdbhavām».
Ath' âināṃ abruvaṃ, «caṇḍi śrutam ehi śayāvahai
na hi tāmra|śikhaṇḍānām ady' âpi sphurati dhvaniḥ.
Aham api dhaval'|êndu|vaṃśa|janmā
kuliśa|kaṭhora|kaniṣṭhikā|prakoṣṭhaḥ.

the journey of a friend going to a lover should be like that of thought—direct!'

After the courtesan said this to me, I flew here immediately and found Your Lordship crying out, 'Oh! Where are you?' Thinking that it was a blameless way of presenting myself, I showed myself to you in the form of the courtesan. When you wanted to embrace her and were repulsed, it was the fault of my virginity, born as I am into a virtuous family. The reason I had the marriage carried out (which was supposedly to fulfill the promise to the *yakṣa*) was to make myself ready for womanhood. And anyway, how could a *yakṣa* have had anything to do with a courtesan? The reason you were forced to drink alcohol when you did not want
to should now be obvious. I forbade you from looking at 14.120
me when I was asleep in order to arouse your curiosity: children are contrary by nature! But that's enough beating about the bush! The courtesan Madanamanjuka has been abducted by Manasavega, and it is as though the goddess of fortune has been abducted by a sinner.

So just ask me and I will bring back Madanamanjuka, like good governance bringing back the wealth of a kingdom after it has been stolen by enemies."

I thought to myself, "It is not right for a husband to employ his highborn wife in a job fit for servants," so I said to her, "My dear, I have heard enough. Come, let us go to sleep for the call of the red roosters is yet to sound. I was born into the lineage of the dazzling moon and the tip of my little finger is as fearsome as Indra's thunderbolt! A

priya|samara|par'|âvarodha|ruddhān
  a|hata|ripuḥ katham āhareya dārān?»

iti Bṛhatkathāyāṃ Ślokasaṃgrahe
Vegavatīdarśano nāma caturdaśaḥ sargaḥ

bellicose foe has detained my wife in his harem—how can I bring her back without killing him?"

Thus ends the fourteenth canto in the
Long Story Abridged into Sanskrit Verse,
called Vegavatī Revealed.

CANTO 15
THE WINNING OF VEGAVATĪ

PARIPĀṬYĀ TATAḤ PRĀPTĀS
trayo Hariśikh'|ādayaḥ
prabhāte mām avandanta na tu Vegavataḥ sutām.
Gomukhas tv a|cirāt prāptaḥ prathamaṃ mām avandata
asmad|āsannam āsīnāṃ bhaktyā Vegavatīṃ tataḥ.
Asau Hariśikhen' ôktaḥ, «suṣṭhu khalv asi paṇḍitaḥ
vandy'|â|vandya|vicāre hi paṇḍitāḥ sama|darśinaḥ».
Ath' ôktaṃ tena, «matto 'sti bhavān ev' âti|paṇḍitaḥ
vandya|lakṣaṇa|yuktāṃ yo vandyām api na vandate.
Bhaṇa kena na pūjy" êyaṃ yā naḥ pūjyena pūjitā?
nanu manda|mate lokaḥ pūjya|pūjita|pūjakaḥ?
Svāminī svāmi|saṃbandhāt svām" îv' ârhati vandanām
candr'|āsannair hi nakṣatrair lokaḥ kāryāṇi kāryate!»
Ity|ādi vadatas tasya pakṣam utkarṣayann iva
ahaṃ Vegavatī|vṛttaṃ tad|varṇitam avarṇayam.
«Vidyā|dhara|kumārīṇāṃ pravṛtt" âvartan" îti» te
vandato muditā gatvā senā|bhartre nyavedayan.
Ten' âpi tāta|pādebhyas tair ambābhyāṃ niveditam
harṣa|dundubhi|vṛndais tu nadadbhir Vṛtra|śatrave.
15.10 Gambhīr'|ôtpāta|jīmūta|saṃpāta|hrāda|bhīṣaṇe
pramoda|dhvanite yātaṃ tanyamāne divā|niśam.
Atha senā|patiḥ prāptaḥ prāto mām idam abravīt

IN THE MORNING Harishikha and the other two arrived and greeted me one after the other, but they did not greet Vegavan's daughter. Gomukha arrived soon after, greeted me first and then respectfully greeted Vegavati, who was sitting next to me. Harishikha said, "You really must be very learned, for when it comes to deciding whom to greet and whom not to, learned people do not discriminate."

Gomukha replied, "You must be even more learned than me, since you are not even greeting a woman who is to be greeted and has the attributes of someone who is to be greeted. Tell me, who is not obliged to respect she whom he whom we must respect respects? You dimwit, does not everyone respect those who are respected by those who should be respected? Because of her relationship with our master she is our mistress and deserves to be greeted like him: everyone does what they have to do according to which constellation is in conjunction with the moon!"

As he said all this and more, I, seeming to take his side, told Vegavati's story as she herself had told it. They were delighted and said that Avartani, the *vidyā* of the sorcerer princesses, had been put into action. They then went and informed the leader of the army. He told my revered father and he told his two queens. A resounding chorus of celebratory drums told Indra. For a day and a night the sky was 15.10
filled with sounds of celebration that were as awe-inspiring as the sounds of rumbling earthquakes and clashes of thunder.

In the morning the leader of the army came to me and said, "Just now the two queens said to the king, 'A second

«idānīm eva devībhyāṃ devo vijñāpito yathā,
‹Dvitīyayā vadhukayā gṛhīto dārakaḥ svayam
kasyāś cid api n' âsmabhir dṛṣṭaḥ pariṇay'|ôtsavaḥ.
Tena prasādo yady asti Vegavatyā tataḥ saha
Naravāhanadattasya vivāhaḥ kāryatām iti.›
Devena tu vihasy' ôktam, ‹evam astu! kim āsyate!
mam' âpi hi manasy āsīd ayam eva mano|rathaḥ.
Kiṃ tu mātā varasy' âtra devī bhavatu Māgadhī
pit" âhaṃ vara|pakṣe 'sya samastam avarodhanam.
Astu Vāsavadattāyāḥ sutā Vegavataḥ sutā
Rumaṇvad|ādayaḥ pakṣe tasyā evaṃ bhavantv iti.›»
Ath' ântaḥ|puram ambāyāḥ Padmāvatyāḥ suhṛd|vṛtaḥ
nīto 'haṃ citra|vinyāsa|ratna|maṅgala|maṇḍalam.
Sa|bhartṛ|bahu|putrābhir nārībhir Vegavaty api
jyeṣṭh'|âmbā|bhavanaṃ nītā keli|kolāhal'|ākulam.
Tapantakas tu Māgadhyā preṣitaḥ prekṣituṃ vadhūm
maṣī|kāla|mukh'|ôraskaḥ kārito jyeṣṭhay" âmbayā.
15.20 Kampamānaś ca kopena tataḥ pratyāgato 'bravīt
«arya|putra khalī|kāraṃ paśyat' êmaṃ mam' ēdṛśam!
Śvaśrūs te māṃ khalī|kṛtya s'|ântar|hāsam avocata
‹kva yāsi jālma? labdho 'si! preṣitas tvaṃ caraḥ kila!
Ek" âiva mama bāl" êyam āyācita|śat'|ârjitā
asyāḥ saubhāgyam utpādyam a|vaśyaṃ kārmaṇair mayā.
Mātā jāmātṛkasy' âiva mahā|kārmaṇa|kārikā
yayā hasta|tale bhartā guru|dhairyo 'pi nartitaḥ!
Vardhayantyāś ciraṃ putraṃ tasyāḥ kārmaṇa|mālayā
kiṃ mayā preṣitaḥ kaś cid bhavān iva caras tayā?›

girl has married the boy and we have not seen the wedding celebrations of either of them, so please be so kind as to arrange for Naravahanadatta's wedding with Vegavati to be celebrated.'

The king laughed and said, 'So be it! Why delay! I too have had this very wish in mind. Now, let's have queen Padmavati be the mother of the groom. I shall be his father and the entire harem will be his party. Vegavati will be the daughter of Vasavadatta, and Rumanvan and the other ministers will be in her party.'"

Then I and my friends were taken to queen Padmavati's apartment. It was full of wonderful pictures, jewels and auspicious objects. Vegavati was taken by ladies who had husbands and lots of children to the palace of the eldest queen, which was filled with tumultuous sounds of celebration.

Padmavati sent Tapantaka to see the bride and the eldest
queen had his face and chest covered in black ink. Shaking 15.20
with rage, he came back and said, "Prince, look how I have been insulted! After this effrontery your mother-in-law said to me with a smirk, 'Where are you going, you wretch? You have been captured! It seems you were sent as a spy! This girl is my only daughter and she was obtained by hundreds of prayers; I must use magic to ensure her marriage is happy. My son-in-law's mother uses powerful sorcery: she has made her heavyweight husband dance in the palm of her hand! For a long time she has been using a string of spells to bring up her son. Have I sent any spy like she has sent you?' After saying this she had me seized by the neck and passed in the same way through a

Ity uktv" ālambhito bhīmām ardha|candra|paraṃ|parām
devyā niṣkramitaḥ svasmād aham antaḥ|purād iti.»

Tapantakena yā prāptā tatra gatvā viḍambanā
tām an|eka|guṇāṃ prāpañ jyeṣṭh'|âmbā|preṣitāś carāḥ.
Iti pravṛtta|vṛtt'|ânte matte 'ntaḥ|pura|sāgare
mayā Vegavatī|pāṇir gṛhīto mantra|saṃskṛtaḥ.

Atha gatvā svam āvāsaṃ vās'|āvāsaṃ praviśya ca
anyādṛśa|prapañc" êva dṛṣṭā Vegavatī mayā.
Vyāhṛtā vacanaṃ n' ādād agād ālambit'|âṃśukā
śayanaṃ ca nav'|ōḍh" êva sevate sma parāṅ|mukhī.
15.30 Upasṛtya śanaiś c' âināṃ bravīmi sma vilakṣakaḥ
«vrīḍā|krīḍā|kṛtā pīḍā dur|bhagā! tyajyatām iti!»

Tayā tu katham apy uktaṃ sphuṭita|smita|candrikam
«arya|putra kutaḥ krīḍā? gurv|ājñ" êyaṃ garīyasī.
Mayā hi śvaśur'|ādeśād asmin vīvāha|nāṭake
duṣ|karā kṣipta|vel" âpi vadhūkā|bhūmikā kṛtā.
Tathā nāṭayitavy" êyam ujjvalā jāyate yathā
tasmād guru|niyogo 'yam a|laṅghyaḥ kṣamyatām iti!»
Tayā saha visarpantyā vivāha|kathay" ânayā
anayaṃ kṣaṇa|saṃkṣiptām āyātām api yāminīm.

Gate tu n' âti|saṃkṣipte kāle caṭula|sambhramaḥ
tvarāvān skhalad|ālāpo mām avocat Tapantakaḥ,
«Arya|putra mayā dṛṣṭāś catasraḥ pura|devatāḥ
bhrāmyatā nagar'|ôdyāne dainya|mlān'|ānan'|êndavaḥ.
Nṛpasy' ân|iṣṭam āśaṅkya manye kim api dāruṇam

terrifying succession of hands before being thrown out of her apartment."

The spies that were sent by the eldest queen received several times over the abuse that Tapantaka had received in her apartment. While the expansive inner apartments were going crazy in this way, I took Vegavati's hand, which had been sanctified with mantras, and married her.

When I reached my house and entered the bedroom, I discovered Vegavati seemingly up to some new tricks. On being spoken to she did not answer and when I grabbed her robe she moved away. She lay in bed with her face averted
like a new bride. Perplexed, I went up to her and whispered, 15.30
"Your play of modesty is torturous and unseemly! Stop it!"

With the moonlight of her smile bursting forth, she somehow managed to say, "My husband, what do you mean 'play'? I am obeying our parents' orders and they carry great weight. At my father-in-law's command, I have played the difficult role of a new bride in this play of a wedding even though my time for that has passed. It must be played to perfection. This is our parents' order, and it has to be obeyed—please be patient!" As the pretense of a wedding stretched on, the long night that I spent with her passed in an instant.

A few days later, Tapantaka, trembling and upset, hurriedly said to me in a faltering voice, "My lord, while strolling in the public gardens I saw four city-goddesses. Their moon-like faces were wan with wretchedness. In fear of some dreadful calamity befalling their king they must have abandoned their city to flee somewhere else."

anyad uccalitāḥ sthānaṃ vihāy' êmāṃ purīm iti.»
Mayā Vegavatī pṛṣṭā, «kās tā iti» tay" ôditam
«krodhān Mānasavegena mama sakhyo vivāsitāḥ.
Mama prasādaḥ kriyatāṃ svayam ādāya tāḥ sakhīḥ
nayan'|ônmeṣa|mātreṇa paśya mām āgatām iti.»
15.40 Utpatantī mayā dṛṣṭā vegād Vegavatī nabhaḥ
āsīnā c' āsane svasmin sakhībhiḥ parivāritā.
Tad|āgamana|vārttā ca vyāpaj jhagiti medinīm
sadyaḥ svobhānu|muktasya tārā|bhartur iva prabhā.
Senā|patir ath' āgatya pravīṇair brāhmaṇaiḥ saha
prīti|snigdha|viśāl'|âkṣaḥ sa|praṇāmam abhāṣata,
Rājā Vegavatīm āha: «pratyāsanna|kara|grahāḥ
catasraḥ kila tiṣṭhanti bhaginyaḥ kanyakās tava.
Mam' âpy a|kṛta|vīvāhā yuvāno ramya|darśanāḥ
putrās tiṣṭhanti catvāraḥ śastra|śāstra|kalā|vidaḥ.
Yadi saṃbandha|yogyān no manyate rāja|dārikā
tatas tā dārikās tebhyaḥ putrebhyo me dadātv iti.»
Tay" ôktaṃ dhīra|gaṇikā|vaktra|saṃkrānta|vākyayā
«deven' ânugṛhīt" âsmi prasādaiḥ phalitair iti!»
Abhūc ca dārikā|pakṣe tadā devī kanīyasī
ahaṃ ca vara|pakṣe tu tātaḥ s'|ântaḥ|puro 'bhavat.
Yā samṛddhis tadā dṛṣṭā Vatsa|rāja|kule mayā
tām ady' âpi na paśyāmi prāpy' âpi śriyam īdṛśam.
Vidyā|dhara|kumārīṇāṃ tato hariśikh'|ādayaḥ
agrahīṣata sa|svedān ambho|ruha|rucaḥ karān.
15.50 Nivartita|vivāhās tu rāja|rāja|sutā iva
rāja|rāja|gṛhāṇ' îva gatāḥ pitṛ|gṛhāṇi te.
Prabhāte tān ahaṃ prāptān sa|vrīḍān iva pṛṣṭavān

I asked Vegavati who they were and she said, "In his anger Manasavega has banished my friends. Be so kind as to let me fetch those friends myself and you will see me return in the blink of an eye."

No sooner had I seen Vegavati fly quickly up into the sky 15.40
than she was sitting on her seat surrounded by her friends. The news of their arrival spread throughout the earth in an instant, like the light of the moon being suddenly released by the demon of the eclipse. The leader of the army arrived with some learned brahmins. His wide eyes sparkled with happiness, and with a bow he relayed a message from the king to Vegavati: "Apparently there are four marriageable maiden sisters of yours here. I have four unmarried boys who are young, handsome and versed in military matters, scholarship and the arts. If Your Highness considers us worthy of being her relatives then please give those girls to those boys."

With words that might have come from the mouth of a clever courtesan, she replied, "I thank His Majesty for his fruitful favors!"

The younger queen and I were in the girls' party; in the grooms' party were my father and his harem. Even now, despite my having obtained such wealth, I do not see the riches that I saw then in the court of the king of Vatsa.

Then Harishikha and the others took the shiny, perspiring lotus-like hands of the sorcerer girls and were married.
When their weddings were over they went to their fathers' 15.50
houses, like the sons of Kubera going to Kubera's palaces.

On their arrival in the morning they seemed embarrassed.

«yātā yasya yathā rātriḥ sa tathā varṇayatv iti.»
Gomukhena tataḥ proktam uccais tāḍita|pāṇinā
«tath" âiteṣāṃ gatā rātrir mā sma gacchad yathā punaḥ!
Ayaṃ Hariśikhas tāvat kany"|ārādhana|kovidaḥ
‹avehi mantri|putr' êti!› bhāryayā bhartsitaḥ spṛśan.
Tataḥ śayyāṃ samāliṅgya kūrma|saṃkoca|piṇḍitaḥ
dāruṇām anayad rātriṃ nidray" âpi nirākṛtaḥ!
Ayaṃ tu ghaṭṭyamāno 'pi bhāryayā Marubhūtikaḥ
‹śūro 'ham iti› bhāryāyāḥ pāda|sthānaṃ na muktavān!
Tapantakaḥ punaḥ śayyāṃ tyaktvā supto mahī|tale
prakṣālanādd hi paṅkasya dūrād a|sparśanaṃ varam!
Tad evaṃ dur|bhagān etān kāntā|saṅgama|kātarān
pragalbhā ramayiṣyanti kathaṃ vidyā|dhar'|âṅganā?»

Tato Hariśikhen' ôktam, «aho nāgarako bhavān
bhāryayā yo 'ti|saubhāgyād gṛhād api nirākṛtaḥ!
Yo hi vāsa|gṛhe suptaḥ prītayā saha kāntayā
sa kathaṃ para|vṛtt'|ântaiḥ kṣapāṃ kṣapitavān iti?»
15.60 Tath" ôpahasatām eṣām ālāpair apayantraṇaiḥ
ramamāṇaḥ kṣaṇaṃ sthitvā sa|suhṛt pānam ācaram.

Ath' âparasmin divase Vegavatyā nimantritāḥ
sa|bhāryāḥ suhṛdas te 'pi tābhir eva sah' āgatāḥ.
May" ôktaṃ, «yasya yasyāś ca pānaṃ saha na duṣyati
sa tayā sā ca ten' âiva pānam āsevatām iti.»

Bhāryāṃ Hariśikhasy' âpi pāṇāv ākṛṣya Gomukhaḥ
śobhā|jita|mṛṇālinyāṃ pāna|bhūmāv upāviśat.

I asked each of them to tell me how the night had gone, to which Gomukha clapped his hands and cried aloud, "They spent the night in a way that they don't wish to repeat! As soon as Harishikha, an expert at winning over girls, touched his wife, she scolded him, saying, 'Get back, minister's boy!' He made himself into a ball, like a tortoise drawing in its limbs, and clung on to the bed. Deprived of sleep to boot, he had a dreadful night! As for Marubhutika, he, despite being kicked by his wife, did not leave the foot of the bed, and thought how brave he was! Tapantaka, however, left his bed and slept on the ground. It is better to stay clear of dirt than to have to wash! So how are the proud sorcerer girls going to enjoy themselves with pathetic boys like these who are too timid to make love to their sweethearts?"

Then Harishikha said, "Aren't you quite the man-about-town, you whose marital bliss was such that your wife threw you out of the house! For how does someone who has slept in his bedroom with a satisfied sweetheart end the night
knowing what has happened to others?" I stayed for a while 15.60
and had a drink with my friends, enjoying the easy banter with which they mocked one another.

The next day my friends and their wives came over at Vegavati's invitation. I said, "Each boy must drink with a girl, and each girl with a boy, with whom they don't mind drinking!"

Gomukha took by the hand the wife of Harishikha, no less, and sat down in a drinking-place more beautiful than a lotus pond.

Bhāryayā Gomukhasy' ôktaṃ,
«yadi labhyaḥ svayaṃ|grahaḥ
gṛhītas tarhi niḥ|śaṅkaṃ
mayā Hariśikhaḥ svayam.»
Āsīnāyāṃ tatas tasyāṃ tena s'|ârdham an|antaram
Tapantakasya gṛhiṇīm agṛhṇān Marubhūtikaḥ.
Marubhūtika|bhāryā tu samupetya Tapantakam
abravīt, «pariśeṣo 'yaṃ kim anyat kriyatām iti?»
Evaṃ saha suhṛd|dāraiḥ suhṛdaḥ śuddha|buddhayaḥ
vayaṃ ca sahitā dāraiḥ krīḍantaḥ sukham āsmahi.
Kadā cit kupitā mahyaṃ yena ken' âpi hetunā
may" ânunīyamān" âpi suptā Vegavatī pṛthak.
Jāgaritvā ciraṃ suptas tato 'haṃ gāḍha|nidrayā
sahasā pratibuddhaś ca sphural|locana|tārakaḥ.
15.70 Unmīlya ca cirān netre bāla|nidrā|kaṣāyite
ken' âpy apaśyam ātmānaṃ nīyamānaṃ vihāyasā.
«A|mar'|âsura|gandharva|piśāca|preta|rākṣasām
ko nu mā nayat' îty?» āsaṃ saṃdeh'|âdhīna|mānasaḥ.
Dev'|ādīnām ayaṃ sparśo lakṣaṇair na hi vidyate
tasmād vidyā|dhareṇ' âhaṃ gṛhīto duṣṭa|buddhinā.
Śatru|haste gatasy' âpi kṣatriyasya na śobhate
hasta|pād'|âstra|mitrasya paṅgor iva mudhā vadhaḥ.
Tasmād, «ahaṃ yathā|śakti vyāyamya dviṣatā saha
mariṣyām' îti» nirdhārya taṃ tāḍayitum udyataḥ.
Atha tena vihasy' ôktaṃ, «sādhu kṣatriya|kuñjara!
svasyāḥ su|sadṛśaṃ jāteḥ karma vyavasitaṃ tvayā.
Vandhyas tu tava saṃkalpaḥ phūt|kāro Vāsuker iva

Gomukha's wife said, "If we are to take our partner of choice then I have no hesitation in taking Harishikha for myself."

Since she was sitting next to him, Marubhutika chose Tapantaka's wife.

As for Marubhutika's wife, she went up to Tapantaka and said, "He's all that's left: I've got no choice!"

Thus we spent some time relaxing and enjoying ourselves, my friends, whose intentions were pure, with their friends' wives, and I with my wife.

Once Vegavati was angry with me for some unknown reason. Despite my pleading, she slept apart from me. I stayed awake for a long time before falling into a deep
sleep. I woke with a start; my pupils were throbbing. After 15.70
a long while I opened my eyes, which were red from lack of sleep, and I found that someone was carrying me through the sky. I had no idea whether it was a deity, a demon, a Gandharva, a goblin, a ghost or a ghoul that was carrying me. It didn't feel like any sort of divine being, so it had to be an evil-minded sorcerer that had seized me.

It is wrong for a warrior, even in the hands of an enemy, to die in vain like a cripple when he has his hands and feet as weapons and allies, so I decided that I would fight my enemy as best I could before I died, and started to strike him.

He laughed and said, "Bravo, brave warrior! You have decided upon a course of action well suited to your caste. But your efforts are as vain as Vasuki's hissing when his powers were curbed by the spell! So say your prayers! Your

mantra|yantrita|vīryasya! tasmāc cintaya devatām!
Prītaś c' âsmi tav' ânena śaurya|śauṇḍena cetasā
tasmād dadāmi te 'bhīṣṭaṃ dvayor anyataraṃ varam.
Brūhi kiṃ mriyase dṛṣṭvā priyāṃ Madanamañjukām
kiṃ mahā|sāgar'|ādhāraiḥ pāṭyase makarair iti?»

Mama tv āsīd, «mṛṇāl" îva cikkhilāt kaluṣād iyam
a|rāter api niryātā bhāratī svaccha|komalā!
15.80 Yadi nāma priyāṃ dṛṣṭvā nyaseyaṃ kāya|śṛṅkhalām
tato me śatru|mitreṇa bhaved upakṛtaṃ mahat.
Yaṃ yam eva smaran bhāvaṃ tyajaty ante kaḍevaram
taṃ tam eva kil' āpnoti tadā tad|bhāva|bhāvitaḥ.
Yas tu paśyan puraḥ prītyā priyāṃ prāṇair viyujyate
tay" ân|antaram ev' âsau su|kṛtī saṃprayujyate.»

Iti saṃkalpayann eva raṇantīṃ kiṅkiṇīm adhaḥ
śṛṇomi sma prabhāt'|êndoḥ paśyāmi sma tanu|prabhām.
Tāṃ diśaṃ prahit'|âkṣeṇa dṛṣṭā Vegavatī mayā
nivāra|bāṇa|nistriṃsa|prabhā|dalita|candrikā.
Pīvara|krodha|saṃjāta|prajvalaj|jvalana|dyutiḥ
lokān iva didhakṣantī pralay'|ânala|saṃtatiḥ.
Sāndraṃ mad|darśanād eva prīti|niśvasit'|ânilaiḥ
krodh'|ânalam a|vicchinnaiḥ sthūlaiś ca niravāpayat.

Ath' âṃsayoḥ samāsajya natayor asi|carmaṇī
mūrdhni c' âñjalim ādhāya lajjā|dīnam abhāṣata,
«Vatsa|rāja|sutaṃ dāntam ākāreṇa tam īdṛśam
yuva|rājaṃ mahā|rāja mā vadhīr bhaginī|patim!
Yath" âhaṃ tava mātuś ca tath" âyaṃ mama vallabhaḥ
sva|dāra|sahitas tasmād a|kṣato mucyatām iti!»

crazed devotion to heroism has pleased me, and I am giving you a choice of two boons. Tell me, do you want to see your beloved Madanamanjuka before you die, or do you want to be ripped apart by the monsters that live in the great ocean?"

I said to myself, "This pure and tender speech has come from an enemy, like a lotus emerging from a filthy quag-
mire! If indeed I do see my sweetheart when I cast off this 15.80
physical fetter then this friendly foe will have done me a great favor. A man is conditioned by whatever thought he has in the final moment before he abandons his body, and he is certain to have that thought again. The wise man who dies while fondly looking at his sweetheart is immediately reunited with her."

While I was having these thoughts I heard bells ringing below me and noticed the faint light of the morning moon. As I looked in its direction I saw Vegavati. The brilliance of her armor and her sword dispersed the light of the moon. Like the fires of doomsday about to engulf the universe, she shone with a blazing brilliance born of her intense anger. As soon as she saw me she blew out the raging fire of her wrath with the stiff steady breeze of her sighs of happiness.

She hung her sword and shield from her bowed shoulders and brought her joined palms to her head. Then with embarrassment and sadness she said, "You have captured the son of the king of Vatsa! You can see what he is like from his appearance: he is a crown prince, o great king. Don't kill your sister's husband! In the same way that I am

15.90 Tataḥ sa|prabal'|âkṣepo daṣṭa|danta|chadaḥ sphuran
svasāram abravīd vācā siṃha|phūt|kāra|ghorayā,
«Svayaṃ|gṛhīta|nirvārya|dharā|gocara|bhartṛkām
dhik tvāṃ śārada|candr'|ābha|Manaḥ|putrika|pāṃsanīm.
Tasyāḥ puro nihaty' âinaṃ y" âsau mām avamanyate
tāṃ ca tvāṃ ca tatas tasya gamayiṣyāmi pṛṣṭhataḥ!»
«Idānīṃ nihato 's' îti!» sā bhrātaram abhāṣata
ten' âpi tvariten' âham abhra|madhye nipātitaḥ.
Atha Vegavatī dhyātvā kula|vidyām abhāṣata
«bhagavaty ārya|putro 'yaṃ! sva|putra iva rakṣyatām!
Vāta|maṇḍalik'|ôtkṣiptaṃ yathā pattraṃ bhramad bhramat
śanaiḥ śanair mahīṃ yāyāt tath" âyaṃ nīyatām iti!»
Atha nistriṃśam udgūrya nir|dharm'|â|karuṇaḥ khalaḥ
hantuṃ Vegavatīm eva pravṛttaḥ prārthitas tayā,
«Strīṣu svasṛṣu bālāsu lālitāsv aṅka|vakṣasi
nipatanti na nistriṃśāḥ śūrāṇāṃ tvā|dṛśām iti!»
Sa tu Vegavatī|madhye dukūla|sparśa|bhīluke
vajra|sthambha|chidā|dakṣām asi|dhārāṃ nyapātayat.
Atha Vegavatīr aṣṭau pracaṇḍ'|āyudha|maṇḍalāḥ
apaśyaṃ yuddha|saṃnaddhā Caṇḍikā|gaṇikā iva.
15.100 Ekā Mānasavegasya madhyaṃ kuliśa|karkaśam
rambhā|sthambham iv' â|sāram alunād asi|dhārayā.
Tato Mānasavegau dvau vikarāl'|âsi|bhāsurau

dear to you and our mother, he is dear to me. Therefore please release him and his wife unharmed!"

Shaking violently, biting his lip and twitching, he said to 15.90
his sister in a voice as terrifying as the roar of a lion, "Manahputrika is as pure as the autumn moon: shame on you for sullying her by choosing someone unsuitable as your husband, someone who walks the earth! After I have killed him in front of this girl that has been humiliating me, I shall send both her and you after him!"

She said to her brother "Now you shall die!" and he hurled me down through the clouds. Then Vegavati invoked the clan's *vidyā* and said, "O goddess, this man is my husband! Look after him like your own son! Please guide him so that he slowly flutters down to earth like a leaf that has been picked up by a whirlwind!"

Then the lawless, heartless wretch raised his sword and started to attack Vegavati. She begged him, "The swords of heroes like you do not fall on women... on sisters... on little girls whom they have played with in their laps and cherished in their hearts!"

However, he brought down his sword, which could cut a pillar of diamond, on Vegavati's middle, which feared the touch of the finest cloth. Then I saw eight Vegavatis bearing an array of fearsome weapons, like a troop of Chandika's followers ready for battle. Manasavega's middle was 15.100
as hard as Indra's thunderbolt, but one of them cut through it with her sword as though it were the hollow trunk of a banana tree. Then two whole Manasavegas sprung forth from the two parts of his body, both shining bright with

utpannau sa|kalāv eva śarīra|sakala|dvayāt.
Ekā Vegavatī kṛttā bhavanty aṣṭau tathā|vidhāḥ
tathā Mānasavegau dvau pragalbhānām itas tataḥ.
Evaṃ Mānasavegānāṃ vṛndair ambaram āvṛtam
kṣaṇād Vegavatīnāṃ ca yudhyamānaiś catur|guṇaiḥ.
Ahaṃ tu tan mahā|yuddhaṃ paśyann eva śanaiḥ śanaiḥ
proṣit'|âmbhasi gambhīre patitaḥ kūpa|sāgare.
Tatas tīvra|viṣādo 'pi vihasya smṛtavān idam
Saṃjayasya vacaḥ kaṣṭe vartamānasya saṃkaṭe:
«Dhṛṣṭadyumnād ahaṃ muktaḥ kathaṃ cit krānta|vāhanaḥ
patitaḥ Sātyak'|ânīke duṣ|kṛtī narake yathā!»
«Kathaṃ dur|uttarād asmān mam' ôttāro bhaved iti»
upāyaṃ cintayann eva smarāmi sma kathām imām.
Babhūvur bhrātaraḥ ke cit trayo brāhmaṇa|dārakāḥ
Ekataḥ pūrva|jas teṣāṃ madhyam'|ântyau Dvita|Tritau.
Taiś c' âdhīta|trayī|vidyair gurur vijñāpitaḥ kila
«gurave dātum icchāmaḥ kāṅkṣitāṃ dakṣiṇām iti.»
15.110 Ten' ôktaṃ, «sva|gṛhān gatvā kṛtvā dāra|parigraham
utpādyatām apatyaṃ ca kratubhiś c' êjyatām iti.»
Tair uktam, «a|parā kā cid dakṣiṇā mṛgyatām iti.»
Ten' ôktam, «alam etena graheṇa bhavatām iti!»
Tasmān n' âiv' âti|nirbandhān nivartante sma te yadā
tadā kruddhena guruṇā yācitā dakṣiṇām imām:
«Ekataḥ śveta|karṇānāṃ gavāṃ kokila|varcasām
kumbh'|ôdhnīnāṃ sahasraṃ me datta sthāta ca mā ciram!»
Te tu bhrāntvā mahīṃ kṛtsnām ārūḍhās tuhin'|â|calam
jñātāḥ kila Kubereṇa kauverīṃ prasthitā diśam.

their terrifying swords. Each Vegavati, when cut, became eight more the same, and in the same way, for each of those Manasavegas boldly moving about the place, two more would appear. Suddenly the sky was filled with hordes of Manasavegas fighting with four times their number of Vegavatis. While I watched the epic battle I wafted down into a vast well that was deep and dry.

Despite my severe distress, I laughed as I recalled the words of Sanjaya in a dangerous and difficult situation: "Having somehow escaped in my chariot from Dhrishtadyumna, I have fallen among the forces of Satyaka, like a sinner falling into hell!"

As I wondered how I might find my way out of the predicament, I remembered the following story. There were three brothers, brahmin boys, the firstborn of whom was Ekata, the middle Dvita, and the last Trita. When they had finished learning the three Vedas they told their teacher that they would like to give him as his fee something he wanted. He said to them, "Go home, get wives, have children and 15.110
perform sacrifices."

They replied, "Please ask for some further payment."

He said, "Stop being insistent!" When they didn't stop insisting the teacher became angry and demanded the following fee: "Give me a thousand cows as black as *koyal* birds but with one white ear and udders like pots—and don't be long!"

They wandered the entire earth before climbing the Himalayas and heading north toward the land of Kubera, who knew that they were coming. What does Kubera not

Kuberasy' âpi kiṃ n' âsti? tena te guru|dakṣiṇām
dattvā prasthāpitāḥ prītās tuhin'|âdrer avātaran.
Saṃcaranto bahūn deśāṃś cārayantaś ca gāḥ śanaiḥ
prāptā Caṇḍeśvar'|āsannāś caṇḍ'|ârka|kiraṇāḥ sthalīḥ.

Kadā cit Ekaten' ôktau gāḥ saṃprekṣya Dvita|Tritau
«lobhanīyam idaṃ dravyaṃ na parityāgam arhati.
Sādhu|kāra|śruter lubdhaḥ kaś cid unmattako yathā
agni|praveśaṃ kurvīta tath" êdaṃ naś cikīrṣitam.
Ten' êdam upapannaṃ ca guruṇā ca may" ôditam
ramaṇīya|vipākaṃ ca vākyaṃ naḥ kriyatām iti!»

15.120 Ath' ôvāca Dvitaḥ prīto, «yuktam āryeṇa cintitam
na hi sv'|ârtheṣu muhyanti buddhayas tvā|dṛśām iti.»

Ekatas tu Tritaṃ dṛṣṭvā tūṣṇīm āsīnam uktavān
«yad atra yuktaṃ tad brūtāṃ kim udāste bhavān iti?»

Ten' ôktaṃ, «ninditaṃ kurvan na kaś cin na nivāryate
pit" âpi hi viṣaṃ khādan n' âiva putrair upekṣyate!
Tena vijñāpayāmi tvāṃ kriyatāṃ ca vaco mama
buddhi|vṛddhena hi grāhyaṃ bālād api su|bhāṣitam.
An|ārya|priyam āryeṇa na kāryaṃ kāryam īdṛśam
kāryaṃ cen mahyam ātmīyam aṃśam āryaḥ prayacchatu.
Tam ahaṃ gurave dattvā dakṣiṇāy' ôpakāriṇe
pratijñā|bhāra|vikṣepād yāsyāmi laghutām iti.»

Tataḥ kruddhau ca lubdhau ca

have? After he had given them their teacher's fee and sent them happily on their way, they came down from the Himalayas. As they slowly herded the cows they crossed several countries before reaching the plateaux near Chandeshvara, where the sun's rays are fierce.

One day Ekata looked at the cows and said to Dvita and Trita, "This is a valuable asset: we must not give it away. What we are supposed to do is like a madman walking into a fire because he wants to hear cries of 'Bravo.' What I am proposing is appropriate, spoken by your senior and will have an agreeable outcome, so let's do it!"

Dvita was happy and said, "What you think is right, 15.120
sir. People like you don't make mistakes in matters of self-interest."

But Ekata noticed that Trita was silent and said, "Tell us what you think is right in this matter. Why are you not giving your opinion?"

He replied, "There is nobody who should not be dissuaded from doing something that is wrong. Even a father eating poison is not ignored by his sons! So I ask you to do as I say. Those advanced in wisdom should accept good advice, even from a child. A good man should not do something agreeable to a bad man, such as this deed. And if you, a good man, are going to do it, please give me my share now. I shall give it to our wise and beneficent teacher. Getting rid of the burden of my promise will be a weight off my shoulders."

Then the eldest and middle brothers became angry as well as greedy. Their minds were blinded by a desire for

kaniṣṭhaṃ jyeṣṭha|madhyamau
dugdha|gardh'|ândha|buddhitvāt
pramāpayitum icchataḥ.
Taiḥ kadā cit pipās"|ândhaiḥ pāntha|saṃhāta|saṃkulam
a|dṛśyamāna|pānīyaṃ dṛṣṭaṃ kūpa|rasātalam.
«Jalam atr' âsti n' âst' îti» saṃdeha|vinivṛttaye
teṣām anyatamaḥ pānthaḥ kūpe loṣṭum apātayat.
Tataḥ, «ṣvād iti!,» kṛtvā tad jarjaraṃ ghaṭa|karparam
babhañja sa ca saṃdehaḥ pathikānāṃ nyavartata.
15.130 Avatīrya tataḥ kūpaṃ Tritaḥ karuṇay" āvṛtaḥ
pānthair uttārayām āsa rajjubhir bhāṇḍa|maṇḍalam.
Tena gāvaś ca pānthāś ca bhrātarau ca mah"|ātmanā
uttāry' ôttārya pānīyaṃ kṛtāḥ snāpita|pāyitāḥ.
Pathikeṣu tu yāteṣu kṛt'|ârthāv Ekata|Dvitau
kūpa eva Tritaṃ tyaktvā sa|go|yūthau palāyitau.
Tritas tu ghaṭam ālokya rajjv" âiva saha pātitam
nir|āśiś cintayām āsa kṣaṇam uttāra|kāraṇam.
«Āṃ! smṛtaṃ! labdham!,» ity uktvā veda|vṛtt'|ânta|peśalaḥ
māh"|êndrīm akarod iṣṭiṃ manas" âiva mahā|manāḥ.
Ath' ân|antaram unnamya niśītha|dhvānta|karburāḥ
dhanuṣmantas taḍitvanto ghanā jalam apātayan.
Śanakaiḥ śanakaiḥ kūpāt pūryamāṇān nav'|âmbubhiḥ
prataran prataran dhīraṃ go|lehyād utthitas Tritaḥ.
Gatvā ca stokam adhvānaṃ gaḥ|khurālīṃ nirūpayan
apavargam iv' âdrākṣīn mūrtimantaṃ tri|daṇḍinam.
Abhivādya tam aprākṣīd, «mārge bhagavatā kva cit

milk, so they wanted to kill the youngest brother.

One day when they were numb with thirst they came across a well as deep as the underworld, where travellers were crowded around and no water could be seen. To find out whether or not there was water in it, one of the travellers threw a piece of clay into the well. When the potsherd broke with a splashing sound, the travellers' uncertainty vanished.
The kindly Trita then went down into the well and used 15.130
ropes to help the travellers bring up several pots of water. The generous fellow went on bringing up water, enabling the cows, travellers and his two brothers to be washed and watered.

When the travellers had gone, Ekata and Dvita got what they wanted: they left Trita in the well and ran away with the cows. When Trita saw that the rope and the pot had fallen in together, he was desperate and wondered for a while how he was going to get out. He said, "Ah! I remember! I've got it!," and then that exalted expert in Vedic episodes mentally performed the Great Indra sacrifice.

Speckled clouds as black as night suddenly appeared, complete with rainbows and lightning, and they poured forth rain. Trita slowly and steadily rose as the well filled up with the fresh rain. When the water was at the level where cows could have drunk it, he climbed out. After following the cows' tracks a short way along the path he saw carrying three staffs an ascetic who looked like liberation personified.

He greeted him and asked, "Your Reverence, you haven't seen somewhere on the path two brahmins like me with a na dṛṣṭāv evam|ākārau sa|go|yūthau dvi|jāv iti?»

Ten' ôktaṃ, «na mayā dṛṣṭau tau mahā|pāpa|kāriṇau
yau tvāṃ pātāla|gambhire kūpe bhrātaram aujjhatām.
15.140 Praṣṭavyāv api na kṣudrau draṣṭavyāv api na tvayā
yāv evaṃ nindit'|ācārau praṣṭavyau kuta eva tau?»

Tam uvāca Tritaḥ krodhād, «dhūrtaṃ kaluṣa|mānasam
duṣṭa|maskariṇaṃ dhik tvāṃ sādhu|nindā|viśāradam!
Jñān'|êndu|kiraṇa|vyasta|saṃmoha|dhvānta|saṃcayāḥ
tā|dṛśā eva jānanti sādhavaṃ na bhavā|dṛśāḥ.»

Tatas tasya parivrājaḥ śuci|tāmra|ghaṭ'|âruṇam
jātaṃ vikasita|jyotiḥ kirīṭ'|ābharaṇaṃ śiraḥ.
Śarīraṃ ca sahasr'|âkṣaṃ karaṃ ca kuliś'|ākulam
kṛt'|âivam|ādik'|ākāraḥ sa jātaḥ sarvathā Hariḥ.
«Varaṃ brūh' îti,» ten' ôktaḥ Tritas tuṣṭas tam abravīt
«bhrātarau me sa|pāpau ced a|pāpau bhavatām iti!»

«Punar brūh' îti» ten' ôktaḥ punar apy abravīt Tritaḥ
«gurū me gurave gās tāḥ prītau vitaratām iti!»
Punaḥ prītatamen' ôktaṃ Hariṇā, «yācyatām iti!»
«paryāptam iti,» ten' ôkte prītaḥ Śakro divaṃ yayau.

Evaṃ Mahendra|daivatyām iṣṭiṃ nirvartya mānasīm
tasmāt pātāla|gambhīrād avaṭād uttithaḥ Tritaḥ.
Tath" âham api tām iṣṭiṃ kiṃ na kuryāṃ mano|mayīm?
yājakais tu vinā yajñaṃ kṣatriyasya virudhyate.
15.150 Tasmād asmād upāyena ken' ôttiṣṭheyam? ity aham

herd of cows?"

He replied, "No, I haven't seen those great sinners who abandoned their brother in a well as deep as hell. You 15.140
shouldn't ask after nor meet those two wretches. There's no reason whatsoever to ask after two men who behave as badly as that!"

Trita angrily said to him, "Shame on you, you mean-minded mischievous mendicant, so skilled at vilifying the virtuous! Only those who have scattered the dense darkness of delusion with the moonbeams of wisdom recognize the virtuous, not people like you."

Then the ascetic's head became as red as a pot of pure copper, haloed with light and crowned with a diadem. His body was covered with a thousand eyes and his hand held a thunderbolt. Taking on these and other attributes he had completely transformed into Indra. He told Trita to ask for a boon, to which he happily replied, "If my brothers have sinned, remove their sins!"

When he was told to ask for another boon, Trita said, "May my elder brothers be happy to give the cows to our teacher!" Indra was very pleased and told him to make another request. When he said that he had had enough, Indra was satisfied and flew to heaven.

After thus performing a mental sacrifice to the great god Indra, Trita was saved from that hole as deep as hell. So why don't I also perform that mental sacrifice? But without
priests it is forbidden for a warrior to offer a sacrifice. So 15.150
how am I to escape? As I thought about this over and over again, I remembered Amitagati. When I released him from

iti c' êti ca nirdhārya smṛty" Âmitagatiṃ gataḥ.
Śaṅku|bandhana|muktena ten' âhaṃ yācitas tadā
«kaṣṭām āpadam āpanno vidhaye māṃ smarer iti!».
A|soḍha|prārthanā|duḥkhaṃ varaṃ tyaktaṃ śarīrakam
na tu pratyupakār'|āśā|rujā jarjaritaṃ dhṛtam.
Evaṃ ca cintayann eva kūpe kūpa|taros tale
apaśyam aham ātmānaṃ taṃ c' Âmitagatiṃ puraḥ.
Māṃ c' âvocat sa vanditvā harṣa|ghargharayā girā
«yuṣmat smaraṇa|pūto 'yaṃ janaḥ kiṃ kurutām iti?»
«Khe saṃgrāmayamāṇāyāḥ saha bhrātrā balīyasā
Vegavatyāḥ sahāyatvam ācar' êti» tam ādiśam.
Ten' ôktam, «arya|duhitur Vegavatyāḥ sahāyatām
kartum icchati yo mohān Mahā|gaurīṃ sa rakṣati!
Ājñā tu prathamaṃ dattā kartavy" âiv' ânujīvinā
ājñā|saṃpatti|mātreṇa bhṛtyād bhartā hi bhidyate.
Tāvat saroja|jala|ja|dhvaja|vajra|lakṣmyā
tvat|pāda|paṅka|ja|yugaṃ na namāmi yāvat
śatror galad|gala|sirā|rudhireṇa mūrdhnā
n' âbhyarcitaṃ mad|asi|lūna|śiro|dhareṇa.

iti Vegavatīlābho nāma
pañcadaśaḥ sargaḥ.

being impaled, he asked me to think of him for help if I was in a difficult situation. But it is better to abandon a body that has not had to suffer the pain of begging than to hold on to one stricken with the sickness of waiting to repay a favor. The very moment that I was thinking this, I found myself under a tree in the well and saw Amitagati in front of me. He greeted me and said with a joyous guffaw, "I have been blessed by your thinking of me. What may I do for you?"

I ordered him to help Vegavati as she fought in the sky with her mighty brother. He replied, "Anyone deluded enough to want to help noble Vegavati might as well be protecting the great goddess Gauri! Nevertheless, a servant must carry out an order once it has been given; a master is distinguished from his servant merely by having the right to give orders. I shall not honor your lotus feet with the royal insignia of the lotus, the fish, the flag or the thunderbolt until I have worshipped them with the head of your enemy, chopped off by my sword and dripping blood from the veins in its throat."

Thus ends the fifteenth canto,
called the Winning of Vegavati.

CANTO 16
THE ENTRY INTO CAMPĀ

Ath' âsau mām avanditvā
nistriṃśa|kara|kaṇṭakaḥ
ārohad ambaraṃ kāle mand'|êndu|graha|candrike.
Taṃ c' ôtpatantam ākāśaṃ śaraṃ v" ālambita|tvaram
na pṛcchāmi sma panthānaṃ deśaṃ nagaram eva vā.
Gāhamānaś ca valmīka|sthāṇu|kaṇṭaka|saṃkaṭām
aṭavīṃ siṃha|mātaṅga|puṇḍarīk'|ākulām agām.
Ath' Âmitagati|krodha|vahni|bhās" êva bhāsitām
apaśyaṃ lohitāyantīṃ prācīm aruṇa|śociṣā.

Kaṃ cic c' âdhvānam ākramya deśe n' âti|ghana|drume
vivādi|dhvani|ghaṇṭānām apaśyaṃ maṇḍalaṃ gavām.
Anumāya tatas tena vasantaṃ deśam antike
jāt'|āśvāsa|matir gacchan kṣaṇen' āraṇyam atyajam.
Tuṣāra|samay'|ārambha|bhīy" êva kamal'|ākarān
apaśyaṃ dhūsara|chāyān gacchan dina|kar'|ôdaye.
Ath' âli|kula|nīl'|âgra|vilasat|kunda|kānanam
ālavāla|parikṣipta|mūlam udyānam āsadam.

Tatra saṃmārjana|vyagram udyāna|paricārakam
pṛṣṭavān asmi, «kasy' êdam udyānam iti» so 'bravīt,
16.10 «Kiṃ ca deva|kumāro 'pi divya|jñān'|âmal'|āśayaḥ
asmad|ādīn a|bodh'|ândhān saṃdihann iva pṛcchati?
Atha vā kiṃ na etena mah"|ātmano hi mā|dṛśaiḥ
krīḍanti? tena devena svayaṃ vijñāyatām iti!»

Atha dvitīyam udyānaṃ ramaṇīyataraṃ tataḥ

THEN, WITHOUT SAYING GOODBYE TO ME, he rose into the sky with his sword in his hand, at the hour when the light of the moon and the planets is faint. He flew up into the sky as fast as an arrow. I hadn't asked him the way or what country I was in or where the nearest city was. I pressed on through a jungle thick with termite mounds, tree stumps and thorns, and teeming with lions, elephants and tigers. Then I saw that the east was becoming red from the light of the dawn, as though lit up by the glow of Amitagati's burning rage.

When I had gone some way along the path, I saw in a clearing a herd of cows whose bells were ringing discordantly. I surmised from this that there was inhabited land nearby. My spirits raised, I walked on and after a while I emerged from the jungle. While walking along at sunrise, I noticed a mass of lotuses that looked gray, as though they feared the onset of winter. Then I reached a garden with banks of jasmine whose buds looked black from the swarms of bees, and where the trees had water basins around their feet.

A gardener was busy sweeping there. I asked him whose the garden was and he replied, "What? You are a prince, a 16.10
dazzling depository of divine knowledge, and you're questioning someone blind with ignorance like me, as though you were in the dark! But anyway, I'm having nothing to do with this, for great men play games with people like me. Find out yourself, Your Majesty!"

Then I went into another, more beautiful garden and saw a pavilion with a tall gateway. When I went in a doorkeeper

praviśy' âpaśyam udyāna|mandiraṃ tuṅga|toraṇam.
Praviśāmi sma tatr' âham eko dauvārikaś ca mām
antare vetram ādhāya, «tiṣṭh' êti!» dvāry adhārayat.
Ath' âvocad dvitīyas taṃ,
«dhik tvāṃ! nirbuddha|cakṣuṣam
nivārayasi yo mohād
enam ambara|cāriṇam!
Kiṃ kadā cit tvayā dṛṣṭaḥ śruto vā kaś cid īdṛśaḥ
evaṃ vā praviśan dhīraṃ dharaṇī|dhīra|dhīr iti?»
Ten' ôktam, «an|anujñātaṃ bhartrā Nāradam apy aham
viśantaṃ n' ânujānāmi kiṃ punaḥ saumyam īdṛśam.
Ayaṃ tu dhriyamāṇo 'pi dig|danti|gati|dhīrataḥ
praviśaty eva pāruṣya|mātra|sārā hi mā|dṛśāḥ.»
Atha niṣ|kāraṇ'|ôtkaṇṭhā|karam udyāna|mandiram
prāviśaṃ nisvanad|vīṇaṃ vinīt'|âṇḍa|ja|vānaram.
Tatr' āsīnaṃ śilā|paṭṭe citra|paṭṭ'|ôpadhānake
apaśyam a|mar'|ākāraṃ naraṃ nāgarak'|ēśvaram.
16.20 Upasṛtya tam ābhāṣya, «bhoḥ sādho! sukham āsyate?
kaccid vā pratyavekṣyante bahu|kṛtvaḥ kalā iti?»
Vīṇā|vyāsakta|cittatvāt paśyati sma na māṃ asau
avakṣiptaṃ hi dṛśyāni manaḥ paśyati n' ēkṣaṇe.
Mayā tu calitā vīṇā gṛhītv" âgre yadā tadā
vīṇātaś cakṣur ākṣipya mayi nikṣiptavān asau.
Tataḥ saṃbhrāntam utthāya sraṃsamān'|ôttar'|âmbaraḥ
māṃ upāveśayat prītas tasminn eva śil"|āsane.
Pāda|cāra|pariśrāntam aṅgaṃ saṃvāhya māmakam
prakṣālya ca svayaṃ pādau datt'|ârghaḥ samupāviśat.
Anuyuktaś ca sa mayā, «ko 'yaṃ jana|padas tvayā
bhūṣitaḥ katamac c' êdaṃ puraṃ sac|caritair iti?»
Atha tena vihasy' ôktaṃ, «saṃbhāvyā nabhasā gatiḥ

raised his cane and stopped me at the gate, saying, "Wait!"

Then a second doorkeeper said to him, "Shame on you! You can't have a very discerning eye if you're foolish enough to obstruct this sky-rover! Have you ever seen or heard of a man like this, going in so confidently, his resolve as firm as the earth?"

He replied, "Without my master's permission I cannot allow even Narada to enter, let alone a mild man like him. But, despite his way being barred, this man is going in all the same, as confidently as a celestial sentinel: men like me are made of nothing but harsh words."

For no apparent reason the pavilion had aroused my curiosity and I went inside. A lute was being played and there were tame birds and monkeys. Sitting on a stone slab covered with colored cloth and cushions, I saw a man who
looked like a god, a prince among gentlemen. I went up to 16.20
him and said, "Hello, good sir! How do you do? Do you often study the arts?" His mind was so absorbed in the lute that he did not see me. The mind, not the eyes, has to be focussed on visible objects for them to be seen. But when I took the lute by its end and moved it, he shifted his gaze from the lute and cast it on me. His shawl slipped off as he hurriedly got up and graciously had me sit on the stone bench. After massaging my limbs, which were exhausted from walking, and washing my feet himself, he welcomed me with water and sat down next to me.

I asked him, "What is this country that you adorn, and which city is this that you decorate with your good deeds?"

He laughed and said, "It is possible that a child of the gods

tvā|dṛśāṃ deva|putrāṇām a|jñānaṃ tu na yujyate!
Yo hi deś'|ântaraṃ yāti mugdho 'pi dharaṇī|caraḥ
agrato bhāvitaṃ deśaṃ n' â|buddhvā saṃprapadyate.
Deśaś candra|prakāśo 'yaṃ candrikā|prakaṭā purī
na jñātā pathiken' êti duḥ|śliṣṭam iva dṛśyate.
Ten' â|mara|kumāras tvam avatīrṇo vihāyasaḥ
a|jñāna|chadmanā channaḥ krīḍituṃ mad|vidhair iti.»
16.30 Ath' âhaṃ cintayitv" êdam uttar'|ābhāsam uktavān
«dvi|jo 'haṃ Vatsa|viṣaye vasataḥ pitarau mama.
So 'haṃ karṇa|sukh'|ācāraḥ! kadā cin mantra|vādinām
śrutvā dārair a|saṃtuṣṭo yakṣīṃ kāṃ|cid asādhayam.
Sā c' âhaṃ ca tataḥ prītau śaile śaile vane vane
yad vā yad rucitaṃ tasyai tatra tatr' âramāvahi.
Cintitaṃ ca mayā rātrau, ‹na me yakṣyā prayojanam
pātāla|mantram ārādhya ramayāmy asurīm iti!›
Ath' ērṣyā|dūṣita|dhiyā tay" âhaṃ yakṣa|kanyayā
ānīya nabhasā nyastaḥ pure 'smin bhavatām iti.»
Ten' ôktaṃ, «na na|saṃbhāvyā yakṣa|rakṣaḥsu caṇḍatā
paścāt|tāpa|gṛhītā tu na sā yusmān vimokṣyati.
‹Ko 'yaṃ jana|padaḥ syāt kā pur" îti› ca yad ucyate
Aṅgā jana|padaḥ sphītaś Campā c' êyaṃ mahā|purī.
Ahaṃ ca Dattako nāma vaṇik paura|puras|kṛtaḥ
prasiddhaḥ priya|vīṇatvād Vīṇādattaka|nāmakaḥ.»
Ath' āhūy' âbravīd ekaṃ sa karṇe paricārakam

such as yourself might travel through the air, but ignorance does not befit you! Any terrestrial traveller who visits a foreign land, even a fool, does not set out without finding out about the countries that lie ahead. This country is as famous as the moon; the city is as well known as moonlight. It seems very unlikely that a traveller would not know of them. You must be a divine prince who has come down from the heavens pretending to be ignorant in order to tease people like me."

After some thought I gave a false answer: "I am a brahmin; 16.30
my parents live in the kingdom of Vatsa. How did I come to be here? It's a good story! One day I listened to some magicians chanting spells. I was unhappy with my wife so I conjured up a *yakṣī*. She and I were happy together and enjoyed ourselves in various favorite mountain and forest haunts of hers. One night I thought, 'There's no point in my being with a *yakṣī*; I shall use the hell-spell and have some fun with a demoness!' Jealousy tainted the *yakṣī*'s mind. She took me through the sky and cast me down in this city of yours."

He replied, "It is not impossible for *yakṣa*s and demons to be cruel. However, she will be seized with regret and will not abandon you. As for your question about this country and city: the prosperous country is Anga and this great city is Champa. I am a merchant called Dattaka, an eminent citizen. Because of my love for the lute I am known as Vinadattaka.*"

Then he called over an attendant and said something in his ear. The attendant hitched up his tunic and hurried

gāḍhaṃ parikaraṃ badhnan dhāvamānaḥ sa c' âgamat.
Kṣaṇena ca parāvṛtya śvasita|spandit'|ôdaraḥ
«svāmi pravahaṇaṃ prāptam iti» Dattakam abravīt.
16.40 Ath' âvatārya muditaḥ sv'|âṅguler aṅgulīyakam
dattavān Dattakas tasmai śīghra|preṣaṇa|kāriṇe.
Kṛt'|âñjalir ath'|ôvāca, «yakṣī|kāmuka dhāvyatām
pāvanair dāsa|bhavanaṃ pāda|nikṣepaṇair iti.»

Ath' āruhya pravahaṇaṃ Vīṇādattaka|vāhakam
gṛhīta|cāru|saṃcāraṃ Campām abhi|mukho 'gamam.
Śṛṇomi sma ca paurāṇāṃ jalpatām itar'|êtaram
«ciraṃ|jīvadbhir āścaryaṃ pṛthivyāṃ kiṃ na dṛśyate!
Kva nāgaraka|senā|nīr Dattakas tuṅga|mastakaḥ
kva ca kasy' âpi pānthasya rajju|bhāge vyavasthitaḥ?»

Ath' âpareṇa tatr' ôktam, «ata ev' âyam uttamaḥ
yena lok'|ôttamasy' âsya rajju|bhāge vyavasthitaḥ.
Ākār'|ânumitaṃ c' âitad guṇa|saṃbhāra|bhāriṇaḥ
nanu c' âsya Vasanto 'pi sārathyena vikatthate!»

Dṛṣṭavān paritaś c' âhaṃ kva cid utsṛṣṭa|lāṅgalān
hālikān hala|mūleṣu vīṇā|vādana|tat|parān.
Kva cid uddāma|govargaṃ vaṭe gaḥ|pāla|maṇḍalam
vitantrīs tāḍayad vīṇāḥ karṇa|śūla|pradāyinīḥ.
Āsannaś ca pura|dvāraṃ vikrayāya prasāritām
vīṇ"|âvayava|saṃpūrṇām apaśyaṃ śakaṭ'|āvalīm.
16.50 Vijarjarita|karṇaś ca vitantrī|dhvani|mudgaraiḥ
vyasta|padma|nidhān'|ābhaṃ prāpnomi sma vaṇik|patham.
Kuṅkumaṃ kretum āyātaḥ kaś cid vāṇijam abravīt

off. He was back in no time. Panting, he said to Dattaka, "Master, the carriage has arrived."

16.40 Dattaka was delighted. He took a ring from his finger and gave it to the man for carrying out his duties so quickly. Putting his palms together, he said to me, "O *yakṣī*'s beau, please purify your servant's house with your holy footsteps."

I climbed into the carriage and Vinadattaka drove us toward Champa at a comfortable pace. I heard the citizens chattering to one another, "If you live long enough there aren't many marvels on the earth that you won't get to see! Who would have thought that proud Dattaka, our foremost gentleman, would sit in the driver's seat for some unknown traveller?"

Someone else said, "Dattaka must be a great man to be sitting in the driver's seat for this exceptional fellow. One can tell from the appearance of the man with his wealth of virtues that even Vasanta would boast of being his carriage-driver!"

I looked around me. Here, there were plowmen who had put down their plows and were sitting by them intently playing the lute. There, I saw a herd of cows roaming free and a group of cowherds under a banyan tree playing out-of-tune lutes that were painful on the ears. On reaching the city gates I saw a row of carts full of lute parts laid out
for sale. My ears were battered from their pounding by the 16.50
sound of out-of-tune lutes. I reached a market that looked like an array of Kubera's treasure. A man had come to buy saffron. His mind was preoccupied by lutes and he said to the merchant, "Give me a lute."

vīṇā|vikṣipta|cetasko, «vīṇā me dīyatām iti.»
Cirād ākarṇya tad vākyaṃ kupitaḥ sa tam abravīt
«vaṇijo 'nye kim utsannā yena khādasi mām iti?»
Evaṃ vardhaki|karmāra|kulāla|varuḍ'|ādayaḥ
nikṛṣṭa|janma|karmāṇaḥ saktā vīṇām avādayan.
Atha prāyaṃ ciraṃ dvāraṃ Vīṇādattaka|veśmanaḥ
śātakumbha|mayaiḥ kumbhair ambho|garbhaiḥ su|maṅgalam
Tatra yānād avaplutya prāviśaṃ gṛham ṛddhimat
utthāsnur iva medhāvī viśālaṃ hṛdayaṃ śriyaḥ.
Dattakas tu puro 'smākaṃ dāsī|dāsam abhāṣata
«ady' ārabhy' âsya yuṣmābhir ājñā saṃpādyatām iti!»
Atha vyajñāpayan prahvāḥ sūpa|kārāḥ sametya mām
«ājñāpayata yuṣmākaṃ kaḥ pākaḥ sādhyatām iti?»
Mama tv āsīd, «mayā tāvad brāhmaṇatvaṃ prakāśitam
brāhmaṇāś ca ghṛta|kṣīra|guḍ'|ādi|madhura|priyāḥ.
Tad idaṃ yuktam» ity etac cintayitv" êdam uktavān
«nanu hasta|puṭa|grāhyaṃ pāyasaṃ sādhyatām iti.»
16.60 Atha hastaṃ vidhūy' ôktaṃ sūpa|kāreṇa gacchatā
«anna|saṃskāra|śāstra|jñāḥ kāṃ diśaṃ yāntu saṃprati?
Bhīmasen'|ādibhir yāni sūda|śāstrāṇi cakrire
karma|karyo 'pi tāny asmin gṛhe prāyeṇa jānate.
Yakṣī|kāmukam āsādya prabhuṃ bhojana|kovidam
an|arthakāni jātāni carit'|ârthāni pāyase.
Aho nāgarakaḥ svāmī svayaṃ pravahaṇena yaḥ
ālekhya|yakṣam ādāya yakṣī|kāmukam āgataḥ.
Sarvathā dhig a|kārya|jñam aiśvarya|janitaṃ madam
gamitaḥ preṣyatāṃ yena mā|dṛśo 'p' īdṛśām iti!».
Atha mardana|śāstra|jñas taruṇaḥ paricārakaḥ

On hearing this request, the enraged merchant, after a long pause, said to him, "Have the other merchants shut up shop? Is that why you are preying on me?" The carpenters, blacksmiths, potters, cane-splitters and other lowborn workers were similarly obsessed with playing the lute.

I finally arrived at the door of Vinadattaka's house, which was most auspiciously adorned with golden pots full of water. I got down from the carriage there and entered the sumptuous house, like a diligent wise man entering the huge heart of the goddess of wealth. In my presence Dattaka told his male and female servants, "From today you are to take orders from this man!"

As a group, the cooks bowed and asked me to tell them what food they were to cook for me. I said to myself, "I have told everyone that I am a brahmin and brahmins like sweet food with ingredients like ghee, milk and jaggery." Thinking it would be appropriate, I asked for a handful of rice pudding to be prepared.

The cook wrung his hands and said on his way out, 16.60
"Where are the masters of the culinary art to go now? Even most of the maids in this house know the cookery books composed by Bhimasena and the rest. Now that we have a gourmet like the *yakṣī*'s beau as our master, our expertise is wasted on making rice pudding. Oh how sophisticated of our master to have personally brought here that picture of a *yakṣa*, the *yakṣī*'s beau. Curse the ignorant arrogance that wealth produces—it has reduced a man like me to such servitude to a man like him!"

Then a young servant who was an expert masseur gave

mam' âṅgaṃ gandha|tailena mṛdnāti sma yathā|sukham.
Paścād udvartanaṃ snānam a|hat'|âmbara|dhāraṇam
kṛtvā deva|praṇāmaṃ ca prāyaṃ bhojana|maṇḍapam.
Tatra bhojana|bhūmi|ṣṭhaṃ māṃ namas|kṛtya Dattakaḥ
sa|bhrātṛ|bhāginey'|ādi|paṅkti|madhya upāviśat.
Kulāla|cakra|pātrī ca pātrī mama hiraṇmayī
pāyasen' êndu|varṇena sūpa|kāreṇa pūritā.
Pārśve pāyasa|pātryāś ca tejasvi|maṇi|bhājane
mahā|sāra|musāra|sthe sthāpite madhu|sarpiṣī.

16.70 Cintitaṃ ca mayā, «jāto mahān ayam upadravaḥ!
madhu|māṃs"|ôcitaḥ kv' âhaṃ kva c' êdaṃ ghṛta|pāyasam!
Kena nāma prakāreṇa tyajeyam idam?» ity aham
vicārya pāyasa|grāsaṃ, «dagdho 'sm' îti!» nirastavān.
Teṣāṃ saṃpratyay'|ârthaṃ ca haran dāha|rujaṃ kila
śīta|pānīya|gaṇḍūṣair mukhaṃ muhur aśītayam.

Ballavas tu puraḥ sthitvā Vīṇādattakam uktavān
«n' âyaṃ vipraḥ! kathaṃ vipraḥ pradviṣyād ghṛta|pāyasam?»
Ācaṣṭa mardakaś c' êdam, «āsav'|āmoda|vāsitaḥ
niśvāso 'sya mayā ghrātaḥ śanakair niścaran iti!»

Dattako 'pi kar'|âgreṇa pidhāya mukham ātmanaḥ
kampayitv" ôttam'|âṅgaṃ ca taṃ bruvantaṃ nyavārayat.
Abravīc ca, «payaḥ|pānaṃ yūyaṃ pibata pānakam
pānakasy' âpi pānena goṣṭhī saṃmānyatām iti!»

Mayā tu jāta|tarṣeṇa pāne pariṇatiṃ gate
tat pītaṃ pāna|sādṛśyāt pāna|buddhy" âiva pānakam.
Khaṇḍa|māṃsa|prakār'|ādyaṃ nān"|âdhiṣṭhāna|saṃkulam

me a delightful massage with scented oil. I removed the oil with shampoo, took a bath and put on new clothes. Then I bowed before the gods and went to the dining hall. When I had sat down to eat Dattaka greeted me respectfully and sat down in the middle of a row between his brothers, his sisters' sons and other men of his family. Their plates, which were made on the potter's wheel, and mine, which was made of gold, were filled by the cook with rice pudding the color of the moon. Next to the plate of rice pudding, in a cup made of dazzling gems on a priceless emerald base, were put honey and ghee.

I thought, "This has gone from bad to worse! I'm used to 16.70
wine and meat and I've got rice pudding with ghee!" After wondering how on earth I was going to get rid of it, I spat out a mouthful of the rice pudding and said, "I've burnt myself!" To convince them, I repeatedly cooled my mouth with sips of cold water, pretending to soothe the burn.

But the cook stood in front of Vinadattaka and said, "This man is not a brahmin! How can a brahmin not like rice pudding with ghee?" And the masseur said, "His breath smells of alcohol—I got a slight whiff of it."

Dattaka put a finger in front of his mouth and shook his head to stop him from continuing. He said, "Do have a drop of punch: it's like water, and we will be honored by your drinking it with us!"

The wine I had drunk earlier had been digested and I was thirsty. I was in the mood for drinking wine, so, because it was like wine, I drank the punch. After eating an exquisite meal of assorted pieces of meat and so forth mixed with

sevitv" āhāram a|grāmyam udatiṣṭhaṃ sa|Dattakaḥ.
Saṃmṛṣṭa|bhojana|sthāne puṣpa|churita|kuṭṭime
kāntam adhyāsi paryaṅkaṃ nyastaṃ tatr' âiva maṇḍape.
16.80 Karpūra|tri|phalā|nābhi|lavaṅg'|âilā|su|gandhinā
mukhasya gandha|rāgau ca tāmbūlen' ôdapādayam.
Evaṃ ca sukham āsīno Vīṇādattakam abravam
«vīn"|ônmattir iyaṃ kasmāc Campāyāṃ kathyatām iti.»
Ten' ôktam, «iha Campāyāṃ Sānudāso vaṇik|patiḥ
tasya Gandharvadatt" êti sutā trailokya|sundarī.
Sa ca tāṃ priyamāṇo 'pi varair vara|guṇ'|ākaraiḥ
abhiprāyeṇa ken' âpi na kasmai cit prayacchati.
Pratyākhyātum a|śaktena yācitena kṣaṇe kṣaṇe
tena śulkam upanyastaṃ duḥ|saṃpādaṃ surair api.
‹A|pūrvaṃ kila gāyantyās tasyāḥ kim api gītakam
yo 'nuvādayitā vīṇāṃ pariṇetā sa tām iti.›
‹May" êyaṃ pariṇetavyā may" êyam iti› nis|trapaḥ
na kaś cid yo na Campāyāṃ vīṇay" ônmattakaḥ kila.
Puro nāgarakāṇāṃ ca catuḥ|ṣaṣṭes tad|arthinām
ṣaṣṭhe ṣaṣṭhe gate māse sā tad gāyati gītakam.
Anena ca prakāreṇa yātaḥ kālo mahān ayam
na c' âpi vīṇayā kaś cid anugacchati tām iti.»
Etat|kath"|âvasāne ca puruṣau śrotriy'|ākṛtī
Vīṇādattakam abrūtāṃ sthavirau vetra|dhāriṇau,
16.90 «Śreṣṭhinā preṣitāv āvāṃ saṃdeśena tvad|antikam
yadi sajjā suhṛd|goṣṭhī samasyā kriyatām iti.»
Ten' ôktaṃ, «suhṛdaḥ sajjā yadi vaḥ su|sthitā gṛhāḥ

various condiments, I and Dattaka stood up. After the dining room had been swept and the inlaid floor strewn with flowers, I sat on a beautiful bed that had been put right there in the hall. I scented and reddened my mouth 16.80
with betel nut delightfully spiced with camphor, nutmeg, areca, cloves, musk and cardamom.

Thus sitting comfortably, I said to Vinadattaka, "Tell me why there is such a craze for the lute in Champa."

He replied, "Here in Champa the head of the merchants is Sanudasa. He has a daughter called Gandharvadatta, who is the most beautiful girl in the three worlds. Despite being propitiated by suitors replete with the finest virtues, for some reason he won't give her to anyone. Unable to refuse their constant requests, he has laid down a bride-price that even the gods would find hard to meet. When the girl sings a certain song that it seems nobody has heard before, the man that accompanies her with the lute will have her hand in marriage. Now every single man in Champa is completely crazy about the lute, and dares to think that he will be the one to marry her. Every six months she sings that song before sixty-four gentlemen who want to marry her. A long time has passed like this and nobody has yet managed to accompany her with the lute."

When this story was over, two educated-looking old men
carrying canes said to Vinadattaka, "The chief merchant 16.90
has sent us to you with the message that if all your friends are ready, they should gather together."

He replied, "My friends are ready. If your house is in order and Gandharvadatta is happy, let's meet tomorrow!"

kalyā Gandharvadattā vā śva eva kriyatām iti!»
Tatas taṃ pṛṣṭavān asmi mah"|ôtsāhena cetasā
«rūpaṃ Gandharvadattāyāḥ kīdṛg ity?» atha so 'bravīt.
Tasyāḥ sva|kānti|pariveṣa|paṭ'|âpidhānaṃ
netra|prabhā|prakara|sārita|harmya|garbham.
utkṛṣṭa|vismaya|vimohita|mānasena
rūpaṃ nirūpayitum eva mayā na śakyam!

iti Bṛhatkathāyām
Gandharvadattālābhe
Campāpraveśo nāma ṣoḍaśaḥ sargaḥ.

Then, with great interest, I asked him to describe Gandharvadatta's beauty. He replied, "It is hidden behind the veil of her loveliness and fills the inside of her house with the dazzling light from her eyes. My mind is so completely transported by adoration that I am at a loss to describe her beauty!"

Thus ends the sixteenth canto in the Long Story,
called the Entry into Champa
in the Winning of Gandharvadatta.

CANTO 17
MARRIAGE TO GANDHARVADATTĀ

Atha Gandharvadattāyās
tāṃ guṇ'|ākāra|saṃpadam
samākarṇy' âiva karṇābhyāṃ mano nītaṃ vidheyatām.
Pṛcchāmi sma ca bhūyas tam, «api śakyā bhaven mayā
draṣṭuṃ Gandharvadatt" êti» tena c' ôktaṃ, «na śakyate.
A|gāndharveṇa sā draṣṭuṃ deven' âpi na śakyate
yadi c' êcchatha tāṃ draṣṭuṃ gāndharvaṃ śikṣyatām iti.»
May" ôktaṃ, «nāradīye 'pi nirvṛtte kila labhyate
gāndharva|śabdas tat tasmād asmākaṃ kāryatām iti!»
Tato vyāharitas tena vīṇ"|ācāryaḥ khara|svaraḥ
naṣṭa|śruti|svara|jñāno Bhūtiko nāma dur|bhagaḥ.
Āsīc ca mama taṃ dṛṣṭvā vikṛtaṃ nara|vānaram
«alaṃ me nāradīyena! kṛtaṃ Gandharvadattayā!
Īdṛśāṃ śiṣyatāṃ gatvā rājya|lābho 'pi garhati
a|nyāy'|āgatam aiśvaryaṃ nindanty eva hi sādhavaḥ!»
Abhyutthān'|âbhivādābhyāṃ taṃ Vīṇādattak'|ādayaḥ
apūjayan mayā c' âsau na draṣṭum api pāritaḥ.
Atha ruṣṭa|kaṭ'|âkṣeṇa lohit'|âkṣaḥ sa vīkṣya mām
Vīṇādattaka|dattāyāṃ pīṭhikāyām upāviśat.
17.10 Abravīd Dattakas taṃ ca, «yakṣī|bhartur dvi|janmanaḥ
bhavān asy' ôpapannasya nāradīyaṃ karotv iti.»
Ten' ôktaṃ, «s'|âbhimānatvād ayaṃ māṃ avamanyate
na ca pārayate dātuṃ dāridryāt kākaṇīm api!
Guru|śuśrūṣayā vidyā puṣkalena dhanena vā
na c' âsminn ekam apy asti yady asti pratipadyatām.»

AS SOON AS THEY HEARD of Gandharvadatta's perfect virtues and beauty, my ears turned my mind into a slave. I asked him another question: "Might I be able to see Gandharvadatta?" He replied, "You cannot. Unless he is a musician, even a god can't see her. If you want to see her you must learn to play music."

I replied, "They say that on completing the study of lute-playing as taught by Narada, one is called a musician, so please arrange that for me!" At this he summoned a lute teacher called Bhutika, an ugly man with a harsh voice and no knowledge of scales or notes.

When I saw that hideous ape of a man I said to myself, "I don't need to learn to play the lute! Forget Gandharvadatta! Even winning a kingdom would be reprehensible if it entailed becoming the pupil of someone like him: good men pour nothing but scorn on ill-gotten wealth!"

Vinadattaka and the others showed him respect by standing up and saluting reverentially. I could not even look at him. With red eyes he cast me angry side glances before sitting in a seat offered by Vinadattaka. Dattaka said to 17.10
him, "This man is the husband of a *yakṣī* and a brahmin. He has come to you as a student. Please teach him Narada's method of lute-playing."

He replied, "He insults me with his arrogance and is so poor that he can't pay me even a penny! Knowledge is acquired either through obedience to a teacher or with abundant wealth, and this man has neither. If he does have what's required, he should hand it over!"

Dattaken' ôktam, «ācārya virūpaṃ mantritaṃ tvayā
ko yakṣī|kāmukaṃ śakto daridram iti jalpitum?
Yasya dāsaḥ sa|dāso 'haṃ tvaṃ jānāsy eva mā|dṛśaḥ
sa yakṣī|kāmukaḥ kasmād daridra iti bhaṇyate?
Su|varṇānāṃ śataṃ v" âpi gṛhyatāṃ tvā|dṛś'|ôcitam
patite droṇa|meghe 'pi na tiṣṭhati jalaṃ sthale.»

Nārad'|ādi|parīvārāṃ sa c' âbhyarcya Sarasvatīm
dur|vyavasthita|tantrīkāṃ vīṇāṃ mahyam upānayat.
Mayā tu sā viparyak|sthā sthāpit" âṅke yadā tadā
Bhūtiko māṃ, «dhig!» ity uktvā Vīṇādattakam uktavān:
«Na yakṣī|kāmuko mandaḥ śakyaḥ śikṣayituṃ mayā
vīṇā|grahaṇam apy eṣa na jānāti sukh'|âidhitaḥ.
Na nāma svayam etena yadi vīṇā na vāditā
ālekhya|vādakāḥ ke 'pi na dṛṣṭā naṣṭa|dṛṣṭinā?»

17.20 Iti saṃtakṣya māṃ vāgbhir ātodyaṃ parivartya ca
sa niṣādo niṣādaṃ me, «ṣaḍ|ja ity,» upadiṣṭavān.
Ath' āmarṣa|parītena dṛḍhaṃ tāḍayatā mayā
catasraḥ pañca vā tantryaś chinnāś, «caḍ iti!,» vi|svarāḥ.

Ath' ôkto Dattakas tena, «tantrī|vartaka|saṃgraham
a|kṛtvā kiṃ karoty asya nāradīyaṃ bhavān iti?»

Ahaṃ tu vismṛta|chadmā chinna|tantrīm api kṣaṇam
śruti|vāsita|karṇatvān mṛdu vīṇām avādayam.
Atha visphāritair netrair ut|karṇā Dattak'|ādayaḥ
«kim etad iti?» jalpanto mām aikṣanta sa|vismayāḥ.
Bhūtikas tu bhaya|krodha|lajjā|vismaya|niṣ|prabhaḥ
«kākatālīyam!» ity uktvā gata eva sa|dakṣiṇaḥ.

Dattaka said, "Teacher, what you have said is unseemly. Who can call the *yakṣī*'s beau poor? I, who have servants, am his servant. You are well acquainted with people like me, so how can the *yakṣī*'s beau be called poor? Take a hundred gold coins, an appropriate amount for someone like you: even after a torrential cloudburst water does not remain in the highlands."

The teacher then worshipped Sarasvati with her retinue of Narada and others, and gave me a lute with badly fitted strings. When I put it in my lap the wrong way round Bhutika cursed me and said to Vinadattaka: "The *yakṣī*'s beau is a dimwit! I cannot teach him: he is so decadent he does not even know how to hold a lute! He may not have played the lute himself, but has he never seen any pictures of people playing it? Is he blind?"

After insulting me like this, the philistine turned it over 17.20
and struck the bottom note, telling me it was the top one. I was furious and vigorously strummed the out-of-tune strings. With harsh twangs four or five of them snapped!

He said to Dattaka, "You should have made a store of lute strings before having this man learn to play."

I, however, forgot my assumed persona, and, because I have a good ear for harmony, managed to play the lute delicately for a moment, even though its strings were broken. Dattaka and the others pricked up their ears, jabbered "What's this?" and looked at me in astonishment with bulging eyes. Bhutika, however, turned pale with fear, anger, shame and surprise. Saying, "It's a fluke!," he left with his fee.

Evaṃ ca divasaṃ nītvā kṛta|prādoṣik'|âśanaḥ
āvasaṃ śayan'|āvāsaṃ mālā|dhūp'|âdhivāsitam.
Haṃsa|pakṣ'|âṃśuka|prāya|komal'|āstaraṇ'|āstṛtam
bhāsvad|vajra|śilā|pādam āseve śayanaṃ tataḥ.
Rūp'|ākṛṣṭa|jagan|netre yuvatī sāra|bhūṣaṇe
rūp'|ājīve śanaiḥ pādau samavāhayatāṃ mama.
Sahaj'|āhārya|mādhurya|ramaṇīyatar'|âkṣaraiḥ
vacobhiḥ kila te cittaṃ madīyaṃ hartum aicchatām.
17.30 Vegavatyā vimuktaṃ ca pratibhānti sma tāni mām
rāsabhī|rasitān' îva vi|rasāni sva|karṇayoḥ.
Tāni c' â|śrotu|kāmena nidrā|vyājaḥ kṛto mayā
atha prasupta ev' âsmi nir|āśe te ca jagmatuḥ.

Ardhe yāte ca yāminyāḥ śvās'|ânumita|cetane
dṛṣṭa|tattva iv' â|vidyāṃ nidrām atyajam utkaṭām.
Citra|paṭṭa|pidhānāyāṃ tiṣṭhantyāṃ nāga|dantake
Vīṇādattaka|vīṇāyāṃ tato dṛṣṭiṃ nyapātayam.

Mama tv āsīd, «a|vaśyaṃ māṃ netā śvas tatra Dattakaḥ
vīṇā ca vādanīyā syāc cir'|ôtsṛṣṭā ca sā mayā.
Vidyā c' ārādhyamān" âpi duḥkhena paricīyate
bhaktyā mātuḥ sa|patn" îva nisarga|kuṭilā hi sā.
Vīṇā saṃnihitā c' êyaṃ velā c' êyaṃ nir|ākulā
jijñāse tāvad ity» enāṃ vicāry' âhaṃ gṛhītavān.

Utkarṣann apakarṣaṃś ca kāś cit kāś cin manāṅ manāk
vyavasthāpayituṃ tantrīḥ kara|śākhabhir aspṛśam.
Ath' âśṛṇavam ālāpān svasmād vāsa|gṛhād bahiḥ

After spending the day thus, I had an evening meal and went to my bedroom, which was scented with flower garlands and incense. The bed was covered with a quilt as soft as the down on a swan's wing, and its legs were made of sparkling diamonds. I lay down on it. Their beauty overshadowing that of the moon, two young and expensively adorned courtesans gently massaged my feet. They tried to steal my heart with words whose beautiful syllables were both naturally sweet and enhanced by artifice. But in my 17.30
separation from Vegavati their words were as unpleasant to my ears as the braying of she-asses. I didn't want to listen to them so I feigned tiredness and as soon as I was asleep the disappointed girls left.

In the middle of the night, when life has to be inferred from breathing, I abandoned my deep sleep like one who has seen the ultimate reality abandoning ignorance. My gaze fell on Vinadattaka's lute, which was hanging on a hook, wrapped in a colored cloth.

I said to myself, "I'm sure Dattaka is going to take me there tomorrow, and I may have to play the lute, which I gave up years ago. Even when practiced assiduously, skill develops with difficulty, for it is naturally capricious, like a married man's mistress. There is a lute handy and at this hour there is no one about. I'll just see what happens." Having made my decision, I took hold of it.

As I tightened some strings a little to tune it and likewise loosened others, I touched them with my fingers. I heard people speaking outside my bedroom: "Samudrasena! Go-datta! Run, run, friend! Quick! Lucky Vinadattaka! His

«Samudrasena! Godatta! dhāva dhāva sakhe! drutam!
Vīṇādattaka|bhadrasya gṛheṣu kṛta|karmaṇaḥ
Sarasvatī bhagavatī vīṇāṃ sārayati svayam!
17.40 Vīṇāyāḥ sāryamāṇāyāḥ svanasy' ôdaya īdṛśaḥ
samāpta|sāraṇāyās tu kī|dṛn nāma bhaviṣyati?
Tasmāt Sarasvatī|vīṇe dṛṣṭvā śrutvā ca saṃhate
netra|śrotrāṇi no yānti pavitra|taratām iti!»
Ath' âvalambya tāṃ vīṇāṃ tvarayā nāga|dantake
prāvṛtya sa|śiraḥ|pādaṃ kāyaṃ nidrāṃ kil' āgamam.
Nāgarās tu nyavartanta jalpanto dīna|cetasaḥ
«kathaṃ Sarasvatī kṣudrair dṛśyate 'smad|vidhair iti?»
Yāpitāyāṃ tu yāminyāṃ kṛta|pūrv'|âhṇika|kramam
māṃ an|ulbaṇa|veṣaṃ ca vanditvā Dattako 'bravīt,
«Amī nāgarakāḥ prāptāś citra|yāna|prasādhanāḥ
tad gandharva|samasyāyai yuṣmābhir api gamyatām.
Ājñāpayata yānaṃ ca kareṇu|turag'|ādikam
yena vo rocate gantuṃ tena prasthīyatām iti!»
May" ôktaṃ, «gacchatu bhavān vāhanena yathā|sukham
ahaṃ tu pāda|cāreṇa gacchāmi śanakair iti.»
Ath' âsmad|anurodhena māṃ purodhāya Dattakaḥ
prasthitaḥ pāda|cāreṇa sa|nāgaraka|maṇḍalaḥ.
Amantrayanta yāntaś ca kruddhā nāgarakā mithaḥ
«yakṣī|kāmuka|rūpo 'yam an|artho 'smān upāgataḥ.
17.50 Vayam asya prasādena tyakta|maṇḍita|vāhanāḥ
āśā|dīrghāsu rathyāsu caraṇaiḥ saṃcarāmahe!»
Meror droṇīr iv' âkraman viśikhā vistṛt'|āyatāḥ
apaśyaṃ veśmanāṃ mālās tasy' âiva sirasām iva.
Prāsādeṣu ca jalpantīr gav'|âkṣa|prerit'|ēkṣaṇāḥ
kokilā|su|bhag'|ālāpāḥ śṛṇomi sma kul'|âṅganāḥ:

work is done! The goddess Sarasvati herself is tuning a lute in his house! If the lute makes a sound like this when it is 17.40 being tuned, what on earth will it be like when the tuning is complete? By seeing Sarasvati and hearing her lute at the same time, our ears and eyes will be particularly blessed!"

I quickly hung the lute on the hook, covered myself from head to toe, and pretended to go to sleep. The citizens went away disappointed, saying, "How are lowly people like us going to see Sarasvati?"

When the night was over and I had done my morning duties and was suitably dressed, Dattaka greeted me and said, "The gentlemen have arrived in their various vehicles and get-ups; you too should be on your way to the musicians' gathering. Say how you would like to travel—by elephant, horse or otherwise—and set forth!"

I replied, "You should go in the vehicle of your choice. As for me, I shall go quietly, on foot."

In deference to my wishes, Dattaka set out on foot behind me, together with all the gentlemen. On the way the angry gentlemen talked among themselves, saying, "This man that has arrived in the guise of a *yakṣī*'s beau is bad news for us. Thanks to him we have abandoned our decorated 17.50 vehicles and are travelling on foot along roads as long as our odds!"

I walked along avenues as wide and long as the valleys of mount Meru, and saw rows of houses that were like the chains of its peaks. I could hear noblewomen on the terraces looking out of the round windows and chattering

«Ayi Māgadhi! Vaidehi! Malayāvati! Yāvani!
yakṣī|kāmukam āyātaṃ sakhyaḥ paśyata! dhāvata!
Khalayā kila yakṣy" âyam īrṣyā|muṣita|cetasā
ākāśāt pātitaḥ prāpto Dattakena su|janmanā.»
«Dhruvaṃ sā rākṣasī yakṣī yadi vā mṛttikā|mayī
kruddhayā mugdhayā v" âpi yayā sv'|ârtho na cetitaḥ!»
«Atha vā sarvam ev' êdam alīkaṃ pratibhāti mām
kva yakṣī|kāmikaḥ kv' âyaṃ Kāmaḥ kāmī Rater iva?»
Iti nirdiśyamāno 'ham aṅgulībhir itas tataḥ
nayan'|ôtpala|mālābhir arcyamānaś ca yātavān.
Atha nāgarakāḥ prāpan sudhāṃ gṛha|pater gṛham
aṅgaṃ Gandharvadattāyās teṣām iva mano|rathāḥ.
Maṇi|hāṭaka|dant'|ādyair aṅgais tair eva kalpitam
sphurad|divya|prabhāvāt tu na vidma kiṃ|mayair iti.
17.60 Tataḥ prathama|kakṣāyām apaśyaṃ saṃnidhāpitām
āsanānāṃ catuḥ|ṣaṣṭiṃ mahā|paṭṭ'|ōrṇa|veṣṭitam.
Teṣu nāgarakaḥ kaś cit kāṃś cid āha sma sa|smitam
«aho! mahā|khalī|kāro yakṣī|kāmukam āgataḥ!
Sānudās'|âbhyanujñātāḥ suhṛdo Dattak'|ādayaḥ
samāyātāś catuḥ|ṣaṣṭis tāvanty ev' āsanāny api.
Yakṣī|kāmukam ālokya pañca|ṣaṣṭam an|āsanam
yat satyaṃ lajjito 'sm' îti!»
Tataś c' ôktam, «ṛjur bhavān
Āyatto Dattako yasya sa|putra|paśu|bāndhavaḥ

delightfully, like *koyals*: "Oh Magadhi! Vaidehi! Malayavati! Yavani!* The *yakṣī*'s beau has arrived, friends: have a look! Hurry! It seems that jealousy seized the wicked *yakṣī*'s mind. She hurled him down from the sky and he was found by the noble Dattaka."

"Surely she must be a demoness—or, if a *yakṣī*, made of clay—to have been so angry or stupid that she didn't realize what was good for her!"

"But all this seems unlikely to me. How could this man love a *yakṣī* when he is like Kama, the lover of Rati?"

I continued on my way, all the while being pointed out like this by fingers from either side, and worshipped by rows of eyes as if they were garlands of lotuses. Then the gentlemen arrived at their host's whitewashed house, and it was as if their desires had arrived at the ambrosial nectar that was Gandharvadatta's body.* Parts of it were constructed from materials like jewels, gold, and ivory, but because of their dazzling brilliance we could not be sure what they
were made of. In the first hall I saw sixty-four seats arranged 17.60
next to one another, each covered with a sheepskin.

One of the gentlemen smiled and said to a few of the others, "Oh dear! The *yakṣī*'s beau has suffered a great insult! Dattaka and the rest of the friends that Sanudasa invited make sixty-four, and that is exactly how many seats there are. Seeing the *yakṣī*'s beau, number sixty-five, without a seat, I am truly embarrassed!"

Someone answered, "You are being naïve. For a man who has Dattaka and his sons, animals and relatives at his disposal, Gandharvadatta herself is easily obtainable, to say tena Gandharvadatt" âpi su|labhā kim ut' āsanam!»

Pañca|ṣaṣṭam a|dṛṣṭvā tu nikṣiptaṃ tatra Dattakaḥ
dattavān svayam ākṛṣya mahyam ātmīyam āsanam.
Te 'pi nāgarakāḥ śeṣāḥ sthite tiṣṭhati Dattake
tiṣṭhanti sma sthitā eva bhṛtakā iva bhartari.
Ath' ânyad āsanaṃ dattaṃ Dattakāy' ôjjvala|prabham
sa tad adhyāsta śeṣāś ca yath" āsanam upāviśan.
Tatas triṃśac|chataṃ tasmād gaṇikānāṃ vinirgatam
gṛhād asura|kanyānāṃ mah"|âsura|purād iva.
Ātta|śṛṅgāra|bhṛṅgārā kā cid āvarjayaj jalam
tāsāṃ praty|ekam ek" âikā teṣāṃ pādān adhāvata.
17.70 Madīyas tu yayā pādaḥ pāṇibhyām avalambitaḥ
tayā sveda|jalen' âiva dhautaḥ ślatha|śarīrayā.
Āvarjitavatī yā ca jalaṃ lulita|locanā
visrasta|hastayā hastād bhṛṅgāraḥ pātitas tayā.

Praviśan dhauta|pādaś ca śṛṇomi sma prajalpitāḥ
prāṃśu|prākāra|garbha|sthāḥ śruti|hāri|giraḥ striyaḥ

«an|artho 'yam upanyastaḥ Sānudāsena dāruṇaḥ.
śulkaṃ Gandharvadattāyā vīṇā|vādana|nāmakam.
Yadi rūpam upanyasyec chulkaṃ gṛha|patis tataḥ
na yakṣī|kāmukād anyaṃ prāpnuyād bhartṛ|dārikā.
Vīṇāyāṃ tu prayuktāyāṃ bhagno 'yaṃ no mano|rathaḥ
hyo yasmād Bhūtiken' âsya nāradīyaṃ kṛtaṃ kila.
Idaṃ tāvan mahad duḥkhaṃ yad yakṣī|kāmuko 'nayā
ayaṃ n' â|su|labhī|bhūtaḥ śulka|doṣān na labhyate.
Idaṃ tu duḥ|sahataraṃ yad imāṃ bakul'|āvalīm
an|ātma|jño balāt ko 'pi gale tāṃ lambayiṣyati.

nothing of a seat!"

When Dattaka saw that there was no sixty-fifth seat he pulled his own across and gave it to me. With Dattaka remaining standing, the rest of the gentlemen stood too, like servants for their master. Then another seat was given to Dattaka, a beautifully dazzling one. He sat down on it and the others took their seats. One hundred and thirty courtesans emerged from the house, like *Asura* maidens coming out from a great *Asura* fortress. There were two for each man. One of them held an ornate golden pitcher and poured water while the other washed his feet. But the 17.70
girl who held my feet in her hands washed them with her sweat and her body went slack. The eyes of the girl who was pouring the water were rolling about. Her hand went limp and she dropped the golden pitcher.

On my way in after having my feet washed I heard women with enchanting voices talking behind the high walls.

"By stipulating lute-playing as Gandharvadatta's bride-price, Sanudasa has made a terrible mistake. If our master had announced good looks to be the price then his daughter would be getting none other than the *yakṣī*'s beau as her husband. But with the lute being used for the purpose our hopes have been shattered, because apparently it was yesterday that Bhutika started teaching him to play. It is indeed a great shame that because the bride-price is wrong she will not get the *yakṣī*'s beau as her husband, when he could have been easily obtainable. But what is even harder to bear is that some ignorant fellow will get to hang this garland of *bakula* flowers around his neck against her

Vīṇā|vādana|śulk" êyaṃ s'|âbhiyogāś ca nāgarāḥ
Prajāpatiś ca dur|lagnaḥ sarvathā śivam astv iti!»
Atha niṣkampa|kālindī|salila|svaccha|kuṭṭimām
jvalan|maṇi|śilā|stambhāṃ viśālāṃ prāviśaṃ sabhām.
17.80 Sabhā nāgarakaiḥ s" âbhād bhinna|prabha|vibhūṣaṇaiḥ
upatyakā|sthalī Meroḥ phullaiḥ kalpa|drumair iva.
Atha haṃsa iv' ôtsārya nalinī|dala|maṇḍalam
nirgataḥ kañcukī prerya tiras|kariṇik'|âmbaram.
Sa nāgaraka|saṃghātam avocad vinay'|ānataḥ
«vijñāpayati vaḥ śreṣṭhī sv|āgataṃ guṇa|rāgiṇām.
Bhavadbhir varṇa|saṃpannair antaḥ|sārair idaṃ gṛham
śāta|kumbha|mayaiḥ pūtaṃ Gaṅg"|âmbhaḥ|kalaśair iva.
Yadi sarve samāyātā yāto v" āgamana|śramaḥ
tato Gandharvadattāyai nirdeśo dīyatām iti!»
Te paras|param ālokya vidrāṇa|vadana|prabhāḥ
hrītāḥ sa|diśam ākāśam apaśyan proṣit'|ôttarāḥ.
Tataḥ kañcukinā vaktraṃ kṣaṇād dīnatayā kṛtam
samare kātarasy' êva sanna|cakṣuṣ|kapolakam.
Praty|ekaṃ ca mukhāny eṣām avalokya ciraṃ ciram
sa yadā yātum ārabdhas tad" āhūya may" ôditaḥ,
«Samāpta|pratikarmā vā kalyā vā yadi sā tataḥ
āgacchatu! kim ady' âpi dṛṣṭair nāgarakair iti!»
Etāvat" âiva Dattasya tat tādṛṅ|mlānam ānanam
jātam ucchvasitaṃ svinna|kapola|sthala|pīvaram.
17.90 Alapat Sānudāsasya prītaḥ parijanas tataḥ

will. Her bride-price is lute-playing, the citizens have been practicing it and Prajapati is set unfavorably—let's hope it all turns out for the best!"*

I went into a huge hall that had an inlaid floor as clear as the calm waters of the Yamuna and columns of sparkling
crystal. Like the terraces at the foot of Mount Meru with 17.80
their flowering wish-fulfilling trees, the assembly hall sparkled with the gentlemen in their various dazzling decorations. Then, like a swan parting a bank of lotus leaves, the chamberlain pushed the curtain aside and came forward.

He bowed politely and addressed the assembled gentlemen: "The chief merchant welcomes you lovers of music and merit. With your nobility and virtue you have sanctified this house like the beautiful golden pots brimming with Ganga water. If everyone is here and has recovered from the journey then you must call for Gandharvadatta!"

They looked at one another and the color drained from their faces. Embarrassed, they stared into space and no one answered. The face of the chamberlain soon took on a wretched expression, his eyes and cheeks as sunken as those of a coward in a battle. He stared for a long time into the face of every man. Then, when he was about to go, I called him and said, "If she has finished doing her makeup and is ready, then have her come! There is no need to wait for the gentlemen any longer!"

Dattaka's sweaty, chubby-cheeked face, which had been
as pale as everyone else's, immediately filled with color. Sa- 17.90
nudasa's servant was delighted and said, "*Yakṣī*'s beau, I salute you! You have done a great deed! After an age you

«yakṣī|kāmuka vandyo 'si! sarvathā śobhitaṃ tvayā!
Vāṅ|mātreṇ' âpi bhavataś cirād ucchvasitā vayam
avagrahe hi jīmūto visphūrjann api śobhate!
Tad evaṃ yādṛśaṃ rūpaṃ yādṛśī c' âti|dhīratā
tādṛśaṃ yadi vijñānaṃ bhavet kiṃ na bhaved iti?»
Eko nāgarakaś c' âikam avocad darśita|smitaḥ
«uddāmita|mukhā loke sukhaṃ jīvanti nis|trapā!
Ko hi veda|jaḍaṃ muktvā chāndasaṃ chāttram a|trapam
madhye mahā|manuṣyāṇām evam uddāmayen mukham?
Yakṣī|kāmuka|śabdo 'pi śabda ev' âsya kevalam
kva ca priya|guṇā yakṣī guṇa|hīnaḥ kva c' ēdṛśaḥ.
Yat kiṃ cid api bālānāṃ cetas|toṣāya kalpate
utkaṭena hi nāmn" âpi prāyas tuṣyanti ḍiṇḍikāḥ!»
Śrutv" êdam itareṇ' ôktaṃ,
«mā sma nindad bhavān imam
ko jānāti manuṣyāṇāṃ
caritaṃ gūḍha|cāriṇām?
Yakṣī|kāntaḥ prakṛṣṭena dhārṣṭyen' ājñāpayann api
yathā paricita|śrīkas tathā māṃ prati śobhate.»
Tato javanikāṃ prerya kanyā kañcukibhir vṛtā
devī Gandharvadatt" āgād abhibhūta|sabhā|prabhā.
17.100 Kathayāmi kathaṃ rūpaṃ tasyāḥ? saṃkṣiptam ucyate
pravrajyām āsthitā nūnam idānīm apsarogaṇāḥ!
Kalpitaṃ ca sabhā|madhye padma|rāga|śilā|mayam
candra|lekh" êva saṃdhy"|âbhram adhyāsta catur|antakam.
Tejaso 'bhibhavāt tasyāḥ saṃkucanti sma nāgarāḥ
bālāyāḥ śaśi|lekhāyāḥ puṇḍarīk'|ākarā iva.
S" âtha prajñā|vacaḥ|śūnyāṃ rūpa|mātraka|śālinīm

have revived me with mere words: in a drought a cloud simply has to rumble to look beautiful! So, if your talent is like your good looks and courage, then you want for nothing!"

One of the gentlemen smiled and said to another, "These days loose-tongued and shameless people have a fine time! Who but a shameless scholar of the Veda stupefied by its hymns would let loose his tongue like this in the company of men of rank? Even his name, '*yakṣī*'s beau,' is just that, a name. *Yakṣīs* are fond of virtue—what would one want with a man like him who has no virtues*? Any old trifle satisfies the simple: a lofty-sounding name is usually enough to satisfy a 'peripatetic mendicant'!"

On hearing this another man said, "You shouldn't ridicule this fellow: who can know what men who travel incognito get up to? Even though the *yakṣī*'s beau did speak with extraordinary audacity, he was so charming that he seemed decent to me."

Then her attendants pushed aside the curtain and Lady Gandharvadatta came in surrounded by them. Her radi-
ance put that of the assembly to shame. How can I describe 17.100
her beauty? Suffice it to say that all the heavenly nymphs must surely have left home to become wandering nuns! A square seat of red marble had been set up in the middle of the assembly hall, and when she sat on it, it was like a sliver of a moon setting into a cloud in the twilight. The gentlemen shrank back at her brilliance, like a mass of lotuses before the brilliance of a crescent moon. The assembly was

paribhūtavatī goṣṭhīṃ sabhā|stambh"|âvalīm iva.
Atha dakṣiṇam utkṣipya karaṃ kañcukin" ôditam
«śrūyatāṃ śreṣṭhino vākyaṃ bho nāgaraka|kuñjarāḥ!
Āste Gandharvadatt" êyam iyaṃ vīṇā ca sāritā
yo vo vādayituṃ śaktaḥ sa kiṃ tiṣṭhati ḍhaukatām!
A|śeṣair na ca kartavyā paripāṭir apārthikā
sā hi yuṣmākam asyāś ca lajjā|kheda|prayojanā.
Tataḥ svayaṃ bhavadbhiś ca yasmin vo bhāvan" āhitā
yuṣmān ātmānam etāṃ ca sa kleśān mocayatv iti!»
Atha nāgarakāḥ sarve Vīṇādattakam abruvan
«tvaṃ naḥ pūjyaḥ pravīṇaś ca tasmād utthīyatām iti.»
Sa yadā kampita|śirā n' êcchati sma tad" âparaḥ
saṃbhāvitatamas teṣāṃ gatvā vīṇām avādayat.
17.110 Tasmin doṣair a|saṃkīrṇān guṇān madhurat"|ôttarān
saṃpādayati śabdo 'bhūd uccakaiḥ, «sādhu! sādhv iti!»
Tato Gandharvadattāyāṃ pragītāyām abhūn mama,
«Are! jñātaṃ may" êdānīṃ ten' âiv' âmī vṛthā|śramāḥ
purā vāmana|rūpeṇa Baliṃ chalayatā kila.
tri|viṣṭapaṃ tribhiḥ krāntaṃ vikramaiś cakra|pāṇinā.
Taṃ ca Viśvāvasur nāma gandharva|gaṇa|sevitaḥ
krāmantaṃ gaganaṃ vegāt triś cakāra pradakṣiṇam.
Tena ca svayam utpādya stuvatā Garuḍa|dhvajam
Nārāyaṇa|stutiṃ nāma gītaṃ gītakam adbhutam.
Nāradena tataḥ prāptaṃ Nāradād Vṛtra|śatruṇā
Arjunena tatas tasmād Virāṭa|sutayā kila.

completely overcome by her. Dumbstruck, they were there only in form, like one of the hall's rows of columns.

Then the chamberlain raised his right hand and said, "Eminent gentlemen, listen to the words of the chief merchant! Here sits Gandharvadatta and here is a tuned lute! Whoever among you can play it should not hesitate to come forward! You must not all come one by one. That would be pointless and lead only to embarrassment for you and discomfort for her. Therefore, if there is a man among you that believes in himself and is believed in by the rest of you, let him put you, himself and her out of their misery!"

As one, the gentlemen said to Vinadattaka, "You are the most worthy and skillful among us, so stand up!" When he shook his head and declined, the next most highly thought
of among them went and played the lute. When he pro- 17.110
duced a performance that was faultless, virtuose and melodious, there were cries of "Bravo! Bravo!"

Then Gandharvadatta started to sing and I said to myself, "Ah! Now I understand why these men's efforts are in vain. Vishnu, in the form of a dwarf, once crossed the three worlds in three steps, thereby outwitting Bali. A certain Vishvavasu, who was attended by a host of celestial musicians, circled him reverentially three times as he sped across the sky. He glorified Vishnu with a remarkable song called the Hymn to Narayana , which he had composed himself. Narada learned it from him, Indra from Narada, Arjuna from Indra, and from him, so it is said, it was learned by Virata's daughter. Parikshit learned it from his mother, and Janamejaya learned it from him. Being handed down like

Parīkṣit prāpnuyān mātus tato 'pi Janamejayaḥ
iti kram'|āgataṃ tātas tātād āgamitaṃ mayā.
Gāndhāra|grāma|saṃbaddhaṃ
kva gāndhāraḥ kva mānuṣāḥ
‹svargān n' ânyatra gāndhāraḥ›
ity āhur Nārad'|ādayaḥ.
Tena yo 'yaṃ na jānāti na ced abhyupagacchati
tad a|saṃpādayann eva jāyate doṣavān asau.
Ahaṃ punar idaṃ jānan sadyaḥ|pariṇamat|phalam
puro nāgarakāṇāṃ ca yathā|sāmarthyam utsahe!»
17.120 Mayi saṃkalpayaty evam asau nāgaraka'|rṣabhaḥ
smayamāno vilakṣyatvāt svam ev' âbhajat' āsanam.
Tataḥ pratihate tasmin suhṛn|maṇḍala|maṇḍane
raṅgo bhaṅgam agṛhṇāt sa nihata|jyeṣṭha|mallavat.
Atha māṃ janit'|ôtsāham uttiṣṭhāsantam āsanāt
dṛṣṭvā saṃbhāvit'|â|jñānaṃ lajjay" âgrāhi Dattakaḥ.
Anyena ca nimittena calito 'haṃ kil' āsanāt
ten' ôktaṃ, «saṃkaṭ'|āsthānād anyatra sthīyatām iti.»
Tatas tam uktavān asmi, «kim idaṃ na tvayā śrutam
‹pathā sakṛt pravṛttāyāḥ kiṃ karoty avaguṇṭhanam?›
Praviṣṭo 'haṃ suhṛd|goṣṭhīṃ yath" âiva baṭu|cāpalāt
tathā Gandharvadatt" âpi dhṛṣṭam ājñāpitā mayā.
Tad asyā baṭu|vidyāyāḥ prāntam a|prāpya mā|dṛśaḥ
‹hā kaṣṭaṃ! vañcito 'sm' îti!› paścāt|tāpena khedyate.
Yatra c' âmī na lajjante sa|lajjāḥ suhṛdas tava
tatra nir|lajjatā|ślāghī lajjay" âiva hi lajjate!»
Samarthayati mayy evaṃ Dattako 'pi niruttaraḥ

this, it reached my father and I learned it from him. It is composed in the *gāndhāra* scale, which is impossible for humans to follow. Narada and other sages have said that the *gāndhāra* scale comes from nowhere else but heaven. So if one of these men is ignorant of it, does not accompany it and fails to master it, he commits a sin. I, however, know it and know that it will bear fruit immediately, so I shall show the gentlemen what I am capable of!"

As I was making my mind up, the gentlemen's champion 17.120
returned to his seat, smiling at his disappointment. With that fellow, the finest of all the friends, unsuccessful, the audience thought that all was lost, as if their finest wrestler had been slain. Then Dattaka saw that I had become keen and was starting to get up from my seat. Supposing me to be misguided, he was seized with embarrassment. Thinking that perhaps I had got up from my seat for some other reason, he asked me to sit somewhere other than my uncomfortable place.

I replied, "Have you not heard the saying, 'What use is a veil for a woman who is already travelling along the road?' Just as youthful insolence made me enter this assembly of friends, so too did it make me brazenly issue the command to Gandharvadatta. When someone like me fails to take this youthful logic to its conclusion, he is pained by regret and thinks, 'Oh no! I've missed out!' When these friends of yours, who are easily embarrassed, are not embarrassed, a man who takes pride in not getting embarrassed should be embarrassed by his embarrassment!"

While I was showing my enthusiasm in this way, all Dat-

«aho sāhasam!» ity uktvā tūṣṇīṃ|bhāvam upeyivān.
Aham apy āsanaṃ tyaktvā tiryak paśyati Dattake
pārśve Gandharvadattāyā dattam āsanam āsthitaḥ.
17.130 Atha kañcukin" ānītāṃ vīṇāṃ dṛṣṭv" âham uktavān
«apar" ānīyatām ārya n' âitāṃ spṛśati mā|dṛśaḥ!
Udaraṃ dṛṣṭam etasyā lūtā|tantu|nir|antaram
jaḍatāṃ gamitā yena paṭu|tantrī|paraṃparā.»
Smita|darśita|dant'|âgrair anyataḥ kṣipta|dṛṣṭibhiḥ
māṃ ālokya tathā|bhūtam uktaṃ nāgarakair iti,
«Brāhmaṇaḥ pūjyatām eṣa nir|lajj"|âgra|patākayā
yena sāhasam ārabdhaṃ sva|guṇ'|ākhyāpan'|ôpamam.
Tantrī|kiṇa|kaṭhor'|âgrā viśīrṇa|karaj'|ātatāḥ
kara|śākhāś ca no jātā na ca saṃbhāvan" ēdṛśī.
Ayaṃ tu komal'|âgrabhis tantrīr aṅgulibhiḥ spṛśan
kadā vādayitā vīṇāṃ veda|ved'|âṅga|pāra|gaḥ?
Sarvath" âyam abhiprāyo may" âitasy' ôpalakṣitaḥ
‹prītim utpādayiṣyāmi tāvad locanayor iti!›
Yāvad utsāryate vīṇā yāvac c' ānīyate 'parā
tāvad Gandharvadattāyā rūpaṃ paśyāmy a|vāritaḥ.
Rathyā|catvara|yātrāsu vakṣyāmi jana|saṃnidhau
īdṛśī tādṛsī dṛṣṭā rūpiṇī yuvatir mayā.
Lūtā|tantu|tataṃ c' âyaṃ vīṇā|karparam āha yat
kiṃ tat satyaṃ mṛṣ" êty etad devair vijñāyatām iti!»
17.140 Udveṣṭite ca tat tasmin dṛṣṭaṃ veṣṭana|carmaṇi
tantu|cakraṃ bhay'|ôdbhrānta|lūtā|maṇḍala|saṃkulam.
Atha Gandharvadattāyā jātam aṅgaṃ nirīkṣya mām

taka could say before falling silent was "Oh, the temerity!" He looked on askance as I left my seat and sat in the one that had been placed at Gandharvadatta's side.

The chamberlain brought in a lute and after I examined 17.130
it I said, "Sir, please bring another. A man like me wouldn't touch this one! I can see that its interior is thick with spiders' webs, making the strings for the high notes stiff."

When the gentlemen saw me behaving like this, their smiles revealed the ends of their teeth. They looked away and said, "This brahmin has shown such audacity in singing his own praises that he should be honored with a banner proclaiming him to be the ultimate in shamelessness! Our fingertips are calloused and coarse from the strings, our nails have fallen out and our fingers have stretched, yet we do not have anything like such a high opinion of ourselves. But when is this master of the Vedas and their ancillary disciplines ever going to use his tender fingertips to touch the strings and play the lute? I've got it! I've realized what his plan is: he just wants to feast his eyes! While the lute is being taken away and another one being fetched, he will be free to look at Gandharvadatta's beauty. On highways, at crossroads and at festivals he will tell people in detail about the beautiful young girl he saw. Let these honorable men find out whether or not the bowl of the lute really is, as he says, covered with spiders' webs!"

When the leather cover was opened, a web teeming with 17.140
frightened spiders was found. Then Gandharvadatta looked at me and became uncomfortable: her body quivered, perspired and tingled with embarrassment. When I strummed

vepathu|sveda|rom'|âñca|lajjā|vidhuram ākulam.
Apar" âpi mayā vīṇā samāsphālya paṭu|kvaṇā
keśa|dūṣita|tantrīkā pratham" êva vivarjitā.
Sānudāsas tato vīṇāṃ su|gandhi|kusum'|ârcitām
kacchap'|ākāra|phalakām ādāya svayam āgataḥ.
Māṃ ca pradakṣiṇī|kṛtya sa|vikāra|tanū|ruhaḥ
Gandharvadattām iva tām adadāt su|bhaga|svanām.
Mayā tu dhauta|pādena vīṇāṃ kṛtvā pradakṣiṇām
a|bhukt'|âmbara|saṃvītaṃ pīṭha|pṛṣṭham adhiṣṭhitam.
Manāk saṃspṛṣṭa|mātrāś ca kara|śākhā|mukhaiḥ svayam
tantrī|bandhā yathā|sthānam asaran dhaivat'|ādikam.
Tatas tantrīṣu gāndhāre jṛmbhamāṇāsu mantharam
Gandharvadattām avadaṃ, «bhīru saṃgīyatām iti!»
Sā pragalbh" âpi gāndhāram ākarṇy' â|mara|gaś|caram
tathā ca dhṛṣṭam ādiṣṭā bāl'|āśā|līnatāṃ gatā.
Tāṃ ca pravartayan bhītāṃ trapā|janita|mūkatām
tad eva gītakaṃ divyam ahaṃ mandam avādayam.
17.150 Hṛte tasyās trapā|setau saṃdarśita|pathā yathā
lokaṃ pāvayituṃ puṇyā prāvartata Sarasvatī.
Vṛttibhir dakṣiṇ'|ādyābhis tad gītaṃ gītakaṃ tayā
upary upari pāṇy'|ântaiḥ pāṇibhir yojitaṃ mayā!
Āsīd idaṃ tamo|bhūtam a|prajñātam a|lakṣaṇam
tad|gīta|mātra|viṣaya|śrotra|mātra|jagat tadā!
Sabhāyāṃ gāḍha|mūrcchāyāṃ mṛdu tad gīta|vāditam
paṭubhir dundubhi|dhvānair abhibhūtaṃ vimāninām.
Patitāsu sa|ratnāsu divaḥ kusuma|vṛṣṭiṣu
kañcukī cetanā|prāptān abhāṣata sabhā|sadaḥ:

the second lute, I rejected it like the first because its strings were spoiled with hair, giving it a sharp tone. Sanudasa then appeared in person carrying a lute that had been worshipped with fragrant flowers and had a bowl shaped like a tortoise shell. His body rippled with delight as he reverentially walked around me before handing me that lovely-sounding lute as though it were Gandharvadatta herself. I had my feet washed, walked respectfully around the lute and then sat on the seat, which had been covered with a fresh cloth. Merely by being brushed with my fingertips the strings sounded in the correct order, *dhaivata* first.

When the strings were softly playing the *gāndhāra* scale, I said to Gandharvadatta, "Sing, sweet lady!" She was a proud girl, but on hearing the *gāndhāra* scale—which is the preserve of the gods —and being commanded so audaciously, she became as shy as a child. The girl was anxious and had been silenced by her bashfulness, so to encourage her I softly played the divine song. When the dam of her 17.150
modesty was removed, it was as if the sacred Sarasvati had been shown the way and was flowing forth to purify the world. She sang that song in the southern and other styles, and with my fine fingertips I accompanied them all!

Everything became dark, obscure, unrecognizable; every living being was all ears and heard nothing other than that song! With the assembly in a deep trance the delicate music was drowned out by the heavy rumbling of the drums of heavenly travellers. Showers of flowers and jewels fell from the sky, and the chamberlain addressed the now con-

«Bho bho nir|matsarāḥ santaḥ satyam ākhyāta sādhavaḥ
gītaṃ yad anay" ânena kiṃ tat saṃvāditaṃ na hi?»
Ath' ôdyamita|hastais taiḥ samastair uktam uccakaiḥ
«dharmya|śulk'|ârjitām eṣa kanyakāṃ labhatām iti!»
Tiras|kariṇikāṃ nītvā tataḥ kañcukin" ântarā
bahiṣ|kṛtā nāgarakā nāstikās tri|divād iva.
Nirgacchanti hata|chāyās te khaṇḍita|mano|rathāḥ
sv|abhyasta|guṇa|vaiphalyaṃ guṇinaḥ kān na tāpayet?
Sa|Vīṇādattako 'haṃ tu śreṣṭhin" âbhyantarī|kṛtaḥ
parīkṣya bahuśo rājñā sacivo guṇavān iva.
17.160 Abhāṣata ca nirgacchat teṣu nāgarak'|arṣabhaḥ
«yakṣī|kāmuka devas tvam a|mānuṣa|parākramaḥ!
Vayaṃ Gandharvadattā ca Sānudāsaś ca s'|ânugaḥ
kṛcchrām āpadam āpannā līlay" âiva tvay"|ôddhṛtāḥ!
Kāśmaryaḥ khadirāḥ śākāś campakāś ca sa|veṇavaḥ
ātody' âṅg'|ârtham utkhātāḥ prarohantu yathā purā!
Agni|hotrāṇi hūyantāṃ dvijāḥ saṃdhyām upāsatām!
kumāryaḥ pariṇīyantāṃ prasūyantāṃ kula|striyaḥ!
Parivrājaka|nir|grantha|bhikṣu|pāśu|pat'|ādayaḥ
guru|vaktr'|âbhisaṃkrāntān sva|siddh'|ântān adhīyatām.
Śānta|vīn"|ôpasargatvāt s' ēra|nagarāḥ sukham
sa|Campā|Magadhāś c' Âṅgāḥ svasth'|âṅgāḥ śeratām iti.»
Tato gṛha|patir dīnaḥ prārthanā|bhaṅga|śaṅkayā
Vīṇādattakam ālokya prāvocan nīcakaistarām,
«Praśastaṃ dinam ady' âivaṃ ten' âyaṃ pauruṣ'|ârjitaḥ

scious assembly: "O gentlemen, do not be envious: speak the truth! Did he or did he not accompany her song?"

They all raised their hands and cried, "The right bride-price has been paid—let him have the girl!" Then the chamberlain drew the curtain across the hall and the gentlemen were sent out, like atheists being expelled from heaven. They left downcast, their dreams shattered. What artist is not tormented by failure in an art that he has practiced assiduously? As for me, I, together with Vinadattaka, was led inside by the chief merchant, like a good minister being accepted by a king after repeated examination.

On his way out, the gentlemen's champion said, "O 17.160
yakṣī's beau, with your unearthly powers you must be a god! We and Gandharvadatta and Sanudasa and his retinue were in dire straits; you have rescued us as if on a whim! May the *kāśmarī*, acacia, teak, *campaka* and bamboo trees, which have been chopped and uprooted to make lute parts, grow as they did before! May brahmins offer fire sacrifices and make the three daily prayers! May young girls get married and wives have babies! May Brahmin, Jaina, Buddhist, Shaiva and other ascetics study their doctrines from the mouths of their teachers! Now that the lute mania is over, the people of Anga, the citizens of Kira* and Champa and the people of Magadha can calm down and return to normal."

Then our host, worried that his request might be refused, looked at Vinadattaka and said very quietly, "Today is an auspicious day, so this man must immediately take in marriage the celebrated hand of Gandharvadatta, which he has

ślāghyo Gandharvadattāyāḥ karaḥ saṃskrīyatām iti.»
Ahaṃ tu s'|âbhilāṣo 'pi darśit'|âlīka|dhīrataḥ
avocaṃ smita|saṃkīrṇām an|āsthā|mantharāṃ giram,
«Dvijo 'ham Meru|Kailāsa|tuly'|â|mala|kul'|ôdbhavaḥ
pariṇetuṃ na me yuktam a|sa|varṇām imām iti.»
17.170 Ath' ôktaṃ Sānudāsena, «viśrabdhaṃ pariṇīyatām
yuṣmākaṃ hi sa|varṇ" êyam utkṛṣṭā vā bhaved iti.»
Āsīc ca mama, «kiṃ mattaḥ? kim unmattaḥ? kim ārjavaḥ?
ayaṃ yasmād a|saṃbaddham a|buddhir iva bhāṣate?
Ahaṃ c' êyaṃ ca yady asya brāhmaṇāv iti niścayaḥ
tato mat katham utkṛṣṭā brāhmaṇī brāhmaṇād iyam?
Ath' êmāṃ brāhmaṇīm eṣa manyate kṣatriyaṃ tu mām
tathā sati kath" âpy eṣā kriyamāṇā virudhyate.
Kiṃ tu saṃbhāvyate n' âyam a|saṃbaddhaṃ prabhāṣitum
yena dharm'|ârtha|śāstr'|ârtha|kṣuṇṇa|dhīr iva bhāṣate.
Agra|jo 'vara|jāṃ bhāryāṃ svī|kurvan na praduṣyati
‹te ca svā c' âiva nṛ|pater› ity uktaṃ Manunā yataḥ.
Pratyākhyānaṃ ca nitarām iyaṃ n' ârhati ninditam
yasmād a|khaṇḍit'|ājñena dāpitā guruṇ" âiva me.
Yad ahaṃ grāhitas tena vijñānam ati|mānuṣam
dāpitā yena ten' âiva tena ten' âiva dāpitā.
Na c' â|vaśya|parigrāhyā kumārī ciram arhati
s'|âbhilāṣā viśeṣeṇa pratyākhyāna|kad|arthanām.
Tasmād alaṃ mam' ânena nirbandhen' êti» niścitam
arthitāṃ Sānudāsasya, «tath" êti!» samamānayam.
17.180 Atha Vaiśravaṇasy' êva sūnor Ākhaṇḍal'|ātma|jaḥ

won with his valor."

But even though I was keen, I pretended not to care. Smiling, I said in a voice heavy with indifference, "I am a brahmin from a family as pure as Meru and Kailasa. It is not right for me to marry this girl—she is not of my caste."

Sanudasa replied, "Marry her with confidence, for she is 17.170
of the same caste as you, or perhaps superior."

I said to myself, "Why is he talking nonsense as if he were an idiot? Is he drunk? Is he crazy? Is he simple? If he thinks that we are both brahmins, then how can she, a brahmin lady, be superior to me, a brahmin man? If he is taking her to be a brahmin lady but me a warrior, then what he is saying doesn't make sense. But it is unlikely that he is talking nonsense, because he speaks like someone who has often reflected upon the meanings of the treatises on law and behavior. A highborn man who takes as his wife a lower-born woman does no wrong, since Manu has said that brahmins can take a wife from their own caste or from that of a king. At all events, the girl should not be rejected. That would be sinful, because it is my father that has caused her to be given to me, and I have never disobeyed his orders. It was from him that I received the superhuman skill that caused her to be given to me, so in effect it is he who has given her. A girl whom one is obliged to marry should not be tortured with refusals for long, particularly when she is eager. So I must stop being obstinate!" Having decided this, I told Sanudasa that I agreed to his request.

I then took Gandharvadatta's hand in marriage, like In- 17.180
dra's son taking that of Kubera's daughter.

karaṃ Gandharvadattāyāḥ sa|saṃskāram upādade.
Mandaṃ pāda|talena tālam anayā
yat kuṭṭayanty" â|ciraṃ
gītaṃ mām abhi visphurat|kuharitaṃ
tāraiḥ su|bhugna|bhruvā
ten' âiva pratanū|kṛtām apaharann
asyāḥ kramena trapāṃ
nirvāṇān mahat" ântareṇa su|bhagaṃ
saṃsāram ajñāsiṣam.

iti Bṛhatkathāyāṃ Ślokasaṃgrahe
Gandharvadattā|vivāhaḥ

As I gradually removed her shyness (which had already lessened when she, with her beautifully arched eyebrows, had briefly sung for me in a tremulous soprano while gently tapping out the rhythm with her foot), I came to realize that worldly existence was vastly superior to liberation.

Thus ends the Marriage to Gandharvadatta
in the Long Story Abridged into Sanskrit Verse.

NOTES

1.4 ***Mahākāla*** is both an epithet of Śiva and the name of one of his attendants.

1.7 ***Bṛhaspati*** is the preceptor of the gods.

1.8 The ***four sciences*** are knowledge of the Vedas, logic and government, and practical knowledge (of agriculture, medicine, business and so forth).

1.36 ***Pradyota*** is another name for Mahāsena.

1.60 ***Savior from hell:*** The birth of a son is supposed to spare his parents from a hell named *Puṃnaraka*. See *Bṛhaspatismṛti* 1.26.81, *Viṣṇusmṛti* 15.44.

2.41 ***King of Vatsa*** refers to Udayana, whose tale is told in cantos 4 and 5.

2.70 Shiva acquired the epithet ***Nīlakaṇṭha*** ("Blue-throated") when, in order to save the world, he drank the poison Halāhala produced at the churning of the ocean of milk but did not swallow it.

2.92 The text says only ***son***, not "Gopāla's son," but the former does not make sense. LACÔTE (1908:20–21) suggests that this could be *"une contamination d'une autre forme de l'histoire—celle qu'on trouve dans les versions cachemeriennes."*

3.10 ***Saṅghamardana*** means "Crowd-crusher."

3.33 ***From afar:*** Outcastes were forbidden too close contact with the higher castes.

3.42 The ***gandharvas*** are a class of celestial musicians.

3.47 I have emended the text presented by LACÔTE (which reads Saptavarṇapure) because of 20.179ff. which describes the city of ***Saptaparṇapura***, where there is a park containing *saptaparṇa* trees and a famous judge called Vāyumukta.

3.69 The ***water-offering festival*** is a festival in which water is offered to the spirits of dead ancestors.

3.77 In this and some subsequent verses, only Avantivardhana is mentioned as being abducted. However, verse 88 makes it clear that Ipphaka, as one would expect, has abducted Surasamañjarī too.

3.92 LACÔTE (1908:30) suggests the emendation of ***vardhamānaka°***, "saucer," to *vadhyamānaka°*. A *vadhyamālā* is "a garland placed on the head of one sentenced to death" (MONIER-WILLIAMS 1899:s.v.).

3.93 The word ***āryuṣ-*** is not found in other texts. It is an epithet of Kāśyapa and may be related to *ārya*. I have thus chosen to translate it with "noble." Naravāhanadatta's ***maternal uncle*** is Pālaka, the brother of Vāsavadattā.

3.100 The ***rohita*** rainbow is Indra's unbent bow, usually invisible to mortals.

4.19 The four *upāyas* or ***means to success*** against an enemy are fomenting dissent, diplomacy, bribery and attack.

4.58 Budhasvāmin is here making a pun on the name of the ***aśoka*** tree, *a-śoka*, "without grief."

4.90 ***Prāptavarām***. It is also possible that we should read *prāptavayasām,* "despite her having come of age," but that would require further changes to the verse.

5.51 A *vidyā*, or ***magical science***, is both a magical technique and a spell or mantra. It can be acquired through practice or as a gift.

5.61 Budhasvāmin is here making a pun on the two meanings of ***guṇa***: ***string*** and ***(good) quality***. The *ṣāḍguṇya* is a particular set of six *guṇas*, referring to acts of foreign policy. They are, according to Manu 7.160, *sandhi, vigraha, yāna, āsana, dvaidhībhāva* and *saṃśraya* (peace, war, advancing, halting, duplicity and taking refuge).

5.71 This verse is missing in all the witnesses. As LACÔTE (1908:54) suggests, the accusatives *dṛṣṭaṃ, svapnaṃ* and *kathitaṃ* in verse 70 indicate that verse 71 perhaps started with a phrase like *āsthāpayad dvijaḥ*, and it must have described how the brahmin interpreted Vasantaka's dream.

5.108 ***Udayana*** means "sunrise."

5.123 The ***yakṣa***s are demigods who serve Kubera, the god of wealth. *Piśāca*s are demonic, goblin-like creatures.

5.180 ***Manoramā*** means "charming woman."

5.183 ***Dānavas*** are a type of demon.

5.188 The ***lion of the Yādavas*** is Kṛṣṇa.

5.198 LACÔTE (1908:462) relates FOUCHER's interpretation of these ***four types of machine***: the first is a noria (a machine for raising buckets of water), the second is a winch, the third a mill, and the fourth a machine for pressing sugarcane to extract the juice.

5.204 Budhasvāmin is making a pun on the name ***Ratnāvalī***, which means "garland of precious stones."

5.219 Budhasvāmin is making the same pun on ***Ratnāvalī***'s name (cf. 5.204).

5.230 The translation follows LACÔTE (1908:463) in taking ***tacca*** to be a Prakrit form of Sanskrit *takṣa*. One might rather have expected *taccha*, so alternatively one might emend to *tatra*, "there", or read *tac ca*.

5.279 ***Garuḍa*** is a great bird of prey, the vehicle of Viṣṇu.

5.293 ***Udayana*** stole queen Vāsavadattā from Mahāsena and was imprisoned in a penance grove.

5.300 The ***guhyaka***s are semi-divine attendants of Kubera, similar to *yakṣa*s.

5.320 A ***Yakṣī*** is a female *yakṣa*. An *Apsaras* is a type of celestial nymph. The reference to Indra is obscure.

5.326 The ***rite of parting the hair*** is usually carried out during the eighth month of pregnancy.

7.16 ***Rati*** is the consort of Kāma, the god of love.

7.18 The word *ācā* is not found in other texts, but seems likely to refer to Udayana and mean "father." Cf. 10.192, 193 *āci/ācī*, which appears to mean "mother," note also Newar *ājimā*, "grandmother," and *āju*, "grandfather."

7.24 It seems likely that this verse is a later addition to the text: it is omitted in NM, found after verse 26 in A, and in the margin of B with a sign indicating that it is to be read after verse 26; furthermore, its inclusion makes verse 25 tautological.

7.76 On the word ***cetasya***, which I have translated as "mindful," see the note to 10.36.

8.40 Here I have conjectured ***dhārā°*** for *dvārā°* (which is the reading found in all the witnesses, but whose meaning is unclear), and taken the former to mean rain [of arrows].

9.1 As LACÔTE notes (1908:99), the rapid and unexplained change of setting between cantos 8 and 9 suggests there may be a lacuna.

9.19 The word ***nāgaraka*** occurs many times in the text. It is derived from *nagara*, "city," and describes someone who is at once clever, sophisticated and gentlemanly.

9.86 ***Vidyādhara, "sorcerer,"*** literally means "possessor *(°dhara)* of magical science *(vidyā°)*."

9.105 ***Because I had just helped him:*** By accepting the *vidyā* he would have been reduced to the status of a paid helper. Additionally, there are *Dharmaśāstra* laws forbidding the sale of knowledge *(vidyāvikraya)*.

10.18 ***Gomukha*** means "cow-faced."

10.31 Budhasvāmin is making a pun on the word ***varṇa***, which can mean either "color" or "social class."

10.34 The word ***cetasya***, which I have translated as "mindful man," has been coined by Budhasvāmin.

10.142 A "***poison-maiden***" (*viṣakanyā* or *viṣakanyakā*) is a girl who is fed poison in ever-increasing doses from her early childhood. She then becomes lethal to anyone who touches her and is employed to kill men by seducing them.

10.176 The river ***Vaitaraṇī*** flows between this world and the underworld of the dead.

10.182 The ***three ends of man*** are *kāma, artha* and *dharma:* pleasure, material gain and religious duty.

10.187 *Mahā-* means "great" and *gaṇa* means "troupe," hence *mahāgaṇikā*, ***great courtesan***.

10.192 On the word ***ācā/āci/ācī***, cf. 7.18.

10.208 ***Yama*** is the god of death.

11.9 ***Rambhā*** and ***Menakā*** are Apsarases, heavenly nymphs.

11.15 ***Lakṣmī, Kīrti*** and ***Kānti*** are the goddesses of wealth, fame and beauty, respectively.

11.20 There is clearly at least one verse missing between 20 and 21, in which Naravāhanadatta must have asked Gomukha to visit Madanamañjukā and he refused.

11.34 Budhasvāmin is making a pun on two meanings of ***guṇa***, "rope" and "virtue."

11.58 In jest, Marubhūtika wants to worry Naravāhanadatta by taking a long time to return from his errand.

11.78 A ***muhūrta*** is forty-eight minutes long.

11.96 The arrival of Gomukha and the beginning of Hariśikha's speech are missing from the witnesses.

11.107 The ***cakravāka***, or ruddy goose, is said to be happy during the day and sad at night.

12.9 The seat of Lakṣmī, the goddess of wealth, is a ***lotus***.

12.29 This episode is described in Kathāsaritsāgara 15–16.

12.40 The original ***Sāvitrī*** is the daughter of Sūrya, the god of the sun. She is also the wife of Brahma, and embodies the Gāyatrī mantra.

12.77 I.e., on the occasion of her marriage.

12.82 The first half of verse 82 is missing from the witnesses.

13.28 The toponym ***Vaitarddha*** is probably connected with the word *vitarda* and its cognates *vitardī, vitarddhī* and *vitarddhikā*, which mean "high plateau." It would thus refer to the Himalayan region, where the sorcerers dwell.

14.5 Budhasvāmin is making a pun on the queen's name: ***Pṛthivī*** means "the earth."

14.29 The ***three powers*** of a king are *prabhutva, mantra* and *utsāha*, "sovereignty," "good counsel" and "'enthusiasm."

14.41 The witnesses here have an extra half-verse. LACÔTE omits it from his edition, noting, *"il n'est qu'un autre rédaction de 41cd et il n'y a pas à supposer de lacune ici"* (1908:167 n.410). However, it in fact appears to consist of a reply from Vegavatī, and translates as "'My affairs have nothing to do with your affairs!' she said." The extra half-verse has *so 'bravīt,* "he said," but this is tautological after 41a's *tenoktam* and needs to be emended to *sābravīt*. Thus it seems that there is probably half a verse missing here.

14.56 Vegavān has been wearing a loincloth woven from dried ***kuśa*** grass and it has chafed his thighs.

14.74 The ***five ancillaries*** of a *vidyā*, or spell, are (i) the way to start it, (ii) the necessary materials, (iii) where and when it is to be practiced, (iv) solutions to any problems that may arise and (v) how to complete it.

14.104 Udayana is the king of the ***lunar race***.

Col. 14 Both this and the previous canto are called Vegavatīdarśana, ***Vegavatī Revealed***, in their colophons.

16.37 ***Vīṇā*** means lute.

17.53 The noblewomen's names indicate their diverse origins: modern-day eastern Bihar, the Terai region of the Uttar Pradesh-Nepal border, Kerala and Greece.

17.58 Budhasvāmin is making a play on the two meanings of ***sudhā:*** "nectar" and "whitewash."

17.78 The astrological omens for a wedding are good (cf. 17.167), but the speaker does not want a wedding to happen, so she thinks that ***Prajāpati*** is set unfavorably.

17.95 Budhasvāmin uses the ***kva*. . . *kva*. . .** construction to contrast incongruities. Thus we need an adjective meaning "without virtues" in the fourth *pāda* and I have diagnostically conjectured *guṇahīnaḥ* accordingly.

17.165 ***Kīra*** usually refers to a people inhabiting a region near Kashmir, but such a meaning is impossible here, and it must refer to a town in ***Aṅga***, a region corresponding to present-day eastern Bihar and Bengal.

INDEX

k	ṭ	t	p	ṅ	n	m	ḥ/r (Except āḥ/aḥ)	āḥ	aḥ	Initial letters:
k	ṭ	t	p	ṅ	n	ṃ	ḥ	āḥ	aḥ	k/kh
g	ḍ	d	b	ṅ	n	ṃ	r	ā	o	g/gh
k	ṭ	c	p	ṅ	ṃś	ṃ	ś	āś	aś	c/ch
g	ḍ	j	b	ṅ	ñ	ṃ	r	ā	o	j/jh
k	ṭ	ṭ	p	ṅ	ṃṣ	ṃ	ṣ	āṣ	aṣ	ṭ/ṭh
g	ḍ	ḍ	b	ṅ	ṇ	ṃ	r	ā	o	ḍ/ḍh
k	ṭ	t	p	ṅ	ṃs	ṃ	s	ās	as	t/th
g	ḍ	d	b	ṅ	n	ṃ	r	ā	o	d/dh
k	ṭ	t	p	ṅ	n	ṃ	ḥ	ā	aḥ	p/ph
g	ḍ	d	b	ṅ	n	ṃ	r	ā	o	b/bh
ṅ	ṇ	n	m	ṅ	n	ṃ	r	ā	o	*nasals* (n/m)
g	ḍ	d	b	ṅ	n	ṃ	r	ā	o	y/v
g	ḍ	d	b	ṅ	n	ṃ	*zero*[1]	ā	o	r
g	ḍ	l	b	ṅ	l̃[2]	ṃ	r	ā	o	l
k	ṭ	c ch	p	ṅ	ñ ś/ch	ṃ	ḥ	āḥ	aḥ	ś
k	ṭ	t	p	ṅ	n	ṃ	ḥ	āḥ	aḥ	ṣ/s
gg h	ḍḍ h	dd h	bb h	ṅ	n	ṃ	r	ā	o	h
g	ḍ	d	b	ṅ/ṅṅ[3]	n/nn[3]	m	r	ā	a[4]	*vowels*
k	ṭ	t	p	ṅ	n	m	ḥ	āḥ	āḥ	*zero*

Permitted finals: (header above first ten columns)

[1]ḥ or r disappears, and if a/i/u precedes, this lengthens to ā/ī/ū. [2]e.g. tān+lokān=tāl̃ lokān.
[3]The doubling occurs if the preceding vowel is short. [4]Except: aḥ+a=o '.